Enterprise and Integration

In post-Brexit Europe, it has never been more important to understand who benefits from the European Union and its Single Market. In this innovative history of European integration, Grace Ballor reconstructs the making of the Single Market in the 1980s and 1990s through the lens of multinational business. She both shows how policymakers viewed big business as an ally in market integration and uncovers the diverse responses of European companies, ranging from enthusiastic support for the market to opposition to its attendant social and environmental policies. Drawing on institutional and corporate archives and interviews with key policymakers and business leaders, Ballor demonstrates how businesses adapted their strategies to the new realities of integration and how these adaptations in turn shaped international markets. This is essential reading for anyone wishing to make sense of contemporary European economics and the complex relationships between business and policymaking, economy and society.

Grace Ballor is Assistant Professor of History at Bocconi University and faculty fellow at the Institute for European Policymaking. Her research examines the political economy of contemporary Europe and the historical intersections of global capitalism and global governance.

CAMBRIDGE STUDIES IN THE EMERGENCE OF GLOBAL ENTERPRISE

The world economy has experienced a series of globalizations in the past two centuries, and each has been accompanied and shaped by business enterprises, their national political contexts, and new sets of international institutions. *Cambridge Studies in the Emergence of Global Enterprise* focuses on those business firms that have given the global economy many of its most salient characteristics, particularly regarding how they have fostered new technology, new corporate cultures, new networks of communication, and new strategies and structures designed to meet global competition. All the while, they have accommodated changes in national and international regulations, environmental standards, and cultural norms. This is a history that needs to be understood because we all have a stake in the performance and problems of global enterprise.

A complete list of titles in the series can be found at: www.cambridge.org/globalenterprise

Enterprise and Integration

Big Business and the Making of the Single European Market

Grace Ballor
Bocconi University

CAMBRIDGE
UNIVERSITY PRESS

CAMBRIDGE
UNIVERSITY PRESS

Shaftesbury Road, Cambridge CB2 8EA, United Kingdom

One Liberty Plaza, 20th Floor, New York, NY 10006, USA

477 Williamstown Road, Port Melbourne, VIC 3207, Australia

314–321, 3rd Floor, Plot 3, Splendor Forum, Jasola District Centre,
New Delhi – 110025, India

Cambridge University Press is part of Cambridge University Press & Assessment, a department of the University of Cambridge.

We share the University's mission to contribute to society through the pursuit of education, learning and research at the highest international levels of excellence.

www.cambridge.org
Information on this title: www.cambridge.org/9781009209359

DOI: 10.1017/9781009209366

When citing this work, please include a reference to the DOI 10.1017/9781009209366

First published 2026

A catalogue record for this publication is available from the British Library

A Cataloging-in-Publication data record for this book is available from the Library of Congress

ISBN 978-1-009-20935-9 Hardback
ISBN 978-1-009-20934-2 Paperback

For D & M

Contents

Figures

Tables

Abbreviations

ABECOR	Associated Banks of Europe Corporation
ACEA	European Automobile Manufacturers' Association
AFB	Association française des banques
AMS	Associated Marketing Services
AMUE	Association for the Monetary Union of Europe
ASEAN	Association of Southeast Asian Nations
BIA	business interest association
BMW	Bayerische Motoren Werke
BNP	Banque nationale de Paris
CBI	Confederation of British Industry
CCD	Committee on Commerce and Distribution
CCMC	Committee of Common Market Automobile Constructors
CECD	Confédération européenne du commerce de détail
CEN	Comité européen de coordination des norms
CENELEC	European Committee for Electrotechnical Standardization
CEPS	Center for European Policy Studies
CIES	Comité internationale des entreprises succursales
EBF	European Banking Federation
EBIC	European Banking Industry Committee
EBRD	European Bank for Reconstruction and Development
ECJ	European Court of Justice
ECSC	European Coal and Steel Community
ECU	European Currency Unit
EEC	European Economic Community
EFTA	European Free Trade Association
EIB	European Investment Bank
ELEC	European League for Economic Cooperation
EMD	European Marketing Distribution
EMS	European Monetary System
EMU	Economic and Monetary Union

EPA	Environmental Protection Agency
EPC	European Political Cooperation
ERM	Exchange Rate Mechanism
ERRT	European Retail Round Table
ERT	European Round Table of Industrialists
ETSI	European Telecommunication Standards Institute
ETUC	European Trades Union Confederation
EU	European Union
EURATOM	European Atomic Energy Community
FEWITA	Federation of European Wholesale and International Trade Associations
FSU	Forward Studies Unit
GEDIS	Groupement européen des entreprises de distribution integrée
ICC	International Chamber of Commerce
IMF	International Monetary Fund
ISO	International Organization for Standardization
MERCOSUL	Mercado comum do sul (Southern Common Market)
MERCOSUR	Mercado común del sur (Southern Common Market)
NAFTA	North American Free Trade Agreement
OECD	Organization for Economic Cooperation and Development
PCF	Parti communiste français
PHARE	Poland and Hungary: Assistance for Restructuring their Economies
SEA	Single European Act
SEAT	Sociedad española de automóviles de turismo
SME	small and medium-sized enterprise
SOE	state-owned enterprise
UNCTAD	United Nations Conference on Trade and Development
UNECE	United Nations Economic Commission on Europe
UNICE	Union of Industrial and Employers' Confederations of Europe
VW	Volkswagen

Introduction

Business and European Political Economy

Throughout the second half of the twentieth century, economic cooperation and market integration were favorite tools to rebuild Europe after war, culminating in the completion of the Single European Market in the 1990s, on the foundation of which the European Union (EU) and its single euro currency were formed. As former European Commission President (1985–1995) Jacques Delors reflected in 2012, "Purely political projects had not worked [to unite Europe], but the economy made it possible to launch the European construction process. The trouble with the economy is that it is very distant from the man in the street. It does not speak to him with the same immediacy as a political or as an institutional reform."[1] By wrestling with that problem, this business history of the Single European Market is a story about whether and how capitalism can be reconciled with democracy, examined in the context designed to bring capitalism and democracy together on the largest possible scale: in a regional polity with an integrated market aimed at maximizing growth.[2]

By the twenty-first century, the Single European Market had become both the crowning achievement of the EU and a lightning rod for its critics. Europhiles celebrated the creation of the largest economy in the world, pointing to the region's global competitiveness and the waiting list of candidate states as signs of success and promises of further growth. Although it is not a state, Euroskeptics denounced the persistence of the EU's "democratic deficit" and accused its supranational institutions of insulating economies from accountability. Despite their divergent views, supporters and skeptics alike saw the internal market as a boon for European business, and the rise of European multinational companies

[1] Jacques Delors, "The Single Market, Cornerstone of the EU," *Notre Europe* (2012): 1–2.

[2] Several books have addressed the relationship of capitalism and democracy, notably: Naomi Oreskes and Erik M. Conway, *The Big Myth: How American Business Taught Us to Loathe Government and Love the Free Market* (New York: Bloomsbury, 2023); Martin Wolf, *The Crisis of Democratic Capitalism*, 1st ed. (London: Allen Lane, 2023). My book engages with that scholarship and contributes to that literature by tackling the issue in the context of contemporary Europe.

from the 1980s to 2000s seemed to bear out the shared conclusion, for better and worse. The progressive liberalization of goods, services, capital, and labor enabled firms to operate across member state borders. But some observers worried that widespread neoliberalism had allowed business to "set the agenda" for the Single Market Program in a struggle of "transnational capitalism" that had corrupted the very core of the Union.[3] Such debates came to a head in the UK's referendum on EU membership in 2016 and its fraught departure in 2020. Brexit proved the market to be the single most popular aspect of regional integration for both the "Leave" and "Remain" camps.[4] It simultaneously revealed the complexity of business perspectives and the limits of their influence, demanding a new analysis of the internal market and the firms that operate in it.

What does it mean to study business in European political economy? Since Susan Strange's landmark work on states and markets, scholarship on the development and regulation of the international economy has paid particular attention to the unprecedented developments of contemporary Europe.[5] That Europe became shorthand for the European Economic Community (EEC) by the 1970s and the EU by the 1990s reveals how successfully Europe was constructed as a political, economic, and cultural entity – an "uncanny" outcome, given the many other regional international organizations formed in the postwar period.[6] Not only was regional market integration among the first initiatives undertaken

[3] On these arguments, see: Maria Green Cowles, "Setting the Agenda for a New Europe: The ERT and EC 1992," *JCMS: Journal of Common Market Studies* 33, no. 4 (1995): 501–526; Bastiaan Van Apeldoorn, *Transnational Capitalism and the Struggle over European Integration* (London: Routledge, 2002); Magnus Ryner and Alan Cafruny, *The European Union and Global Capitalism: Origins, Development, Crisis* (London: Palgrave, 2016).

[4] Even chief Brexiteer Nigel Farage favored access to the Single Market. In a June 2016 speech at the European Parliament, he asked the EU to cut a "sensible, tariff-free deal" with the UK, giving it preferential market access subjecting it to the EU's rules, after which, he claimed, Britain would be Europe's "best friends in the world." Farage also framed the Brexit result as "the little people" having "rejected the multinationals … the merchant banks … big politics." See: Jon Stone, "Nigel Farage delivers first post-Brexit speech to the European Parliament in full," *The Independent*, June 30, 2016.

[5] Susan Strange, *States and Markets*, Reprint ed. (London; New York: Bloomsbury Academic, 2015); *The Retreat of the State: The Diffusion of Power in the World Economy*, Cambridge Studies in International Relations 49 (Cambridge; New York: Cambridge University Press, 1996); *Mad Money: When Markets Outgrow Governments* (Ann Arbor: The University of Michigan Press, 1998). Strange's earlier work dealt with the relationship of firms to governance: "States, Firms and Diplomacy," *International Affairs (Royal Institute of International Affairs 1944–)* 68, no. 1 (1992): 1–15; "Big Business and the State," in *Multinationals in the Global Political Economy*, ed. Lorraine Eden and Evan H. Potter (London: Palgrave Macmillan, 1993), 101–107.

[6] Kiran Klaus Patel, *Project Europe: A History* (Cambridge: Cambridge University Press, 2020).

by postwar organizations in the 1950s, but the Single Market Program launched in the summer of 1985 and concluded in December 1992 laid the foundation for subsequent economic and political cooperation in the region in the 1990s, 2000s, and beyond. Scholars agree on the centrality of an internal market to European integration, just as it was to nineteenth century efforts to transform the nascent US from a developing country into an economic powerhouse.[7] But they disagree on its agents. Neofunctionalists maintain that integration in one domain inevitably "spilled over" into others, that exogenous forces like crises can advance integration, and that interest groups have effectively pressured national governments to pursue cooperation.[8] Liberal intergovernmentalists insist instead on the agency of nation states in making "grand bargains" according to their own interests.[9] Still others theorize the matrix of multi-layered governance by states and supranational institutions in the political and economic development of the region.[10] The ensuing contest between these theories has dominated scholarship on contemporary Europe for almost as long as there has been a Europe to debate.[11]

[7] For comparisons of the European and US single markets, see: Michelle P. Egan, *Single Markets: Economic Integration in Europe and the United States* (Oxford: Oxford University Press, 2015); Craig Parsons, "The Extraordinary, Taken-for-Granted Achievement of Europe's Single Market," in *European Studies: Past, Present, Future,* ed. Erik Jones (Newcastle upon Tyne: Agenda Publishing, 2020). See also the ongoing ARENA project directed by Craig Parsons. On reinterpreting the US as a developing country, see: Stefan Link and Noam Maggor, "The United States as a Developing Nation: Revisiting the Peculiarities of American History," *Past & Present* 246, no. 1 (2020): 269–306.

[8] Ernst B. Haas first developed the theory of neo-functionalism and the language of "spillover." Among his many works, see: *The Uniting of Europe: Political, Social, and Economic Forces, 1950–1957* (Notre Dame, IN: University of Notre Dame Press, 2004). Neo-functionalists like Wayne Sandholtz, John Zysman, Neil Fligstein, and Alec Stone Sweet have advanced the theory. See: Sandholtz and Zysman, "1992: Recasting the European Bargain," *World Politics* 42, no. 1 (1989): 95–128; Fligstein and Stone Sweet: "Constructing Polities and Markets: An Institutionalist Account of European Integration," *American Journal of Sociology* 107, no. 5 (March 1, 2002): 1206–1243.

[9] Andrew Moravcsik, *The Choice for Europe: Social Purpose and State Power from Messina to Maastricht* (Ithaca, NY: Cornell University Press, 1998). While Moravcsik asserted the primacy of nation states, his *Choice for Europe* is among the few works of political science to address the interests of business on issues like the Common Agricultural Policy and European Monetary System. Before the publication of his book, Moravcsik applied his liberal intergovernmental analysis to the Single European Act of 1986: "Negotiating the Single European Act: National Interests and Conventional Statecraft in the European Community," *International Organization* 45, no. 1 (1991): 19–56.

[10] Liesbet Hooghe and Gary Marks, *Multi-Level Governance and European Integration* (Lanham, MD: Rowman & Littlefield Publishers, 2001).

[11] Catherine De Vries skillfully reviewed the influence of these narratives on EU politics: "How Foundational Narratives Shape European Union Politics," *JCMS: Journal of Common Market Studies* 61, no. 4 (2022): 867–881.

What these literatures share is a relative neglect of economic actors in European integration in favor of a focus on states and, to a lesser extent, on labor, which drew attention during the Marxist moment of ultimately unrealized optimism for a "social Europe."[12] Many studies of business in contemporary Europe have worked to measure the influence of business interest associations (BIAs) on European policymaking and trace the impact of market integration on the structure of organized interests.[13] Indeed, the activities of interest groups and lobbies in Brussels offer one important perspective on business and European political economy. But understanding the complexity of market integration also requires a close analysis of the actors that make up the market, from the many small and medium sized enterprises (SMEs) doing business in the EEC to the national champions of EEC member states to the multinational corporations operating within and beyond the region.[14] This book addresses a range of business perspectives by embedding discussions of interest group influence within case studies of individual firms. Business strategies reveal the ways companies shaped the functioning of the market, and BIA activities illuminate both the power and the limits of business influence.

My narrative reconstructs the making of the Single European Market through the lens of European business. It shows European firms – especially

[12] Vivien Schmidt noted growing interest in business in the early twenty-first century after decades of scholarly focus on labor and states: "European Political Economy: Labour Out, State Back In, Firm to the Fore," *West European Politics* 31, no. 1–2 (2008): 302–320. This interest seems to have since waned, however. To be sure, neofunctionalists have focused on economic actors more than any other group of scholars. On the rise and fall of social Europe, see: Aurélie Dianara Andry, *Social Europe, the Road Not Taken: The Left and European Integration in the Long 1970s*, Oxford Studies in Modern European History, 1st ed. (Oxford, New York: Oxford University Press, 2022).

[13] The majority of this literature has been written by political scientists and economic sociologists. See, for example: Justin Greenwood, *Interest Representation in the European Union*, 4th ed. 2017 edition (London: Palgrave, 2017); Wolfgang Streeck et al., eds., *Governing Interests: Business Associations Facing Internationalism* (London: Routledge, 2006).

[14] Several business historians have tackled the question of corporate nationality, which is particularly important in the context of the EEC, in the markets of which companies headquartered in the US and Japan invested heavily in the twentieth century. This book focuses on companies headquartered in the EEC, even as it explores the complexities of determining which firms were "European." On corporate nationality, see: Geoffrey Jones, "Nationality and Multinationals in Historical Perspective," Harvard Business School Working Paper 00-052 (2006); Alfred Reckendrees, Boris Gehlen, and Christian Marx, "International Business, Multinational Enterprises and Nationality of the Company: A Constructive Review of Literature," *Business History* 64, no. 9 (2022): 1567–1599; Boris Gehlen, Christian Marx, and Alfred Reckendrees, "Ambivalences of Nationality – Economic Nationalism, Nationality of the Company, Nationalism as Strategy: An Introduction," *Journal of Modern European History* 18, no. 1 (2020): 16–27.

multinational enterprises – were central to the market's policy design in the 1980s, contributed to the public–private process of integration throughout the EEC's program to complete an internal market by its 1992 deadline, and progressively regionalized their operations and political activities in response to the changing business environment of the 1990s. As a result, and by drawing on scholarship on the "European experience" of big business, I argue multinational businesses shaped the Single European Market during the crucial decades of its formation. They exerted policy influence through formal channels of lobbying and elite exchange, and they exerted market influence through their corporate structures, supply chains, and operations in the region. Not only did many firms expand their operations across EEC member states in the late twentieth century, but some also used the internal market as a springboard from which to globalize in the twenty-first, thereby repositioning Europe in the global economy. My narrative also explains why and how the internal market, motivated by a desire to recover the growth rates of the postwar boom, reflected the interests of labor-intensive industry more than those of the emergent service economy and was thus already outdated before it was completed.

Such findings raise serious implications for the other dimensions of economic and political integration that rest on the market, including the creation of a single currency and the formation of the EU. But my narrative also shows the Single Market was more than a mere liberalization project and did not always favor business interests, nor did firms always support integration. Consequently, this is not a European case of what Naomi Oreskes and Erik M. Conway have described in the American context as *The Big Myth* of market fundamentalism, even if the market was core to the creation of the contemporary EU.[15] Indeed, instances of business opposition to regulatory, social, and environmental policies underscore the market's embeddedness in the wider regulatory frameworks of the EEC and EU. Already by 1991, the EEC described the Single Market as the source of its global soft power, including on the increasingly salient issue of climate change: "With the completion of the Internal Market, the European Community will be the biggest economic/trading partner in the world with the potential to exercise an important level of moral, economic and political influence and authority."[16]

[15] Naomi Oreskes and Erik M. Conway, *The Big Myth: How American Business Taught Us to Loathe Government and Love the Free Market* (New York: Bloomsbury, 2023).

[16] European Commission, "A Community Strategy to Limit Carbon Dioxide Emissions and to Improve Energy Efficiency. Communication from the Commission to the Council" SEC (91) 1744 final, October 14, 1991.

In scholarship and beyond, the term "business" is used to gesture broadly to economic entities engaged in production and commerce for profit, whether privately controlled or state owned. It appears in the singular to refer to industrial or commercial actors as a group nearly as frequently as it appears in the plural to refer to specific firms. This language reflects the usual treatment of business as a monolith and the assumption that the interests of capital are cohesive and common. Beyond the "varieties of capitalism," however, is an even broader diversity of firms.[17] Differences in size and structure, management and market segment determine how firms experience business environments and their capacity to influence policies and policymakers. Multinational companies are distinct among these many forms of enterprise. Their origins within early merchant empires as what Geoffrey Jones has called "proto-multinational" companies – and their differentiation from the free-standing companies Mira Wilkins identified as firms engaged only in foreign direct investment – position them as key actors in both home and host countries.[18] Through their expansion into international markets and development of international supply and value chains, multinationals have honed the ability to adapt to new economic and regulatory environments and navigate political risks, especially by establishing networks of subsidiary firms, as well as supply and value chains.[19] As a result, they have been powerful drivers of globalization even in the face of economic nationalism. And by availing themselves of the benefits of tax havens and through innovations in legal structures like incorporation,

[17] Peter A. Hall and David Soskice introduced the framing of "varieties of capitalism" in their: *Varieties of Capitalism* (Oxford: Oxford University Press, 2001). See also: Georg Menz, *Varieties of Capitalism and Europeanization: National Response Strategies to the Single European Market* (Oxford; New York: Oxford University Press, 2008). For a management perspective on the diversity of firm types, see: Richard R. Nelson, "Why Do Firms Differ, and How Does It Matter?" *Strategic Management Journal* 12, no. 2 (1991): 61–74.

[18] On the origins of multinationals and their role in globalization, see the many works of Geoffrey Jones, especially: *Multinationals and Global Capitalism: From the Nineteenth to the Twenty-First Century* (Oxford; New York: Oxford University Press, 2005). On free-standing companies, see: Mira Wilkins, "The Free-Standing Company, 1870–1914: An Important Type of British Foreign Direct Investment," *The Economic History Review* 41, no. 2 (1988): 259–282; Mira Wilkins and Harm Schroter, eds., *The Free-Standing Company in the World Economy, 1830–1996* (Oxford: Oxford University Press, 1999).

[19] On multinationals and political risks, see: Sabine Pitteloud, *Les multinationales suisses dans l'arène politique, 1942–1993* (Geneva: Droz, 2022); Christina Lubinski, *Navigating Nationalism in Global Enterprise: A Century of Indo-German Business Relations* (Cambridge: Cambridge University Press, 2022). On multinationals and value chains, see the many works of Gary Gereffi, including: Timothy Sturgeon, Johannes Van Biesebroeck, and Gary Gereffi, "Value Chains, Networks and Clusters: Reframing the Global Automotive Industry," *Journal of Economic Geography* 8, no. 3 (2008): 297–321.

multinationals have developed ways to shield owners and shareholders from legal liability, affording them considerable latitude in their international operations.[20]

Given their characteristics and role in globalization, multinational corporations might seem the most likely supporters of regional market integration, equally advocates and beneficiaries of efforts to remove tariff and nontariff barriers between geographically proximate countries. Many European multinationals, incentivized by changing market conditions, entered other countries in the region and established regional production and distribution, subsidiaries and chains. As my narrative shows, however, European multinationals varied almost as much in their perspectives on and experiences of the Single Market as they did in their countries of origin and industries. Consequently, the transnational BIAs in which they participated functioned as forums for consensus and instruments of influence as often as they devolved into arenas of conflict, sometimes to the point of group collapse.[21] At other times, BIAs joined similarly skeptical groups of firms together in collective defense against the perceived threat of an integrated region. Ironically, even organizing against Europe contributed to European integration.

To scholarship on international business, this history of European political economy offers a detailed picture of the complex context in which firms and their chairmen operated. Not only are supranational governance and intergovernmental decision making idiosyncratic as the *sui generis* elements of the European Communities and EU, but the processes of designing the market and its policies were opaque, sometimes obscured even from member state governments.[22] Companies had

[20] Gabriel Zucman measured the economic effects of corporate and private tax havens in his *The Hidden Wealth of Nations: The Scourge of Tax Havens*, trans. Teresa Lavender Fagan and with a foreword by Thomas Piketty (Chicago: University of Chicago Press, 2016). On the global histories of tax havens and their regulation, see the many works of Vanessa Ogle, including: "Archipelago Capitalism: Tax Havens, Offshore Money, and the State, 1950s–1970s," *The American Historical Review* 122, no. 5 (2017): 1431–1458; and "Governing Global Tax Dodgers: The 'Group of Four' and Taxation of Multinational Corporations," *Business History Review* 97, no. 3 (2023): 547–574.

[21] Wolfgang Streeck and Philippe C. Schmitter have written extensively about the sociology of organized interests in the context of the Single Market. See their: "From National Corporatism to Transnational Pluralism: Organized Interests in the Single European Market," *Politics & Society* 19, no. 2 (1991): 133–164.

[22] One such example of efforts to obscure supranational governance from member states was the secretive trade agreement made between the EEC and Japan in the early 1990s. See: Grace Ballor, "Liberalisation or Protectionism for the Single Market? European Automakers and Japanese Competition, 1985–1999," *Business History* 65, no. 2 (2022): 302–328; Alice Milor, "Non-documents for Big Decisions: The Commission and the EEC-Japan Automotive Agreement (1991)," *JCMS: Journal of Common Market Studies* 62, no. 6 (2024): 1654–1671.

to navigate still wider information asymmetries and a rapidly changing regulatory landscape. Together with the records of regional policymaking, the deliberations that drove business decisions in those circumstances have remained sealed by archival closure rules until recently.[23] Access to institutional and corporate documents – together with interviews of officials and executives – now makes it possible to uncover the ways policymakers thought about companies in their designs for the Single Market as well as the ways firms adapted their strategies and political activities to it. By embedding case studies of business strategy into a larger narrative history of market integration, I aim to reassert the agency of corporations, executives, and BIAs in the making of the market and to show how business responded to the aspects of market policy that contradicted their interests.

To scholarship on contemporary Europe, this business history of European political economy challenges the linear teleology of European integration and reinforces its historical contingency in four ways. First, my narrative provincializes the Single Market by framing market integration as part of a long and contingent historical process, inflected by global events and affected by global actors like multinational corporations. Second, a focus on firms pluralizes the actors involved in market integration, expanding the scope of agency from nation states and supranational institutions to interest associations, companies, and even individual executives. Third, granular analyses of a wide range of firms problematize business influence on the market by uncovering instances in which business interests eclipsed those of the demos and by demonstrating the broad spectrum of firm perspectives on regional market integration – from active proponents to "business Eurosceptics."[24] Fourth, engagement with arguments about the market's winners and losers and the need for reform politicizes the history of market integration and situates this book among present debates about the future of regulating and doing business in Europe.

Provincializing the Single Market

Is the Single European Market unique and distinct from other efforts to integrate regional markets? Where should we place it among other

[23] The Historical Archives of the European Union maintains a 30-year rule, as do many corporate archives, meaning access to the final year of documents from the 1992 Program became available in 2022.

[24] On the framing of "business Eurosceptics," see: Grace Ballor, "Business Eurosceptics: British Industry on Economic and Monetary Union, 1978–1999." *Business History* (2026).

modern eco-political projects?[25] Furthermore, is the Single European Market a vision of a post-national future? In the mid-eighteenth century, Enlightenment thinkers like Montesquieu and Charles de Villers advocated for more robust regional trade and outlined plans for a "European" customs union, centered on the Western, Christian, industrialized part of continent.[26] The German *Zollverein* – established in the 1830s to remove tariffs between and coordinate the economic policies of German states – put those Enlightenment ideas into practice, albeit on a smaller scale. That the nascent German nation state was already an industrial powerhouse by the 1870s demonstrated the potential of a customs union to nation-build and spur economic development.[27] After the Great War shocked the globalized world of the *fin de siècle* and a new world order took shape in the League of Nations, groups of European federalists advocated for the creation of a regional polity, a "United States of Europe."[28] For eclectic visionaries like Richard von Coudenhove-Kalergi, such regionalism could restructure the outmoded worlds of nations and empires into five global superstates pictured in Figure 0.1,[29] each complete with its own customs union.[30] He imagined the sprawling "Pan-Europa," after which he named the first international organization for European unity, would bind together the imperial continent and its overseas colonies – notably excluding Britain and its empire – while shielding Christian, democratic Europe and its capitalist interests from the threat of Eastern

[25] On twentieth-century eco-political constructions, see: Charles S. Maier, *The Project-State and Its Rivals: A New History of the Twentieth and Twenty-First Centuries* (Cambridge, MA: Harvard University Press, 2023). This language of "project" also draws on the work of Kiran Klaus Patel. See his *Project Europe: A History* (Cambridge: Cambridge University Press, 2020).

[26] For excerpts of these writings, see the anthology edited by Catriona Seth and Rotraud von Kulessa on early ideas of Europe: *The Idea of Europe: Enlightenment Perspectives* (Cambridge: Open Book Publishers, 2017).

[27] For more on the Zollverein and its legacy, see: Rolf H. Dumke, "The Political Economy of German Economic Unification: Tariffs, Trade and Politics of the Zollverein Era," *The Journal of Economic History* 38, no. 1 (1978): 277–278; W. O. Henderson, "The German Zollverein and the European Economic Community," *Zeitschrift Für Die Gesamte Staatswissenschaft / Journal of Institutional and Theoretical Economics* 137, no. 3 (1981): 491–507; W. R. Lee, "Economic Development and the State in Nineteenth-Century Germany," *The Economic History Review* 41, no. 3 (1988): 346–367.

[28] Calls for the creation of a "United States of Europe" have a long and contested history, from early modern political philosophers to nineteenth century On European federalist movements, see: Walter Lipgens, *A History of European Integration: 1945–1947* (Oxford: Clarendon Press, 1982).

[29] Redrawn from: Coudenhove-Kalergi, *Europa Erwacht!* Many thanks to Dan Sauer for the visualization.

[30] Richard von Coudenhove-Kalergi's outlined his vision in: *Europa Erwacht!* (Paris; Vienna; Zürich: Paneuropa-Verlag, 1932).

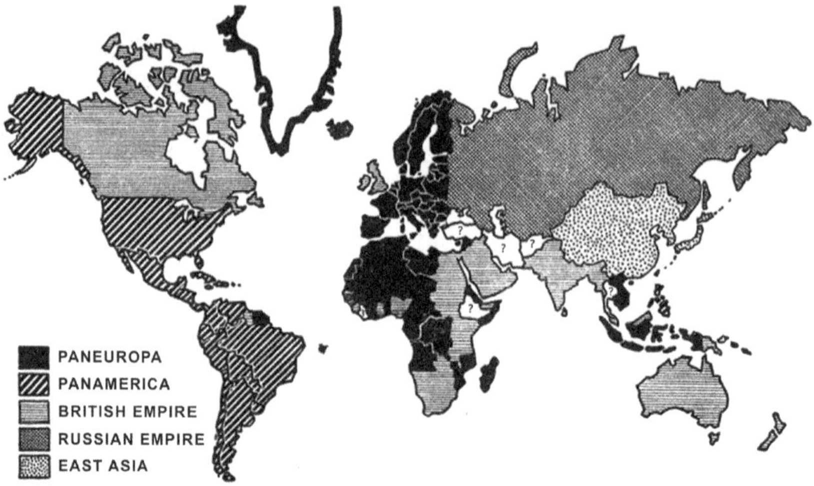

Figure 0.1 Coudenhove-Kalergi's world of superstates.

Bolshevism.[31] In reality, while the League organized the political world by nation rather than region or empire, it facilitated a restructuring of the global economy into various scalar units through "most favored nation" agreements, the arbitration of which was delegated to the new global business organization, the International Chamber of Commerce (ICC).[32] To the federal, superstate, and international organization visions for a united Europe alike, an integrated market was essential. Few of these regionalists had personal experience in commerce, however, and the early twentieth-century world in which they developed their thinking was dominated by empires and state-owned enterprises.

In the crucible of the 1930s, a group of central European economists developed more expansive ideas about the relationships of states and markets. The wartime collapse of landed empires and emergence of international organizations motivated members of what Quinn

[31] Although Coudenhove-Kalergi's superstates and their integrated markets went realized amid the economic tumult of the Great Depression and the conflict of the Second World War, his Pan-Europeanism enjoyed new support in the war's aftermath. British statesman Leopold Amery, likewise saw the "world in blocs," with markets organized into imperial economic unions with preferential tariffs. On Amery, see: Liane Hewitt, "The World in Blocs: Leo Amery, the British Empire and Regionalist Anti-Internationalism, 1903–1947," *Journal of Global History* 17, no. 2 (2022): 1–23.

[32] Patricia Clavin and Madeleine Dungy, "Trade, Law, and the Global Order of 1919," *Diplomatic History* 44, no. 4 (2020): 554–579; Madeleine Lynch Dungy, *Order and Rivalry: Rewriting the Rules of International Trade after the First World War* (Cambridge: Cambridge University Press, 2023).

Slobodian named the "Geneva School" to remake the relationship between *imperium* and *dominium* by encasing markets in structures that would insulate them from democratic intervention.[33] For "globalists" like Wilhelm Röpke, the globe was the only acceptable unit of post-nation political economy, and the outbreak of a Second World War provided the clean slate necessary to construct a new order of global markets embedded within global institutions. Debates about scale in international political economy only intensified when the postwar creation of European customs unions and then the launch of a program to create an internal market further divided regionalist and globalist neoliberals for and against Europe.[34] In the subsequent creation of the European Free Trade Association (EFTA) in 1960, Association of Southeast Asian Nations (ASEAN) in 1967, Southern Common Market (MERCOSUR/L) in 1991, North American Free Trade Agreement (NAFTA) in 1994, and thousands of preferential free trade zones around the world, globalists found plenty of targets to criticize "crack-up capitalism" beyond the EEC.[35]

Nor was the timing of Europe's market embrace coincidental. By the early 1980s, protracted economic downturn had supplanted the founding rhetoric of European integration as a postwar peace project with the new primacy of the growth imperative. Repeated recessions weakened national GDPs and state tax revenues, seemingly sealing the fate of Keynesian economics and characterizing the 1970s to early 1980s as a period of "crisis," debates about which are addressed in Chapter 1.[36] Following the elections of Margaret Thatcher as British prime minister in 1979 and Ronald Reagan as US president in 1980, the Anglo–US alliance and the international organizations they led launched a double campaign to persuade the rest of the world to deregulate, liberalize,

[33] Quinn Slobodian, *Globalists: The End of Empire and the Birth of Neoliberalism* (Cambridge, MA: Harvard University Press, 2018).

[34] Quinn Slobodian and Dieter Plehwe have written about these dialectics in their: "Neoliberals against Europe," in *Mutant Neoliberalism: Market Rule and Political Ruptures.*, ed. William Callison and Zachary Manfredi (New York: Fordham University Press, 2019), 89–111. On the globalist critiques of the EEC, see: Slobodian, *Globalists*, 146–181.

[35] Quinn Slobodian, *Crack-Up Capitalism: Market Radicals and the Dream of a World Without Democracy* (New York: Metropolitan Books, 2023). On multinationals and market integration in many regions of the globe, see: Grace Ballor, "Multinationals and Market Integration," in *The Cambridge Companion to Multinationals and Society*, ed. Geoffrey Jones and Sabine Pitteloud (Cambridge: Cambridge University Press, 2026).

[36] Due to simultaneously high inflation, some nominal GDPs grew during this period, as was the case for the UK. See: World Bank, "National Accounts Data – United Kingdom, 1960–2022."

and privatize (by enforcing "the Washington Consensus") – and to simultaneously outcompete them.[37] In response, officials in many EEC member states adopted their own neoliberal agendas to keep pace, putting their faith the market's ability to remedy economic and social woes. To optimists, the "end of history" in 1989–1991 seemed to confirm the liberal triumph.[38] But setting common economic policy proved less cut and dried. Laurent Warlouzet uncovered the difficult legislative compromise the EEC had to chart between French dirigisme and industrial policy on the one hand and German ordoliberalism and competition policy on the other.[39] Not only did European policymakers have to "battle" through the development of common economic thought, but they were as susceptible to internal tensions as they were to outside influence, including from business interests.[40]

Set against this expanded backdrop, the making of the Single European Market in the 1980s and 1990s becomes just one chapter in a longer, larger story of twentieth-century political economy, further provincialized through the lens of business.[41] Especially for multinationals, the 1992 Program, named for the Single Market completion deadline, informed decisions about investment, acquisitions, mergers, and supply chain development even more intensively than the EEC's

[37] On neoliberalism in the US, see: Gary Gerstle, *The Rise and Fall of the Neoliberal Order: America and the World in the Free Market Era* (Oxford; New York: Oxford University Press, 2022).

[38] Francis Fukuyama, "The End of History?" *The National Interest* no. 16 (1989): 3–18.

[39] See Laurent Warlouzet's many works on European political economy, including: *Governing Europe in a Globalizing World: Neoliberalism and Its Alternatives Following the 1973 Oil Crisis*, 1st ed. (New York; London: Routledge, 2017); "The EEC/EU as an Evolving Compromise between French Dirigism and German Ordoliberalism (1957–1995)," *JCMS: Journal of Common Market Studies* 57, no. 1 (2019): 77–93; *Europe contre Europe: Entre liberté, solidarité et puissance* (Paris: CNRS Editions, 2022). For an overview of European competition policy, see his: "La politique de la concurrence européenne depuis 1950: Surveiller les entreprises et les États," *CVCE*, University of Luxembourg (2012): 1–11. See also the PhD dissertation of Dorothea Todd at the University of Glasgow, "The Freiburg School and the Making of the Euro" (2023).

[40] Gilles Grin, *The Battle of the Single European Market: Achievements and Economic Thought, 1985–2000* (London: Kegan Paul, 2003).

[41] In 2013, Kiran Klaus Patel appealed to scholars of European integration to use a historical lens to situate contemporary Europe in its larger context; progress had been made by 2019, he argued, and encouraged historians to increasingly incorporate work from other disciplines: "Provincialising European Union: Co-Operation and Integration in Europe in a Historical Perspective," *Contemporary European History* 22, no. 4 (2013): 649–673; "Widening and Deepening? Recent Advances in European Integration History," *Neue Politische Literatur* 64, no. 2 (2019): 327–357. Such work builds on the important scholarship of Dipesh Chakrabarty, who identified the "imaginary Europe" at the center of social science research. See his: *Provincializing Europe: Postcolonial Thought and Historical Difference* (Princeton, NJ: Princeton University Press, 2007).

common market had in the 1950s and 1960s. Companies based in European member states were confronted with the equal challenge and opportunity of an enlarged internal market in which state aids and protections were no longer permitted and public procurement and contract competition were regional not national. Firms headquartered outside the EEC in countries like Japan also perceived the advantages of access to a large market with just a single set of common standards, so long as they could get beyond the potential commercial policy barriers of "Fortress Europe." Meanwhile, SMEs throughout the region had their own experiences of the market: some faced heightened competition as firms increasingly did business across member state borders, and many became nodes in the networks of European multinationals, especially after German reunification and the collapse of the Soviet Bloc opened central and eastern Europe to international business.[42] In fact, as historians Angela Romano, Federico Romero, and Aleksandra Komornicka have shown, entrepreneurs and enterprises had long engaged in business across the Iron Curtain, affecting both Soviet and EEC economies during the crucial years of the 1992 Program and opening of the East and reflecting the embeddedness of Europe and its market in the global economy.[43]

Business experiences of the Single European Market also shed light on the history of globalization and the role that companies have played in integrating economies and markets across and between regions. While conventional narratives assume multinational companies increasingly globalized their operations in the late twentieth century, international business scholars like Alan Rugman and Alain Verbeke argue instead that most of the world's largest firms do business within just one region.[44] Beyond the methodological issues inherent in the data provided as evidence for "regional multinationals" and the limitations of a focus on sales rather than production, their conclusions raise two sets of questions: Did

[42] On the ways policymakers viewed SMEs in the 1970s, see the PhD thesis by Laurens-Jan Danen completed at the European University Institute in 2025.

[43] See the volume edited by Angela Romano and Romero Federico: *European Socialist Regimes' Fateful Engagement with the West: National Strategies in the Long 1970s*, 1st ed. (Abingdon, Oxon; New York: Routledge, 2021); Aleksandra Komornicka, *Poland and European East-West Cooperation in the 1970s: The Opening Up* (London: Routledge, 2023).

[44] See: Alan M. Rugman and Alain Verbeke, "A Perspective on Regional and Global Strategies of Multinational Enterprises," *Journal of International Business Studies* 35, no. 1 (2004): 3–18; Alan M. Rugman, *The Regional Multinationals: MNEs and "Global" Strategic Management* (Cambridge; New York: Cambridge University Press, 2005); Benjamin Rosa, Philippe Gugler, and Alain Verbeke, "Regional and Global Strategies of MNEs: Revisiting Rugman & Verbeke (2004)," *Journal of International Business Studies* 51, no. 7 (September 1, 2020): 1045–1053.

multinationals organize their operations regionally to align with preferential regional trade frameworks, or did multinational preferences shape the geometry of international political economy into regions? Chapter 3 of this book builds on scholarship by Kerry Chase and Shannon O'Neil about the "myth of globalization" and "why regions matter" by presenting the Single European Market as an ideal case in which to examine these questions, answers to which require a closer analysis of business strategy and the relationship of companies to those designing and regulating the markets in which they operate.[45]

Pluralizing Market Actors

Was the Single Market designed by and for profit, or people? Answering that crucial question requires identification of the market's architects and their motivations. The regional international organizations that proliferated in the aftermath of the Second World War shared two common features: Their objectives were overwhelmingly oriented around international economic cooperation as a means of preserving peace and advancing collective prosperity, and their signatories were nation states. Through international agreements, these nation states became member states of the new United Nations Economic Commission for Europe (UNECE), Organization for European Economic Cooperation (which later became the OECD), and Council of Europe – to name just a few of the organizations created in the late 1940s.[46] In the 1950s, six European countries formed closer-knit communities, beginning with the European Coal and Steel Community (ECSC) established in 1951 to secure peace by jointly managing strategic resources and facilitating economic integration through a limited customs union, originally outlined in a plan developed by Robert Schuman in 1950 in collaboration with Jean Monnet. Not only did the ECSC stabilize international relations among the erstwhile enemies of France, Italy, West Germany, and the Benelux states, but historian Alan Milward argued that regional cooperation actually "rescued the nation state" from the deleterious effects of world war and the intensive social demands of the postwar period.[47] Figures like Jean Monnet, Robert Schuman, Alcide de Gaspari, and Paul-Henri

[45] Kerry A. Chase, *Trading Blocs: States, Firms, and Regions in the World Economy* (Ann Arbor: University of Michigan Press, 2005); Shannon O'Neil, *The Globalization Myth: Why Regions Matter* (New York: Council on Foreign Relations, 2022).

[46] In the first chapter of his *Project Europe*, Kiran Klaus Patel counted a global total of 1,255 international organizations created in the postwar period (p. 15).

[47] Alan S. Milward, *The European Rescue of the Nation-State*, 2nd ed. (London; New York: Routledge, 2000).

Spaak loomed large in the hagiography of mid-twentieth-century Europe, but they acted on behalf of and as officials representing their countries of origin within early regional organizations.[48] In short, in the history and historiography of early regional economic cooperation, nation states were both the primary actors and chief beneficiaries.[49]

Non-state and non-European actors were rarely constrained by national borders, however, nor were they mere observers of twentieth-century regional cooperation. The emergence of the Cold War positioned Europe in the crosshairs of another global conflict between East and West. Rising tensions motivated the US to extend Marshall Aid funds to European countries for reconstruction and development already in the late 1940s, the stipulations of which confirmed the US's capacity for international economic and political influence even to the point of institution-building.[50] It also motivated Europeans to pursue regional economic cooperation within postwar organizations like the ECSC. And it motivated the EEC and its member states to engage increasingly in economic exchange with both the US and the Soviet Bloc throughout the decades-long conflict until German reunification paved the way for former Bloc states to join the EU and its Single Market.[51]

If the establishment of the ECSC represented a shift toward endogenously motivated regionalism, it also marked a transition from sovereign cooperation to transnational integration.[52] This more intensive form of regional interdependence included the active dismantling of select tariffs and quotas, the joint management of strategic resources, and the creation of the first supranational institutions: the High Authority, Common

[48] In his *European Rescue of the Nation-State*, Milward used the language of "hagiography" to criticize the tendency of scholarship to make "great saints" of the "founding fathers" of the early European organizations and communities.

[49] For a longer discussion of the early role of nation states and nationalism, see: Grace Ballor, "Europe between Nationalism and Neoliberalism," in Cemil Aydin et al., "Rethinking Nationalism," *The American Historical Review* 127, no. 1 (2022): 311–371.

[50] The OEEC, for example, was created in 1948 to administer the Marshall Aid. Shortly after, the US dollar's primacy as the world's reserve currency required OEEC countries to create the European Payments Union in 1950, demonstrating the US's direct and indirect influence on the creation of European organizations. The US also stipulated that countries receiving Marshall funds should engage in regional economic cooperation.

[51] For more on the evolution of EC international relations during the Cold War, see: Angela Romano, "The EC and the Socialist World: The Ascent of a Key Player in Cold War Europe," in *Europe's Cold War Relations: The EC Towards a Global Role*, ed. Ulrich Krotz, Kiran Klaus Patel, and Federico Romero (London: Bloomsbury, 2020), 51–71; Angela Romano and Federico Romero, eds., *European Socialist Regimes' Fateful Engagement with the West: National Strategies in the Long 1970s*, 1st ed. (Abingdon, Oxon; New York: Routledge, 2021).

[52] Laurent Warlouzet has critiqued the disciplinary usage of these terms in his: "European Integration History: Beyond the Crisis," *Politique europeenne* 44, no. 2 (2014): 98–122.

Assembly, Special Council, and Court of Justice.[53] After the failure of the proposed European Defense Community in 1954, the Messina Conference and subsequent signing of the Treaty of Rome in 1957 created two more Communities among ECSC member states: the European Atomic Energy Community (EURATOM) and the EEC, the improbable predecessor of the EU.[54] Outlined in the Treaty was the promise of "an ever-closer union," the first step of which was to extend the ECSC's coal and steel customs union to the whole economy by 1970, a progression then theorized by Béla Belassa in his five-stage evolution of economic integration: free trade area, customs union, common market, economic union, and total integration.[55] The regional common market of the EEC's "inner six," completed two years ahead of schedule, stood in stark contrast to the mere free trade zone of the EFTA's "outer seven."

The Treaty of Rome also concretized the integrative role of the newly renamed and newly common supranational institutions of the three Communities: the European Commission, European Parliament, European Council, and Court of Justice (ECJ).[56] In several decisions in the 1960s and 1970s, the ECJ worked to realize the market objectives of the Treaty. Most notably, in its 1979 ruling on the *Cassis de Dijon* case about national standards for products like alcoholic beverages, the Court implemented the principle of mutual recognition, requiring member states to allow goods that met the technical specifications of the member state of origin to move freely between borders.[57] But even this legal precedent did not address the foundational issues of common standards and system compatibility required for an internal market. In the mid-1980s, the Commission devised a plan to "relaunch" the EEC and bolster "European competitiveness" by completing an internal market free from even non tariff barriers to trade.[58] The 1992 Program aimed to create a business environment in which European companies could restructure, re-strategize, and eventually reemerge as leaders in the

[53] In his *Project Europe*, Kiran Patel notes that the Economic Cooperation Administration responsible for the Marshall Plan was the first to use the term "integration" in reference to postwar European cooperation (pp. 35–36).

[54] In 1955–1956 following the Messina Conference, Paul-Henri Spaak oversaw the work of the intergovernmental committee studying further integration between the six member states of the ECSC, including the creation of a common market, which was presented in the eponymous Spaak Report of 1956.

[55] Béla Balassa, *The Theory of Economic Integration* (Homewood, IL: RD Irwin, 1961); Commission of the European Communities, *The Treaty of Rome*, preamble.

[56] The Merger Treaty of 1965 consolidated the institutional frameworks of the three European Communities (EC).

[57] For an overview of the ruling's legacy, see: Albertina Albors-Llorens, Catherine Barnard, Brigitte Leucht, eds., *Cassis de Dijon: 40 Years On* (Oxford: Hart Publishing, 2021).

[58] European Commission, "White Paper on Completing the Internal Market," 1985.

global economy. It also aimed to advance the progress toward monetary union begun in the 1970s.[59] Whether market integration was its ultimate goal or the Commission was merely "playing the market" as a means to more political ends as Nicolas Jabko has argued, its members bore the institutional responsibility for the market's policy design.[60] Their work was expedited by the 1986 Single European Act (SEA), which created the institutional framework for market making by increasing the powers of European institutions and their mandates, especially to remove all nontariff barriers in the EEC. With the SEA and under its president Jacques Delors, the Commission gained even more responsibility over the design of the market and its policies, and the Council, comprised of the heads of member states, controlled the approval and implementation of the Commission's proposals, a responsibility conditionally shared with the Parliament after 1979.[61]

Beyond the institutional foundation laid by treaties like Rome and the SEA, European law created the framework for market integration. International law is already a critical link between global capitalism and global governance.[62] But Renaud Dehousse and Joseph H. H. Weiler argued that common legislation in the European Communities forged a union like no other force could and provided the structure for cross-border business activity.[63] For Antoine Vauchez, it was not just the force of the law, but the judges, attorneys, law firms, and legal scholars working in and on the European Communities that realized a transnational polity and its integrated market.[64] While landmark legal cases

[59] Emmanuel Mourlon-Druol, *A Europe Made of Money: The Emergence of the European Monetary System*, Cornell Studies in Money (Ithaca, NY: Cornell University Press, 2012); Harold James, *Making the European Monetary Union* (Cambridge, MA: Belknap Press, 2012). See also Mourlon-Druol's ERC Project: "EURECON: The Making of a Lopsided Union: Economic Integration in the European Economic Community, 1957–1992."

[60] Nicolas Jabko, *Playing the Market: A Political Strategy for Uniting Europe, 1985–2005* (Ithaca, NY: Cornell University Press, 2006).

[61] Laurent Warlouzet traced the evolution of the Parliament and its role in market integration in his *Completing the Single Market: The European Parliament and Economic Integration, 1979–1989* (Luxembourg: Publications Office of the European Union, 2020).

[62] On the relationship of capitalism and global governance, see: Sabine Pitteloud et al., "Capitalism and Global Governance in Business History: A Roundtable Discussion," HBS Working Paper No. 22-081 (2022): 1–57.

[63] Renaud Dehousse and Joseph H. H. Weiler published their arguments about the role of law in European integration in: "The Legal Dimension," in *The Dynamics of European Integration*, ed. William Wallace (London: Pinter Publishers, 1990): 242–259.

[64] Among his many works, see: Antoine Vauchez, *Brokering Europe: Euro-Lawyers and the Making of a Transnational Polity* (Cambridge: Cambridge University Press, 2015).

like the *Cassis de Dijon* ruling underscore the vital role of the ECJ and actions of the court reinforce its role in ongoing economic governance, they also highlight where the limits of the law leave room for – and even require – other actors to shape the market.[65]

The creation of the European Communities in the 1950s dramatically changed the regional business environment, prompting responses from companies doing business in Europe. As Chapter 1 explains, some firms based in Western European member states viewed the EEC's creation of a regional common market with intense skepticism and worried about what increased competition would mean for their business. Others saw regional integration as a growth opportunity and immediately organized themselves to benefit from close contact with the new institutions of regional governance. Just after the Treaty of Rome took effect in December 1958, European business leaders wrote to Commissioner for Industry and the Economy Paul de Groote to explain that it is "extremely important that we are able to establish very close and permanent contacts with your institution."[66] De Groote welcomed collaboration with the region's leading industrialists and helped shape the business group into the "Chamber of European Commerce for the Three Communities," which met frequently with the Commission to discuss economic policy.[67] Perhaps the most enthusiastic observers of early European market integration were US multinationals, who keenly followed the development of the customs union, ripe for their investment, and expanded into European markets with the help of representation in business organizations like the US Council of the ICC.[68] US multinationals were such successful entrants into EEC markets that some Europeans worried, as

[65] Paul Dermine, *The New Economic Governance of the Eurozone: A Rule of Law Analysis*, Cambridge Studies in European Law and Policy (Cambridge: Cambridge University Press, 2022).

[66] Letter from Chamber of Commerce to High Authority, December 16, 1958. BAC 118/1986, Historical Archives of the European Union (hereafter HAEU).

[67] Note A. M. Meugens (Cabinet de M. de Groote) signed Giorgio Smoquina (Porte-parole de la Commission), January 23, 1959. BAC 118/1986, HAEU; Letter from E.G. Stijkel to European Chamber of Commerce, January 21, 1959. BAC 118/1986, HAEU. The European Chamber of Commerce for the Three Communities, a derivation of the Belgian Chamber of Commerce for the Common Market, was created in 1958 to facilitate contacts between private companies, industry, exporters and importers with the European Communities. It did not have a liaison with the International Chamber of Commerce or with UNICE. See: "Fiche de Documentation sur la Chambre de commerce européenne pour les trois communautes," Brussels, January 23, 1959. BAC 118/1986, HAEU.

[68] Janick Marina Schaufelbuehl's work on US companies and their investment in Europe highlights the global nature of business interests in the EEC. See her "'The Advantage of Being inside the Wall When It Is Built:' US Multinationals' Direct Investments in the Common Market, the Balance of Payments Deficit and Bretton Woods (1958–74),"

French politician Jean-Jacques Servan-Schreiber did, that "le défi américain" might pose an existential threat to European businesses if they did not band together to mount their own counter-challenge.[69]

European companies did intensify their cooperation with one another in the postwar period, both through bilateral partnerships and by increasingly participating in BIAs through which they exerted policy influence. In the postwar landscape of new international organizations, rising global competition, and regional integration, the national interest associations formed in the late nineteenth and early twentieth century progressively turned their attention to international developments.[70] Neil Rollings has shown, for example, how the Confederation of British Industry (CBI) recognized the significance of early European economic integration and played a role in the integration process independently from the British state.[71] He has also traced the global development of transnational BIAs, which became increasingly powerful in the latter half of the twentieth century as they united firms from various national contexts around shared interests and strove to exert collective influence on international economic governance, especially in the context of the EEC.[72]

In addition to national BIAs like the CBI and global associations like the ICC, the regional groups created in the postwar period worked to broker business interests in European political economy.[73] As Yohann

Journal of European Integration 43, no. 6 (2021): 667–682; "Becoming the Advocate for US-Based Multinationals: The United States Council of the International Chamber of Commerce, 1945–1974," *Business History* 65, no. 2 (2023): 284–301; *Crusading for Globalization: US Multinationals and Their Opponents since 1945* (Philadelphia: University of Pennsylvania Press, 2025).

69 Jean-Jacques Servan-Schreiber, *Le Défi américain* (Paris: Denoël, 1967).

70 Grace Ballor and Sabine Pitteloud, "Introduction: Capitalism and Global Governance in Business History," *Business History Review* 97, no. 3 (September 2023): 459–479. On Nordic business clubs, see: Niklas Jensen-Eriksen, "Industrial Diplomacy and Economic Integration: The Origins of All-European Paper Cartels, 1959–72," *Journal of Contemporary History* 46, no. 1 (January 1, 2011): 179–202; Niklas Jensen-Eriksen, "Creating Clubs and Giants: How Competition Policies Influenced the Strategy and Structure of Nordic Pulp and Paper Industry, 1970–2000," *Business History* 62, no. 5 (July 3, 2020): 763–781.

71 Neil Rollings, *British Business in the Formative Years of European Integration 1945–1973* (Cambridge: Cambridge University Press, 2007).

72 Neil Rollings, "The Development of Transnational Business Associations during the Twentieth Century," *Business History* 65, no. 2 (2023): 235–259.

73 A special issue of *Business History* addressed the role of transnational business associations in international political economy and introduced the language of "brokering globalization." See the introduction of the issue: Pierre Eichenberger, Neil Rollings, and Janick Marina Schaufelbuehl, "The Brokers of Globalization: Towards a History of Business Associations in the International Arena," *Business History* 65, no. 2 (2023): 217–234. On the ICC, see the many works of Thomas David and Pierre Eichenberger, including: "Business and Diplomacy in the Twentieth Century: A Corporatist View," *Diplomatica* 2 (2020): 9; Thomas David and Pierre

Morival has shown, the Union of Industrial and Employers' Confederations of Europe (UNICE), now known as "Business Europe," is one such association originally founded within the OEEC that quickly adapted to the new political environment of the EEC to help firms lobby the new supranational institutions.[74] The relatively small bureaucracy of the Commission relied on the outside expertise of business leaders to develop policy prescriptions, and commissioners like Étienne Davignon and François-Xavier Ortoli courted input from such business groups and even facilitated the creation of several transnational BIAs in the 1970s and 1980s. The Commission also welcomed engagement by regional business forums like the European League for Economic Cooperation (ELEC) and Association for the Monetary Union of Europe (AMUE), peak sectoral associations like the Committee of Common Market Automobile Constructors (CCMC), and transnational industry groups like the European Round Table of Industrialists (ERT).[75] Not only did the ERT meet regularly with the Commission, but the overlap between its roster and those of other transnational business and private global governance forums like the Bilderberg Group and Groupe des Présidents has granted a small set of executives outsized influence in histories of European and global economic policymaking. Moreover, the revolving door of individual elites between business and Brussels maintained the close connections between "capitalism and its brokers" in this "economic milieu" and

Eichenberger, "'A World Parliament of Business?' The International Chamber of Commerce and Its Presidents in the Twentieth Century," *Business History* 65, no. 2 (2022): 1–24.

74 Yohann Morival, "Reassessing the Historical Dynamics of European Business Associations: The Genesis of UNICE, Late 1940s to 1970s," *Business History* (published online October 26, 2022): 1–18.

75 On ELEC, see: Michel Dumoulin and Anne-Myriam Dutrieu, *La ligue européenne de coopération économique (1946–1981): Un groupe d'étude et de pression dans la construction européenne* (Bern: Peter Lang, 1993); Alexis Drach, "The Forgotten Currency: The European Currency Unit Private Market and European Integration," paper presentation at the *World Economic History Congress (WEHC) 2022* (Aubervilliers, France, 2022). On the CCMC, see work by Sigfrido Ramírez Pérez, including: "Embedding the Market during Times of Crisis: The European Automobile Cartel during a Decade of Crisis (1973–1985)," *Business History* 62, no. 5 (2020): 815–836; Samuel Klebaner and Sigfrido Ramírez Pérez, "The European Automotive Industry: A Strategic Sector in Search of a New Industrial Policy," in *EU Industrial Policy in the Multipolar Economy*, ed. Defraigne Jean-Christophe et al. (Cheltenham: Edward Elgar Publishing, 2022): 304–331. And in addition to work on the ERT by Maria Green Cowles and Bastiaan van Apeldoorn, see: Benjamin Bürbaumer, "TNC Competitiveness in the Formation of the Single Market: The Role of European Business Revisited," *New Political Economy* 26, no. 3 (2020): 1–15.

strengthened the impact of collective and bilateral business lobbying in Europe, particularly during the making of the Single Market.[76]

But the "vast and unsolved enigma" of business power in the EEC extended beyond the political influence of elites and interest groups.[77] In addition to their lobbying functions, peak associations like UNICE) and transnational industrial federations like served as forums for social networking and information exchange.[78] Hélène Michel found that by facilitating synergies and convergences across Europe, these associations contributed to a fundamental kind of regional integration, necessary for cross-border business and indispensable to a true internal market.[79] By facilitating cooperation among firms in the region, sectoral BIAs also created early "European champions," according to Alexis Drach.[80] Multinationals with subsidiaries, branches, and suppliers across the region were positioned to contribute to European integration in an even more direct way. They developed company-wide technical specifications, which functioned as de facto standards given their size and scale.[81] And through consolidation, vertical integration, and the expansion of their supply and value chains, multinationals both became "more European," and, as the following chapters show, they made the market "more

[76] Sylvain Laurens, *Lobbyists and Bureaucrats in Brussels: Capitalism's Brokers* (London: Routledge, 2018); Éric Bussière et al. eds., *Milieux économiques et intégration européenne au XXe siècle: La relance des années quatre-vingt (1979–1992)* (Paris: Comité pour l'Histoire économique et financière, 2008). On business as a political actor in the EEC/EU, see the many works of David Coen, including his co-authored book: David Coen, Alexander Katsaitis, and Matia Vannoni, *Business Lobbying in the European Union* (Oxford: Oxford University Press, 2021).

[77] Neil Rollings made a strong case for studying business power in his BHC Presidential Address: "'The Vast and Unsolved Enigma of Power': Business History and Business Power," *Enterprise and Society* 22, no. 4 (2021): 893–920. Rollings draws this quotation from Adolf Berle's *Power Without Property: A New Development in American Political Economy* (New York: Harcourt, Brace & Co., 1959): 87.

[78] On industrial federations, see: Neil Rollings and Matthias Kipping, "Private Transnational Governance in the Heyday of the Nation-State: The Council of European Industrial Federations (CEIF)," *The Economic History Review* 61, no. 2 (2008): 409–431. Sabine Pitteloud has also written extensively about these dynamics in her 2022 book on Swiss multinationals and in her article "Let's Coordinate! The Reinforcement of a 'Liberal Bastion' within European Industrial Federations, 1978–1987," *Business History* 65, no. 2 (2021): 345–365.

[79] Hélène Michel, "Businesseurope au-delà du 'lobbying': Le travail d'intégration européenne d'une organisation patronale," *Critique internationale* 59, no. 2 (2013): 133–155.

[80] Alexis Drach, "An Early Form of European Champions? Banking Clubs between European Integration and Global Banking (1960s–1990s)," *Business History* 66, no. 1 (2022): 287–310.

[81] See: Wolfram Kaiser and J. W. Schot, *Writing the Rules for Europe: Experts, Cartels, and International Organizations*, Making Europe: Technology and Transformations, 1850–2000 (Houndmills, Basingstoke, Hampshire: Palgrave Macmillan, 2014).

European" as well.[82] Recognizing the role of business affirms the market as historically contingent and co-constructed by a multiplicity of market actors, including individual firms and the BIAs in which they participated.[83]

Problematizing Business Influence

Do corporations control politics? While answering this question is important at all levels and has been addressed in some national contexts, it is urgent to address it on the largest scale of regional supranational governance.[84] Moreover, business influence on the EU and its Single Market delimit the possibilities for European reform.

In addition to provincializing Europe and pluralizing market actors, a business history perspective of the 1992 Program also exposes the methodological and political problems of business influence. The first set of problems, originating in assumptions about business influence in European political economy, risks a flat, two-dimensional view of the Single Market and the firms operating in it. The second set reflects the real dangers business influence poses to democracy. By addressing the methodological issues, I argue, we can better attend to the political ones.

Many scholars have uncovered evidence of private influence in the public domain. Benjamin Waterhouse and Sabine Pitteloud have each demonstrated the considerable sway elite business groups enjoyed over national economic policymaking in the US and Switzerland respectively, and several others have traced the rise of private global governance whereby elites have wielded economic power and scrutinized the corporate control of the "transnational capitalist class."[85] But specific cases of

[82] For an overview of "merger mania" in Europe in the late twentieth century, see: Ivan T. Berend, *The History of European Integration: A New Perspective*, 1st ed. (London; New York: Routledge, 2016): Chapter 4, pp. 118–157.

[83] Among other economic sociologists, Neil Fligstein and Iona Mara-Drita provided the theoretical framework for markets as co-constructions. See their: "How to Make a Market: Reflections on the Attempt to Create a Single Market in the European Union," *American Journal of Sociology* 102, no. 1 (1996): 1–33.

[84] On corporate influence in the US, see: Adam Winkler, *We the Corporations: How American Businesses Won Their Civil Rights* (New York: Liveright, 2018).

[85] Benjamin C. Waterhouse, *Lobbying America: The Politics of Business from Nixon to NAFTA* (Princeton, NJ: Princeton University Press, 2013); Pitteloud, *Les multinationales suisses dans l'arène politique (1942–1993)*. On critical theory approaches to this topic, see: William K. Carroll, *The Making of a Transnational Capitalist Class: Corporate Power in the 21st Century*, Illustrated ed. (London; New York: Zed Books, 2010). On private governance, see: Tim Büthe and Walter Mattli, *The New Global Rulers: The Privatization of Regulation in the World Economy* (Princeton, NJ: Princeton University Press, 2011).

business influence have also been marshalled to make generalist claims: that capital loves liberalization and that business always favors market integration. Applied to contemporary Europe, such assumptions require two methodological corrections. First, just as "business" does not represent a cohesive set of interests, firms and their management viewed the EEC and its 1992 Program very differently, even within the same industries and sectors. Diversity of size, structure, and geography resulted in equally varied operational experiences of the internal market. While some firms and BIAs pushed for further integration and successfully shaped regional economic policymaking as Benjamin Bürbaumer has argued, this book finds that others were deeply skeptical of and even opposed to market integration, requiring a nuanced approach to business influence.[86] Second, the Single Market is much more than a framework for trade liberalization. Not only was its design an intergovernmental amalgam of different economic traditions, but the implementation of its flanking economic, social, and environmental policies created a regional business environment far more complex than its mere free trade area counterparts. In the wide range of business perspectives, the market's dimensions become clearer.

Unsurprisingly, many of the most energetic business supporters of the 1992 Program were executives of large multinational corporations. Some were so enthusiastic about the prospect of removing all barriers to trade within the EEC that they became activist proponents of an enlarged internal market. Despite not being from an EEC member state, Pehr Gyllenhammar of the Swedish carmaker Volvo so strongly supported regional market integration that he found a loophole to allow his company to become a member of the sectoral association for European carmakers, the Committee of Common Market Automobile Constructors (CCMC), giving him a seat at the table of producers in the EEC. He also helped create the ERT in 1983, bringing industrial executives and Commissioners together to advocate for business interests in an integrated market. In 1985, Gyllenhammar's likeminded ERT colleague, Wisse Dekker of the Dutch Philips company, wrote a manifesto advocating for the urgent completion of an internal market by 1990, two years ahead of even the Commission's ambitious schedule.[87] Executives like Gyllenhammar and Dekker already moved within the same social networks as national politicians and regional officials. But their political access and potential for influence were augmented by the fact that both

[86] Bürbaumer, "TNC Competitiveness in the Formation of the Single Market."

[87] Wisse Dekker, "Europe 1990 An Agenda for Action," *European Management Journal* 3, no. 1 (1985): 5–10.

domestic and European policymakers viewed the success of big business as essential to recovery from the economic and social crises of the 1970s.

Not all corporate executives supported the Single Market, however. Jacques Calvet of the French PSA Group so vehemently opposed regional integration on nationalist grounds that the CCMC ultimately collapsed and had to be remade without him and his company, as Chapter 4 shows. The episode proved just how widely perspectives could differ even within the same interest group, especially on issues like foreign investment and common technical standards.[88] Personality mattered, as did company size. For SMEs, the potential for increased competition in the internal market posed a greater threat, and big businesses could better absorb the costs of regulatory changes than their smaller counterparts. Even some of the largest firms struggled to adapt to the exigencies of an integrated market. Geoffrey Jones and Peter Miskell described the difficulty with which the giant multinational Unilever, seemingly well positioned to benefit from regional market integration, struggled to restructure its business amid the development of the common and then single European markets.[89] Unilever's awareness of the differences in consumer preferences across the region also reveals the inherent challenges of integrating international markets. Still other firms approached the internal market with initial skepticism, only gradually becoming "reluctant Europeans," as Alexis Drach described the British and French commercial banks that traded their doubts about the banking integration for an appreciation of the opportunities offered by the Single Market.[90] Companies and BIAs expressed concern, too, about how the market's attendant policies – especially the social and environmental protections developed by the Delors Commission – would affect their operations and revenues. Such divergences in firm

[88] One of the richest sectoral studies of business and European integration is the PhD thesis of Sigfrido Manuel Ramirez Pérez: "Public Policies, European Integration and Multinational Corporations in the Automobile Sector," PhD dissertation, European University Institute, 2007.

[89] Geoffrey Jones and Peter Miskell, "European Integration and Corporate Restructuring: The Strategy of Unilever, c.1957–c.1991," *The Economic History Review* 58, no. 1 (2005): 113–139. For another example of corporate restructuring, see: N. A. Phelps, *Multinationals and European Integration: Trade, Investment, and Regional Development*, Regional Policy and Development 14 (London; Bristol, PA: J. Kingsley Publishers; Regional Studies Association, 1997).

[90] Alexis Drach, "Reluctant Europeans? British and French Commercial Banks and the Common Market in Banking (1977–1992)," *Enterprise & Society* 21, no. 3 (2020): 768–798. The language of "reluctant Europeans" has also been used by: Alan MacKinlay, Helen Mercer, and Neil Rollings, "Reluctant Europeans? The Federation of British Industries and European Integration, 1945–63," *Business History* 42, no. 4 (2000): 91–116.

opinions reflect the many facets of the market beyond the free movement of goods and capital.

The heterogeneity of their market perspectives notwithstanding, corporations and BIAs strove to influence European policymaking. Political scientists and sociologists continue to debate the efficacy of business influence, however. In successive studies, David Coen has chronicled decades of business lobbying in the EEC and EU, demonstrating the range of technical and personal mechanisms at their disposal.[91] Bastiaan van Apeldoorn focused on the ERT and its privileged access to regional policymakers, which enabled industrial elites to set the very agenda of the SEA, as Maria Green Cowles argued.[92] Despite his disagreements with such neofunctionalist views, Andrew Moravcsik recognized the way business interests supported national governments in their liberal intergovernmental grand bargaining.[93] Indeed, national studies like Christakis Georgiou's work on French firms in the EU support Moravcsik's point that companies used national governments as mouthpieces to advance their interests in regional policymaking and did so effectively.[94] But Andreas Dür, David Marshall, and Patrick Bernhagen challenge many of these assertions about capitalist influence by showing that in the boardrooms of Brussels, information was power, and BIAs were no more informed nor effective in shaping European policy than any other lobbying groups.[95]

Still, for supporters of labor rights, trade unions, and the integrity of democracy, business influence on European politics exacerbated the

[91] Among his many works, see: David Coen, "The Evolution of the Large Firm as a Political Actor in the European Union," *Journal of European Public Policy* 4, no. 1 (1997): 91–108; David Coen, "The European Business Interest and the Nation State: Large Firms Lobbying in the European Union and Member States," *Journal of Public Policy* 18, no. 1 (1998): 75–100; David Coen and J. J. Richardson, eds., *Lobbying the European Union: Institutions, Actors, and Issues* (Oxford; New York: Oxford University Press, 2009). For a data-driven approach to the topic, see: David Coen, Alexander Katsaitis, and Matia Vannoni, *Business Lobbying in the European Union* (Oxford: Oxford University Press, 2021).

[92] See: Bastiaan Van Apeldoorn, "Transnational Class Agency and European Governance: The Case of the European Round Table of Industrialists," *New Political Economy* 5, no. 2 (2000): 157–181; *Transnational Capitalism and the Struggle over European Integration*; Cowles, "Setting the Agenda for a New Europe."

[93] Moravcsik, *The Choice for Europe.*

[94] Christakis Georgiou, *Les grandes firmes françaises et l'Union Européenne: Economie politique de la construction du capitalisme européen intégré, de l'Acte Unique à la crise de la zone euro* (Vulaines sur Seine: Editions du Croquant, 2017). On the French case, see also: Stela Raytcheva et Gilles Rouet, eds., *Les Entreprises et l'intégration européenne* (Paris: Harmattan, 2016).

[95] Andreas Dür, David Marshall, and Patrick Bernhagen, *The Political Influence of Business in the European Union* (Ann Arbor: University of Michigan Press, 2019).

perceived democratic deficit many saw as the EU's "birth defect."[96] Moreover, the efforts of multinationals and their BIAs to undermine consumer protections and a more social Europe draw further attention to the problems of big business in the making of the Single Market. The failure of early efforts to regulate multinationals in Europe, like the proposed Vredeling Directive discussed in Chapter 1, inspired concerned observers of ever-larger corporations to draw bestiary analogies, likening multinationals – from the United Fruit company in the mid-twentieth century to the partnership of the German Dresdner and the French Banque Nationale de Paris (BNP) banks mentioned in Chapter 5 – to the mythical tentacled seamonster Kraken.[97] Already in the 1990s, critics like Wolfgang Streeck and Philippe Schmitter recognized democratic collapse and rising inequality as just some symptoms of the perversion of regional cooperation by corporate interests.[98] Then the protracted crises of the twenty-first century expanded the circle of detractors significantly. From alarm about the corporate control of "surveillance capitalism" to proposals for regulating human rights violations across multinational supply chains, even "business lounge intellectuals" came to acknowledge the "crisis of democratic capitalism" in the EU and beyond.[99]

While business interests did exert some influence on regional policy-making, I argue multinationals also shaped the market through their operations. The cases included in this book demonstrate how manufacturers, banks, distributors and retailers expanded throughout the region. As they regionalized, they made investments and acquisitions, integrated supply chains, and established common norms, and facilitated economic transformations. Through economies of scale and partnerships, they also contributed to the homogenization of goods and services as well as price convergence. In many ways – and sometimes inadvertently – they facilitated market integration, requiring us to reframe our thinking about

[96] See, for example, Koen van Zon's work on labor, consumers, and the regulation of European multinationals: "Battleground Brussels: The EU and the Regulation of Multinationals" (Utrecht: Utrecht University, 2021).

[97] Not only were these analogies made by commentators about multinationals in the twenty-first century, but Robert Fredona and Sophus A. Reinert developed a "politico-philosophical" argument for such analogies in their: "Leviathan and Kraken: States, Corporations, and Political Economy," *History and Theory* 59, no. 2 (2020): 167–187.

[98] Among their many works, see: Schmitter and Streeck, "Organized Interests and the Europe of 1992."

[99] Shoshana Zuboff, *The Age of Surveillance Capitalism: The Fight for the Future at the New Frontier of Power*, 1st ed. (London: Faber and Faber, 2019); Martin Wolf, *The Crisis of Democratic Capitalism*, 1st ed. (London: Allen Lane, 2023); William Davies, "Martin Wolf: The Business-Lounge Intellectual," *New Statesman*, January 14, 2023.

business influence and posing new questions for ongoing political debates about the market and its reform.

Politicizing the Market

Given the market's origins, what are the possibilities for reform to make it more humane, equitable, and democratically accountable? Is the market necessary to maintain peace and cooperation in the region, as its architects argued?

Debates about the future of Europe, its market, and the firms that operate in it came to a head in Britain's referendum on EU membership in 2016, the result of which some observers read as part of a wider backlash against globalization and the crises of the early twenty-first century, not a "bolt from the blue."[100] As has become increasingly clear in the intervening years, the Brexit result reflected the state of domestic politics in the UK and its "special relationship" with Europe more than it was a barometer of wider support for or opposition to the EU.[101] However, the referendum did illuminate several of Europe's most serious challenges, including regional cohesion, the democratic deficit, and the need to effectively regulate multinational corporations. And it politicized the most popular aspect of regional integration: the Single Market. While Euroskeptics supporting the Leave campaign demanded the reclamation of sovereignty over market policymaking, they also expressed support for the economic benefits of retaining access to the internal market. Brokering even better trade deals would be easy, and, as Perry Anderson argued in a series of essays in the *London Review of Books*, more democracy would allow the British public to prioritize people over business profits.[102]

[100] See, for example: Italo Colantone, Gianmarco I. P. Ottaviano, and Piero Stanig, "The Backlash of Globalization," SSRN Scholarly Paper (Rochester, NY, September 3, 2021); Italo Colantone and Piero Stanig, "Global Competition and Brexit," *American Political Science Review* 112, no. 2 (May 2018): 201–218. On Europe and the Global Financial Crisis, see: Ivan Berend, *Europe in Crisis: Bolt from the Blue?* (London: Routledge, 2012).

[101] On Brexit and British politics, see: Geoffrey Evans and Anand Menon, *Brexit and British Politics* (Chichester: John Wiley & Sons, 2017); William Davies, *This Is Not Normal: The Collapse of Liberal Britain* (London: Verso, 2020). On the "special relationship," see the many works of N. Piers Ludlow, including: "The Discomforts of Life on the Edge: Britain and Europe, 1963–1975," *International Affairs* 88, no. 6 (November 1, 2012): 1331–1340.

[102] Perry Anderson, "The European Coup," *London Review of Books*, December 17, 2020; Perry Anderson, "Ever Closer Union?" *London Review of Books*, January 7, 2021; Perry Anderson, "The Breakaway: Goodbye Europe," *London Review of Books*, January 21, 2021.

Here again, businesses perspectives of the EU and its Single Market diverged, with some chairmen signing open letters in support of the Remain campaign, some – like home appliance tycoon Sir James Dyson – who traded his early advocacy for British entry into the Eurozone for strong support of Brexit before relocating to Singapore in 2019, and many others electing not to take any public position at all for fear of brand damage and consumer retribution.[103] Some British firms, critical of regulatory overreach by nonelected international officials, saw the referendum as a way to finally be free from oppressive product health and safety standards and labor protections, nevermind the seeming inescapability of what Anu Bradford termed the "Brussels effect" and the UK's many exceptional concessions.[104] Business Euroskepticism raised questions about critical theory perspectives of the internal market and revived arguments about how to interpret the "social Europe" some firms opposed: Was market integration a necessary means to achieve a humane society, or a thin veil for encased capitalism?[105]

This book was, in large part, motivated by Brexit and its aftermath. What began as a broad study of business and European integration became an attempt to answer questions at the center of the referendum and other contemporary political debates: Was the Single European Market a creation by and for capitalist elites, as its critics claimed? If so, what would that mean for the aspects of economic, monetary, and political integration which rest on the foundation of the market? By reconstructing the market through a business historical lens, my narrative locates big business at the very center of market integration in policy design, standard setting, the development of regional supply and value chains, and the practical functioning of the market at the heart of the European project. And it finds efforts to offset the consequences of a market designed for and built, in part, by big business through cohesion funds and social and environmental regulations were important, but ultimately insufficient, to reconcile capitalism and democracy in the EU, resulting in backlash, fragmentation, and the need for reform.

[103] "EU Referendum: More than 1,280 Business Leaders Sign Letter," *BBC News*, June 22, 2016, sec. Business; "EU Referendum: CBI Warns of UK Exit 'Serious Shock,'" *BBC News*, April 14, 2016. After supporting Brexit, Dyson was lambasted for announcing the move of his company headquarters from Britain to Singapore.

[104] Anu Bradford, *The Brussels Effect: How the European Union Rules the World* (New York: Oxford University Press, 2020).

[105] On these competing visions, see: Eric Bussière, Michel Dumoulin, and Sylvain Schirmann, *Europe organisée, Europe du libre-échange?: Fin XIXe siécle - années 1960* (Bern: Peter Lang, 2006); Quinn Slobodian, "Demos Veto and Demos Exit: The Neoliberals Who Embraced Referenda and Secession," *Journal of Australian Political Economy* 86 (2020): 19–36.

After the Brexit referendum, negotiations between the UK and EU revolved around how to cleanly excise the UK from the internal market, given its porous land border with the Republic of Ireland after the Good Friday Agreements of 1998. Neither the UK's own Internal Market Act in 2020 nor the Brexit Withdrawal Agreement and subsequent Windsor Framework settled between the UK and EU have given Britain the sovereign-but-liberal market Brexiteers promised. Fallout from the Covid-19 pandemic and Russia's invasion of Ukraine have only exacerbated the economic effects of leaving the Single Market. And under a dizzying succession of prime ministers, the UK has promoted further liberalization rather than regulation, making good on Margaret Thatcher's vision in her famous Euroskeptic speech at Bruges in 1988: "We have not successfully rolled back the frontiers of the state in Britain, only to see them reimposed at a European level with a European superstate exercising a new dominance from Brussels."[106]

The first three chapters of this book examine business in European political economy. Chapter 1 examines the ways policymakers in the Commission thought about European companies as they designed the market. Chapter 2 describes the role big business played in developing the standards at the center of market integration, thereby co-producing core elements of the internal market and its connections to other international markets like the EFTA. And Chapter 3 develops a case study approach for examining the economic geography of European firms and their business strategies and the relationship between globalization and regionalization.

Chapters 4, 5, and 6 build on the framework and findings of the first three chapters to offer detailed case studies of multinationals headquartered in different EEC member states and operating in different economic sectors. The companies selected represent a broad cross section of the European economy, even as they provide crucial access points for themes of nationalization and state patronage, family business and managerial capitalism, supply chains and consumer relations, multi-level regulation and organized interests. Their chairmen also espoused diverse perspectives on the Single Market, each of which brings the nuances of the market into focus. Chapter 4 studies German carmakers Volkswagen and BMW, who supported market integration as an interim step toward further globalization and whose market segments and BIA membership offer insight into the ways a wide range of European manufacturers developed supply chains in the Single Market and approached issues of

[106] Margaret Thatcher, "Speech to the College of Europe," Bruges, September 20, 1988.

foreign competition and environmental regulation. Chapter 5 examines the French merchant bank Paribas and its active role in economic transformations across Europe especially after the opening of Central and Eastern – and Northern – Europe. Chapter 5 also explores the bank's ambivalence about other dimensions of economic integration and its mobilization through a BIA against the regulatory dimensions of the Single Market. And Chapter 6 uncovers how concerns about the Single Market motivated food retailers like the Belgian grocer Delhaize to form defensive regional buying clubs and BIAs, which consequently and paradoxically made European retail more European. Together, these cases reveal the complex relationship of big business to the 1992 Program and of the Single Market to its larger global context. The Conclusion reflects on the implications of this business history of European political economy for understanding economic and monetary integration and discusses how this history can inform current debates about reforming the EU and its market to be more equitable and humane in the future through effective regulation of multinational corporations and more economic policy coordination across member states, informed by input from social stakeholders.

1 How to Make a Market

In January 1985, the newly appointed members of the European Commission gathered around their conference table at the institution's Berlaymont headquarters in Brussels to determine how to make a single market (Figure 1.1).[1] Their primary objectives under Commission President Jacques Delors were to shepherd the EEC out of the crises of the previous decade and reinvigorate the "stalled" European project. Even before officially taking up his position, Delors offered several proposals to achieve those ends, ranging from common defense to monetary union. Above all, it was the agenda of full internal market integration that won unanimous approval among member state governments looking to Brussels for solutions to widespread economic and social problems. By facilitating the free movement of goods, services, capital, and people across the EEC's member state borders, an internal market could remedy the region's economic and social crises, reenergize growth and employment, and relegitimize the Community, reasoned national officials and regional policymakers. They believed the right market policies could also bolster European competitiveness in a global economy full of rivals from other regions and lay a foundation for further integrative aims like political, economic, and monetary union. Success required a diverse cohort of commissioners to design a regional business environment that would incentivize firms to engage in intensive cross-border trade and investment, to pursue mergers and develop supply chains, to hire new employees, and to carry out commercial activity. In short, the Europeanization of business was fundamental to the objectives of the

[1] Delors Commission I, 1985–1988: European Commission, "Meeting of the Delors Commission (1985)" June 1, 1985, Centre virtuel de la connaissance sur l'Europe (hereafter CVCE): © Union européenne, 2025, CC BY 4.0. In this image, Commission President Jacques Delors is seated on the far-right middle of the conference table, and Arthur Cockfield, Commissioner for the Internal Market, is across from him on the far left.

Figure 1.1 Delors Commission I, 1985–1988.

Single Market Program. But how did European policymakers view the companies at the center of the market they were making? What methods did they deploy to energize and constrain business activity in their efforts to create and, in turn, regulate an internal market?

Answers to these questions are complicated by the same diversity that plagued debates among commissioners as they worked to develop policies for the internal market. Not only did the institution's composition change often given the four-year terms of its members during the late 1950s to early 1990s, but enlargements also increased the number and widened the perspectives of its policymakers.[2] Commissioners hailed from countries with drastically different economic systems and policy approaches, ranging from German ordoliberalism to French dirigisme to British neoliberalism, competition between which played out in policy meetings about market integration in the 1980s as much as it had in the EEC's efforts to develop a collective response to the problems of the

[2] The Maastricht Treaty, signed in 1992 and effective in 1993, extended Commission terms to five years in line with those of the European Parliament.

1970s.[3] When they designed the Single Market, few of the Commission's then eighteen members had training in economics. Some, like the Dutch Frans Andriessen and Manuel Marín from Spain, were lawyers before entering civil service; others, like António Cardoso e Cunha from the new member state of Portugal, had corporate careers before joining the Commission.[4] Such diverse national and professional backgrounds informed their many views on the place of business in the Single Market. For liberal commissioners like Peter Sutherland, who later became the founding Director General of the World Trade Organization (WTO), regulation posed a threat to the primary goal of growth; for those of more socialist persuasions like the Italian environmentalist Carlo Ripa di Meana, the market was only worth pursuing if it could provide a path to humane, cohesive, and equitable development – not guaranteed by the "invisible hand" of market forces.[5] In some ways, these diverse perspectives enriched the work of market making. At the same time, discrepancies within the institution underscored the challenges of intergovernmental consensus and left its policymaking endeavors open to outsized influence from those with vested interests in certain market outcomes.[6] Despite their differences, however, policymakers in the Commission developed a comprehensive program for market integration that relied on the regionalization of business, even

[3] Laurent Warlouzet examined the origins of and relationships between these approaches in his *Governing Europe in a Globalizing World: Neoliberalism and Its Alternatives Following the 1973 Oil Crisis*, 1st ed. (New York; London: Routledge, 2017).

[4] For a detailed institutional history of the Commission, see the multivolume work: Michel Dumoulin et al., *The European Commission 1973–86: History and Memories of an Institution* (Luxembourg: Publications Office of the European Union, 2014); Éric Bussière et al., *The European Commission 1986–2000: History and Memories of an Institution* (Luxembourg: Publications Office of the European Union, 2019).

[5] Laurent Warlouzet discussed some of these political and ideological differences within the Commission in his "A Social Europe with a Greener Perspective: The Evolution of the Delors Commission around 1989," *Studi Storici: Rivista Trimestrale Dell'Istituto Gramsci* 62, no. 1 (2021): 189–209.

[6] The most salient works on lobbying European institutions in general and business lobbying in particular include: Justin Greenwood, *Interest Representation in the European Union*, 4th ed. 2017 edition (London: Palgrave, 2017); Pepper D. Culpepper, *Quiet Politics and Business Power: Corporate Control in Europe and Japan* (Cambridge; New York: Cambridge University Press, 2011); David Coen, Alexander Katsaitis, and Matia Vannoni, *Business Lobbying in the European Union* (Oxford: Oxford University Press, 2021); Sylvain Laurens, *Lobbyists and Bureaucrats in Brussels: Capitalism's Brokers* (London: Routledge, 2018); Sonia Mazey and J. J. Richardson, eds., *Lobbying in the European Community*, Nuffield European Studies (Oxford; New York: Oxford University Press, 1993); Wolfgang Streeck and Philippe C. Schmitter, "From National Corporatism to Transnational Pluralism: Organized Interests in the Single European Market," *Politics & Society* 19, no. 2 (June 1, 1991): 133–164.

if, as Chapters 4, 5, and 6 show, their views were not always aligned with those of European firms.

This chapter locates business in the economic thinking of the Single Market Program, which transformed regional economic, commercial, competition, industrial, and social policies and remade the relationship between firms and European governance. It examines the wide-ranging approaches European officials took to enterprise as they made collective Community agreements and designed policies for the internal market. Cabinet documents and speeches from regional policymakers in the European Commission shed light on the tensions between promoting the regional economic activity of firms on the one hand and increasingly regulating the market and its actors to protect consumers, workers, and the environment on the other.[7] In the body of scholarship that has risen to the challenge of Euroskeptics past and present to evaluate the birth defects, social failures, and business capture of European integration, this chapter uncovers the debates between treating business as a market-making ally on the one hand and prioritizing social concerns on the other.[8] Ultimately, it argues, the Commission saw Community-wide business activity as the key to achieving the market and its wider economic and social objectives. By supporting cross-border mergers, acquisitions, investment, partnerships, and the development of regional supply and value chains, regional policymakers aimed to reassert the power and influence of a united Europe in the global economy.

To trace the evolution of policy approaches to business in the Single Market, this chapter begins by contextualizing the challenges that motivated the EEC to pursue market integration as a means of economic and social "crisis management." Once the agenda of relaunching the Community through market integration took shape in the European Council and the introduction of qualified majority voting accelerated

[7] In that sense, this chapter avoids the tendency to make "great saints" of European officials in the "hagiography of European integration," as critiqued by Alan Milward in his *The European Rescue of the Nation State*, with George Brennan and Federico Romero (Los Angeles: University of California Press, 1992): 318.

[8] Key texts in this literature include: Laurent Warlouzet, "The EEC/EU as an Evolving Compromise between French Dirigism and German Ordoliberalism (1957–1995)," *JCMS: Journal of Common Market Studies* 57, no. 1 (2019): 77–93; Quinn Slobodian and Dieter Plehwe, "Neoliberals against Europe," in *Mutant Neoliberalism: Market Rule and Political Ruptures*, ed. William Callison and Zachary Manfredi (Fordham University Press, 2019), 89–111; Bastiaan Van Apeldoorn, *Transnational Capitalism and the Struggle over European Integration* (London: Routledge, 2002); Bastiaan Van Apeldoorn, "Transnational Class Agency and European Governance: The Case of the European Round Table of Industrialists," *New Political Economy* 5, no. 2 (2000): 157–181.

collective decision making, the Commission began designing policies for a regional business environment strongly oriented toward the big businesses and multinational corporations best positioned to operate across member state borders. Given the diversity of economic thinking and the rapid evolution of the Single Market Program, these policies were, at times, in concert with one another, and at other times in conflict. Institutional reform enabled the Commission to engage in a new form of industrial policy to create European champions through economies of scale. But the context of market making also gave rise to a new competition policy, which strove to increase the number of European firms and make them more globally competitive through liberalization.[9] Commercial policy subsequently wrestled with universal liberalism on the one hand and protectionist tendencies toward "Fortress Europe" on the other.[10] During Delors' second term as president, as the primacy of market integration gave way to the new aims of Economic and Monetary Union, and the reunification of Germany and subsequent collapse of the Soviet Union drastically remade the economic and political landscape, the EEC's policy agenda became even more complex. Some Commissioners in the new cohort insisted on fully liberalized trade, while others – including Delors – strove to achieve a social market economy with robust social and environmental policies and increasing attention to stakeholders like SMEs.[11] To this rapidly changing policy environment, European multinational companies reoriented their institutional relationships and adapted their business strategies, thereby coproducing a regional market and its attendant economic, social, and political consequences.[12]

[9] On the bargains between planning and competition, see Laurent Warlouzet, "Competition versus Planning: A Battle that Shaped European Integration (1945–2022)," in *The Cambridge History of the European Union, Volume 2, European Integration Inside-Out*, ed. Mathieu Segers and Steven Van Hecke (Cambridge: Cambridge University Press, 2023): 234–260.

[10] I thank the directors and fellows of the KFG on Universalism and Particularism in Contemporary European History at LMU Munich for challenging me to think about universalism and particularism in economic policymaking.

[11] The occasion of Delors' death in December 2023 prompted several scholars to eulogize him from a variety of critical and supportive perspectives. See, for example: Aurélie Dianara, "Jacques Delors Was the Gravedigger of 'Social Europe,'" *Jacobin* January 8, 2024. See also this book's Conclusion.

[12] Economic sociologists have developed arguments about the public–private process of market creation and the "cultural frame" of institution-building. See, for example: Neil Fligstein and Iona Mara-Drita, "How to Make a Market: Reflections on the Attempt to Create a Single Market in the European Union," *American Journal of Sociology* 102, no. 1 (1996): 1–33. I made similar arguments about the coproduction of the common and internal markets in: Grace Ballor, "Agents of Integration: Multinational Firms and the European Union," *Enterprise & Society* 21, no. 4 (December 2020): 886–892.

Crisis Management

European economies floundered in the early 1980s. Three decades of economic integration since the Treaties of Paris and Rome in the 1950s had removed tariff barriers, created a customs union, and increased trade between EEC member states. But the momentum of postwar economic miracles stalled by the late 1960s. The searing hot 6–8 percent growth rates of postwar reconstruction cooled to 3–5 percent by the end of the 1960s, and the volume of trade between EEC member states plateaued. Amid the successive energy shocks and geopolitical tensions of the 1970s, traditional manufacturing collapsed, inflation and unemployment both surged. These "crises" of relative if not absolute downturn forced the EEC to trade its ambitious Werner Plan to achieve economic and monetary union by 1980 for a short-lived stopgap measure – the "Snake in the Tunnel" – to bolster the region against the rising value of the free-floating dollar after the US withdrew from the Bretton Woods agreement in 1971.[13] Meanwhile, nontariff barriers to trade persisted even after the Court of Justice's ruling in the *Cassis de Dijon* case in 1979, which introduced the principle of mutual recognition and facilitated the free movement of alcoholic beverages much more than that of complex industrially manufactured goods.[14] Capital and services moved even less freely. That European economies lagged their counterparts in other regions – and that foreign companies, especially from the US and Japan, increasingly claimed greater market shares in the EEC – only heightened the sense of urgency for a collective policy response lest Europe be relegated to the margins of the globalizing economy.[15] Some observers argued that the European project itself had stalled with the region's economies. "Eurosclerosis" gave way to "Europessimism": If the world's only supranational institutions could not solve such problems, then what was the EEC good for? Such

[13] Giuliano Garavini has examined the oil crises of the 1970s and their connections to European integration. See his *After Empires: European Integration, Decolonization, and the Challenge from the Global South, 1957–1986* (Oxford: Oxford University Press, 2012); *Counter-Shock: The Oil Counter-Revolution of the 1980s*, (S. I. Bloomsbury Academic, 2018); *The Rise and Fall of OPEC in the Twentieth Century*; Elisabetta Bini, Giuliano Garavini, and Federico Romero, eds., *Oil Shock: The 1973 Crisis and Its Economic Legacy* (S.l.: Bloomsbury Academic, 2016).

[14] Jacques Pelkmans, "Mutual Recognition in Goods and Services: An Economic Perspective," European Network of Economic Policy Research Institutes, Working Paper no. 16, March 2003.

[15] In the 1960s, Jean-Jacques Servan-Schreiber famously warned of the threat American investment in Europe posed to the continent. Within a decade, his *Le Défi américain* (Paris: Denoël, 1967) had become a Japanese challenge, too, thanks to Japan's rapid postwar industrial development. See: Chalmers Johnson, *MITI and the Japanese Miracle: The Growth of Industrial Policy, 1925–1975* (Stanford: Stanford University Press, 1982).

Figure 1.2 EEC real growth rate, 1960–1985.

criticism came from politics, academia, and the general public, whose support for the EEC had dwindled to just 25 percent in 1980 and for whom the introduction of direct elections and new powers for the European Parliament still did not solve what they saw as the Community's fundamental democratic deficit.[16]

European officials and policymakers met frequently during the late 1970s and early 1980s to triage both the region's economies and the EEC's legitimacy. They were particularly concerned about solving widespread unemployment and "stagflation," the dangerous combination of high inflation and slow growth, which averaged just 0.6 percent across the EEC in 1981, as shown in Figure 1.2.[17] Uneven development also

[16] On critiques of the EEC in this period, see: Andrew Moravcsik, "Negotiating the Single European Act: National Interests and Conventional Statecraft in the European Community," *International Organization* 45, no. 1 (1991): 19. For polling data on Europessimism, see: European Commission, *Together since 1957: 35 Years of Eurobarometer: European Integration as Seen by Public Opinion in the Member States of the European Union*, 2009. Use of the language of "democratic deficit" intensified after the Treaty of Maastricht, signed in 1991 and effective in 1993.

[17] Notably, documents from European institutions in the late 1970s and early 1980s rarely include mention of global economic competition in thinking about the EEC's challenges and policy aims. Figure 1.2 shows the EEC real growth rate, 1960–1985: European Commission, "European Economy: 1998 Broad Economic Policy Guidelines" (Directorate General for Economic and Financial Affairs, 1998): 70–85. This graph reflects the membership composition of the EEC year over year.

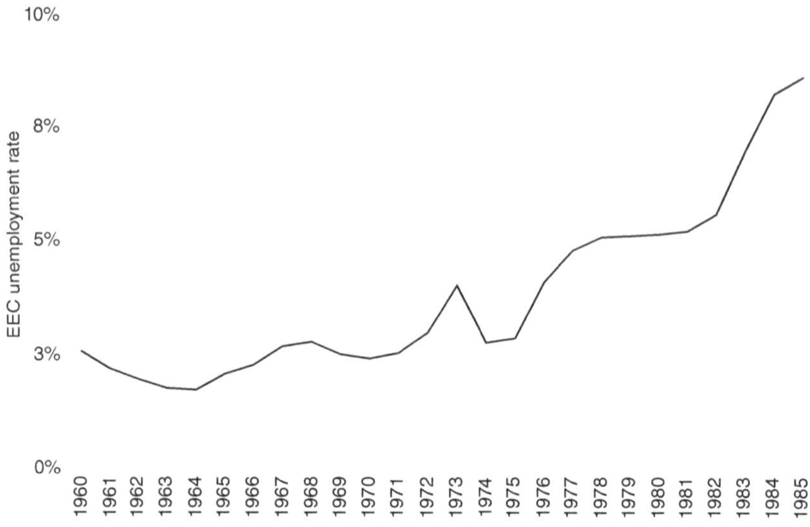

Figure 1.3 EEC unemployment rate, 1960–1985.

troubled the European Parliament and the consultative body of the Economic and Social Committee, both of which drafted recommendations on cohesive economic policy. Meanwhile, consumer price inflation soared, reaching 12 percent in 1980.[18] As shown in Figure 1.3, unemployment rates increased steadily throughout the 1970s, too, averaging 6.5 percent by late 1980 as manufacturing productivity increased and then gave way to services.[19] As relatively new entrants to European labor markets, women fared far worse than their male counterparts in finding work. In Italy, for example, female unemployment topped 10.2 percent at the height of the recession following the 1979 oil shock.[20] Social tensions manifested in mass protests, and industrial action became a frequent mode of expression for frustration and dissatisfaction with

[18] European Commission, "Annual Economic Report 1980–81: COM(80)596 Final," October 15, 1980, Archive of European Integration (hereafter AEI).

[19] European Commission, "European Economy: 1998 Broad Economic Policy Guidelines" (Directorate General for Economic and Financial Affairs, 1998). Figure 1.3 shows EEC unemployment rate, 1960–1985: This data is derived from the economic survey report: European Commission, "European Economy: 1998 Broad Economic Policy Guidelines" (Directorate General for Economic and Financial Affairs, 1998): 64–69.

[20] "Unemployment Statistical Telegram: Monthly Statistics of Registered Unemployed in the Community" (Eurostat, February 15, 1980), AEI.

national governments, especially where the Keynesian economics of state intervention seemed to have failed.[21]

Many EEC officials experienced these economic and social challenges as natural disasters, as unavoidable and unforeseen exogenous shocks, rather than as cumulative consequences of business cycle undulations, policy decisions, and geoeconomics, let alone as the structural collapse or "malaise" of capitalism Charles Maier examined and Robert Brenner described in his "economics of global turbulence."[22] Few discussed the cycle theories of Clément Juglar, Nikolai Kondratiev, and Thorstein Veblen when growth plateaued and unemployment rose in the 1960s and 1970s.[23] They engaged only slightly more with contemporary economic theorists, although they did so seemingly indiscriminately, with no clear ideological bias.[24] Reflecting the diversity of thought within the region and its institutions of transnational governance, they invoked liberal and state interventionist, supply side and demand side, marketeer and monetarist thinkers in nearly equal, although small, measures. Just six working papers mentioned Friedrich Hayek in assessments of agriculture and consumer protections. Joseph Schumpeter's writing on innovation made its way into a modest dozen policy documents produced by the EEC before the mid-1980s.[25] Milton Friedman was marginally more popular, with citations in sixteen documents on purchasing

[21] Göran Therborn et al., "The 1970s and 1980s as a Turning Point in European History?" *Journal of Modern European History / Zeitschrift Für Moderne Europäische Geschichte / Revue d'histoire Européenne Contemporaine* 9, no. 1 (2011): 8–26; Grahame Thompson, "The Evolution of the Managed Economy," *Economy and Society* 21, no. 2 (1992): 129–151.

[22] Trevor Jackson's rich monograph on financial crises explores the longrun evolution of thinking about economic and financial crises as unavoidable natural disasters, rather than the consequences of corruption, greed, or ineffective policies. See: Trevor Jackson, *Impunity and Capitalism: The Afterlives of European Financial Crises, 1690–1830* (Cambridge: Cambridge University Press, 2022); Robert Brenner, *The Economics of Global Turbulence: The Advanced Capitalist Economies from Long Boom to Long Downturn, 1945–2005* (London: Verso, 2006); Charles S. Maier, "'Malaise': The Crisis of Capitalism in the 1970s," in *The Shock of the Global*, ed. Niall Ferguson et al. (Cambridge; London: Belknap Press of Harvard University Press, 2010); Charles S. Maier, "Two Sorts of Crisis? The Long Seventies in the West and East," in *Koordinaten Deutscher Geschiste in Der Epoche Des Ost-West Konflikts*, ed. Hans Gunter Hockerts (Munich: Oldenburg, 2004).

[23] Two Commission documents, one from 1966 and the other from 1972, cited Veblen. One footnote referenced Juglar in: European Commission, "Programme de recherche et d'action sur le developpement du marche de l'emploi," 1982.

[24] The digital AEI makes tracking such references possible.

[25] One policy paper from 1982 referenced the work of Kondratiev, Schumpeter, and Keynes to explain the recession in Europe in the early 1980s; it also cited the work of Mancur Olson in positing that "distributional coalitions … reduce the rate of economic growth." See: Alfred Steinherr, "The Great Depression: A Repeat in the 1980s? Economic Papers No. 10, November 1982," EU Commission – Working Document, 1982.

power parity, world hunger, inflation, and labor markets. John Maynard Keynes loomed largest in EEC economic thinking; nearly ninety working papers, speeches, and official texts cited his work in relation to postwar political economy and monetary union. Overall, though, those making economic policy decisions for the EEC rarely referenced economic theory in their attempts to make sense of – and manage – the region's economic challenges.

By contrast, the mythos of Jean Monnet's famous maxim permeated European institutions. More than 5,000 EEC documents across the EEC's official languages addressed the urgency of "crisis/es" from the 1950s to early 1980s. By that time, European officials seemed convinced of their responsibility to rise to the occasion and manage the "crises" out of which they believed Europe would continue to be "forged."[26] Challenges had indeed driven regional cooperation, giving rise to a new economic and monetary consensus already in the mid-1970s, which created the European Monetary System (EMS) and its Exchange Rate Mechanism (ERM) in 1979 and laid a path for further economic and political union.[27] The ongoing conflict of the Cold War also motivated the strengthening of European Political Cooperation (EPC) first established in 1969. In 1981, West German Foreign Minister Hans-Dietrich Genscher and his Italian counterpart Emilio Colombo drafted a joint proposal to reinforce political cooperation and collective foreign policy by weakening member state veto power. This Genscher-Colombo Plan for a European Act concluded that the solidarity of the Community and its strength on the world stage was contingent on solving the region's economic and social problems, for which "the common market must not only be maintained: it must be brought to completion." Full economic integration, the plan argued, would position the Community to realize the "potential of the European economic area, increase its competitiveness, improve investment opportunities and reduce the level of unemployment."[28] Even the success of

[26] In his memoir, one of the early architects of the European Communities, Jean Monnet, argued that "Europe will be forged in crises and will be the sum of the solutions adopted for those crises." See: Jean Monnet, *Memoires* (Paris: Artheme Fayard, 1976). Monnet's words laid the foundation for a "Crisis Theory" of European integration, the disciplinary consequences of which Laurent Warlouzet has written constructively: Laurent Warlouzet, "European Integration History: Beyond the Crisis," *Politique européenne* 44, no. 2 (2014): 98–122.

[27] For an authoritative history of the EMS, see: Emmanuel Mourlon-Druol, *A Europe Made of Money: The Emergence of the European Monetary System*, Cornell Studies in Money (Ithaca, NY: Cornell University Press, 2012).

[28] Hans-Dietrich Genscher and Emilio Colombo, "Draft European Act Submitted by the Governments of the FRG and Italy, 6 November 1981," *Bulletin of the European Communities*, November 1981, No. 11. Luxembourg: Office for Official Publications of the European Communities: 87–91.

European foreign policy required internal market integration. And the narrative and responsibility of crisis management drove the Council to call on the Commission to look for new, remedial policy avenues to reenergize economic growth. Since the crises of the 1970s called the viability of economic planning into question, the Commission began to adopt a new approach to its economic policymaking: risk management, imported from business practices and based largely on forecasting.[29]

Relaunching the Community

In 1982, just after Greece joined the EEC and amid discussions about another enlargement to include Spain and Portugal, the heads of member states on the European Council cited the convergence of external and internal pressures in their appeals to "relaunch" the Community, however anachronistically framed given the achievements of the preceding years. After several months of meetings, including deliberations on the Genscher-Colombo Plan, the Council held a summit in Copenhagen, at which it endorsed the "need for a comprehensive strategy for achieving a marked improvement in the employment situation through the creation of durable new jobs" through a broad range of interlinking member state and regional policies.[30] Notably, as Chapter 4 explains, manufacturing seemed to the Commission best placed to deliver "durable" jobs and recapture the employment rates and industrial economy of the postwar boom. Furthermore, reduced interest rates could encourage productive activity; investing in new industries could prepare young people to take advantage of high-tech jobs; reorganizing working hours and facilitating mobility could afford Europeans more flexibility; removing market barriers could boost trade; dynamic energy policy could simultaneously offer savings and diversify supply; and strengthening the EMS could increase international cooperation. In short, growth and employment were the goal. Whatever policy agenda they settled on to these ends would also have to align with their objectives for international trade in the ongoing negotiations of the General Agreement on Tariffs and Trade (GATT) and collective foreign policy. The EEC was eager to develop East–West relations with the

[29] For more on risk management in European economic governance, see my "Marketizing Climate Risk: An Actuarial History of the European Emissions Trading System," *European Review of History*, June 5, 2025.

[30] European Council, "The Presidency's Conclusions on the Proceedings of the European Council, Copenhagen 3–4 December 1982," 1982.

Soviet Union through its EPC mechanism.[31] And because tensions with the USSR had spilled over into the Middle East after the Soviet invasion of Afghanistan in 1979, conflict in that region added to the EEC's foreign policy concerns. Moreover, the Council included ongoing economic competition with the US and Japan in its agenda setting calculus.

When the Council met in Stuttgart in June 1983, its members not only identified their priorities for relaunching the Community, but they made a Solemn Declaration to create the European Union they determined was necessary "to meet the dangers of the world situation" and ensure "social progress."[32] To achieve the vision of a union bound by the "common destiny" of democracy and human rights, the Council laid out four major spheres of work to be completed, chief among which were solving employment and inflation and strengthening the EMS and common commercial policy.[33] The Declaration secondarily aimed to complete the unfinished internal market, develop a common industrial strategy to make European business more globally competitive, and facilitate legal approximation to protect industrial and commercial property, ensure consumer protection, and achieve a common company law.[34] While the revised institutional division of labor compelled the Council to consult with the Parliament on its plans, it was the Commission that the Council turned to as the "driving force in the process of European integration," empowering it to develop policy proposals that could give new life to the Community and eventually constitute a Treaty on European Union.[35]

[31] Angela Romano's detailed narrative of East–West relations explains these dynamics well. See: Angela Romano, "The EC and the Socialist World: The Ascent of a Key Player in Cold War Europe," in *Europe's Cold War Relations: The EC Towards a Global* Role, ed. Ulrich Krotz, Kiran Klaus Patel, and Federico Romero (London: Bloomsbury, 2020): 51–71.

[32] European Council, "Solemn Declaration on European Union," Stuttgart, June 19, 1983. In January 1983, the EEC created an "Internal Market Council."

[33] The Declaration offered no definitions for its conception of universal – or even European – human rights, but instead seemed to rely on the body of European law with which all member states and applicant countries had to comply. That body of law was later formulated as the *acquis communautaire* to facilitate negotiations for the fourth and fifth enlargements.

[34] Finding the level of especially youth unemployment intolerable, the Council had previously issued a resolution on unemployment, which argued for industrial restructuring, greater attention to SMEs, and youth training programs in order to respond to the Community's crises. See: Official Journal of the European Communities, "Resolution du conseil du 12 julliet 1982 concernant une action communautaire pour combattre le chômage," No C 186/1, BAC 174/1999 n. 2505 (1985), Historical Archives of the European Commission (hereafter HAEC).

[35] European Council, "Solemn Declaration," 5. The Tindemans Report of 1976 had worked to clarify the language of "European Union" and its many dimensions. See, Leo Tindemans, "European Union: Report by Mr. Leo Tindemans, Prime Minister of

Under Gaston Thorn, Luxembourgish politician and Commission president from 1981 to 1985, the Commissioners responsible for internal market (Karl-Heinz Narjes, Germany), industry (Étienne Davignon, Belgium), and competition policies (Frans Andriessen, Netherlands) renewed their efforts to achieve the economic aims set by the Council. Thorn, who, according to his successor Jacques Delors, "submitted about fifteen very interesting plans to deepen the single market" – none of which were ever adopted because of the unanimity rule, also encouraged business groups like the Chambers of Commerce to reinforce its political support for more market integration, lest Europe succumb not only to competition from the US and Japan but also to what he described as the dirigiste inclinations of European officials.[36] Despite his extensive career experience in the Community and his efforts to reanimate the EEC, Thorn's leadership was quickly eclipsed by the charisma of his vice-president and erstwhile rival Viscount Étienne Davignon, whose long career in Belgian politics, European institutions, and business included serving as the attaché of Paul-Henri Spaak, architect of the common market in the 1950s.[37] Davignon also authored a report on the future of collective foreign policy and the problems of political unification in 1970.[38]

Charisma also earned Davignon the nickname "Stevie Wonder" for his political efficacy and his large rolodex, which included many corporate executives.[39] For Davignon, businesses – multinational firms in particular – were essential to the objectives of market integration; they had the

Belgium, to the European Council," 1976, *Bulletin of the European Communities*, Supplement 1/76, AEI.

[36] European Commission, "Une perspective europpéenne: Intervention de Gaston Thorn, Lors d'un dejeuner, Causerie organise par la chambre de commerce de Bruxelles," April 1984: 13; Jacques Delors "The Single Market: Cornerstone of the EU," *Notre Europe* November 22, 2012.

[37] After serving as Spaak's chef de cabinet, Davignon stayed on in the same post under Foreign Minister Pierre Harmel (1966–1969), during which time his reputation as a driving force inspired memes about him pulling the puppet strings behind the backs of those nominally in power. This reputation was advanced by his promotion in 1969 to Director General for Policy in the Belgian Foreign Ministry, where he authored the "Davignon Report" (1970) on the problems of political unification in Europe. In 1974, he became Chairman of the Executive Committee on the International Energy Agency, a position that groomed him for his leading role in the Thorn Commission.

[38] This report is often called the "Davignon Report." Bulletin of the European Communities. November 1970, no. 11. Luxembourg: Office for Official Publications of the European Communities. "Davignon Report (Luxembourg, 27 October 1970)," 9–14.

[39] European Voice, "Belgium's Driving Force," *Politico*, March 26, 1997, www.politico.eu/article/belgiums-driving-force/. For more on the sociology of global economic elites, see: Sabine Pitteloud and Grace Ballor, "The Rise and Fall of Private Advocacy Forums from 1945 to the Twenty-first Century," *Socio-Economic Review*, 2025.

incentive and capacity to regionalize and, importantly, to bring the SMEs in their supply and value chains along with them.[40] He was keen to bring European multinationals into the EEC's political process by creating a forum similar to the US Business Roundtable.[41] He had cultivated his business contacts from 1977 to 1981 when he held the position of commissioner for an unprecedented portfolio combination: Internal Market and Industrial Affairs, the Customs Union, the Information Market and Innovation, Energy, the Euratom Supply Agency and International Nuclear Relations.[42] In that capacity, he designed a plan to restructure the European steel industry to make it more globally competitive, which contributed to the development of Community industrial policy.[43] Then, as Director General for Industrial Affairs, Energy, Research, and Science and de facto Commission president during Thorn's term, he championed policies to strengthen the EEC's common market and the region's global competitiveness.[44] Noting Europe's decline relative to the US and Japan in producing high technology, Davignon created the Big Twelve Round Table of technology business leaders in 1980 – also called the Davignon Round Table – and pushed for a six-fold increase in Community funding of technology R&D and for the Commission to foster collaboration among European technology firms so they could compete globally.[45] To that end, he was instrumental in establishing

[40] Grace Ballor, Interview with Étienne Davignon, Audio recording. Brussels, June 16, 2016. On Davignon's role in the creation of European business forums, see: Rasmus Salén and Grace Ballor, "In Search of Unicorns: Lessons from Past European Industrial Policy and Business Forums in High Tech," presented at the Council for European Studies conference in Lyon, France in July 2024.

[41] Edwin Artzt (Procter & Gamble Company), "Letter to Viscount Étienne Davignon on a European Business Roundtable, 10 May 1979," INV 0015/2019 no. 7 (1977–1983), HAEC. For more on the US Business Roundtable, see: Benjamin C. Waterhouse, *Lobbying America: The Politics of Business from Nixon to NAFTA* (Princeton, NJ: Princeton University Press, 2013).

[42] In this role, Davignon addressed the need for extensive restructuring for European industries like auto manufacturing and steel and secured EEC funding to facilitate such changes. See: "Address by Viscount Étienne Davignon at the [International Iron and Steel Institute] Board Luncheon of the Rome Cavalieri Hilton, Rome, on Sunday 9 October 1977," INV 00015/2019 no. 8 (1977–1983), HAEC.

[43] European Commission, "Proposition of Council Regulation (EEC) on Community Aid for Industrial Restructuring and Conversion Operations," Brussels, October 26, 1978; COM(78) 532 final. On the steel industry, see the work of Dimitri Zurstrassen.

[44] For a history of the Thorn presidency, see: Piers Ludlow, "Gaston Thorn: An Embattled Visionary," in *The European Commission 1973–86: History and Memories of an Institution*, ed. Michel Dumoulin et al. (Luxembourg: Publications Office of the European Union, 2014): 201–206.

[45] On the Big Twelve Roundtable, see: Margaret Sharp and Claire Shearman, *European Technological Cooperation* (London: Chatham House Papers, 1987): 47–49; On Davignon's focus on technology investment and joint research and development,

the framework programs for European research policy and the European Strategic Program on Research Information Technology (ESPRIT) to promote shared research and development and share industry information and create common industry norms, like the Open System Interconnection Model (OSI) to facilitate the interfacing of computer networks.[46] He also contributed to the creation of the Strategic Program for Innovation and Technology Transfer (SPRINT) to foster technological innovation and help European companies implement the just-in-time logistics systems fueling the success of their Japanese rivals and to support the development of effective management practices across the EEC.[47] With his aides, Pierre Defraigne and Michel Carpentier, Davignon also hosted regular conferences, roundtables, and bilateral meetings of business leaders in Brussels, a "centerpiece of the resurgent Europe movement in the early eighties" in the eyes of some observers.[48]

Davignon found strong support for his views about the role of business in market integration among the executives of major European multinationals like Siemens, Shell, Nestlé, FIAT, and Renault, as well as the dynamic Swedish CEO Pehr Gyllenhammar from Volvo. Despite not being from an EEC member state, Gyllenhammar secured a place for himself within the auto sector interest associations of the EEC, described in Chapter 4, and worked with Davignon and former Commission President-turned-CEO François-Xavier Ortoli to form the European Round Table of Industrialists (ERT) in April 1983.[49] "Not just another lobby group," according to Gyllenhammar, the ERT functioned as a platform for leading European industrial firms to bring their interests straight to EEC policymakers in regular, biannual meetings at Berlaymont. That business was given a seat at the Commission's table – and that Davignon regarded ERT

see: Joel Goodfader, "European Unity: Pursuing the Vision: An Interview with Viscount Étienne Davignon," n.d., 4.

46 European Commission, "Communication from the Commission to the Council on Laying the Foundations for a European Strategic Programme of Research and Development in Information Technology: The Pilot Phase. COM (82) 486 Final/2, 13 August 1982," August 13, 1982. For more on the Commission's technology programs, see: Pierre-Henri Laurent, "The European Technology Community, the Meeting of the Elites, and the Completion of the Internal Market," *Il Politico* 52, no. 2 (1987): 310; On European research policy, see the PhD research of David Irion at LMU Munich.

47 European Council, "Council Decision of 25 November 1983 Concerning a Plan for the Transnational Development of Supporting Infrastructure for Innovation and Technology Transfer," *Official Journal of the European Communities*, 83/624/EEC.

48 Laurent, "The European Technology Community," 310.

49 For more on Gyllenhammar's role within EEC associations, see: Grace Ballor, "Liberalisation or Protectionism for the Single Market? European Automakers and Japanese Competition, 1985–1999," *Business History* 65, no. 2 (2022): 302–328.

members as "policy consultants" – has led some scholars to credit this bastion of "transnational capitalism" with "setting the agenda" for market integration in the following years.[50] Regardless of the extent to which industrialists shaped market policies, the participation of current and former commissioners in the ERT's formation and meetings reveals the increasing importance with which regional policymakers like Davignon treated business interests as they worked to relaunch the Community in the wake of recession.[51] The ERT was asked to advise the Commission on how to stimulate the European economy.

In meetings with the Commission in June 1985, the captains of European industry discussed the "Obstacles to European Industrial Growth," including low returns on investment, heterogeneous regulation, a lack of common standards, and other fiscal, legal, and political obstacles. They did not discuss capitalism itself being in crisis or the structural decline of their own economic and social importance. Among the remedies they suggested to Europe's economic woes and "improve Europe's position in world markets" were tax reductions, fiscal measures, support for risk or venture capital, the standardization of technical specifications, the deregulation of public markets, investment in public infrastructure, and the harmonization of economic policies. Additionally, reducing the cost of transborder flows and facilitating the emergence of transnational industrial structures to compete on world markets by eliminating the fiscal impediments to company mergers while maintaining a competitive environment in Europe would, in the minds of industrialists, help Europe remain globally competitive and solve its economic and social problems.[52] In subsequent meetings with the Commission, the ERT stressed the need for a European venture capital initiative and support for risk capital, through a program called "Euroventures" and to collectivize R&D in technology and computer science through a European Technology Institute (ETI), based on the Silicon Valley model of university research in partnership with industry. They also called for European investment in transportation links, like a

[50] Here, I am quoting the strongest of these arguments: Bastiaan Van Apeldoorn, *Transnational Capitalism and the Struggle over European Integration* (London: Routledge, 2002); Maria Green Cowles, "Setting the Agenda for a New Europe: The ERT and EC 1992," *JCMS: Journal for Common Market Studies* 33, no. 4 (1995): 501–526.

[51] Geoffrey Garrett's earlier work attributed less influence to business interests than Cowles, giving rise to a lively debate about the extent to which the market agenda was shaped by the ERT. See: Geoffrey Garrett, "International Cooperation and Institutional Choice: The European Community's Internal Market," *International Organization* 46, no. 2 (1992): 533–560.

[52] European Roundtable of Industrialists, "Foundations for the Future of European Industry," June 1985, PSP-385, HAEU: 6–7.

"EuroRoute" tunnel under the English Channel the "Chunnel" and better rail connections over the Alps and through Scandinavia "Scanlink," emulating the Japanese rail network.[53] Through these initiatives, the ERT argued, "European industry can improve its position in world markets if government and business work further toward the integration of European markets so as to allow greater economies of scale in research and development, manufacturing and distribution."[54] The commissioners who engaged in meetings on these topics with the ERT, including Peter Sutherland and Stanley Clinton-Davis broadly supported these proposals. Indeed, several ERT proposals were included in the Commission's 1985 "White Paper on Completing the Single Market" and in the initiatives launched in the early stages of the 1992 program.

Beyond the ERT, commissioners met frequently with many sectoral BIAs to solicit industry input on policy proposals and encourage business groups to embrace the EEC's economic agenda. Forums like the Center for European Policy Studies (CEPS) in Brussels also brought public and private interests together expressly for the purpose of advancing their common policy objectives. At CEPS in 1984, Wisse Dekker, Chairman of the Dutch multinational Philips, outlined a five-year plan to complete an internal market by removing physical, technical, and fiscal barriers to trade. Developing common European policies seemed far too burdensome to meet Dekker's 1990 deadline; instead, collective deregulation offered a much more expedient path to policy convergence. And with Dekker's crisis clock reading mere minutes to the metaphorical midnight of Europe losing the contest of global competition, he argued: "there is really no choice ... The only option left for the Community is to achieve the goals laid down in the Treaty of Rome. Only in this way can industry compete globally, by the exploiting of economies of scale for what will then be the biggest home market in the world."[55] At the same time, the European Parliament passed a resolution on the need to implement the internal market for the benefit of all stakeholders.[56]

[53] These discussions are contained in the files of Commissioner Peter Sutherland: PSP-385, HAEU.

[54] European Roundtable of Industrialists, "Foundations for the Future of European Industry," June 1985, PSP-385, HAEU.

[55] Dekker published his 1984 plan in an academic journal the following year: Wisse Dekker, "Europe 1990: An Agenda for Action," *European Management Journal* 3, no. 1 (March 1, 1985): 5–10.

[56] Klaus Löffler, "More of a Heavyweight Than It Looks: The European Parliament's Role in Setting Up the Internal Market," *Commission of the European Communities: Monthly Newsletter on the Single Internal Market*, April 4, 1992. For more on the role of the Parliament in market integration, see: Laurent Warlouzet, *Completing the Single*

When the Council met at Fontainebleau in June 1984 to adopt "new guidelines for the re-activation of European cooperation" by resolving budget issues, creating a "People's Europe," and commissioning an ad hoc Committee for Institutional Affairs under Irish representative James Dooge, it also had to nominate a new cohort of commissioners and determine who should serve as the body's next president.[57] Despite Davignon seeming the obvious choice to lead the EEC's executive body given his extensive experience, French President François Mitterrand and West German Chancellor Helmut Kohl made a "backdoor deal between Paris and Bonn" over breakfast one morning that Mitterrand's former Minister of Economics, Finance, and Budgetary Affairs, Jacques Delors, should assume the role.[58] Before his ministerial career at the Banque de France, Delors had a long career in French civil service and entered the European Parliament in its first round of democratic elections in 1979, where he chaired the Economic and Monetary Affairs Committee. Despite his political affiliation with the French socialist party, he was confirmed as Thorn's successor at the Commission with the support of Margaret Thatcher, who favored him for the job after he helpfully brokered a rebate for the UK's contributions to the EEC budget. Thatcher had not liked Davignon, who subsequently left the Commission altogether, in what some described as a "serious loss" of his stature and expertise.[59]

Delors' presidential mandate was clear: relaunch the Community. It was his responsibility, together with his cabinet chief Pascal Lamy, to develop the Commission's policy agenda for how best to do that and to allocate policy portfolios to his fellow commissioners accordingly.[60] Given his career experience in central banking, Delors argued that a single currency would most effectively propel the EEC forward out of crisis and toward the ever closer union promised in Rome. He was

Market: The European Parliament and Economic Integration, 1979–1989 (Luxembourg: Publications Office of the European Union, 2020).

57 European Council, "Fontainebleau Summit," 1984. On the appointment of commissioners, see: Alexandra Devantier, "Appointment of the Commission: Parliament's Role before 1995" (European Parliament: Briefing).

58 Paul Cheeseright, "All Change as European Commission Old Guard Is Replaced," *Financial Times* January 4, 1985, JD-17, Fondation Jean Monnet pour l'Europe (hereafter FJME).

59 "A Good Choice for Brussels," *Financial Times*, JD-17, FJME. For a detailed explanation of the contested appointment of Delors, see: Grace Ballor, "Agents of Integration: Multinational Firms and the European Union" PhD dissertation, UCLA, 2018: 63–107.

60 After his work in the Delors Commission, Lamy was CEO of Crédit Lyonnais, then returned to Brussels as trade commissioner before helming the WTO from 2005 to 2013. For more on Lamy at the Commission, see the ongoing work of Éric Bussière.

careful, however, to temper his ambition with pragmatism. To ensure member state support for his policy agenda, he shopped four proposals around member state capitals in the fall of 1984, asking heads of state what major project they thought would best reinvigorate the region and reenergize its economy: developing common defense, creating a monetary union, pursuing institutional reform to resolve the EEC's persistent democratic deficit, or completing the internal market? Only market integration earned the unanimous support of Council members, so Delors resolved to complete the internal market as the foundation on which his other aims could be achieved.[61] Consequently, beyond managing secular stagnation and social strife, market making was motivated by a constellation of diverse economic, political, and social ambitions for the EEC, some of which were eventually incorporated into efforts to create a single market.

Portfolio allocation had always been a complicated set of negotiations, and the objective of successfully relaunching the Community by completing an internal market that could lay the foundation for economic and monetary union only raised the stakes.[62] In this, too, Delors proved himself to be both highly pragmatic and an effective diplomat. In October 1984, he went to London to meet Thatcher, who insisted that her Commission appointee Francis Arthur Cockfield – a London School of Economics law graduate who worked in both private sector finance and government taxation and served as UK Minister for Trade under the Conservatives – be given responsibility for the internal market.[63] Thatcher wanted to position British interests at the center of the Commission's policy agenda and limit Delors' other ambitions. Delors agreed and even made Cockfield a vice-president of the institution, further cementing a good working relationship with the British prime minister committed to market liberalization at home and abroad and skeptical of the overreach of regional governance. In theory, Davignon's departure from the Commission meant that his behemoth portfolio could be reapportioned. But even after the separation of energy and nuclear policy from industrial affairs, Cockfield secured a capacious brief including the internal market, financial services, company law,

[61] For more on the complexity of Delors' economic thinking, see: Dermot Hodson, "Jacques Delors: Vision, Revisionism, and the Design of EMU," in *Architects of the Euro: Intellectuals in the Making of European Monetary Union*, ed. Kenneth Dyson and Ivo Maes (Oxford: Oxford University Press, 2016): 212–232.

[62] Michel Dumoulin, "The Commission as a Body," in *The European Commission 1973–86*, 77–97.

[63] Gilles Grin, *The Battle of the Single European Market: Achievements and Economic Thought, 1985–2000* (London: Kegan Paul, 2003): 110. Cockfield reportedly hated his first name and being called "Frank"; he went by Arthur instead.

taxation, the customs union, manufacturing, pharmaceutical and chemical industries, construction, and distribution, allowing him to expedite his development of market policies unimpeded by colleagues with intersecting responsibilities. The remaining portfolios were delegated at a preparatory meeting of the new commissioners and their cabinets at the Royaumont Abbey outside Paris in December 1984, where German Karl-Heinz Narjes was charged with Industrial Affairs.[64]

Within a week of the Commission officially convening in early January 1985, Delors formally announced the "thrust" of his institution's agenda to the European Parliament: to endow Europe with economic, technological, financial, and monetary strength through a "large market and industrial cooperation, the strengthening of the European Monetary System, and the convergence of economies to lead to higher growth and more jobs."[65] He emphasized – and perhaps exaggerated – the crises Europe faced to underscore his point.[66] The Community had not yet realized the objectives of the Treaty of Rome, he argued, because the "engineers of European integration are fumbling not over 'what has to be done' but rather over 'how to go about it.'"[67] The *what* was clear: to create a "tangible Europe, a real Community," to restore Europe's credibility by rediscovering the path to economic growth, and "to eliminate all frontiers in Europe by 1992," within two of the Commission's four-year terms.[68] He cited Davignon's ESPRIT Program as a model of how an integrated market could throw open the doors to innovation, competition, and growth, simultaneously expanding choices and reducing prices for consumers. Although Delors assured the Parliament that he was realistic about the challenges of creating a single currency right away, he argued that the market's objectives could be accelerated by economic and monetary union. Regardless of the economic means, he promised that the Commission, as "engineer of this European construction project" and "guardian of the public interest," would attend to the needs of all stakeholders – business and commerce, firms and workers – whose

[64] "Delors and his 13 Apostles," *Economist*, May 17, 1984, JD-17, FJME.

[65] European Commission, "The Thrust of Commission Policy: Statement by Jacques Delors, President of the Commission, to the European Parliament" January 14–15, 1985, Strasbourg (Bulletin of the European Communities): 9.

[66] Wayne Sandholtz and John Zysman, "1992: Recasting the European Bargain," *World Politics* 42, no. 1 (1989): 98.

[67] European Commission, "The Thrust of Commission Policy," 4.

[68] Ibid., 5–6. Subsequently, there was some debate about whether the deadline should be January 1992, when a new cohort of commissioners would take up their positions, or December 1992, allowing more time to complete the unprecedented Single Market Program. It quickly became clear that the later deadline was best, even if it did not align with the Commission's terms.

participation and collaboration would be essential to the market's success.[69] But devising a plan to achieve a true internal market – the *how* – would take "a little time," perhaps until March. It would also require institutional reform, since the unanimity principle established in Article 100 of the Treaty of Rome had hampered progress toward market integration in the past and, as Delors discovered on his tour of member state capitals a few months before, national priorities differed widely.

Although not all parliamentarians welcomed Delors' agenda in January 1985, Cockfield wasted no time in tackling the question of method that had frustrated earlier efforts to integrate member state markets. Over the following months, he developed an extensive three-pillared plan, not unlike the brief proposed by Dekker, to remove all physical, technical, and fiscal barriers to trade through 279 measures of legislative harmonization, like developing a common value added tax, regulating state aids, and opening public procurement contracts across the EEC. These measures were to be implemented through directives – legislative acts drafted by the Commission and approved by the Council with input from the Parliament – that outlined results to be achieved by each member state. As Chapter 2 explains, Cockfield's plan also included a "New Approach" to standardization, the process of creating common norms and technical standards, around which policymaker and big, especially industrial, business interests converged. By June, the Commission submitted Cockfield's "White Paper on Completing the Internal Market" to the Council for approval at its Milan Summit, where it was also considering the Dooge Committee's March 1985 report on institutional reform and the strategy of using market integration as a means of political unification.[70] The White Paper described Europe at a crossroads, facing the choice between embracing the future of a Single Market with resolution and determination or simply allowing Europe to slip into the mediocrity of being nothing more than a free trade area, rather like the EEC's economic rival in the region, the EFTA.[71] And it

[69] European Commission, "The Thrust of Commission Policy," 10.

[70] European Council, "Ad hoc Committee for Institutional Affairs Report to the European Council (Brussels, 29–30 March 1985) [Dooge Report]," March 29, 1985. For an analysis of how policy entrepreneurs used market integration in a "quiet revolution" of coalition-building, see: Nicolas Jabko, *Playing the Market: A Political Strategy for Uniting Europe, 1985–2005*, Cornell Studies in Political Economy (Ithaca, NY: Cornell University Press, 2006).

[71] European Commission, "White Paper from the Commission to the European Council on Completing the Internal Market (COM(85)310 final)," Milan, June 28–29, 1985: 55. The EFTA was formed in 1960 as an alternative to the EEC. During the 1990s and 2000s, many EFTA countries became EEC and EU member states, and in 1994, the EU and EFTA joined to form the European Economic Area (EEA).

argued that Europe could only retain its place in the global economy "by enabling industries to make economies of scale and therefore to become more competitive."[72] Council members, who had already unanimously supported Delors' proposed agenda of market integration, readily accepted the White Paper and its completion deadline of December 31, 1992, giving Cockfield the confidence to declare the Single Market Program the "flagship of the enterprise" at the core of the EEC and himself the architect and "Father of the Single Market."[73]

That the EEC had barely managed a handful of legislative harmonization measures each year before 1985 made the 1992 Program's timeline look like an unwinnable "steeplechase," however.[74] Only institutional reform could accelerate the process. With the market as motive and the Dooge Report as a guide to the comprehensive economic and social objectives of market making, the Council agreed to an unprecedented Intergovernmental Conference in September 1985 on amending the Treaty of Rome.[75] Among the many interventions achieved by the fraught negotiations over the resulting Single European Act (SEA), signed in February 1986 and effective in July 1987, were augmenting the agenda-setting authority of the Commission, increasing the power of the European Parliament to make decisions with the Council about the internal market, and entrusting the Economic and Social Committee – consisting of representatives from industry, labor, and the general public – with commenting on policy proposals.

Most importantly, the SEA replaced the cumbersome unanimity principle, which had impeded earlier efforts to remove nontariff barriers and integrate Community markets, with an extension of qualified majority voting (QMV) first established in the Luxembourg Compromise of 1966.[76]

[72] European Commission, "White Paper," 6.

[73] Cockfield, who was knighted in 1973 for his public service to the UK's Price Commission to control inflation, wrote a memoir detailing his contributions to the Single Market: Arthur Cockfield, *The European Union: Creating the Single Market* (Chichester: Wiley Chancery Law, 1994). By 1989, Thatcher ousted Cockfield from his post in Brussels for betraying his mandate to promote deregulatory trade liberalization with his overzealous Euro-enthusiasm.

[74] Jacques Pelkmans, "The Significance of EC-1992," *The Annals of the American Academy of Political and Social Science* 531, no. 1 (January 1994): 95.

[75] Commissioners weighed in on the Dooge Report in March 1985 and shaped the plan for institutional reform and the EEC's economic and social aims ahead of the intergovernmental conference that produced the Single European Act. See: Commission des Communautes Europeennes, "Comte rendu de la 11ème réunion du comite ad hoc pour les questions institutionelles (Comite Dooge) les 13, 14, et 15 mars 1985," Brussels, March 19, 1985, COM.

[76] Aside from the introduction of direct elections for members of the European Parliament in 1979, no major institutional reforms had been undertaken since the Treaty of Rome created the Communities in 1957. Other proposal for institutional reform had been put

This allowed the Council, in cooperation with the Parliament and with input from the Economic and Social Committee, to move past persistent deadlock and make economic policy decisions on a majority basis. By restricting member state veto power, the EEC could harmonize legislation much more efficiently and embark fully on a Single Market Program. Indeed, the pace of harmonization reported biannually by the Commission quickened in 1988 and beyond. Moreover, combining the principle of mutual recognition outlined in Articles 30–36 of the EEC Treaty and developed further in the ECJ's ruling in the *Cassis de Dijon* case with the new approach to legal harmonization presented in Article 100a, the SEA provided the institutional framework required to complete the White Paper's agenda of legislative harmonization.[77] Even if the SEA was ultimately achieved through interstate bargaining, many business groups had advocated for EEC reform and many more welcomed the resulting acceleration of progress toward an internal market.[78]

According to Jacques Delors, "[The SEA] was based on a triptych ... : competition that stimulates, cooperation that strengthens, and solidarity that unites. ... the missing link ... is cooperation. That can of course be remedied through a total transfer of sovereignty to the European level, but such a prospect is neither possible nor entertained by the member states."[79] However much such a transfer of sovereignty might seem to supplant democracy, Delors argued that the EEC's commitment to cohesion and its focus on social dialogue "which was very much alive between 1985 and 1994," achieved the following economic and social results "between 1986 and 1992: an additional 0.5 percent growth; 11 million new jobs created; a one-third increase in investments; and the development, both internally and externally, of mergers and acquisitions, thus a strengthening of competitiveness."[80]

forward, however, including the so-called Report of the Three Wise Men in 1979 on restructuring the institutions and revising the number and responsibilities of commissioners. See: Council of the European Communities, "Report on European Institutions, Presented by the Committee of Three to the European Council (October 1979)," Centre virtuel de la connaissance sur l'Europe (hereafter CVCE).

77 Official Journal of the European Communities, "Communication on the Free Movement of Foodstuffs within the Community," 89/C 271/03, Vol. 32, (October 24, 1989): Communication, A. Introduction, 1.

78 Moravcsik, "Negotiating the Single European Act," 21. For a comprehensive analysis of the role of interstate bargaining in European integration, see: Andrew Moravcsik, *The Choice for Europe: Social Purpose and State Power from Messina to Maastricht*, Cornell Studies in Political Economy (Ithaca, NY: Cornell University Press, 1998).

79 This triptych is also echoed in Laurent Warlouzet's *Liberty, Solidarity, and Community: Capitalism and European Integration, 1945 to the Present* (Cambridge: Cambridge University Press, 2026).

80 Jacques Delors, "The Single Market: Cornerstone of the EU," *Notre Europe* November 22, 2012.

Business in Single Market Policymaking

As instrumental as the White Paper and SEA were in creating a framework for market integration, policymakers recognized that achieving the Single Market and its economic and social objectives required firms to engage in business activity across EEC member states. From the start of the 1992 Program, the Commission worked to convince European companies of the opportunities afforded by an internal market and to develop programs for facilitating business regionalization. The primary targets for these efforts, especially during the mid and late 1980s, were big European industrial manufacturing companies, multinational corporations already doing business in multiple EEC member states and poised for further expansion in the Community. Policies aimed at business in the Single Market evolved considerably during the 1992 Program due to the diversity of Commissioner perspectives and in response to the changing geopolitical and economic landscape of Community enlargements, the collapse of the Soviet Union, global competition, and Economic and Monetary Union. Through debates about industrial intervention and protectionism on the one hand and open competition and full liberalization on the other, a set of policies took shape around business in the Single Market. By the time Delors began his second term as Commission president with a new cohort of colleagues and new mandates to create a single currency and prepare the EEC for both deeper political union and the potential of Eastern enlargement, policymaker approaches to business took on further social and environmental dimensions.

Immediately following the Milan Council Summit in summer 1985, Cockfield embarked on a speaking tour to promote the internal market to European business. In addition to clarifying elements like intellectual property, insurance, and the recognition of healthcare worker credentials, he used his speeches to court market support from Chambers of Commerce and Confederations of Industry, encouraging their members to "seize Europe's opportunities" and offering advice about how to navigate the challenges and opportunities presented by the Single Market.[81] In many cases, Cockfield's audiences were already strong

[81] Arthur Cockfield, "Seizing Europe's Opportunities, Speech to the Chambers of Commerce of Belgium and Luxembourg," November 11, 1985, HAEC. On other occasions throughout his Commission term, Cockfield addressed groups like the Association of Portuguese Banks; the Kangaroo Group; the European League for Economic Cooperation; the *Financial Times*; the British and American Chambers of Commerce in Belgium; the Confederations of British, Finnish German, and Portuguese Industry; and even the British Biscuit, Cake, Chocolate and Confectionary Alliance.

proponents; as he later recalled in his memoir, "nowhere did the concept of relaunching the Community receive greater support than in the top ranks of European industry."[82] Large corporations and peak BIAs were increasingly engaged in political activity in Brussels, especially after the SEA increased the Commission's capacity to set regional policy.[83] Throughout the 1992 Program, the Commission continued to meet with the ERT, business networks, and sectoral BIAs like those discussed in Chapter 3 to solicit business input on market policies and urge firms to embrace the market.

There were some skeptics, however, especially among SMEs, who worried about the challenges of facing open competition from firms in other member states. To that end, the Commission created a new Directorate General for Enterprise Policy (DG XXIII), to which Heinrich von Moltke was appointed. Recognizing the importance of accurate data on companies in the Community, von Moltke set to work with the EEC's Statistical Office (Eurostat) to measure the number and size of all firms within the EEC and to "provide businesspeople, opinion formers, policymakers and the general public with basic information on business activity by size of enterprises throughout the Community."[84] von Moltke and Eurostat saw statistics as "an integral part of the Community's enterprise policy," aimed as much at "increasing the competitiveness of the European economy, for employment growth and for economic and social cohesion in Europe" as convincing European companies of the opportunities of the internal market.[85] At the same time, Cockfield spearheaded the launch of "Enterprise Europe," a campaign to create a European network of interest associations representing business in Brussels.[86] And the Commission cultivated closer relationships with

[82] Cockfield, *The European Union: Creating the Single Market*, 177.

[83] For more on business interest representation in the EEC and EU, see: Coen, Katsaitis, and Vannoni, *Business Lobbying in the European Union*; David Coen, "The European Business Interest and the Nation State: Large Firms Lobbying in the European Union and Member States," *Journal of Public Policy* 18, no. 1 (1998): 75–100; David Coen, "The Evolution of the Large Firm as a Political Actor in the European Union," *Journal of European Public Policy* 4, no. 1 (1997): 91–108. On "1992" as a compromise between business and European institutions, see: Streeck and Schmitter, "From National Corporatism to Transnational Pluralism."

[84] European Commission, "Enterprises in the European Community," (Office for Official Publ. of the European Communities, 1990).

[85] European Commission, ed., "Enterprises in Europe: Second Report" (Office for Official Publ. of the European Communities, 1992).

[86] Arthur Cockfield, "A More Prosperous Europe, Speech to the Commerce and Industry Group of the European Movement," July 15, 1985, London, BAC 389/1991 no. 277, HAEC. See also: "BC-NET: Business Cooperation Network: réseau informatisé européen de coopération," Brussels, March 11, 1988, HAEC.

UNICE to discuss topics like "The Great Internal Market and Industrial Development."[87]

Because many firms lacked detailed knowledge about the market, the Commission established "Centers of Excellence" at universities, business schools, and research centers throughout the Community to cultivate expertise and facilitate the sharing of information.[88] By bringing together management scholars, economists, and market analysts around research on business and 1992 at these centers, policymakers hoped to convince business of the market's potential. Additionally, the Commission created a network of Euro-Info-Centers (EICs), designed "to ensure that businesses, and in particular SMEs, ha[d] reliable sources of information about Community and national markets, and about the process of completing the internal market."[89] These efforts to boost public relations with European SMEs also supplied the Commission with insight about how firms across the region viewed market integration. Through networks like Enterprise Europe, Euro-Info-Centers, and the consultants contracted to gather data on sectoral and industry performances, the Commission used business feedback to inform market policies.

By the late 1980s, the UK developed its own programs to prepare British business for the Single Market, which it cynically marketed as the "silver lining" of European integration.[90] Its Department for Trade and Industry (DTI) launched a program called "Europe Open for Business" and published a *Single Market News* periodical. It also produced a number of rather humorous videos (wonderfully preserved on YouTube!) featuring celebrity CEOs like Richard Branson with titles like "The Single Market: The Facts" and "An Action Checklist for Business," encouraging interested companies to contact the DTI immediately for their very own "Single Market Information Pack."[91] The DTI warned even the smallest British businesses to be prepared for regional competition lest "1992 be your 1066," comparing the potential invasion of competitors from the continent to the Norman conquest.[92]

87 Arthur Cockfield and Karl-Heinz Narjes, "The Great Internal Market and Industrial Development, 24 January 1985," EN-937, HAEU.

88 European Commission, "Towards a Single Market in Distribution: Internal Trade in the Community, the Commercial Sector, and the Completion of the Internal Market." COM(91) 41 final. Brussels, March 11, 1991, p. 15.

89 European Commission, "Les 'Euro Info Centre,' 1988" 71/025-026, HAEC. See also: COM(87)152 final of April 7, 1987; SEC(89)931 final of June 5, 1989.

90 UK Department of Trade and Industry, "Head for the Silver Lining!" HW-37, HAEU.

91 UK Department of Trade and Industry, "The Single Market: The Facts," HW-37, HAEU.

92 UK Department of Trade and Industry, *Single Market News* no. 4 (Autumn 1989), p. 20, HW-37, HAEU.

Not only were regional policymakers and national governments eager to prepare European firms for the new business environment of the Single Market, but they also wanted to develop companies that could compete on a global scale, especially with rivals from the US and Japan. Global competition intensified in the 1980s thanks to advancements in communications technology, the rise of financialization, and the ascendance of neoliberal policies for deregulation, privatization, and liberalization. Concerned about the survival of European businesses, the most protectionist policymakers in the Commission argued that while the 1992 Program would remove barriers between member states, protections should remain in place against foreign competition. Such protectionist proposals incited international outcries against "Fortress Europe," a betrayal of the Single Market's promise of liberalization and likely a violation of GATT agreements as well.[93] Indeed, the EEC supported some initial protections, with Delors defending the persistence of quotas for Japanese car imports until the European industry could be ready for free competition, as explained in Chapter 4. "Europe is open, but not for the taking," he made clear in an address to Parliament while defending the maintenance of some protections even after market liberalization.[94]

More liberal commissioners claimed instead that such protectionism would only compromise the development of European industry. Peter Sutherland, an Irish lawyer, businessman and Commissioner for Competition from 1985 to 1989, insisted on full liberalization for the internal market. Martin Bangemann – the German Free Democrat who took over as Commissioner for the Internal Market and Industrial Affairs in 1989 after Thatcher refused to renew the appointment of Cockfield for his overzealous Euro-enthusiasm – maintained that only competition could optimize the structure of European industry.[95] Moreover, he believed liberalization could also provide the EEC with the best leverage for negotiating reciprocal access to foreign markets like Japan.[96] By creating the conditions for healthy competition and encouraging research, information exchange, and openness to change, the EEC could not only develop strong globally competitive firms, but it could also incorporate new policy agendas like environmental protections. Belgian

[93] The introduction of Brian T. Hanson's article on "Fortress Europe" uncovers these fears. See: "What Happened to Fortress Europe?: External Trade Policy Liberalization in the European Union," *International Organization* 52, no. 1 (1998): 55–85.

[94] European Commission, "Completing of the Internal Market: Progress Report on the 1st of April 1989," Memo 89/16.

[95] Martin Bangemann, "Yes to the Community's Industrial Policy," *Commission of the European Communities: Monthly Newsletter on the Single Internal Market*, April 4, 1992.

[96] European Commission, "Export Promotion Programme: EXPROM," July 1986, PSP-347, HAEU.

politician Willy De Clerq uttered the strongest defense of liberalism when he argued that Europe's embrace of its "destiny" through its "great adventure in liberalization" would position the EEC to "play a leading role in dismantling barriers to international economic activity around the world … creating a new dynamism in the world economy" and inspiring a global movement of liberalization.[97]

Propelled by these visions, the EEC created several policy programs to incentivize and support regional business activity. Building on Davignon's earlier efforts, the Commission launched EUREKA, an organization to facilitate regional collaborations in technology and R&D and incentivize companies to work together to capitalize fully on the opportunities of the market.[98] It also developed University/Industry Cooperation in Training for Technology (COMETT) to mobilize the resources of higher education for industrial development.[99]

This was a new kind of regional industrial policy. Discussions about industrial intervention had long been a hallmark of the Coal and Steel and Economic Communities' approaches to business, and yet it was only after the reforms of the SEA that the Commission was able to take concrete steps to shape the structure of regional industry.[100] Its emergent strategy was not to protect weak firms with subsidies from Brussels, however, even if the growing challenge of global competition in areas like consumer technology, auto manufacturing, and banking did produce some tendencies toward protectionism, neomercantilism, and support for European champions.[101] Instead, EEC policy ultimately reflected a

97 European Commission, "1992: The Impact on the Outside World, part of The European Community in a Changing World: Speech by Willy De Clercq EC-Commissioner for External Relations and Commercial Policy," Buenos Aires, August 2, 1988, KM-257, HAEU.

98 European Commission, "Recherche et developpement technologique," Brussels, October 2, 1985, BAC 174/1999 n. 2505 (1985), HAEC.

99 European Commission, "University/Industry Cooperation in Training for Technology (COMETT)," Brussels, May 30, 1985, PSP-385, HAEU. The ERT also shared proposals with Commissioner Peter Sutherland in 1985, outlining plans to create a European Technology Institute to advance research in areas of strategic relevance to European industry and catch Europe up to the US' Silicon Valley and to form a collective venture capital firm called Euroventures.

100 For a history of industrial policy in the EEC and EU, see: Eric Bussière, "EU Industrial Policy: Lessons from the Experience of the 1960s to the 1990s," in *EU Industrial Policy in the Multipolar Economy*, ed. Jean-Christophe Defraigne et al. (Cheltenham; Northampton, MA: Edward Elgar Publishing, 2022): 159–172. Several of the volume's chapters provide surveys of industrial policy in relation to specific sectors and industries, like the chapter by Dimitri Zurstrassen on the steel industry.

101 On these protectionist and neomercantilist debates, see: Grace Ballor, "Liberal Environmentalism: The Public-Private Production of European Emissions Standards," *Business History Review* 97, no. 3 (2023); Ballor, "Liberalisation or Protectionism for the Single Market?" *Business History* 65, no. 2 (2022): 302–328.

stronger preference for liberalization as a means to build European companies with the potential to be as competitive abroad as they were in their new regional "home" market.[102] Policymakers still supported regional collaboration between firms, and the Commission encouraged companies to work together on large public procurement projects to build the road, rail, and communications infrastructure needed to realize free movement of goods and services.[103] At times, albeit rarely, the Commission supported mergers too, as happened during the creation of European aerospace champions like Airbus.[104]

But industrial policy in the Single Market Program was much less interventionist than it had been in previous decades. Through regulations on cartels (Regulation 17/62) and mergers (4064/89) as well as the institutional reforms of the SEA, the Commission had centralized its capacity to control trusts and evaluate mergers with the goal of improving the performance of European firms.[105] Merger control was especially important, given the "merger mania" that swept through European industry in the 1980s as companies aimed to fend off global competition by increasing their size and market power. Sutherland and his successor Leon Brittan, Commissioner for Competition Policy from 1989 to 1992, were adamant about the need to apply Treaty rules on competition rigorously in the context of the Single Market. They argued that eliminating interventions like state aids and promoting open competition would incentivize European firms to innovate and rationalize, thereby creating regional businesses that were globally competitive.[106]

[102] On EEC competition policy, see the many works of Laurent Warlouzet: Laurent Warlouzet and Tobias Witschke, "The Difficult Path to an Economic Rule of Law: European Competition Policy, 1950–91," *Contemporary European History* 21, no. 3 (2012): 437–455; Laurent Warlouzet, "The Centralization of EU Competition Policy: Historical Institutionalist Dynamics from Cartel Monitoring to Merger Control (1956–91)," *JCMS: Journal of Common Market Studies* 54, no. 3 (2016): 725–741; Laurent Warlouzet, "Laurent Warlouzet, La politique de la concurrence européenne depuis 1950: surveiller les entreprises et les États," n.d., 11; Neil Rollings and Laurent Warlouzet, "Business History and European Integration: How EEC Competition Policy Affected Companies' Strategies," *Business History* 62, no. 5 (2020): 717–742.

[103] The ERT published a paper in 1984 on "The Missing Links," highlighting industry's need for transcontinental infrastructure. PSP-385, HAEU.

[104] For a history of Airbus, see: Ralf Ahrens, "The Importance of Being European: Airbus and West German Industrial Policy from the 1960s to the 1980s," *Journal of Modern European History* 18, no. 1 (2020): 63–78.

[105] Warlouzet, "The Centralization of EU Competition Policy," 1–3. By this time, cartels, which were once a primary unit of capitalist organization, had come to be seen as "monopoly menaces," as Liane Hewitt framed them in her PhD dissertation: "Monopoly Menace: The Rise and Fall of Cartel Capitalism in Western Europe, 1918–1957," Princeton University, 2023.

[106] Leon Brittan, "Competition Policy Report, 26 July 1989," P/89/44 European Commission. Brittan went on to write a book on competition policy: *Leon Brittan,*

This was also, then, a competition policy with new objectives. Over the course of the late 1980s and early 1990s, the Commission worked to regulate state aids and cartels and harmonize national rules with the goal of full market liberalization to encourage the development of competitive companies, increase consumer choice, and reduce consumer prices.[107] Indeed, several commissioners described their role as architects of the competitive environment in which business could thrive. Delors mused that "companies – even giant corporations – are like plants. They need to plunge their roots into dense and rich soil to have a solid foundation."[108] Global competition had made regionalization all the more important; in his view, "globalization had not outmoded regional groups, but in fact had made them indispensable."[109] And for Delors, competition was the fertile soil firms needed to thrive. For all of their personal political differences, Frans Andriessen added to Delors' vision, confident that the business environment of the internal market could facilitate much-needed industrial restructuring in the region, and that it also served as a kind of "training ground where [firms] can prepare themselves and warm up before the real economic competition on the global market begins."[110] Creating globally competitive "European companies" could not only solve the original growth and unemployment problems in the region, but it could also reassert Europe in the global economy.

The Delors Commission conceived of "European companies" in concrete terms. In 1988, it proposed to finally create a European company statute, a *Societas Europaea* (SE), first discussed in the 1950s and 1960s as a way to complete the original common market and developed in the 1970s when Dutch Commissioner Hank Vredeling proposed to regulate multinationals through stakeholder capitalism by giving labor a place on corporate boards.[111] Amid the crises of that decade, and in the wake of opposition from several member states and influence by large companies,

European Competition Policy: Keeping the Playing Field Level (Brussels: Center for European Policy Studies, 1992).

107 Laurent Warlouzet argues that competition policy became fully neoliberal in the context of the 1992 Program. See: *Governing Europe in a Globalizing World: Neoliberalism and Its Alternatives Following the 1973 Oil* Crisis, Chapter 8.

108 Jacques Delors, "Une strategie efficace pour une France non frileuse," *French Politics and Society* 6, no.1 (1988): 6.

109 Delors, "Une strategie efficace," 6.

110 Commission européenne, "Lettre mensuelle sur l'Europe sans frontières," June 1990. Extrait du discours prononcé à Rotterdam, April 6, 1990.

111 Noëlle Lenoir, "The Societas Europaea (SE) in Europe: A Promising Start and an Option with Good Prospects," *Utrecht Law Review* 4, no. 1 (2008); Warlouzet, *Governing Europe in a Globalizing World*, Chapter 3. For a history of the concept of "European companies," see: Harm G. Schröter, *The European Enterprise: Historical Investigation into a Future Species* (Berlin & Heidelberg: Springer-Verlag, 2010).

the Vredeling Directive was scuttled. Delors revived the issue, which he described as one of the areas in which progress had regrettably been the slowest during the first half of the 1992 Program, arguing that a European company law would create more economic growth and more jobs and would serve as a symbol that workers had not been forgotten in the objectives of European integration.[112] After all, hadn't social concerns and unemployment rates motivated the market in the first place? He promised to realize the stalled proposal in his second term as Commission President.[113] It would take a comeback intervention by Davignon in the early 2000s, however, to finally implement the SE.[114]

As promised by Delors in 1985, the Commission reviewed its progress toward the Single Market at the Program's half-way point in 1988, which was also the end of one Commission term and as appointments were being made for another. As part of the midterm review, Delors tasked Italian lawyer and banker Paolo Cecchini, who had served as deputy director general for the Internal Market and Industrial Affairs under Davignon, to conduct an extensive, sixteen-volume report on the "Cost of Non-Europe," tallying the economic and social consequences of failure to complete the internal market.[115] Volume 3 of the report offered a survey of 11,000 firm perspectives on the market's likely effects on their business, because, as the Commission reiterated: "deriving full success from the creation of a European Community home market depends largely on the reactions of companies to the challenge inherent in it."[116] Policymakers needed to know, before undertaking the remaining legislative measures, whether the prime targets for the 1992 Program were threatened by the internal market, or invigorated by its

112 Jacques Delors, "Press Conference by President Delors before the European Council Summit in Hanover," Brussels, June 23, 1988, AEI.

113 European Commission, "Internal Market and Industrial Cooperation – Statute for the European Company – Internal Market White Paper, point 137. Memorandum from the Commission to Parliament, the Council and the Two Sides of Industry," COM (88) 320 final, June 8, 1988. Bulletin of the European Communities, Supplement 3/88.

114 Ultimately, Regulation 2157/2001 and Directive 2001/86/EC created the statute, which allows firms with at least €120,000 of capital and operations in two or more member states to take advantage of the mechanism for a European limited liability corporation. Response from firms was lackluster, though, with only about 2,200 companies embracing the SE designation as of 2020, a preponderance of them Czech and/or in financial services.

115 Paolo Cecchini, "Research on the Cost of Non-Europe, Basic Findings. The Completion of the Internal Market: A Survey of European Industry's Perceptions of the Likely Effects." Vols. 1–16 (Luxembourg: Office for Official Publications of the European Communities, 1988); Cecchini also co-wrote a book summarizing this report with Alex Jacquemin and Michael Catinat: *The European Challenge, 1992: The Benefits of a Single Market* (Aldershot: Wildwood House, 1988).

116 Cecchini, "Research on the Cost of Non-Europe," Vol. III, 1.

opportunities for investment, cooperation, diversification and competitiveness. The report's introduction cautioned readers that many participant firms answered the survey without full understanding of the market and through a microeconomic lens. Such hedging was wise, given that just 56 percent of respondents thought the internal market would increase opportunities for their company, while 37 percent either expected no change or did not know what to expect at all.[117] Still, Delors remained optimistic about big business support for the market and credited "the success of 1992 Program from the outset to the support we received from the heads of enterprises and trade union organizations even before having political support" from nation states.[118]

Along with the Cecchini Report, Delors commissioned a study on the as-yet unrealized efforts to achieve Economic and Monetary Union (EMU), which he called "the integrating force of all of the major measures of the borderless market."[119] At Hanover in 1988, the Council had reappointed him as Commission President and charged him with "studying and proposing concrete stages leading toward this union."[120] The resulting Delors Report laid the foundation for a three-stage plan for EMU, which, with the Single Market well underway, became his priority in his second term as Commission president.[121] "One market needed one money," the Commission's economists argued in 1990, just as the first stage of abolishing exchange controls was achieved, allowing capital to move freely.[122] Or was it that "one money would create one market?" as one of the same economists would later clarify.[123] Regardless of the answer to this "chicken and egg" question, the Delors Commission closely connected the completion of the internal market with the creation of a single currency. With the signing of the Treaty on European Union in Maastricht in February 1992, EMU became a binding objective, requiring the convergence of member state economic policies and eventually

[117] Cecchini, "Research on the Cost of Non-Europe," Vol. III, 3.

[118] "Interview du President Delors, 1988," JD 84-93, FJME. [119] Ibid.

[120] European Council, "Hanover European Council," June 27–28, 1988, *Bulletin of the European Communities*, No. 6/1988.

[121] In 1989, the Commission reported that it had completed 46 percent of the White Paper's measures for legislative harmonization. See: European Commission, "Completing of the Internal Market: Progress Report on the 1st of April 1989," Memo 89/16.

[122] Michael Emerson, Daniel Gros, and Alexander Italianer, *One Market, One Money: An Evaluation of the Potential Benefits and Costs of Forming an Economic and Monetary Union* (Oxford; New York: Oxford University Press, 1992). The original text was published as a Commission paper in October 1990.

[123] Daniel Gros, "One Market, One Money: A Mistaken Argument (Post Factum)?" Center for European Policy Studies No. 2017/05, February 16, 2017.

introducing a single currency by the end of the decade.[124] The economic process of making a market with a single currency had become a political project – too political, in fact, for member states like Denmark and Britain, which opted out of the currency union even as signatories to the Treaty and even with the new British Prime Minister John Major presiding over both a financial crisis in the UK and the presidency of the European Council.[125]

Toward a Social Single Market

The second half of the Single Market Program was deeply affected by exogenous shocks. Already in 1988, the Soviet Socialist Republic of Estonia declared independence from the Soviet Union, taking advantage of the openings created by Mikhail Gorbachev's tandem policies of glasnost and perestroika. Then, the toppling of the Berlin Wall in November 1989 ruptured the bipolar world order in place since the beginning of the Cold War. For some, it was the "end of history," the victory of liberal democracy.[126] For the European Economic Community, it not only remade relationships between East and West, but also thrust German reunification into the center of the EEC's economic and political agendas. An enlargement outside of the Treaty process posed unprecedented challenges, and the strength of Germany's Deutsche Mark additionally raised concerns for Delors' plans for EMU, ultimately motivating other member state governments to support a single currency lest a strengthened Germany overtake other member states and upset the delicate balance of the EMS.[127] The subsequent opening of Soviet Bloc economies and collapse of the Soviet Union in 1991 radically altered the geometry of the Single Market and future economic and political union. The EEC was quick to declare its intentions to "welcome new members, several of whom have already submitted application bids," and accepted the responsibility for "supporting the difficult process of economic and political reforms in Eastern Europe and the republics of the ex-Soviet Union" through structural and cohesion funds.[128] As discussed in

[124] European Council, "Treaty on European Union," OJ C 191, 29.7.1992.

[125] In the Commission's own words, the integration process began with trade, moved to economics, and then entered the realm of politics. See: European Commission, DG X, *From Single Market to European Union*, Publications Office, 1992.

[126] Francis Fukuyama, "The End of History?" *The National Interest*, no. 16 (1989): 3–18; Fukuyama, *The End of History and the Last Man* (New York: Simon & Schuster 2006).

[127] Several historians have examined the connections between German reunification and EMU, especially: Harold James, *Making the European Monetary Union:* (Cambridge, MA: Belknap Press, 2014): 210–264.

[128] European Commission, *From Single Market to European Union*, 6

Chapters 4 and 5, for Western European firms the opening of the Soviet Bloc offered cheap labor, large consumer markets, and new investment opportunities, especially as the "Shock Therapy" of rapid privatization and liberalization accelerated in the mid-1990s.[129] Many Western European companies, including those covered in the later chapters of this book, capitalized on opportunities in countries like Hungary, Poland, and the new Czech Republic. They made or facilitated acquisitions, established manufacturing, and built distribution in Eastern European countries, connecting those economies to the Single Market long before they became member states in the enlargements of 2004–2007.

In the midst of these changes to the economic, political, and foreign relations landscape, regional policymakers shifted their attention to social and environmental protections. Already in 1985, the Commission had engaged in social dialogue at the Belgian castle Val Duchesse, outlining a desire to create an internal market that reflected the needs of European societies and labor unions.[130] Delors had used his earliest presidential address to the European Parliament to advocate for regional collective bargaining.[131] And with the landmark Schengen Agreement allowing for the free movement of people signed in June 1985 and subsequent Commission discussions about the regional harmonization of labor conditions and creation of an action group on social issues like female employment, it seemed momentum toward a social Europe was building.[132] Even the Council had agreed to prioritize social policy alongside industrial development in 1985.[133] In the following years, discussions about a "People's Europe" remained on the agenda, but

129 For more on the transformation of Central and Eastern Europe, see: Ivan Berend, *From the Soviet Bloc to the European Union: The Economic and Social Transformation of Central and Eastern Europe Since 1973* (Cambridge: Cambridge University Press, 2009).

130 It was also at Val Duchesse that the Treaties creating the European Economic Community and Euratom were drafted in 1956 and 1957 before being signed in Rome.

131 European Commission, "The Thrust of Commission Policy," 9.

132 While the Schengen Agreement was not fully implemented until 1995 when member countries abolished internal border checks, its signing already signaled a shift toward a more social Europe. On Commissions discussions of specific social programs, see: European Commission, "Conclusions de la réunion du groupe restreint union Européenne, en presence de M. le president, le jeudi 12 septembre 1985," Brussels, September 17, 1985, UE (85) 144, BAC 174/1999 n. 2505 (1985), HAEC; European Commission, "Principales résolutions du Conseil pouvant permettre de développer une action communautaire," Brussels, September 18, 1985, BAC 174/1999 n. 2505 (1985), HAEC.

133 Official Journal of the European Communities, "Conclusions du conseil du 22 juin 1984 concernant un programme d'action sociale communautaire à moyen terme," (84/C 175/01), BAC 174/1999 n. 2505 (1985), HAEC.

the Commission focused much more on creating a growth-oriented market for business than on implementing regulations, and the social dialogue between employers in UNICE and the European Trades Union Confederation (ETUC) stalled. But in 1988, Delors and Commission Vice President Manuel Marín worked with the consultative body of the Economic and Social Committee to develop a European social program.[134] Other policymakers, too, began to draft new directives on vehicle emissions and packaging waste in response to environmental concerns, on codes of conduct for banks processing electronic payments, and limits for saturated fats in foods to protect consumers, upsetting European business groups who saw such regulations as a betrayal of the 1992 Program. That same year, Delors delivered a speech to the British Trades Union Congress at Bournemouth, in which he articulated plans for European workers rights, likely catalyzing Thatcher's famous Bruges Speech against the bureaucratic overreach of Brussels.[135] Then, in October 1989, Delors unveiled the landmark "Community Charter of Fundamental Social Rights of Workers" to the Council, which safeguarded collective bargaining, equal treatment for men and women, health and safety in the workplace, and the consultation of workers by employers, among other rights and the adoption of which by the Council's Labor and Social Affairs Committee led the Commission to prepare a forty-seven-point Action Program to be implemented in conjunction with the completion of the internal market.[136]

The Social Charter and the Social Action Program that followed recast the internal market as a social market, as "capitalism with a human face."[137] With the Charter ratification by every member state but Britain, the "road not taken" toward social Europe in the 1970s started to look more like an emergent European welfare state.[138] Delors' socialist politics, Catholic faith, and "discipleship" of personalist philosopher Emmanuel Mounier were finally reflected in European policy with the

[134] European Commission, "Briefing sur la charte communautaire des droites sociaux fondamentaux," 71/025-026, HAEC. Marin is credited with creating the Erasmus educational exchange program in 1987.

[135] Jacques Delors, "1992: The Social Dimension – Address at the Trades Union Congress, Bournemouth 8 September 1988," https://ec.europa.eu/commission/presscorner/api/files/document/print/en/speech_88_66/SPEECH_88_66_EN.pdf.

[136] European Council, "Community Charter of the Fundamental Social Rights of Workers," signed in Strasbourg, December 9, 1989. AEI.

[137] Samuel Brittan, *Capitalism with a Human Face* (London: Edward Elgar, 1995).

[138] Aurélie Dianara Andry, *Social Europe, the Road Not Taken: The Left and European Integration in the Long 1970s*, 1st ed. (Oxford: Oxford University Press, 2022); Laurent Warlouzet, "A Flanking European Welfare State: The European Community's Social Dimension, from Brandt to Delors (1969–1993)." *Contemporary European History* 33, no. 1 (2024): 23–36.

support of member state governments.[139] Over the following years, fellow commissioners, like the Italian environmentalist Carlo Ripa di Meana, championed additional social and environmental policies and contributed to the humanizing and greening of the Single Market.[140] The Commission also introduced training programs, like EUROFORM and FORCE to support convergent skill-building by European workers and facilitate transnational labor mobility, PETRA to provide additional vocational opportunities for young people, and IRIS and NOW to rectify persistent gender imbalances within the European workforce through specific initiatives for female career development. New programs were introduced, too, to support SMEs, which continued to fear the threat of open competition against large multinationals. While some European firms like the German carmakers covered in Chapter 4 saw business opportunities in such initiatives, others like the commercial companies discussed in Chapter 6 responded defensively. Businesspeople like John Hoskyns, Director General of the British Institute of Directors, disparaged the policy shift, arguing that "the Single European Market could turn out to be the biggest defensive merger of all time," its social turn an attempt to mollify corporatist countries unable to compete – as Britain was prepared to – in a fully liberalized market.[141]

In 1989, Delors also created a new economic advisory group within the Commission, called the Forward Studies Unit (FSU) and first led by French economist Jérôme Vignon. The Cellule de prospective, as it was called in French, consisted mostly of economists and reported directly to the Commission president, as its successors have continued to do in the twenty-first century. Under Delors, the FSU anticipated challenges the EEC and EU might face and developed reports to inform Commission policymaking. On many topics, ranging from North–South relations, German reunification, and the economic transformation of former Soviet Bloc states to immigration, demographic change, and climate change, the FSU took a risk management approach, forecasting the economic consequences of various threats as well as the methods and costs of mitigating them, thus "foreseeing like a company," as described by political scientist Hugo Canhihac.[142] Importantly, together with other

[139] See: Benedetto Zaccaria, "Personalism and European Integration: Jacques Delors and the Legacy of the 1930s," *Contemporary European History* 33, no. 3 (2024) 982–1001. Delors explicitly describes his personalist philosophy in his "Commemoration of Christian Philosopher Emmanuel Mounier," JD-201, FJME, as well as his *Mémoires* (Paris: Plon, 2003), 13, and "Speech at Bruges, 17 October 1989," Speech 89/73.

[140] Warlouzet, "A Social Europe with a Greener Perspective."

[141] "Institute of Directors: The Voice of Business Leaders," Press Release, June 12, 1989, HW-37, HAEU.

[142] See the ongoing work of Hugo Canhihac, including: "Forseeing Like a Company: Business and the Emergence of 'Sustainable Competitiveness' at the European Commission's Forward Studies Unit," ECPR Paper, 2024.

bodies in the Commission like the Interservice Group on Business Strategies (GISE), the FSU also examined the strategies of European enterprise and the business view of economic integration to inform the Commission on how to make a market.[143]

Conclusions

Social Europe did not supplant the Single Market Program and its focus on economic growth. Instead, European policymakers like Delors increasingly saw the Single Market and its economic strengths as the solid foundation on which they could develop environmental and social policies.[144] Nor did Social Europe substantively change the Commission's approach to business in the market, which first took shape around its Berlaymont conference table in January 1985. While the inclusion of social and environmental policies in the 1992 Program reflected the personal hopes of commissioners like Delors to create a social market economy for the region, they were only implemented when it became clear that the Single Market would succeed. Ever the pragmatist, Delors remained focused on making a market that could provide growth, jobs, and increased standards of living to all Europeans by encouraging the regionalization of European business. But by designing a market aimed at recovering the economy of the postwar economic miracles, the Commission neglected the structural transformations of the 1970s and created a market that was outdated even before it was complete. Not only did a retrograde focus on industry in the 1980s not serve European workers, but even when celebrating the achievement of the Single Market in 1992, Delors encouraged the European Parliament to be "more attuned to the requirements of the business world" going forward, dismissing hopes that social and environmental policies could balance the primacy of large enterprises in the market.[145]

Big businesses and multinational firms remained the primary targets of policymaker designs for the market throughout the 1992 Program, although with the "social turn," increasing attention was directed to

[143] See, for example: European Commission, "Cellule de prospective et Groupe inter services sur les stratégies d'entreprises (GISE)," BAC 208/1993 37, HAEC.

[144] See, for example, the quotation included in the Introduction about how the Commission in 1991 saw the Single Market as the new source of the EEC/EU's global soft power, especially on the issues of climate change and economic development.

[145] Jacques Delors, "1992, A Pivotal Year: From the Single Act to Maastricht and Beyond, The Means to Match our Ambitions," Strasbourg, February 12, 1992. *Bulletin of the European Communities*, Supplement 1/92, AEI.

SMEs in the EEC, which employed the majority of Europeans. Single Market industrial policies supported the creation of large European firms through acquisitions, greenfield investment, partnerships, and certain mergers. This industrial policy was counterbalanced by a liberal competition policy with two key objectives: simultaneously broadening choices and lowering costs for consumers on the one hand and cultivating more globally competitive firms on the other. As Chapter 4 shows in detail, commercial policies offered some protections for European firms against foreign competition in European markets during the transition phase of market integration, after which policymakers hoped the region's companies would be ready to compete not just against foreign firms in Europe but even in global markets. Indeed, by the time focus on the Single Market Program gave way to Economic and Monetary Union within the new political European Union, regional policymakers and member state officials increasingly saw the internal market as a springboard from which European firms could globalize. The resulting paradoxes between a commitment to competition policy and a view of big business as allies in market making shaped the Commission's economic governance of the Single Market for decades.

This history of Single Market political economy, which situates big business at the center of policymaker approaches to market integration, raises an important question: How did European firms view the regional business environment of an internal market? Chapter 2 finds the interests of both businesses and policymakers converged around efforts to set common European standards and that firms participated in shaping the market through the development of regional technical specifications and norms. Chapter 3 analyzes the extent to which companies Europeanized in response to the Single Market Program as the Commission had intended.

2 Coproducing Common Standards

In 1989, Peter Tracey, the tenacious manager of the UK-based safety systems company Herga Electric Ltd. and avid recreational sailor, dove headfirst into a new initiative: developing standards for products in the new Single European Market.[1] Over the previous decades, he had transformed his small manufacturing company into an award-winning producer of fiber-optic sensing systems, safety foot pedals, pressure valves, and air switches for industrial machinery – most of which were exported to markets outside Britain.[2] But with the 1992 Program underway and the European Commission prioritizing the creation of regional norms for products bought and sold in the Community, Tracey recognized "there are going to be common standards across Europe in 1992," and asked: "how can we make the best of this?"[3] He wanted to guarantee his company's competitive advantage in the new regulatory landscape for goods in the internal market.

The UK's Health and Safety Executive informed Tracey that he could only "do anything" to influence regional standards if he first joined the British Standards Committee, the prerequisite for which was representation in a national trade association.[4] Since no national organization existed yet for producers in his category, he took the initiative in creating one "with the primary purpose of helping [British] safety equipment manufacturers to get their voice heard in Europe."[5] "It was like everything in life," Tracey

[1] This chapter contains some analysis and tables first published in articles in the *Business History Review* and reprinted here with the journal's permission: Grace Ballor. "CE Marking, Business, and European Market Integration," *Business History Review* 96, no. 1 (2022): 77–108.

[2] Herga Electric won two Queen's Awards for Enterprise. See: Andrew Bibby, "The Boss Who Gave Away the Business," *Financial Times*, January 24, 2006.

[3] UK Department for Trade and Industry, "Influencing Safety Standards," *Single Market News*, Autumn 1989. HW-37, Florence, HAEU: 24.

[4] UK Department for Trade and Industry, *Single Market News*, Autumn 1989. HW-37, Florence, HAEU: 20.

[5] UK Department for Trade and Industry, "Influencing Safety Standards," 24.

reflected later of his approach: "if you don't get involved, then don't expect things to go your way."[6] BIAs seemed too bloated and bureaucratic to effectively represent Herga as it faced open competition in an enlarged internal market. Instead, membership in the new Safety Association allowed Tracey and his counterpart manufacturers to participate directly in the British Standards Committee and from there to join the European working groups tasked with establishing new technical specifications for industrial safety products sold in the region. And when all of the national standards associations convened in Berlin some months later for the delegation of regional working groups by member state, the group for safety standards was assigned to the UK, and Tracey was made its chairman. Of a standards meeting over which he presided, he recalled: "When we finally produced the standard, I asked around the room how the different countries proposed to apply it. The Scandinavians said that they would follow it. The Germans said that they would interpret it in their way. The French said that it was a good objective, and the Italians waved their arms in the air and said that the main problem was staying in business."[7]

Tracey assured the dozen members of his working group from other EEC and EFTA countries – including technical directors, engineers, and three rival manufacturers – that establishing common guidelines and characteristics for products in their industry would give "everybody an equal opportunity in the market."[8] But he used his prerogative as chairman to suggest that the group adopt the UK's standards, with which Herga already more than complied, and make them the EEC industry norm. In fact, the standards to be set by his working group would not "just apply across the Common Market countries – [but] across the whole of Europe" because of the EEC's trade agreements with the EFTA.[9] Nor did Tracey's vision end even at the continental boundary: "if we adopt a very strong standard across Europe, then there is a much greater chance that we shall be able to persuade the Americans and the Japanese to use these standards in their own production processes,"[10] thereby creating a single, global norm, with Herga's products leading the way. He "was keen that [his] own product, which was patented and had

[6] Grace Ballor, Interview with Peter Tracey. Audio recording. Milan, April 1, 2023.

[7] Peter Tracey, *My Life, My Business, and My Boats*, 28.

[8] The European Commission defines a standard as a "technical specification relating to a product or an operation which is recognized by a large number of manufacturers and users." See: European Commission, "Intellectual Property and Standardization," Brussels, October 27, 1992. Document: COM(92)445, AEI.

[9] In the late 1980s, EFTA members included: Austria, Finland, Iceland, Norway, Sweden, and Switzerland.

[10] UK Department for Trade and Industry, "Influencing Safety Standards," 24.

some very superior features, should become the product of choice" in Europe and the world.[11] In short, Tracey understood the power of standards to open and close markets and to create international winners and losers. After five years of biannual meetings and a few concessions to his German competitors with whom he eventually made friends, Tracey convinced the working group to adopt standards that closely resembled the specifications of his own company's products, at relatively low cost to competitive companies in the rich regulatory states of Northern Europe but high cost to small manufacturers and firms based in Southern Europe.

In the 1980s and 1990s, many European entrepreneurs and business leaders like Tracey recognized the centrality of common technical specifications to the Single Market Program. Seemingly "arcane technicalities," standards became the building blocks of the new internal market when the integration project was relaunched in 1985 when regional policymakers took a New Approach to creating European norms.[12] Where the Commission's bureaucratic old approach had failed to harmonize the technical specifications that inhibited regional trade, it hoped a revised strategy would finally ensure the free movement of goods between member states. By deploying national, regional, and global standard setting infrastructure, focusing legally-binding technical harmonization only on the "essential requirements," and keeping standards set by private bodies voluntary, the New Approach – and its subsequent reforms – promised a process of market integration much more feasible to accomplish by the deadline of December 1992.[13] It also promised to include business input in the process of normalization and create standards with which firms were more likely to comply.

This chapter uncovers the role of business in coproducing European standards during the 1992 Program. Building on the argument of Chapter 1 that the Commission strove to create a regional business environment in which firms would regionalize, it finds that the interests of European business and European policymakers converged around the issue of standards. The Commission promoted common norms as a means of market integration. While some European companies, executives, and BIAs were skeptical of the potential for standardization

[11] Grace Ballor, Interview with Peter Tracey. Audio recording. Milan, April 1, 2023.

[12] Robert L. Mallett, "Why Standards Matter," *Issues in Science and Technology* 15, no. 22 (1998): 63. For more on the long intellectual history of standards, see: Lawrence Busch, *Standards, Recipes for Reality* (Cambridge, MA: MIT Press, 2011).

[13] European Council, "Council Resolution of 7 May 1985 on a New Approach to Technical Harmonization of Standards," (85/C 136/01) *Official Journal of the European Communities*.

Table 2.1 *Taxonomy of business participation in European standardization*

Type of standardization	Procedure	Firm participation
De jure	Commission directives enumerate essential requirements for products in key categories	Recommendations through business interest associations
Voluntary	With the support of the Commission, regional standards bodies develop European norms to remove trade barriers	Business representatives serve on the working groups of standards bodies and draft common norms
De facto	Firm standards become common norms	Companies standardize their products and production to achieve economies of scale; competitive market pressure encourages adoption by other firms

to function as a form of regulation, they also understood that standards were determinants of market access. And many worked, as Tracey did, to shape new regional norms to their advantage.

Business actively participated in the creation of common European norms in three main ways, outlined in Table 2.1.[14] First, many multinational corporations saw the development of common European de jure standards as a means of securing market advantages, even when the implementation of a new norm was costly, as was the case with the implementation of vehicle emissions standards discussed in Chapter 4.[15] BIAs also lobbied the Commission to adopt global norms wherever possible to facilitate economies of scale. Second, business representatives participated in the working groups of the private standards organizations to which the Commission delegated standard setting for goods and services in the Single Market. Together with representatives of other stakeholder groups – from consumers to labor to technical experts – business representatives contributed to the development of

[14] For a collection of works on business and global standards, see the special issue of *Business History Review* edited by JoAnne Yates and Craig N. Murphy, which is summarized in their: "Introduction: Standards and the Global Economy," *Business History Review* 96, no. 1 (ed. 2022): 3–15. On the "Janus face" of business toward regulation and protectionism, see: Jacques Pelkmans, "Mutual Recognition in Goods and Services: An Economic Perspective," European Network of Economic Policy Research Institutes, Working Paper no. 16 (2003): 25.

[15] For more specifically on the role of business in setting vehicle emissions standards, see: Grace Ballor, "Liberal Environmentalism: The Public-Private Production of European Emissions Standards," *Business History Review* 97, no. 3 (2023): 575–601.

"rules, guidelines, and definitions" for products and production in the European market as well as in the markets of its trading partners.[16] Moreover, business interest groups intervened in reforming regional standardization processes as the deadline to complete the internal market neared. Beyond influence on formal and private standard setting, big businesses operating across EEC markets contributed to standardization through their supply and value chains, service and distribution networks. By consolidating, regionalizing, and incorporating SMEs into their operations, these multinationals facilitated de facto standardization through sheer economies of scale.[17]

To contextualize the ways business coproduced European standards, this chapter uncovers the role of standards in economic integration and traces the evolution of policymaker approaches to standardization in the EEC from the 1950s to the early 1980s. It then turns to the New Approach introduced by the Commission's White Paper on Completing the Internal Market in 1985 and its reception by business groups like the ERT. It discusses the involvement of firms in voluntary standard setting during the early years of the Single Market Program, as well as their contributions to reforming the New Approach when it became clear that the ambitious market completion deadline of December 31, 1992 required an even more streamlined process. Finally, this chapter examines the ways big businesses facilitated standardization through their size and market power. By the time the Single Market was declared complete in January 1993, laying the foundation for the new European Union and its single currency, business had contributed to the harmonization of European legislation, the streamlining of technical specifications, and the creation of common market norms.

Standards and Market Integration

Standards have long functioned as vectors of market access and occupied a central place in international political economy.[18] As JoAnne Yates and Craig Murphy have shown, amid the first wave of globalization in the late

[16] This is the definition of standards offered by CEN.

[17] The differences between de jure and de facto standards have been elaborated by: Stanley M. Besen and Joseph Farrell, "Choosing How to Compete: Strategies and Tactics in Standardization," *Journal of Economic Perspectives* 8, no. 2 (1994): 117–131; Joseph Farrell and Gareth Saloner, "Converters, Compatibility, and the Control of Interfaces," *The Journal of Industrial Economics* 40, no. 1 (1992): 9–35; Jonathan Kazam and David Mowery, "The Commercialization of RISC: Strategies for the Creation of Dominant Designs," *Research Policy* 23, no. 1 (1994): 89–102.

[18] The following sections are adapted from my article on business in the development of CE Marking: Grace Ballor, "CE Marking, Business, and European Market Integration," *Business History Review* 96, no. 1 (2022): 77–108.

nineteenth century, "standards bearers" on both sides of the Atlantic began to develop a "vast, yet inconspicuous global infrastructure of private, consensus-based standard setting."[19] These early standardizers, many of whom were engineers, envisioned a world in which goods could cross borders without any obstacles, thanks to international consensus around product characteristics. After all, the standardization of work and workers had created "unparalleled abundance" and "seemingly infinite" economies of scale, according to father of scientific management Frederick Winslow Taylor. By the early twentieth century, standards were so ubiquitous that economic sociologist Thorstein Veblen remarked on "modern industry's little use for … what does not conform to the standard."[20] After the First World War shocked the liberal imaginary of the so-called golden age of capitalism, the architects of the peace saw in cooperation a way to recover from the devastation of total war. Discussions at the League of Nations revolved around developing frameworks for global economic integration, and business groups like the International Chamber of Commerce advocated for mechanisms to support unfettered trade.[21] For all of these interwar aspirations toward global exchange, however, the systems constructed to manage peace and promote economic growth failed spectacularly at both: The Second Industrial Revolution resulted in uneven development which, coupled with the punitive approach to the transgressors of the first global conflict, led to the Second World War.[22]

When wartime nationalism finally gave way to international cooperation, new postwar organizations offered improved plans for social and economic coordination.[23] These proposed "internationalisms" required institutions to facilitate their objectives, giving rise to a vast network of organizations including the United Nations (UN) and its economic commissions, the Council of Europe, and the Organization for

[19] For a history of global standard setting, see: JoAnne Yates and Craig Murphy, *Engineering Rules: Global Standard Setting since 1880* (Baltimore: Johns Hopkins University Press, 2019): 2–3.

[20] Thorstein Veblen, *The Theory of Business Enterprise* (New York: Charles Scribner's Sons, 1904).

[21] Glenda Sluga, *Internationalism in the Age of Nationalism* (Philadelphia: University of Pennsylvania Press, 2013); Patricia Clavin, *Securing the World Economy: The Reinvention of the League of Nations, 1920–1946* (Oxford: Oxford University, 2013).

[22] Craig Murphy, *International Organization and Industrial Change: Global Governance since 1850* (New York: Oxford University Press, 1994): 136–152.

[23] Craig Murphy explained how the interwar depression had finally convinced European officials to forsake their punitive and imperial approach to the peace and focus instead on development assistance, inclusive social orders, institutional frameworks, industrial growth, and welfare support. See: Murphy, *International Organization and Industrial Change*, 153–218.

Economic Cooperation and Development (OECD).[24] The many and diverse iterations of international integration shared a core objective: the need for common norms and standards and the demand for an apparatus to coordinate such harmonization. By creating larger markets for goods, standards could help producers achieve economies of scale, argued American and British officials working to revitalize global trade in the late 1940s.[25] Corporations aiming to do business in international markets readily agreed. For their part, "globalists" like those in the Mont Pèlerin Society saw standards at the intersection of the worlds of *dominium* and *imperium*, capable of forging a world economy through the use of uniform technical specifications for goods on an international market.[26] To realize the shared objective of common standards, the International Organization for Standardization (ISO) was established in parallel with the UN in the mid-1940s and tasked with providing standards documents to its fellow international organizations. Its prominent place within the concentration of international organizations in Geneva demonstrates just how essential standardization was to cooperation on a global scale.[27]

As the European project took shape in the 1950s and Western European countries developed their own more insular internationalisms, standards acquired a new importance. In addition to being mechanisms for integration by removing barriers to trade, they were equally seen as tools to reinforce the exclusivity of the EEC's agreement for a common market made in the 1957 Treaty of Rome. At the core of their promise of "ever closer union" was the "free movement of goods, services, capital, and labor," dependent on common norms. Articles 30 and 100 of the Treaty sought to overcome the differences in national laws impeding cross-border trade through legislative harmonization, but European officials soon realized that the harmonization of laws could not eliminate the many other barriers keeping goods from crossing borders.[28] Similarly,

[24] Patricia Clavin and Glenda Sluga, eds., *Internationalisms: A Twentieth Century History* (Cambridge: Cambridge University Press, 2016); Kiran Klaus Patel, *Project Europe: A History* (Cambridge: Cambridge University Press, 2020).

[25] Yates and Murphy, *Engineering Rules*, 129–157.

[26] Although Quinn Slobodian does not himself make this argument about standardization, the framework he provides for understanding the economic thought of twentieth century neoliberals aligns closely with documentary evidence on the rationale used to support the formation of a global system of standards. See: *Globalists: The End of Empire and the Birth of Neoliberalism* (Cambridge, MA: Harvard University Press, 2018).

[27] Mark Mazower, *Governing the World: The History of an Idea, 1815 to the Present* (New York: Penguin Books, 2012): 102.

[28] European Council, "The Treaty Establishing the European Community (Treaty of Rome)," March 25, 1957, Rome, Italy. For more on legislative harmonization and legal approximation, see: Carol Cosgrove Twitchett, ed., *Harmonization in the European Economic Community* (London: Palgrave Macmillan, 1981).

the customs union outlined in the Treaty of Rome could only do so much; the negative integration of removing tariffs needed to be paired with the positive integration of developing shared standards.[29] The fledgling Commission had few means at its disposal to advance regional standardization though, and it focused its attention on legal approximation. Meanwhile, seven European countries interested in free trade but not in the EEC's uniform external tariff – namely, Austria, Denmark, Norway, Portugal, Sweden, Switzerland, and the UK – formed the EFTA in January 1960.[30] EFTA member states also recognized the importance of common technical specifications to the free flow of goods and expressed interest in harmonizing norms with the EEC. This broad support for European standards demanded the creation of a system capable of coordinating collective standardization across the region.

It was in this dual context of the EEC and EFTA that "standards entrepreneur" Olle Sturén, a Swedish engineer, spearheaded the creation of the Comité européen de coordination des norms (CEN) in 1961, an organization that could unite the "inner six and outer seven" around the shared goal of free trade in the region.[31] CEN's mission was, from the outset, to promote open trade across the continent through the development of common standards. Sturén expected European governments to turn their attention to the removal of nontariff barriers like competing standards once tariffs had been successfully eliminated, and he aimed to position CEN to facilitate standardization within and ultimately between the blocs.[32] It was important then that CEN was beholden to neither the EEC or EFTA, lest one bloc attempt to use the organization to create exclusionary standards against the other. Nor was it reliant on national governments, which Sturén and his colleagues believed lacked the required expertise. Instead, it was designed to incorporate input from a variety of stakeholder groups, including European companies, governments, and most importantly, the national standards bodies on whose cooperation the organization relied. In fact, the regional body acted as something of a clearing house for national standards, as well as a forum for discussion and negotiation between national bodies like the Deutches

29 Jacques Pelkmans, "The New Approach to Technical Harmonization and Standardization," *Journal of Common Market Studies* 25, no. 3 (1987): 249–269.

30 Theirs was a free trade agreement, but without the obligations of the Treaty of Rome.

31 Yates and Murphy, *Engineering Rules*, 11, 121. From the outset, the EFTA co-funded the budget of CEN together with the EEC and did the same for the budgets of CENELEC and ETSI as well.

32 Yates and Murphy, *Engineering Rules*, 161, 163–164. Yates and Murphy describe Sturén as a principled internationalist. While he had special interests in regional standardization in Europe, he also supported global standards as tools of widespread economic integration.

Institut für Normung (DIN), the Association française de normalisation (AFNOR), and the British Standards Institution (BSI).[33] The inclusion of these various stakeholder groups in the process of standard setting laid the foundation for business representatives to actively participate in shaping regional standards in the following decades.

In 1966, the French government proposed a partnership with the Federal Republic of Germany to create a Franco-German committee on standardization.[34] The Germans agreed, with the caveat that the UK, having been denied EEC membership by France, be included as well. The resulting Tripartite Committee on Standardization, a subgroup of CEN, aimed at accelerating regional progress toward harmonization. Meeting two to three times per year, the Committee tackled such topics as auto safety standards and juridical frameworks for standards enforcement, and it made agreements about norms for key items like office equipment and machine tools.[35] In 1971, as cracks formed in the international monetary system and on the eve of the EEC's first enlargement to include Britain, Ireland, and Denmark, the UK Delegation to the Tripartite Committee urged that "it was now essential to get the CENEL harmonized system into full operation (in the sense of putting components on the market) as quickly as possible."[36] Economic growth demanded free trade, and free trade required standardization.

Despite these supplementary initiatives to accelerate regional normalization, CEN made only modest progress during the 1960s and 1970s. Mounting competition over computer technologies motivated the highly strategic electrotechnical sector to build on the foundation of early agreements and develop a more cohesive regional standards organization called the European Committee for Electrotechnical Standardization (CENELEC), established in December 1972.[37] Similar to CEN, membership in this expanding genealogy of electrotechnical standards organizations included EFTA members from the start, with objectives to promote intra-regional trade and cooperation among European tech firms who were increasingly feeling pressure from their American and Asian rivals. CENELEC benefitted from being focused on fewer, more specific aims than CEN, and it provided the first opportunity for

[33] The BSI is the national standards body in which Peter Tracey participated.

[34] European Free Trade Association, "Tripartite Committee on Standardization," 1972. EFTA-1185, Florence, HAEU.

[35] "Confidential Letter from the United Kingdom Mission (M. A. Wacker) to the Finnish Mission (M. K. Yrjo-Kockinen)," July 5, 1967. EFTA-1185, Florence, HAEU.

[36] "Tripartite Committee for Standardization Meeting in Paris: 14th and 15th October 1971: Note by the United Kingdom Delegation." EFTA/CTE W /1/72 (January 7, 1972), Distribution B.2. EFTA-1185, Florence, HAEU.

[37] CENEL and CENELCOM were the predecessors of CENELEC.

centralized European interests to set the standards agenda for the ISO and the International Electrotechnical Commission (IEC).[38] Fueled by this momentum, the most significant breakthrough in regional standardization came just a few months later when the European Commission issued the Low Voltage Directive (73/23/EEC) of 1973, which harmonized the voltage limits for electrical equipment in the EEC.[39] This "ancestor of regional Directives for technical specifications" paved the way for the Commission to take the lead on standardization for the region in the years that followed, although nearly a decade would pass before the next major milestone directive was approved.[40]

Already in the late 1960s, members of the European Parliament drew attention to the "problems of standardization" in the Community. At a session in 1964, one member asked: "what measures does the Commission intend to take to ensure the widest possible standardization in the common market?"[41] The Commission explained that because it had been disappointed by the results of both Treaty Article 100 to provide for harmonization as well as the ability of private organizations to create standards, it would take direct action "with a view to eliminating barriers to trade resulting from technical specifications" and "encourage the creation of international bodies whose purpose is to carry out standardization, particularly at the Community level."[42]

In its efforts to make up for such shortcomings, the Commission took a highly interventionist approach to regional norms beginning in the mid-1960s. "It felt that its obligation was to harmonize" rules across member states, and it attempted to independently determine what specifications were needed for goods – and later services – to flow freely in the Community.[43] Although it generally supported CEN's work, the Commission's narrower focus on the EEC precluded closer collaboration with the regional body, which was committed to broad inter-

[38] By the twenty-first century, European standard setting was so effectively centralized relative to its fragmented American and Canadian counterparts, that it dominated international standardization. The specifications developed by CEN and CENELEC increasingly set the standards for the ISO and IEC, positioning the European system of standardization at the forefront of global efforts toward harmonization.

[39] Commission of the European Communities, "Low Voltage Directive," 73/23/EEC. Brussels, February 19, 1973.

[40] Florence Nicholas, *Common Standards for Enterprises.* (Luxembourg City: Office for Official Publications of the European Communities, 1995), 86.

[41] European Parliament, "Problèmes de normalisation dans le marché commun: Question from Andre Armengaud," Paris, December 17, 1964. PEO-8689, Florence, HAEU.

[42] Ibid.

[43] Grace Ballor, Interview with Étienne Davignon. Audio recording. Brussels, June 16, 2016.

national cooperation across the EEC and EFTA. The Commission resolved to make its own detailed prescriptions for uniform technical specifications, which it then submitted to the Council for approval. Not only was this drafting process laborious, but because Council decisions required unanimity, few agreements were actually reached.[44] On the whole, this approach of "market integration from above" was "cumbersome, unrealistic, redundant in its disjointedness from standards, slow, poorly implemented, of low priority to the Council, out of touch with the realities of global trade, and had utterly neglected issues of conformity assessment and testing."[45] Arduously bureaucratic on the one hand and lacking the means even to verify compliance on the other, the Commission's efforts represented a great deal of work with dismal results. Furthermore, by the time they were developed and fought over by member states, the Commission's standards were already outdated before they even took effect.

Amid the economic downturn and increasing challenge of globalization in the 1970s, national governments looked for ways to shore up their champion firms from outside competition. Liberal trade agreements at the GATT prohibited the erection of new tariff walls, but states like France and Italy sought recourse through nontariff barriers (NTBs).[46] Through voluntary export restraints (VERs) and new national technical specifications, they attempted to restrict foreign products from their markets. The resulting patchwork of national barriers impeded cross-border business, thwarted the Commission's efforts to eliminate NTBs, and further obscured the promise of EEC market integration.[47] Still, the Community's institutional framework offered few remedies,

[44] UK Institute for European Environmental Policy: Nigel Haigh and David Baldock, "Environmental Policy at 1992," London, 1989. HW-37, Florence, HAEU: 18–19.

[45] On the Commission's early top-down approach, see: Jacques Pelkmans, *Market Integration in the European Community* (The Hague: Martinus Nijhoff Publishers, 1984): Part II. On the shortcomings of the old approach, see: Jacques Pelkmans and A. Vollebergh, "Fifteen Years of Traditional Harmonisation: Accomplishments and Deficiencies," in *Coming to Grips with the Internal Market*, ed. Jacques Pelkmans and M. Vanheukelen, Working Document 85/05, European Institute of Public Administration, Maastricht (1986).

[46] Helen Milner, "Resisting the Protectionist Temptation: Industry and the Making of Trade Policy in France and the United States During the 1970s," *International Organization* 41, no. 4 (1987): 640. Milner explains how these NTBs were gradually reduced over the course of the decade, when liberalization offered more gains than protectionism. In 1980, the GATT enacted its own Standards Code to promote standards mechanisms for trade liberalization and discourage their use as mechanisms for protectionism.

[47] On the potential for standards to both facilitate and impede market integration, see one of the many important works by Michelle Egan on European standards: "Bandwagon or Barriers? The Role of Standards in the European and American Marketplace,"

and the Commission was reluctant to appear overly meddlesome. When presented with a separate proposal to use standardization as a means of supporting social inclusivity in the Community in the late 1970s, Commissioner Hank Vredeling, who subsequently proposed to regulate multinational corporations collectively, responded: "the Commission certainly does not advocate maximum standardization; I do not consider standardization desirable for its own sake. We have tried to achieve standardization only when it was essential to remove certain technical obstacles to trade."[48] Finally in 1979, the European Court of Justice's landmark ruling in the *Cassis de Dijon* case created the legal precedent for the mutual recognition of national technical specifications and allowed for goods produced according to the regulatory guidelines of one member state to circulate lawfully through the others.[49] Even this proved an insufficient mechanism for the free flow of goods, however, since national technical specifications – from product size to adapter compatibility – rendered many products made in one market inoperable in another. European companies looking to scale their business could not afford to produce to the different specifications of each national market.

Business Interests and the New Approach

As Chapter 1 explained, European officials managed the social and economic "crises" of the 1970s by relaunching regional integration in the 1980s through a program to complete the internal market. The 1985 White Paper on Completing the Internal Market identified standards as a central component of its reinvigorated objective of market integration. It proposed that the Community should establish a procedure to coordinate standards and regulations on a regional level to prevent the emergence of new technical barriers. The Mutual Information

University of Pittsburgh: Center for West European Studies, Working Paper no. 1 (1997): 2.

48 In this session, the Parliament was considering a proposal to create a car for handicapped people. Arguments for the project were that standardization of such a vehicle would make economies of scale possible for automakers, who would then be incentivized to make a car that would give a "human face" to capitalism in the EC. See: European Parliament, "Oral questions in Parliament 1977: Normalisation: une Commission à visage humain," January 11, 1977, PEO-6687, Florence, HAEU: 33.

49 European Court of Justice, Judgement of February 20, 1979: Case 120/78. By establishing the legal precedent for the mutual recognition of standards across member states, this ruling helped barriers to intra-EEC trade, but the friction of national differences in technical specifications remained.

Directive (83/189/EEC), passed in March 1983 and implemented on January 1, 1985, became the primary mechanism by which the EEC could synchronize national legislative developments among member states.[50] With this directive, the Commission began to view the regional standards bodies CEN and CENELEC as partners in the harmonization process; these bodies had the information on national technical specifications the Commission so desperately needed in order to eliminate barriers to trade. Notably, just like the Commission, the Secretariat of the EFTA also agreed to cooperate with CENELEC in 1983. Then, in April 1984, the EEC and EFTA signed the Declaration of Luxembourg Agreement, providing for the free circulation of goods among the two groups.[51] The EFTA also developed its own Committee on Technical Barriers to Trade (the TBT Committee), which began meeting regularly with the Commission on matters of harmonization and standards in industrial policy. As a result, by the mid 1980s, trade officials across the European region embraced standards as means to create larger "home" markets so that firms could remain globally competitive.

According to its former Vice President Étienne Davignon, the Commission's relationships with European business became most crucial "once the negotiations were no longer simply about tariffs, but about norms."[52] The shift from negative integration to positive integration – from creating a customs union by removing barriers to building a Single Market through harmonization – required regional policymakers to "deal directly with industry at the European level" and to prioritize standards. During his term as commissioner for Industrial Affairs and several other portfolio responsibilities, Davignon saw in the principle of mutual recognition established by the 1979 *Cassis de Dijon* case a template he "could use to completely change the approach of the Commission; it became very important in terms of standards."[53] Out of discussions with European business groups, he noticed the lack of common norms in the region was exacerbating the loss of European market share by European firms to their global competitors who understood the power of standards to determine market access. "The only lawn mower that meets all European [national] standards is Japanese," Davignon

[50] European Council, "Council Directive on Laying Down a Procedure for the Provision of Information in the Field of Technical Standards and Regulations," Directive 83/189/EEC. *Official Journal of the European Communities*, March 28, 1983.

[51] European Council, "Joint Declaration: Ministerial Meeting between EFTA Countries and the EEC and Its Member States," Luxembourg, April 9, 1984.

[52] Grace Ballor, Interview with Étienne Davignon. Audio recording. Brussels, June 16, 2016.

[53] Ibid.

lamented in 1984.[54] The lack of common European standards extended from consumer goods to worker credentials. Instead of answering how "could a barber be allowed to be a barber in all countries?" by arbitrarily setting one country's registration as the rule for all members, Davignon and his colleagues in the Commission began to look to the principle of mutual recognition. Certification by one member state should be recognized by all others, they argued; "this really was the pattern Jacques Delors used going forward."[55]

Indeed, just a few months into Delors' first term as Commission president, the Commission outlined a New Approach to standardization in its White Paper on Completing the Internal Market. The former practice of "incorporating detailed technical specifications in Directives ha[d] given rise to long delays because of the unanimity required in Council decision making."[56] Beginning in 1985, in sectors where barriers to trade were created by "justified divergent national regulations concerning the health and safety of citizens and consumer and environmental protection, legislative harmonization will be confined to laying down only the *essential requirements*, conformity with which will entitle a product to free movement within the Community."[57] Instead of setting detailed technical specifications for as many products as possible, the Commission resolved to develop targeted directives – similar to the Low Voltage Directive of 1973 – outlining a short list of essential requirements to which products in key health and safety categories had to conform. The Commission resolved to align its legislative aims in "reference to standards," by "combining the total harmonization of the objectives at issue (safety, etc.) with a flexible approach of the means (standardization)."[58] As was the case with the principle of mutual recognition, national public authorities were asked to recognize that all products in accordance with harmonized standards presume to conform to the essential requirements defined by EEC legislation. Through the

54 "Bouscule les habitudes: cabinet multinaional, protefeuilles de la commission repartis en fonction de la competence plus que de la nationalite et de la politique: le nouveau president de la commission europeenne, qui prendra officiellement des fonctions le 6 javier proachin, innove et bouscule les habitudes," November 19, 1984, *Le Matin*, JD-17, HAEU.

55 Grace Ballor, Interview with Étienne Davignon. Audio recording. Brussels, June 16, 2016.

56 European Commission, "White Paper on Completing the Internal Market (COM(85) 310 Final)," June 1985: 19.

57 Commission of the European Communities, "Completing the Internal Market," Milan, June 28–29, 1985: Article 68. In this text, the Commission made a clear distinction between the mandatory nature of essential requirements and the voluntary nature of standards.

58 Pelkmans, "The New Approach," 253, 257.

New Approach, the Commission also supported the development of voluntary regional standards, elaborated by CEN, CENELEC, and other bodies.[59] These changes relieved businesses of the burden of satisfying a patchwork of national norms and of having to meet arcane technical specifications set by the Commission.

The ERT was quick to endorse the New Approach and offer its own suggestions. In June 1985, it issued a memorandum on the "Foundations for the Future of European Industry." To stimulate the technical harmonization and cooperation needed for European firms to rise to the challenge of foreign rivals on scale, price, and productivity, they argued, the EEC needed to develop "common European technical standards."[60] It called on the Commission to harmonize national regulations, deregulate public markets, and "encourage the development of common European and other technical standards for new products and services (automotive, telecommunications, electronics)." These steps would not only facilitate regional integration, but more importantly would "create a common European basis for negotiations of world standards."[61] Moreover, the ERT advocated for the role of business in this process, since "companies can promote standardization" of everything from automotive components to computing software.

The ERT's position on regional standards diverged from those of the Commission, however, in the proposed scope of application: Standards should be "EC-inspired," the ERT argued, but these "new specific policies aiming at European industrial and technological cooperation" ought to be open to non-EEC Europeans and "must be framed to allow for flexibility in developing Europe's links with the rest of the world."[62] After all, companies represented by the ERT hailed from EFTA countries as well as EEC member states. While the Commission remained focused on the potential for standards to remove trade barriers between EEC countries and achieve an internal market as a defense against globalization, business leaders in the ERT saw them as a way of reinforcing Europe's global trade connections. Not only did the New Approach establish a single set of requirements for certain goods in the markets across the EEC and EFTA to the great advantage of firms from both inside and outside Europe, but

[59] Commission of the European Communities, "White Paper on Completing the Internal Market," Article 68.

[60] European Roundtable of Industrialists, "Foundations for the Future of European Industry," June 1985. PSP-385, Florence, HAEU: 6.

[61] European Roundtable of Industrialists, "Foundations for the Future of European Industry," June 1985. PSP-385, Florence, HAEU: 7–8.

[62] European Roundtable of Industrialists, "Foundations for the Future of European Industry," June 1985. PSP-385, Florence, HAEU: 8.

the prospect of harmonizing European standards with those from other parts of the globe promised even larger economies of scale.

The Single European Act signed in 1986 provided the institutional reforms needed to realize an internal market by 1992. It also underscored the White Paper's argument about the need for European standards, especially because Europe was "at a crossroads" in the mid-1980s. In the words of the Commission: "[w]e either go ahead – with resolution and determination – or we drop back into mediocrity. We can now either resolve to complete the integration of the economies of Europe; or, through lack of political will to face the immense problems involved, we can simply allow Europe to develop into no more than a free trade area," like the EFTA.[63] According to the Council, a free trade area, while better than nothing, "would fail and fail dismally to release the energies of the people of Europe; it would fail to deploy Europe's immense economic resources to the maximum advantage; and it would fail to satisfy the aspirations of the people of Europe," albeit undefined.[64] The contrast the Commission subsequently drew between its Single Market and free trade in the EFTA made clear the 1992 Program was not simply a matter of liberalization. Only through legislative harmonization and standardization could the economic and social objectives of market making being achieved.

Setting Standards and Reforming the New Approach

In addition to narrowing the range of essential requirements to be addressed by Commission directives, the New Approach also established a new system for developing voluntary norms, which "laid the groundwork for firms to participate in setting the rules for market access."[65] To the European standards bodies, CEN, CENELEC, and the European Telecommunication Standards Institute (ETSI) established in 1988, the Commission delegated the task of developing standards, both to help products in key categories meet the essential requirements that would allow them to circulate in the European market, and to enable all other goods to move freely across member state borders. Compared with the Commission's nearly 300 agenda items to achieve legislative harmonization before 1992, regional standards bodies developed more than 800 new European-wide norms between 1985 and 1990 – three

[63] The SEA does not explicitly mention the EFTA, but the comparison is strongly implied. European Council, *Single European Act*. (Luxembourg, Office for the Official Publication of the European Communities, 1986): 55.

[64] European Council, *Single European Act* (Luxembourg, Office for the Official Publication of the European Communities, 1986): 55.

[65] Egan, "Bandwagon or Barriers," 5.

times more than they had drafted in the previous twenty years.[66] Per the Commission's estimations in 1990, the completion of the Single Market would require yet another 800 or more standards, about one new standard each day to meet the late 1992 deadline. CEN, CENELEC, and ETSI reported an even heavier workload: some representatives calculated more than 3,000 outstanding work items before standardization could be achieved.[67]

Developing such a huge volume of standards required the regional bodies to include all interested parties in the process. The ETSI worked directly with all groups interested in technology and telecommunications standards, but the "peak associations" CEN and CENELEC adopted a representative structure whereby national standards bodies from EEC and EFTA member states sent delegates to participate in regional working groups, tasked with drafting standards for particular product categories. To tap into a diversity of proficiencies and ensure the broadest acceptance of the standards developed, these groups were comprised of "technical experts" from a wide range of stakeholders: Representatives from trade unions and environmental groups came together to draft standards for products within their respective realms of interest and expertise. But "most of the technical experts represented profit-making companies."[68] Participation in these working groups gave business representatives the opportunity to "write the rules for Europe" and shape the contours of the internal market for goods and services.[69]

Participation in working groups was costly though. Peter Tracey, for example, had to step away from his managerial duties at Herga for several days at a time as he traveled, usually from Britain to Berlin, for group meetings and strove to build international consensus around his company's standards. For multinational firms, export-oriented business, and

66 European Commission, "Green Book on the Development of European Standardization: Action for Faster Technological Integration in Europe," Brussels, October 8, 1990. Document: COM(90)456 final, AEI: 3.

67 Karen Frankel, "The Politics of Standards and the EC," *Communications of the ACM* 33, no. 7 (1990): 42.

68 Yates and Murphy, *Engineering Rules*, 8–10. CEN/CENELEC currently describes its network as including "business federations, commercial and consumer organizations, environmental groups and other societal stakeholders. More than 60,000 technical experts from industry, research, academia and other backgrounds are directly involved in our work." CEN/ELEC, "About CEN," accessed February 2, 2021: www.cencenelec .eu/about-cen/.

69 Wolfram Kaiser and Johan Schot, *Writing the Rules for Europe: Experts, Cartels, and International Organizations* (Hampshire: Palgrave Macmillan, 2014). Another notable work on the privatization of regulation is that by Tim Büthe and Walter Mattli, *The New Global Rulers: The Privatization of Regulation in the World Economy* (Princeton, NJ: Princeton University Press, 2011).

big corporations, however, the reward of securing their market positions by influencing regional standards was well worth the expense. Tracey viewed the cost like buying a "great insurance policy" – a guarantee of his company's access to valuable international markets.[70] Business participation in this standardization system raised problems for EEC competition policy, however, when firms in the same industry colluded to set regional standards that would exclude other competitors. Equally, it complicated the Commission's efforts to protect intellectual property rights, since working groups sometimes adopted standards that gave preference to the patents held by one company while undermining the intellectual property claims of others.

Small businesses often lacked both the resources and high-level expertise required to place representatives on regional working groups. While some saw the use of regional norms as a valuable means of accessing larger markets, many small firms were critical of the Commission's "overly burdensome" requirements, which could add as much as 10 percent to the cost of a good exported in the EEC market under the new rules of the New Approach.[71] Observing the ability of big businesses to "buy their way in" to working groups only exacerbated tensions between company types on the issue of standards.[72] Even firms without working group influence had an opportunity to comment on proposals when the drafts were sent back to national bodies for a six-month deliberation period and approval process. Still, aside from a few notable exceptions like the decision by small companies to "wreak havoc" on efforts to standardize plugs and voltages in the region,[73] the interests of big business usually eclipsed those of their smaller counterparts. The weaker positions of environmental and labor groups fared even worse when stacked against those of large corporations, save for the rare occasions when they found "strength in numbers."[74]

In addition to the disparities between the types of firms able to influence regional standard setting, national origin further differentiated company responses to regional standardization and the willingness of firms to embrace voluntary standards. Reflecting back on his experience as head of the working group for safety equipment standards in 1989, Peter Tracey noted the wide variance of approaches to the new standard

[70] Grace Ballor, Interview with Peter Tracey. Audio recording. Milan, April 1, 2023.
[71] Mallett, "Why Standards Matter," 63; Pelkmans, "The New Approach," 260.
[72] Frankel, "The Politics of Standards and the EC," 51.
[73] The "Europlug" was developed in 1963 and refined in a 1975 technical report by the IEC.
[74] Gunnar Trumbull, *Strength in Numbers: The Political Power of Weak Interests* (Cambridge, MA: Harvard University Press, 2012).

among representatives from different EEC and EFTA member states: While the Scandinavians planned to follow the new common standard, the Germans reserved the right to interpret it for themselves. The Italians, by contrast, expressed concerns about remaining competitive in a market increasingly oriented around standards much more stringent than their previous production.[75] Competition between the interests of working group members resulted in races to the top rather than to the bottom, and companies producing to relatively lower national standards like those of Italy experienced the dual disadvantage of having rivals set the rules and bearing the high costs of retooling production to compete.[76] Exasperated, many small firms and those accustomed to domestic protections chose to retreat into national markets rather than to sink resources into competing against products meeting high international standards.

In biannual reports throughout the late 1980s and early 1990s, the Commission clocked its progress toward the Single Market against its initial objectives for legislative harmonization and technical standardization. By the 1992 Program's half-way mark in 1989, it was clear the 1992 deadline to harmonize the technical specifications covered by directives could not be reached without further reforms to the Commission's approach. One problem was speed: Allowing national bodies six months to deliberate and approve proposed regional standards was simply too long to meet the deadline. A Symposium on Testing and Certification held in Brussels in June 1988 also found the redundancies in the process of conformity assessment to de jure standards covered by the Commission directives were undermining the success of the standardization effort. Under the New Approach, products needing to meet essential requirements had to be certified by notifying bodies in every member state in which they were sold. This repetitive process, which flew in the face of the principle of mutual recognition established in the ECJ's *Cassis de Dijon* case, was time consuming, costly, and a deterrent against international business for many firms. Coupled with these problems, the fall of the Berlin Wall and the opening of Central and Eastern Europe to the West signaled rapid political changes coming in the region. In seeing the potential for these changes to "lead to a larger, and more closely integrated European market economy," the Commission named "common technical standards as one of the means for assuring

[75] Grace Ballor, Interview with Peter Tracey. Audio recording. Milan, April 1, 2023.

[76] Anu Bradford's work on the "Brussels Effect" explains the EEC's "race to the top" phenomenon in global context. See: *The Brussels Effect: How the European Union Rules the World* (New York: Oxford University Press, 2020).

Figure 2.1 The "CE Mark."
Source: Kolonko / iStock / Getty Images Plus.

an orderly transition to that state of affairs" and initiated a number of reforms to ensure they would be achieved.[77]

The first relatively easy reform came with the 1988 De Villamoura Procedure, which cut the national review time in half to three months and expedited the process of approving regional standards. This restricted the time during which firms could challenge drafted standards, but it also expedited the implementation process and accelerated market integration. Problems of assessment proved more difficult to resolve. In 1989, the Commission submitted a proposal to the Council concerning a "Global Approach to Conformity Assessment and Certification." This Global Approach attempted "to bring together all the different elements [of conformity assessment, quality systems, certification, and accreditation] which, when carefully and properly assembled, will give the EEC as a whole a comprehensive quality policy which is an indispensable part of any industrial policy and fundamental to the very concept of an Internal Market."[78] The reform was was comprised of two core elements: "The Proposal for a Council Decision concerning the Modules for the Various Phases of the Conformity Assessment Procedures intended to be used in the Technical Harmonization Directives," and the accompanying "Communication on a Global Approach to Certification." The first established an eight-part "modular system" for assessing conformity to product directives.[79] The second laid out plans for a comprehensive scheme for conformity assessment and certification. Per the Global Approach, products in certain modules would require assessment and testing by notified bodies, which would then affix a "CE Mark" (Figure 2.1) indicating the products' conformity

[77] European Commission, "Green Book on European Standardization," 31.

[78] Commission of the European Communities, "A Global Approach to Certification and Testing," COM(89) 209 final – SYN 208; OJC 89/C/231/3. Brussels, July 24, 1989. PE3–21885, Florence, HAEU: Annex I, 5.

[79] Commission, "Global Approach," Objectives; Commission of the European Communities, "Re-Examined Proposal for a Council Decision," PE3–21885, Florence, HAEU: 11.

to relevant New Approach regulations.[80] Manufacturers of products covered by other modules could affix the CE Mark themselves. Use of standards remained voluntary but was strongly encouraged.

After the Single European Act increased the powers of the European Parliament, its Committee on Economic and Monetary Affairs and Industrial Policy was tasked with reviewing the Global Approach proposals before the Council's vote. Parliamentary deliberation required public feedback on the functioning of the existing system and possible suggestions for reform, and in this case, the "public" concerned with conformity assessment and certification was comprised not of individual citizens, but of the firms operating within the European market. The committee rapporteur solicited industry feedback on the proposal for a global approach from fifteen European-based organizations, including the Committee of Common Market Automobile Constructors (CCMC), the Union des industries de la communauté européenne (UNICE), and the American Chamber of Commerce (AMCHAM).[81] Their sectoral, size, and national diversity notwithstanding, the majority of these associations expressed broad support for the proposals included in the Global Approach but expressed continued frustrations with the system's redundancies, which continued to be plagued by "too many possible methods and undue confusion and legal ambiguity."[82] Not only had the Commission's ad hoc approach to developing its directives caused confusion for producers of the many key products like kitchen appliances and medical equipment that fell under the guidelines of more than one directive, but the disjointed assessment process by national notifying bodies was so burdensome and costly that it deterred firms from doing business in EEC and EFTA markets. Not surprisingly, many of the BIAs that submitted position papers encouraged the use of international ISO standards by regional standards bodies and the Commission wherever possible to allow European firms to achieve the scale and scope required to compete globally.[83]

[80] Figure 2.1 shows the "CE Mark:" European Commission, Directorate General for Internal Market, Industry, Entrepreneurship, and SMEs, "CE Marking," accessed May 2021. For a detailed history of CE Marking and its Global Approach reforms, see: Ballor, "CE Marking, Business, and European Market Integration."

[81] Commission of the European Communities, "Re-Examined Proposal for a Council Decision – concerning the modules for the various phases of the conformity assessment procedures which are intended to be used in the technical harmonization directives," COM(90) 606 final – SYN 208. Brussels, December 7, 1990. PE3–21885, Florence, HAEU: 12.

[82] European Commission, "Re-Examined Proposal for a Council Decision," 12.

[83] Commission of the European Communities, "Memorandum from the Roundtable of Industrialists," June 1985. PSP-385, Florence, HAEU.

As the Parliament synthesized business feedback in early 1990 and prepared its recommendations for a reformed Global Approach, the Commission prepared a "green paper" of proposals aimed at "providing the most complete and updated picture of European standardization possible" and "improving the efficiency of standardization organizations."[84] This document explicitly urged businesses not only to "ask themselves whether they [we]re giving European standardization the attention it deserves," but also to "be motivated enough to seek a place at the negotiating table," to change the conditions of trade in both export and national markets. While the cost of this participation might initially appear high, the Commission acknowledged, and "be perceived by some parts of industry as more of a threat than a benefit," "companies which delay in coming to terms with what is an inevitable process will find themselves at a major disadvantage compared to their more *enlightened* competitors."[85] The Commission urged all European firms to actively participate in standardization in two ways: by releasing "technical experts to assist in the drafting of European standards or in discussion of them in Technical Committees and working groups," and committing "whole-heartedly to the rapid development of common European standards."[86] In recognizing their own limits, regional policymakers explained that the viability of common European standards was directly dependent on the "availability of technical experts from industry," and they claimed "[w]ithout greater commitment from European industry, there can be no significant improvement in the present [economic] situation."[87] With this sense of urgency, the Commission appealed to firms of all sizes to participate in regional standardization, encouraging them to seize the opportunity to shape the regional business environment through the "democratic process" of standard-setting, rather than allowing norms to be "set by the most powerful forces in the market."[88]

Following on deliberations by the Parliament and input from stakeholders including business representatives, the Council finally approved new regulations on conformity assessment and certification in May 1991.[89] Per these reforms, certification of conformity to the essential requirements granted by one national body had to be recognized in

[84] Commission of the European Communities, "Green Paper on the Development of European Standardization: Action for Faster Technological Integration in Europe: Brussels, 8 October 1990," Document: COM(90)456 final, AEI: 1.
[85] European Commission, "Green Book on European Standardization," 21, 20.
[86] Ibid., 20. [87] Ibid., 23. [88] Ibid., 21.
[89] Michelle Egan and Jacques Pelkmans, "Fixing European Standards: Moving Beyond the Green Paper," CEPS Working Document no. 65/ CEPS Standards Programme Paper no. 3, (May 1992). The Vienna Agreements signed by the ISO and CEN in June 1991 promised even closer exchanges of information on standards to integrate not only the markets of European member states, but the Single Market with the globe.

Table 2.2 *EEC directives, 1973–1993*

Year	Product Category	Directive
1973	Low voltage	73/23/EEC
1987	Simple pressure vessels	87/404/EEC (amended 1990)
1988	Toys	88/378/EEC
1988	Constructions	89/106/EEC
1989	Electromagnetic compatibility	89/336/EEC
1989	Machines	89/392/EEC (amended 1991)
1989	Personal protection equipment	89/686/EEC
1990	Nonautomatic weighing machines	90/384/EEC
1990	Implantable medical devices	90/385/EEC
1990	Appliances burning gaseous fuels	90/396/EEC
1991	Telecom terminal equipment	91/263/EEC
1992	Hot water boilers	92/42/EEC
1993	Explosives for civil uses	93/15/EEC
1993	Medical devices	93/42/EEC

all EEC and EFTA markets.[90] The CE Mark subsequently became a symbol of the European trading area, as well as a marketing tool for some firms – not only indicating conformity to European regulations, but also appearing to many consumers as a mark of quality, too, even if it did not function as such legally.[91] With streamlined, "global" assessment and certification procedures in place and increased business participation in the standardization process, the EEC accelerated its progress toward "Europe 1992." Directives for products like telecommunications equipment and medical devices listed in Table 2.2 created the regulatory scaffolding around which the CE Mark was utilized, voluntary standards were developed, and barriers to trade were eliminated with the goal of completing the internal market by the end of 1992.

[90] Standardization across EC/EU and EFTA member states also laid the foundation for the creation of the European Economic Area (EEA) in 1994. See: Commission of the European Communities, Commission of the European Communities. Proposal for a Council Regulation (EEC) concerning the affixing and use of the CE mark of conformity on industrial products. COM (91) 145 final, May 17, 1991, AEI.

[91] David Higgins described the ways firms have embraced marks of conformity as a type of branding. See: David M. Higgins, *Brands, Geographical Origin, and the Global Economy: A History from the Nineteenth Century to the Present.* (Cambridge: Cambridge University Press, 2018). Higgins also cites Mira Wilkins' valuable work on "The Neglected Intangible Asset" – and its constructive critique by Teresa da Silva Lopes – in describing the ways multinationals have often viewed the advantages of trademarks. See: Higgins, *Brands, Geographical Origin, and the Global Economy*, 15; Wilkins, "The Neglected Intangible Asset: The Influence of the Trade Mark on the Rise of the Modern Corporation," *Business History* 34 (1992); da Silva Lopes, *Global Brands: The Evolution of Multinationals in Alcoholic Beverages* (Cambridge: Cambridge University Press, 2007).

Multinationals and De Facto Standardization

While industry groups like the ERT supported the de jure standardization of directives drafted by the Commission and approved by the Council, and business representatives contributed to the development of voluntary standards through regional bodies like CEN and CENELEC, companies made an even greater impact on the 1992 Program through de facto standardization.[92] De facto standards emerged not as regulatory requirements or consensus-driven norms, but as internal technical solutions to firm-level problems with production or operations. These technical solutions became dominant in markets by default, scale, or competition when industry consolidation and international expansion positioned firms to implement internal practices on a large scale. As merger mania and consolidation fueled the rise of ever-larger multinational corporations in Europe in the 1980s, parent companies with widespread subsidiary and value chain networks used internal standards to rationalize production and enable economies of scale, effectively transforming their own private norms into the public goods of standards.[93]

In the context of the Single European Market, de facto standards proved no less coercive than de jure ones. Especially in sectors dominated by a few large firms like telecommunications, market participation often required related businesses to adopt the norms of leading companies. This phenomenon of "bandwagoning" had a dramatic effect on competition in the internal market.[94] Firms producing to the leading standard tended to be rewarded with increasing market share, while other firms were forced either to adopt the leading firm's standards or compete directly against them.[95] Companies also raced to develop and disseminate norms before their competitors. For them, the costs of developing specifications and the potential loss of production flexibility seemed worth the potential gains of securing market advantages by setting a standard.[96] Additionally, because of their coercive market power and because de facto standards were further strengthened through the process of competition, standards bodies and regional regulators alike often adopted de facto standards into formal or de jure ones, further

92 On the process of policymaking in the EEC, see Chapter 1.

93 Charles P. Kindleberger, "Standards as Public, Collective, and Private Goods," *Kyklos* 36 (1983): 377–396.

94 Egan, "Bandwagon or Barriers," 2.

95 Jeffrey L. Funk, *Global Competition Between and Within Standards* (Basingstoke, Hampshire, UK & New York, NY: Palgrave Macmillan, 2001): 1.

96 Grace Ballor, Interview with Étienne Davignon. Audio recording. Brussels, June 16, 2016. Davignon described the first mover advantages enjoyed by firms whose internal norms became de facto standards as well as for those firms that implemented de jure standards earlier than their competitors.

guaranteeing the dominance of firms leading in a product category like Peter Tracey's Herga Electric. Moreover, as the growth ambitions of some European companies extended beyond their "home" region, they developed de facto standards even more global than those set by the Commission, focused on integrating regional markets, and even standards bodies, despite their efforts to align European norms with those of the ISO.

According to Davignon, European multinationals were uniquely positioned to set de facto standards for the Single Market. To rationalize production and optimize business through economies of scale, parent companies homogenized norms across their networks of subsidiaries, which increasingly spanned from Spain to Scandinavia, Britain to Berlin as the EEC enlarged and Eastern Europe increasingly opened to the West during the 1992 Program. Large corporations also required their subcontractors and suppliers to produce according to their internal technical specifications, as Chapter 4 describes through the case of auto production.[97] Even those SMEs not incorporated into the networks of multinationals felt pressure to adapt to the standards of big business to compete. This pressure by corporations on other enterprises encouraged the widespread adoption of common norms.[98] In this way, firm-level specifications became industry-wide standards for the region.

Chapters 4 and 6 examine the ways a variety of European multinationals contributed to de facto standardization. As Chapter 4 explains, carmakers like Volkswagen implemented modular and platform construction, which effectively standardized the production of car components for a huge portion of the European auto industry. Even specialty carmakers like BMW manufactured more than 100,000 genuine parts and accessories across its supply chains by the early 1990s, each one an opportunity to develop industry and market norms. The case of European automakers also reveals how regional standards were used as a mechanism to exclude foreign competitors from the internal market and how producers were willing to accept more stringent rules in exchange for an integrated market. Chapter 6 considers the different ways retailers like Delhaize and the buying clubs food retailers formed in the late 1980s regionalized nutritional, health, and food safety standards, as well as consumer tastes, across their networks of chain stores, supermarkets, and subsidiaries. Through their own regional economies

[97] For more on the impact of formal standards on value chains, see: Knut Blind, Axel Magelsdorf, Crispin Niebel, and Florian Ramel, "Standards in the Global Value Chains of the European Single Market," *Review of International Political Economy* 25, no. 1 (2017): 28–48.

[98] Grace Ballor, Interview with Étienne Davignon. Audio recording. Brussels, June 16, 2016.

of scale and in pursuit of their own profit-driven interests, these multinationals from different sectors facilitated de facto standardization and contributed to the removal of trade barriers and the realization of an internal market.

Conclusions

In the context of the Single Market Program, the interests of regional policymakers and European business converged on standardization. As this chapter has shown, business coproduced the common European standards essential for the completion of the Single Market in three key ways. Business forums like the ERT offered recommendations as the Commission drafted the directives that established de jure standards for both the EEC and EFTA. Business representatives like Peter Tracey also served on the working groups of standards bodies and contributed to the development of common norms as an "insurance policy" and means of securing a strong position in the new internal market. And as multinational corporations pursued economies of scale and acquired greater market share across the region, they exported their product standards and pressured their competitors and firms in their supply and value chains to adopt them as well. Business participated in all three of these forms of standardization enthusiastically because they recognized in the development of common regional norms an opportunity to secure their own market advantages.

Much like its approach to industrial policy as described in Chapter 1, the Commission did not engage in heavy handed governmental standard setting during the 1992 Program. In trading a top-down old approach for the much more flexible New Approach, it created a framework for regional policymakers to intervene only in setting essential requirements in the realms of consumer health and safety. Through that process, the CE Mark indicating conformity to European standards became both a vector for market access and a symbol of a large, internal market in the region. Otherwise, the EEC – and, secondarily the EFTA – deferred to standards bodies like CEN, CENELEC, and the ETSI and their technical committees of experts to develop the voluntary common standards necessary for both market integration and the regulation of industry across a large regional market to provide for the health and safety of European citizens. The New Approach enabled – even incentivized – business participation in the development of regional standards. The Single Market Program also aimed to motivate European firms to regionalize, to engage in business across member states in the Community. Chapter 3 addresses the question of just how regional European companies became during the program to complete the regional internal market.

3 Regional Business Strategies

"It is only at the European level that we can cope with the global challenge," Commission President Jacques Delors reiterated when reflecting on the Single Market Program.[1] But did the Single Market Program incentivize business investment in the EEC as the European Commission intended in its plans to help European firms recover from the downturn of the 1970s and meet the challenge of global competition? What can the economic geography of business operations tell us about how companies viewed the challenges and opportunities of a regional internal market? Furthermore, what does multinational business strategy tell us about the relationship of the region to the globe? Business historical cases offer opportunities to examine the relationships between business strategy and business environments. In the context of contemporary Europe, they also invite us to consider the ways firms based both inside and outside of the EEC perceived regional market integration in relation to the global economy. Building on Chapter 1, which considered how policymakers viewed business as they designed the internal market, and Chapter 2, which described how the European Commission and European multinationals coproduced common standards, this chapter examines business strategy in the context of the 1992 Program.

Scholars and regulators have both attempted to map and measure multinational activity to determine the role of multinationals in globalization and the influence of regional frameworks on multinational business strategy. While acknowledging the ways multinational enterprises have historically navigated diverse business environments – from economic nationalism and political risks to liberalized trade, this chapter engages with the efforts of international business scholars to map

[1] Jacques Delors, "The Single Market: Cornerstone of the EU," *Notre Europe* November 22, 2012.

multinationals and develops instead a case study approach to examine the evolution of business strategy within the context of the Single Market Program. The cases covered here – ranging from pharmaceuticals to retail banking – offer a lens not available to international business scholars, challenge conventional narratives about big business and globalization, and show that many European multinationals regionalized in response to the internal market, often in preparation for eventual expansion into other parts of the globe. They also lay a methodological foundation for the remaining chapters of the book.

Mapping Multinationals

Multinational firms multiplied in number and swelled in size during the second half of the twentieth century. Frameworks for international cooperation, trade agreements, policies of liberalization and deregulation, and technological innovations in transportation and communication all facilitated cross-border business and investment. Multinationals, in turn, deepened interdependence between countries and acted as historical drivers of international economic integration.[2] As a result, multinationals became synonymous with globalization. In the context of postwar Europe, associations between multinationals and globalization were reflected in the ways Europeans viewed US-based multinationals as agents of the "Americanization of the European economy," forces of the "irresistible empire" of American culture, products, and hygiene, and perpetrators of "Coca-colonization."[3] To observers like Robert Reich, the expansion of multinationals had so changed the landscape of the global economy that he answered his own question "Does Corporate Nationality Matter?" with a resounding "no," neglecting the

[2] For research linking multinationals and globalization, see: Geoffrey Jones, *Multinationals and Global Capitalism: From the Nineteenth to the Twenty-First Century* (Oxford; New York: Oxford University Press, 2005). See also: Robert Fitzgerald, *The Rise of the Global Company: Multinationals and the Making of the Modern World*, Reprint ed. (Cambridge: Cambridge University Press, 2016).

[3] Harm G. Schröter, *Americanization of the European Economy: A Compact Survey of American Economic Influence in Europe since the 1880s* (Dordrecht; Norwell, MA: Springer, 2005); Victoria de Grazia, *Irresistible Empire: America's Advance Through Twentieth-Century Europe* (Cambridge, MA: Harvard University Press, 2006); Kristin Ross, *Fast Cars, Clean Bodies: Decolonization and the Reordering of French Culture* (Cambridge, MA: MIT Press, 1996); Reinhold Wagnleitner, *Coca-Colonisation und Kalter Krieg: Die Kulturmission der USA in Österreich nach dem Zweiten Weltkrieg* (Wien: Verl. für Gesellschaftskritik, 1991).

important role played by national corporate boards who shape international strategy decisions.[4]

Beginning in the 1970s, increasingly liberal economic policies and ever-expanding trade frameworks further accelerated the growth of multinationals from a variety of regions and subsequently surged rates of cross-border exchange. The relative deglobalization of the first, war-torn half of the twentieth century gave way to what Geoffrey Jones has called the "Second Global Economy," characterized by rapid economic growth and widening inequality. For all its contributions to "flattening" the world, globalization also had its "discontents."[5] And dual desires to understand multinational behavior and recalibrate the balance sheet of the global economy inspired various attempts by international organizations and by scholars alike to map the economic geography of business activity.

International organizations increasingly assumed responsibility for regulating global capitalism in the second half of the twentieth century.[6] Collective efforts to mitigate the negative social and environmental impacts of globalization focused on regulating multinationals, from proposals to create a New International Economic Order in the 1970s to suggestions about holding companies accountable for human rights abuses across their international supply and value chains.[7] As part of its mission to address the unique needs of developing countries, the United Nations Conference on Trade and Development (UNCTAD) began to monitor multinational enterprises already in the 1960s. In 1975, it

[4] Robert B. Reich, "Does Corporate Nationality Matter?" *Issues in Science and Technology* 7, no. 2 (1990): 40–44; "Multinational Corporations and the Myth of National Origin," *Harvard International Review* 13, no. 4 (1991): 15–17. For a review of business historical literature on corporate nationality, see: Alfred Reckendrees, Boris Gehlen, and Christian Marx, "International Business, Multinational Enterprises and Nationality of the Company: A Constructive Review of Literature," *Business History* 64, no. 9 (2022): 1567–1599. See also Geoffrey Jones' arguments on why corporate nationality does matter: *Multinationals and Global Capitalism: From the Nineteenth to the Twenty-first Century* (Oxford; New York: Oxford University Press, 2005): 50.

[5] Thomas L. Friedman, *The World Is Flat: A Brief History of the Twenty-First Century*, 3rd ed. (New York: Picador, 2007); Joseph E. Stiglitz, *Globalization and Its Discontents*, 2nd ed. (New York: W. W. Norton & Company, 2003).

[6] Grace Ballor and Sabine Pitteloud, "Introduction: Capitalism and Global Governance in Business History," *Business History Review* 97, no. 3 (2023): 459–479.

[7] For a contemporary account, see: Gamani Corea, "Unctad and the New International Economic Order," *International Affairs (Royal Institute of International Affairs 1944–)* 53, no. 2 (1977): 177–187. And on the UN Code of Conduct, see: Jennifer Bair, "Corporations at the United Nations: Echoes of the New International Economic Order?" *Humanity: An International Journal of Human Rights, Humanitarianism, and Development* 6, no. 1 (2015): 159–171. See also the work of Christy Thornton, both her *Revolution in Development: Mexico and the Governance of the Global Economy* (Los Angeles: University of California Press, 2021), as well as her research on economic governance.

created a United Nations Centre on Transnational Corporations to examine corporate responsibility and global governance.[8] And in the early 1990s, UNCTAD developed a "transnationality index" as part of its *World Investment Report*, which ranked the largest 100 multinationals by a weighted average of the geographical distribution of their sales, assets, and employment data. It also launched a journal publishing research on *Transnational Corporations*.[9] Motivated by its own mission to facilitate economic development among its members, the OECD began to follow country- and sector-level flows of multinational investment in the 1990s, from which it produced a database on the "Activity of Multinational Enterprises." Similarly, the European Commission and Eurostat also worked to measure firm activity in the EEC, particularly through the business research centers described in Chapter 1. EEC officials used the data they collected to design the European economy, draft proposals for common regulation, and take stock of business perceptions of the internal market. Consequently, for a wide range of international organizations, statistics about business activities became equally valuable tools of political economy as well as regulation.

Scholars also required firm-level data for their analyses of globalization. Building on Stephen Hymer's foundational theories of multinational enterprises as institutions for international production rather than mere exchange, international business researchers scraped corporate annual reports and the records of regulators like the US Securities and Exchange Commission for data on the locations of multinational production and distribution.[10] Among the first to take a quantitative approach was Raymond Vernon, who launched the multi-year "Multinational Enterprise Project" at Harvard Business School in the 1960s to collect data on 35,000 foreign subsidiaries of major global manufacturers from 1900 to 1971.[11] Vernon was chiefly interested in

[8] Khalil Hamdani and Lorraine Ruffing, *United Nations Centre on Transnational Corporations: Corporate Conduct and the Public Interest* (Abingdon; Oxon; New York: Routledge, 2015).

[9] See, for example, the first report: Centre on Transnational Corporations, ed., *The Triad in Foreign Direct Investment*, World Investment Report 1991 (New York: United Nations, 1991).

[10] Mira Wilkins, "The History of Multinationals: A 2015 View," *Business History Review* 89, no. 3 (2015): 405–414.

[11] This data, which redacted the names of parent companies, has been published in: Joan P. Curhan, William H. Davidson, and Rajan Suri, *Tracing the Multinationals: A Sourcebook on U.S.-based Enterprises* (Cambridge, MA: Ballinger, 1977), James W. Vaupel and Joan P. Curhan, *The Making of Multinational Enterprises: A Sourcebook of Tables Based on a Study of 187 Major U.S. Manufacturing Corporations* (Boston: Division of Research, Harvard Business School, 1969), and James W. Vaupel and Joan P. Curhan, *The World's Multinational Enterprises: A Sourcebook of Tables Based on a Study*

mapping the subsidiaries of US-based parent companies and the headquarter locations of parent companies with US subsidiaries.[12] In 1980, a group including John Dunning and John Stopford expanded on Vernon's project and published *The World Directory of Multinational Enterprises*, which collated firm-level data on the history, structure, products, current situation, and long-range financial information of major multinationals. Over the following two decades, the *World Directory* grew into a five-book, ten-volume collection, including *The World Directory of Multinational Enterprises* (1983), *The MacMillan Directory of Multinationals* (1989), and *The Directory of Multinationals* (1992, 1998). Its volumes laid the foundation for subsequent databases, like the Orbis and Amadeus products offered by Bureau van Dijk, and Refinitiv Worldscope, now called LSEG – all of which underpin contemporary scholarship on international business and industrial organization.

In a series of lectures, economist Paul Krugman revisited Immanuel Wallerstein's paradigmatic world systems analysis and offered some "quick-and-dirty calculations" to explain the dynamics of localization and concentration.[13] In his theory of *Geography and Trade*, Krugman placed the EEC's internal market at the very center of new thinking about trade, growth, and business cycle theories, and he argued it offered an ideal laboratory in which to test the effects of economic policy and firm behavior beyond the level of the nation state but beneath the level of the globe. By the end of the 1990s, the EU and its Single Market were just one such regional proving ground after NAFTA and MERCOSUR joined ASEAN and the EU/EFTA as major regional trade frameworks, demanding answers to new questions about the economic geography of international business: Did multinationals transcend national borders to do business globally, or were their international operations oriented instead around the advantages of regional trade frameworks?[14]

Motivated by such questions, scholars like Allen J. Morrison conducted surveys and interviews to study the management strategies of multinationals. Already in 1991, he and his colleagues found that

of the Largest U.S. and Non-U.S. Manufacturing Corporations (Boston: Division of Research, Harvard Business School, 1973).

12 See his: *Sovereignty at Bay: The Multinational Spread of US Enterprises* (New York: Basic Books, 1971).

13 Paul Krugman, *Geography and Trade*, 1st ed. (Leuven: The MIT Press, 1992): 99; Immanuel Maurice Wallerstein, *World-Systems Analysis: An Introduction* (Durham, NC: Duke University Press, 2004).

14 I explore this question further in a chapter of an edited volume: Grace Ballor, "Multinationals and Market Integration," in *The Cambridge Companion to Multinationals and Society*, ed. Geoffrey Jones and Sabine Pitteloud (Cambridge: Cambridge University Press, 2026).

"globalization is no panacea" because "global imperatives are being eclipsed by an upsurge in regional pressures."[15] Another international business scholar, Alan Rugman, then developed similar thinking about the geography of multinational management through a series of publications on *The Theory of Multinational Enterprises*, *The End of Globalization*, and "The End of Global Strategy."[16] Together with Alain Verbeke, Rugman also compiled a database of his own: the Regional Nature of Global Multinational Activity (RNGMA), comprised of revenue statistics from *Fortune*'s list of the 500 largest firms in the world. They drew on Kenichi Ohmae's geometric framing of global competition between triads and used RNGMA figures to argue that the world's largest companies derive most of their revenue from their "home regions," which afford them the unique advantages of lower transaction costs.[17] In their analysis, 88 percent of multinationals were "home region-oriented," while 10 percent were "host region-oriented" or "bi-regional," and just 2 percent were "global."[18] A subsequent article with Simon Collinson found that European multinationals were overwhelmingly regional.[19] "Globalization is a myth," claimed Rugman and the many others who embraced his line of research.[20] If proven using firm-level data, this provocative claim had the potential to rewrite the history of business in the global economy and reframe globalization as regionalization.

But the "regional multinationals" thesis had its detractors, who levied several points of criticism against its methods – although not against its conclusions. For starters, Rugman conflated big business and multinational companies. That the *Fortune 500* list at the core of his work made no distinction between different company structures raised

[15] Allen J. Morrison, David A. Ricks, and Kendall Roth, "Globalization versus Regionalization: Which Way for the Multinational?" *Organizational Dynamics* 19, no. 3 (1991): 28.

[16] Alan M. Rugman, *The Theory of Multinational Enterprises: The Selected Scientific Papers of Alan M. Rugman* (Cheltenham: Edward Elgar, 1996); Alan M. Rugman, *The End of Globalization* (London: Random House Business Books, 2000); Alan Rugman and Richard Hodgetts, "The End of Global Strategy," *European Management Journal* 19, no. 4 (2001): 333–343.

[17] Alan M. Rugman and Alain Verbeke, "A Perspective on Regional and Global Strategies of Multinational Enterprises," *Journal of International Business Studies* 35, no. 1 (2004): 3–18; Alan M. Rugman, *The Regional Multinationals: MNEs and "Global" Strategic Management* (Cambridge; New York: Cambridge University Press, 2005).

[18] Rugman and Verbeke, "A Perspective on Regional and Global Strategies," 7.

[19] Alan M. Rugman and Simon Collinson, "Multinational Enterprises in the New Europe: Are They Really Global?" *Organizational Dynamics*, Management Challenges in the New Europe 34, no. 3 (2005): 258–272.

[20] Wolfgang Burr and Britta Fischmann, Review of *The Regional Multinationals, MNEs and "Global" Strategic Management* by A. M. Rugman, *MIR: Management International Review* 48, no. 1 (2008): 137–140.

immediate problems for Rugman's argument that "most of the world's largest firms are stay-at-home multinationals."[21] Moreover, Rugman did not clearly delimit the boundaries of triads in developing his geographic categories, nor did he define the very regions at the core of his thesis. Consequently, his analyses shed no light on the differences for multinational business between free trade areas like NAFTA or ASEAN and the interdependent and supranationally governed region of the EEC/EU. In addition, his reliance only on sales data – and only from one year (2001) – marked a departure from half a century of scholarship on multinationals and international production, *à la* Hymer, and seems to have neglected the dramatic spatial restructuring of supply and value chains that characterized the late twentieth century. Together, these shortcomings led D. Eleanor Westney to accuse Rugman of designing a database to fit his hypothesis and "using data as a drunk uses a lamp post: for support, rather than illumination."[22] Perhaps it was this sort of criticism that led to the RNGMA database's abrupt removal from online circulation and to be seemingly lost when the "old computer" on which it was stored was "recycled" by its host institution, the University of Toronto.[23] Still, regionalization remains an active area of international business research. Some scholars have deployed new data sources as evidence and tested the theory on particular sectors.[24] With additional

[21] Yair Aharoni, "Book Review: The Regional Multinationals MNEs and Global Strategic Management," *International Business Review* 14, no. 4 (August 2006): 440.

[22] D. Eleanor Westney, "The Regional Multinationals: MNEs and 'Global' Strategic Management," *Journal of International Business Studies* 37, no. 3 (2006): 446.

[23] This was the fate of the database as described to me by a researcher involved in the project.

[24] Chang Hoon Oh and Jing Li, "Commentary: Alan Rugman and the Theory of the Regional Multinationals," *Journal of World Business* 50, no. 4 (2015): 631–633; Alain Verbeke and Liena Kano, "The New Internalization Theory and Multinational Enterprises from Emerging Economies: A Business History Perspective," *Business History Review* 89, no. 3 (2015): 415–445; Christian Geisler Asmussen, "Local, Regional, or Global? Quantifying MNE Geographic Scope," *Journal of International Business Studies* 40, no. 7 (2009): 1192–1205; Fragkiskos Filippaios and Ruth Rama, "Globalisation or Regionalisation? The Strategies of the World's Largest Food and Beverage MNEs," *European Management Journal* 26, no. 1 (2008): 59–72; Jan-Erik Vahlne and Inge Ivarsson, "The Globalization of Swedish MNEs: Empirical Evidence and Theoretical Explanations," *Journal of International Business Studies* 45, no. 3 (2014): 227–247; Elitsa R. Banalieva and Michael D. Santoro, "Local, Regional, or Global? Geographic Orientation and Relative Financial Performance of Emerging Market Multinational Enterprises," *European Management Journal, Is International Business Strategy Global or Regional?* 27, no. 5 (2009): 344–355; Thomas Osegowitsch and André Sammartino, "Reassessing (Home-)Regionalisation," *Journal of International Business Studies* 39, no. 2 (2008): 184–196; Benjamin Rosa, Philippe Gugler, and Alain Verbeke, "Regional and Global Strategies of MNEs: Revisiting Rugman & Verbeke (2004)," *Journal of International Business Studies* 51, no. 7 (2020): 1045–1053.

dimensions of analysis and robustness checks, others have found that multinationals were regional in previous decades but have since globalized.[25]

Data offers the promise of clear, aggregate answers to the question of whether European companies regionalized around the Single Market as European policymakers had intended. Of all the sources of firm-level data available for the 1970s–1990s, the most complete and the one suggested by Rugman's critics was *The World Directory of Multinationals*.[26] Scans of the ten physical volumes of the directory and manual transcriptions of their data yielded enormous tables.[27] And early analysis of those tables returned time series results more robust than the single year or single factor conclusions offered previously. But, using the directory's data to quantify the regionalization of multinationals in the Single European Market has several limitations and does not provide the business strategy insight afforded by historical case studies for several reasons.[28]

First, the *World Directory*'s data does not reflect the major structural changes the global economy underwent during the 1980s–2000s. "[F]irms predominantly or exclusively in banking, insurance, commodity brokering, retailing, engineering contracting and other service industries [were not] included" in the directory until its final volumes.[29] As a result, the directory neglects the rise of the service sector at the center of Rugman's analysis, impeding the possibility of checking his conclusions.

Second, even if John Stopford remained an advisor to the project for most of the directory's volumes, managing editorship changed over time, resulting in different approaches to the project and different inclusions in the data. Some volumes, for example, provide information for sales in "France" vs. "Abroad." Others offer additional categories, like "Europe," "Western Europe," and "Rest of Europe," without ever defining those boundaries – likely because each company's annual reports defined the

[25] Christoph Czychon, *Regional and Global Multinationals: An Examination of Theory and Empirical Evidence from European MNEs*, MIR ed. (Wiesbaden: Springer Gabler, 2021).

[26] D. Eleanor Westney, "The Regional Multinationals: MNEs and 'Global' Strategic Management," *Journal of International Business Studies* 37, no. 3 (2006): 445–449.

[27] Many thanks to Jessica Boutchie for her research assistance with scanning the volumes and transcribing the tables of data and to Laura Linard at the Baker Library at Harvard Business School for so generously facilitating consultation of these resources amid Covid-19 pandemic restrictions.

[28] Mira Wilkins noted similar methodological problems in Alfred Chandler's *Strategy and Structure* (Cambridge, MA: MIT Press, 1962), in which he did not define regions: Mira Wilkins, "Chandler and Global Business History," *The Business History Review* 82, no. 2 (2008): 251–266.

[29] John M. Stopford, *Directory of Multinationals* (New York, NY: Stockton Press 1992): xii.

region uniquely and because the region and its intersecting sets of international organizations were also evolving rapidly at the same time.

Third, the directory's editors screened the world's largest multinationals using three criteria: having at least 25 percent voting equity in at least three foreign countries, 5 percent of consolidated assets attributable to foreign investments, and at least $50 million (1978) in sales originating abroad.[30] Those criteria resulted in samples of about 500 multinationals per volume. But the firms within those samples changed considerably with each volume as firms ascended to and dropped out of the rankings of largest companies or no longer met the editors' criteria for inclusion, thus making it very difficult to draw any real conclusions about change over time.

In addition to specific critiques of the *World Directory* as a source, a quantitative approach to the economic geography of multinationals runs the risk of reducing business strategy to a limited set of statistics, which may or may not reveal what we expect. Nor can sales and production data be accurately understood in isolation from management decisions, national policies, and macroeconomic developments. That the EEC/EU – with support from Eurostat and the network of Business Information Centers described in Chapter 1 – had not managed to compile accurate data on multinationals operating in its market underscores the challenge of mapping and measuring the regionalization of European multinationals.

Building on other efforts to bring historical approaches to bear on international business scholarship, this chapter examines the business strategy of selected European multinationals in the 1992 Program through business historical case studies on a range of companies operating in the internal market of the EEC.[31] It considers a wide range of firms headquartered both inside and outside the EEC and from a wide range of sectors and industries, including manufacturing, pharmaceuticals, telecommunications, electronics, and retail, chosen for their diversity of experiences and approaches. Not only does this case study approach "bring history (back) into international business" and "put the process

30 Subsequent volumes raised the revenue threshold to account for inflation.

31 Peter J. Buckley, "Business history and International Business," *Business History* 51, no. 3 (2009): 307–333; Peter J. Buckley, "Historical Research Approaches to the Analysis of Internationalisation," *Management International Review* 56, no. 6 (2016): 879–900; Peter J. Buckley, "The Role of History in International Business: Evidence, Research Practices, Methods and Theory," *British Journal of Management* 32, no. 3 (2021): 797–811; Robert A. Burgelman, "Bridging History and Reductionism: A Key Role for Longitudinal Qualitative Research," *Journal of International Business Studies* 42, no. 5 (2011): 591–601. See also the ongoing special issue of the *Journal of International Business Studies* on "Integrating Historical Approaches in International Business: Moving Beyond 'History Matters'" being edited by Stephanie Decker, Geoffrey Jones, Klaus Meyer, and Catherine Welch.

back in" to research on firm internationalization, but through repetition, it also provides for the development of explanatory theories.[32] This, then, is methodological impressionism: Together, the collection of vignette cases presented here paints a bigger picture, revealing patterns about the growth and development of multinationals, their regionalization, and the relationship between regionalization and globalization that data alone could not make clear.[33]

These cases shed light on the diversity of approaches firms from different industries, sectors, and countries took when approaching the opportunities and challenges of the Single European Market: by expanding, investing, consolidating, partnering, merging, and forming regional interest associations.[34] Case method also allows us to study the process, motivations, and timing of managerial decision making in much more detail than geographical data could. In short, European business regionalized around the Single Market in ways that increased both their market power and political influence – at home and in Brussels. And as Chapters 4, 5, and 6 demonstrate through more extensive case studies of multinationals across sectors and countries, even firms skeptical of internal market integration ultimately became more "European" in their opposition to the Single Market and its flanking policies.

Cases of Europeanization

Manufacturing

One of the greatest transformations of European business in the late twentieth century was the restructuring of manufacturing supply chains.

[32] Geoffrey Jones and Tarun Khanna, "Bringing History (Back) into International Business," *Journal of International Business Studies* 37, no. 4 (2006): 453–468; Catherine Welch et al., "Theorising from Case Studies: Towards a Pluralist Future for International Business Research," *Journal of International Business Studies* 42, no. 5 (2011): 740–762: Catherine Welch and Eriikka Paavilainen-Mäntymäki, "Putting Process (Back) in: Research on the Internationalization Process of the Firm," *International Journal of Management Reviews* 16, no. 1 (2014): 2–23; Teresa da Silva Lopes et al., "Organizational Innovation in the Multinational Enterprise: Internalization Theory and Business History," *Journal of International Business Studies* 50, no. 8 (2019): 1338–1358; Catherine Welch et al., "Theory and Context: How the Case Study Can Set a New Agenda for IB Research," *Journal of International Business Studies* 53, no. 1 (2022): 4–26.

[33] Thanks to Rasmus Salén for his research assistance work on the selection of these cases and sources.

[34] Again, on the formation of BIAs, see: Neil Rollings, "The Development of Transnational Business Associations during the Twentieth Century," *Business History* 65, no. 2 (2023): 235–259.

Especially in the auto industry, producers responding to rapidly changing regulation, consumer preferences, and foreign competition increasingly relied on expansive networks of suppliers to provide the wide array of specialized component parts their models required, as described further in Chapter 4. In many ways, the strategies of these suppliers reflected broader economic shifts across the region and globe.

The German engineering and manufacturing company Bosch was one of the most important suppliers of automobile component parts in Europe. The company's early history and the "deep responsibility" of its founder have been chronicled by Geoffrey Jones.[35] Bosch made several acquisitions in Europe in the 1980s, growing its number of factories across nine European countries. In this period, the geography of its business strategy reflected its close ties to Volkswagen as a primary parts supplier. While Bosch operated in other global regions, too, its largest presence outside of Germany was concentrated in the countries of Western Europe because of the advantages of close geographic proximity, the common market of the EEC, and plans for the Single European Market. By 1988, its diversification strategy away from only automobile components and the consumer appliance sector, both hard hit by the crises of the 1970s, led Bosch to develop a telecommunications division for which it acquired companies in France, Italy, Portugal, Spain, and Austria, which it used as a base to supply Central and Eastern Europe with manufactured goods.[36] In the 1980s, it also expanded its auto part production capacity across three different sites in France in anticipation of increased demand for fuel-injection engine components for passenger cars in the wake of the EEC's new stricter emissions standards, which would take effect in 1993.[37] Because labor costs were high in Germany, where a Bosch employee cost about 32.67 Deutsche marks per hour, chairman Marcus Bierich (1984–1993) looked to expand production into cheaper labor markets, like Portugal, where an hour of labor cost just 5.32 Deutsche marks by contrast.[38] Bosch's need to expand production outside Germany to remain competitive aligned with the European Commission's vision for business in the Single Market provided Bosch

[35] Geoffrey Jones, *Deeply Responsible Business: A Global History of Values-Driven Leadership* (Cambridge, MA: Harvard University Press, 2023): Chapter 3.

[36] Johannes Bähr, Paul Erker, and James Amery Underwood, *Bosch: History of a Global Enterprise*, 1. Aufl (München: Verlag C. H. Beck, 2015). Harm G. Schröter, "The German Question, the Unification of Europe, and the European Market Strategies of Germany's Chemical and Electrical Industries, 1900–1992," *Business History Review* 67, no. 3 (1993): 403.

[37] Ballor, "Liberal Environmentalism."

[38] Schröter, "The German Question," 404.

keep its "durable jobs" within the EEC, a primary motivation for the internal market program in the first place.

Bosch's European expansion was also driven by the evolution of the European auto industry and its component sector in the wake of both just-in-time production and growing competition with Japan, which underwent dramatic consolidation into a "leading group of large multinational companies," which partnered with vehicle assemblers on a pan-European basis.[39] For example: "the total sales of the Bosch group-Europe's leading components manufacturer in 1990 amounted to roughly half the world turnover of Volkswagen, Europe's biggest indigenously owned vehicle assembler."[40] As Bosch consolidated automobile component part manufacturing into its vast multinational network of producers, it started demanding quality standards from suppliers, thereby facilitating the kind of standardization described in Chapter 2. Bosch worked to "reshape a national patchwork of companies across Western Europe" into a rationalized "Pan-European system" whereby it could service the entire continent with one particular product – fulfilling the dream of the Single Market.[41]

Ultimately, the globalization of the auto industry required parts suppliers like Bosch to globalize as well. Expansion throughout Europe gave Bosch the springboard it needed to set up manufacturing in Southeast Asia, Malaysia, Iran, and Turkey, to meet the needs of its client carmakers and solve the export problems caused by the high Deutsche Mark exchange rate.[42] Europeanization was the first step in Bosch's emergence as a global enterprise.

Pharmaceuticals

During the late 1980s, the French pharmaceutical company Rhône-Poulenc became "one of Europe's most aggressive acquirers," purchasing several firms in Europe, "including Natterman, a large, family-owned German pharmaceutical company."[43] This 1980s strategy of aggressive expansion and embrace of European integration was a marked contrast from its experience of the 1960s, when its slow reaction to the reduction

[39] David Sadler, "The Geographies of Just-in-Time: Japanese Investment and the Automotive Components Industry in Western Europe," *Economic Geography* 70, no. 1 (1994): 48.

[40] Sadler, "The Geographies of Just-in-Time," 48. [41] Ibid., 55.

[42] Kathrin Fastnacht et al., "The Emergence of a Global Player: The Internationalization of the Bosch Group," *Journal of Bosch History*, n.d.

[43] Ibid.

of tariff barriers after the Treaty of Rome left it vulnerable to the US chemical companies that did as Jean-Jacques Servan-Schreiber feared and posed a "défi américain" by taking advantage of the common market.[44] Recognizing the plight of French pharmaceutical companies like Rhône-Poulenc, the French government attempted to create national champions in the 1970s by reorganizing the industry. Rhône-Poulenc benefitted from this effort through the ability to acquire new assets, but the events of the 1970s demanded further intervention and a new business strategy.

Beginning in 1981, French President François Mitterrand nationalized and recapitalized many key French companies, including Rhône-Poulenc.[45] During its nationalization, Rhône-Poulenc divested from heavy chemicals and invested in pharmaceuticals and fine chemicals. Mitterrand's successor, Jacques Chirac, embarked on a privatization campaign, but stock market turmoil delayed this process, keeping Rhône-Poulenc in the public sector into the 1990s. In the mid-1980s, French management consultant Jean-René Fourtou wrote a report on the chemical industry's future in France, which earned him the position of Rhône-Poulenc's chief executive and chairman in 1986.[46] While still in control of the company and with Fourtou's guidance, the French government doubled down on their champion firm by injecting capital into Rhône-Poulenc "to limit competition between French firms at the national level, and to form large companies capable of competing with their rivals at international level."[47] Fourtou then deployed the strategy of internationalization, both within the EEC and its Single Market and also globally. It was under his leadership that the company became an "aggressive acquirer" of pharmaceutical assets, partner of the large Merck & Company and large investor in Asian vaccine production.

[44] On the early international history of Rhône-Poulenc, see: Christian Marx, *Wegbereiter der Globalisierung: Multinationale Unternehmen der westeuropäischen Chemieindustrie in der Zeit nach dem Boom (1960er–2000er Jahre)* (Göttingen: Vandenhoeck & Ruprecht 2023), Section 2.2.

[45] In her dissertation, Liane Hewitt framed Mitterrand's nationalization campaign as a French effort to deal with corporate power. By contrast, the contemporary German approach was to give workers representation on corporate boards. See: Liane Hewitt, "Monopoly Menace: The Rise and Fall of Cartel Capitalism in Western Europe, 1918–1957," PhD dissertation, Princeton University, 2023.

[46] Joel Kurtzman, "The Passionate Leader: An Interview with Jean Rene Fourtou," *Strategy +Business*, www.strategy-business.com/article/17726. Fourtou's career also demonstrates the importance of what Christopher McKenna called the "world's newest profession"; see: Christopher D. McKenna, *The World's Newest Profession: Management Consulting in the Twentieth Century* (Cambridge: Cambridge University Press, 2010).

[47] Florence Charue-Duboc, "Repositioning of European Chemicals Groups and Changes in Innovation Management: The Case of the French Chemical industry. The Global Chemical Industry in the Age of the Petrochemical Revolution," (Cambridge: Cambridge University Press, 2007): 15.

And it was in this context that Jean-Pierre Tirouflet, the CFO of Rhône-Poulenc, argued: "It is necessary to have the largest market possible to help spread the cost of research, distribution and new investments."[48] Rhône-Poulenc was privatized in 1993. By 1996, it reported revenues exceeding $17 billion and was one of the largest pharmaceutical companies in both Europe and the world.

Meanwhile, many of Rhône-Poulenc's primary competitors were in neighboring Switzerland. The 1970 merger of two Swiss pharmaceutical companies, CIBA and Geigy, created a large multinational drug producer, CIBA-Geigy. Swiss consumers reacted strongly against multinational pharmaceutical companies in the 1980s, given the rising cost of medicine and healthcare, and a 1986 chemical fire at the Sandoz plant. As a result, to shield itself from the increasingly hostile public opinion and regulatory environment in Switzerland, CIBA-Geigy opened a new plant in France where it worked to capitalize on a more friendly regulatory environment and access to the Single European Market, since Switzerland remained in the EFTA but outside of the EEC. It also worked to mobilize politically at the national and European levels against the regulation of multinational corporations.[49] Together with CIBA-Geigy, Hoffman-La Roche and Sandoz, which restructured its operations in 1989 "in anticipation of the EC unification," were dubbed the "Basel MNEs" thanks to their common headquarter location in the Swiss city of Basel.[50] Due to the small size of the domestic Swiss market, these companies had early incentives to expand abroad: While the Swiss market made up just 2–4 percent of sales by the early 1990s, more than one third of sales came from the EEC.[51] Eventually, CIBA-Geigy merged with Sandoz to create the Swiss giant Novartis.

The German pharmaceutical giant Bayer "went further" in its Europeanization, according to historian Harm Schröter; it "included in its strategy the representation of its varied European work force." It also held a European Forum in the six European (not necessarily EEC) countries in which it had the largest presence, not only to build cooperation, but also to export the "German model" more widely within its organization. Bayer also registered its shares on all major European stock exchanges to raise capital more easily, protect itself against potential

[48] Steven Greenhouse, "Merger Mania Strikes Europe as Barrier-Free Market Nears," *The New York Times*, August 26, 1988, sec. Business, https://www.nytimes.com/1988/08/26/business/merger-mania-strikes-europe-as-barrierfree-market-nears.html.

[49] Sabine Pitteloud, "Unwanted Attention: Swiss Multinationals and the Creation of International Corporate Guidelines in the 1970s," *Business and Politics* 22, no. 4 (2020): 587–611.

[50] David J. Collis, Elizabeth Johnson, "Smashing the Cube: Corporate Transformation at Ciba-Geigy Ltd.," HBS Case 9795041 (1995).

[51] Razeen Sally, "The Basel Chemical Multinationals: Corporate Action within Structures of Corporatism in Switzerland," *West European Politics* 16, no. 4 (1993): 563.

hostile takeovers, and expand the company's recognition outside of Germany. In the 1980s, a Bayer representative explained: "Distinctions between Europe and Germany are artificial; for us they no longer play any role."[52] Europe became Bayer's "home market," a sentiment echoed by fellow German company Siemens in 1988, when they called the Single European Market their new home market.[53]

From investment and acquisition strategies to employee and consumer engagement, several pharmaceutical companies based in Europe regionalized during the later decades of the twentieth century. Some were motivated by the business opportunity of a large Single Market, while others saw regionalization as part of their eventual globalization, and others like Bayer saw internal Europeanization to keep national and regional regulators at bay. Still, in 1996, the European Commission recognized that while it was "one of the great success stories of Europe," the competitiveness of the European pharmaceutical industry required the further "dismantling of national regulatory regimes and the development of Community institutions."[54] Of chief concern for the EU at that stage was the harmonization of drug prices across the Single Market, so the Commission launched initiatives to bolster the industry, support common research and development, and facilitate harmonization.[55]

Telecommunications

Spain was governed by fascist dictator Francisco Franco from 1936 to 1975, during which time the Spanish telecommunications company Telefónica, founded in 1924, became a public monopoly. Spain applied to become an EEC associated country in 1962, but following Franco's death in 1975, the new democratic government requested full EEC accession in 1977 and began the transformation of its economy and politics toward liberal democracy requisite for EEC membership.[56] This was a difficult transition period in Spain, exacerbated by the oil

52 Harm G. Schröter, "The German Question, the Unification of Europe, and the European Market Strategies of Germany's Chemical and Electrical Industries, 1900-1992," *The Business History Review* 67, no. 3 (1993): 403.

53 HB8TNB: Harvard Baker Library; Siemens AG 1988 Annual Report.

54 European Commission, "Europe's Pharmaceutical Industry: An Innovation Profile," EIMS Publication no. 32 (August 1996), Director General XIII.

55 On the contest over drug pricing in Europe, see: Sabine Pitteloud and Pierre-Yves Donzé, "Swiss Multinationals versus the French Welfare State? The Social Security Deficit, European Integration, and the Battle for 'Fair' Drug Prices (1970–1990)," *Contemporary European History* (January 24, 2024) 1–20.

56 Eventually, the EEC's norms of democracy and liberalism were enshrined in the EU's *acquis communautaire* in 1993, requiring applicant countries to meet certain economic and political and social criteria to qualify for membership.

and economic crises of the 1970s. During that challenging decade, the Spanish stock market collapsed, and the value of Telefónica stock plummeted, from being so secure they had been called "widow's shares" at 490 pesetas each in 1973 to just 84.5 pesetas a share by 1977.[57] Even though Telefónica remained a public company well after Spain's accession to the EEC as part of the third enlargement in 1986, minority shares of the company were listed on foreign stock exchanges, and it entered into strategic joint ventures with other European technology firms, including Olivetti, Brown Boveri, Philips, Saab-Scania, and Telfin.[58]

Spain's entry into the EEC in 1986 coincided with the Commission's launch of the many business Europeanization programs described in Chapter 1. Telefónica participated in several of these initiatives, including ESPRIT's collaborative R&D projects on microelectronics, information processing systems, and office and business systems.[59] Throughout the Single Market Program, Telefónica also participated in other EEC initiatives like RACE (a spin-off of ESPRIT), ENS, CTS-2, DRIVE, AIM, DELTA, and COST.[60] Telefónica also pursued joint ventures and R&D partnerships with other European telecommunications companies in an effort to compete for the anticipated pan-European telephone market. It also swapped shares with the Italian firm Telettra. In addition to these actions, Telefónica adopted its business strategy to the opportunities of the Single Market Program and began expanding rapidly into other European member states.[61] According to Wayne Sandholtz, who has articulated a neofunctionalist interpretation of European integration, Telefónica's Europeanization helped to integrate Spain into the Single Market and to facilitate market integration across the EEC during its Single Market Program.[62] Others

[57] Judith Clifton, Francisco Comín, and Daniel Díaz-Fuentes, "From National Monopoly to Multinational Corporation: How Regulation Shaped the Road towards Telecommunications Internationalisation," *Business History* 53, no. 5 (2011): 761–781.

[58] Ibid.

[59] European Commission, "1989 Annual Report: ESPRIT – European Strategic Programme for Research and Development in Information Technology," 1989, EUR 12626 (Brussels: Commission for the European Communities, 1990).

[60] "Annual Report 1991: Telefónica de España," Annual Report, 1992, www.telefonica.com/en/shareholders-investors/financial-reports/historical-archive-annual-reports/1991/.

[61] Mauro F. Guillen and Esteban Garcia-Canal, "How to Conquer New Markets with Old Skills," *Harvard Business Review*, November 2010.

[62] Wayne Sandholtz, *High-Tech Europe: The Politics of International Cooperation* (Berkeley: University of California Press, 1992). On neofunctionalism, see: Alec Stone Sweet and Wayne Sandholtz, "European Integration and Supranational Governance," *Journal of European Public Policy* 4, no. 3 (1997): 297–317.

have used this case to explain the development of multinational enterprises.[63]

Retail

Amid the economic crises of the 1970s, many European countries restricted retail expansion to protect SMEs; this forced large retailers to look beyond their national home country borders in search of growth opportunities. Chapter 6 discusses the regional expansion of food retail in detail through the case of Belgian grocer Delhaize. But several other food retailers also regionalized during the Single Market Program, and the diversity of their approaches sheds light on the sector's experience and perspective of market integration.

The French grocer Carrefour pioneered the European supermarket model and expanded widely starting in the 1950s; by the late 1960s, it was operating chain stores and supermarkets in the UK, Belgium, Italy, and Switzerland. Similarly, the German wholesaler Metro AG directed its efforts to building a strong European network of brands with stores across the EEC. British Tesco first moved into Ireland in the 1970s and then France in the 1980s with mixed success before capitalizing on the newly opened markets of Central and Eastern Europe in the 1990s, where, motivated by talks about eventual EEC and Single Market membership for former Soviet Bloc states, it built large stores with goods sourced through its centralized, "lean" supply chains. While internationalization contributed to the growth of these companies and to the economic growth and development of distribution infrastructure in host countries on the European periphery, Delhaize and Tesco were ultimately forced to divest from many of their international acquisitions as competition ate into their profits and transitions to capitalism proved difficult, revealing both the unique challenges of multinational retailing as well as the new obstacles European multinationals faced in a changing global economy. In deciphering the signal from the noise, however, it becomes clear that despite the ambivalent revenue results of their regionalization in this period, Western European multinational investment did play a role in integrating home and host markets through their supply chains, product lines, store layout, consumer services, and pricing schemes.[64] Moreover,

[63] Adoración Álvaro-Moya, "Networking Capability Building in the Multinational Enterprise: ITT and the Spanish Adventure (1924–1945)," *Business History* 57, no. 7 (2015): 1082–1111.

[64] Grace Ballor, "Agents of Integration: Multinational Firms and the European Union," *Enterprise & Society* 21, no. 4 (2020): 886–892.

as Chapter 6 explains, food retailers followed the example of firms in many other sectors and established regional BIAs to maximize their policy influence in Brussels. They also formed defensive regional buying clubs to prepare for the challenges of the Single Market.

In addition to food commerce, other retailers regionalized during the 1980s and 1990s. The Swedish economy slowed considerably in the 1970s when oil shocks beget economic crises and previously high post-war growth rates stagnated. That Sweden's productivity lagged even the OECD average motivated Swedish chairmen like Ingvar Kamprad to look outside their home markets for new growth opportunities. Kamprad's furniture retail company IKEA had already expanded into neighboring Norway and Denmark in the 1960s. In the 1970s and 1980s, Kamprad opened IKEA stores across Europe.

As a result, IKEA was an early European multinational, originating in Sweden with a parent holding company in the Netherlands to be inside the EEC and its Single Market, where "profits were transferred to a charitable foundation [its founder Ingvar] Kamprad had set up in the Netherlands to escape stringent Swedish taxes and foreign exchange regulations."[65] Kamprad, who eventually moved to Switzerland "partly to escape high Swedish taxes" declared: "it is our duty to expand," which he managed to do throughout continental Europe in the turbulent 1970s and 1980s through direct ownership of stores, whereas its expansion outside Europe was done mostly through a franchise model.[66] According to corporate archivist Tony Nilsson, IKEA first expanded into Switzerland because it was an EFTA member, and thus had a free trade treaty with Sweden.[67] Just as the Single Market Program was getting underway in 1986, IKEA reorganized its European assets into "Retail Europe" and moved its headquarters to Denmark, a relatively new EEC member state, inside the Single Market.[68] In the 1980s, it expanded into the UK, Belgium, Austria, France, and Italy, and announced plans to expand further rapidly.

Commonalities across Europe allowed IKEA to achieve economies of scale by offering a homogenous product range, store format, and catalog, and make just small adaptations in advertising to local markets.[69] A 1979

[65] Christopher A. Bartlett and Ashish Nanda, "Ingvar Kamprad and IKEA," Harvard Business School Case 9-390-132 (May 7, 1990).

[66] Ibid.

[67] Tony Nilsson, "The Early IKEA Expansion, by Way of the German Speaking Markets," *Archiv und Wirtschaft* 52, no. 4 (2019): 172–178.

[68] Bartlett and Nanda, "Ingvar Kamprad and IKEA," 9.

[69] Ulf Johansson, "IKEA: The Making of a Global Giant," in *Global Strategies in Retailing: Asian and European Experiences*, Routledge Studies in International Business and the

plan to source locally and adapt to regional markets in Southern Europe, Northern Europe, and beyond failed and generated a dispersed product range that was "in conflict with the IKEA concept," and with the company's successful approach to capturing economies of scale.[70] Its uniform product line has long been a hallmark of IKEA's business model. It also positioned IKEA to play a key role in homogenizing consumer goods and consequently the design of homes and the materiality of daily life across Europe. IKEA's successful expansion in Europe paved the way for "the making of a global giant" in the twenty-first century.[71]

Electronics

In the 1980s and 1990s, companies headquartered outside the EEC were keen to establish a presence in the Community to capitalize on the business opportunity of its Single European Market. As Lauri Ratia, Nokia's vice president for corporate planning put it: "[b]ecause of the size of the markets in the European Community, it is a must to have operations located inside the EC."[72] "Want[ing] to be on the right side of the fence" when the Single Market became a reality. Nokia, a Finnish electronics company, made fourteen acquisitions in the EEC in 1987–1988 alone. Similarly, Electrolux, a Swedish appliance company, made more than twenty-five acquisitions annually in the mid-to-late 1980s.[73]

ABB was created through the merger of two electronics champions from countries in the EFTA, explicitly motivated by the EEC's Single Market Program and their desire to take full advantage of it as a business opportunity. In 1988, when the completion of the Single Market seemed a certainty, Swedish electronics company ASEA merged with its main rival, the Swiss Brown Boveri, to create ABB.[74] The two companies "began to realize that presence in the EC countries was the only way to

World Economy, ed. John A. Dawson and Masao Mukoyama (Abingdon, Oxon; New York: Routledge, 2014): 137–145.

70 Anna Jonsson and Nicolai J. Foss, "International Expansion through Flexible Replication: Learning from the Internationalization Experience of IKEA," *Journal of International Business Studies* 42, no. 9 (2011): 1085–1088.

71 Ulf Johansson, "IKEA: The Making of a Global Giant," in Dawson and Mukoyama, *Global Strategies in Retailing.*

72 Steven Greenhouse, "Merger Mania Strikes Europe as Barrier-Free Market Nears," *The New York Times*, August 26, 1988: www.nytimes.com/1988/08/26/business/merger-mania-strikes-europe-as-barrierfree-market-nears.html.

73 Ibid.

74 Andrew Boynton and Mark R. Eaker, "Abb Asea Brown Boveri (a): The Merger," UVA-BP-0323 (Rochester, NY, October 21, 2008).

guarantee access to EC markets," crucial to escape the economic trouble they faced at home and out of a "rising fear of what [was] brewing in Brussels," leading them to "set up shop in as many countries as possible so they can present themselves as local manufacturers."[75] Thanks to its expansion across the EEC in the 1980s and 1990s, ABB became recognized as one of the "models of the multinational" and an example of how business Europeanized in response to the Single Market Program.[76]

Conclusions

Many European businesses regionalized during the 1980s and 1990s, both because they recognized the business opportunity of the Single Market and because they needed to expand to remain globally competitive. As these business historical cases reveal, while their paths toward and motivations for regionalization differed, they all focused on scale, producing ever larger firms through acquisitions and mergers, and consolidating industries – both horizontally and vertically. The 1992 Program motivated Europe's late 1980s "merger mania" through the interests of industrialists and with the support of financiers; as *New York Times* business reporter Steven Greenhouse explained in 1988: "While industrialists are the driving force behind the deals, aggressive investment bankers – especially from American and British firms – are greasing the wheels."[77] As Chapter 5 explains, merchant banks like Paribas played a key role in facilitating the regionalization of industry required for the completion of the Single Market by financing the infrastructure projects needed to move goods, services, capital, and people throughout the EEC, by funding corporate mergers, acquisitions, investments, and expansion, and by facilitating economic transformations across the region.

In addition to business strategy decisions to expand, invest, merge, and find partners in the EEC, European businesses also regionalized by creating regional BIAs, designed to share information as much as to coordinate policy positions. European multinationals wanted to exert influence over regional policymakers, but they also wanted to reduce information asymmetries and work together to understand and anticipate macroeconomic and geopolitical changes. The vignette cases in this chapter lay a foundation for Chapters 4, 5, and 6, which expand on the

[75] Boynton and Eaker, "Abb Asea Brown Boveri (a): The Merger."

[76] See: Sumantra Ghoshal and Christopher A. Bartlett, "The Multinational Corporation as an Interorganizational Network," *The Academy of Management Review* 15, no. 4 (1990): 603–625. Ghoshal and Bartlett also wrote a book in 1989 on *Models of the Multinational*.

[77] Greenhouse, "Merger Mania Strikes Europe as Barrier-Free Market Nears."

complexity of business approaches to the Single Market in three sectors: manufacturing, banking, and commerce, and discuss various ways European multinationals regionalized in response to the 1992 Program and the effects of their regionalization, in turn, on market integration.

While competition policy remained a chief economic tool of the Commission during the 1992 Program, its lack of explicit legal competence in industrial policy and desire for "European" businesses in the internal market kept antitrust cases to a relatively low dozen per year average during the 1980s and early 1990s. Some of the cases covered in this chapter did attract the Commission's attention, however, as Europeanization produced larger, more powerful multinationals, whose market share became monopolistic. Bosch had already been fined 76,500 ECU by the Commission in 1982 for violating Article 85 of the Treaty of Rome by buying assets for distributing dishwashers and washing machines from the Belgian firm IPTC without proper disclosure.[78] Then, in May 1988, the Commission faulted the German pharmaceutical firm Bayer for engaging in five distribution agreements with BPCL to control supply and set prices for its polyethylene product; such restructuring and rationalizing of European petrochemical business was not warranted, in the view of the Commission, given the ease of transporting polyethylene directly by Bayer, and the de facto specialization and market distortion created by the agreements.[79] Some anticompetitive activity was permitted, however, especially to advance technological capacity in the EEC. For example, when BBC Brown Bovari extended a technical licensing agreement as part of its joint venture (Newco) with the Japanese company NGK Insulators, Ltd., to cooperate exclusively in the research and development of the precision ceramics required to make innovative sodium-sulfur high-performance batteries for electric vehicles and off-peak electricity storage, the Commission, which initially deemed this agreement a "distortion of competition," ultimately granted a fifteen-year exemption, signed by Peter Sutherland.[80] Together, these antitrust decisions by the Commission reveal its policy perspective on the benefits and risks of multinational regionalization.[81]

[78] 82/777/EEC: Commission Decision of November 4, 1982 amending Decision 82/371/EEC relating to a proceeding under Article 85 of the EEC Treaty (IV/29.995 - NAVEWA/ANSEAU).

[79] 88/330/EEC: Commission Decision of May 5, 1988 relating to a proceeding under Article 85 of the EEC Treaty (IV/32.075 - Bayer/BP Chemicals).

[80] 88/541/EEC: Commission Decision of October 11, 1988 relating to a proceeding under Article 85 of the EEC Treaty (IV/32.368 - BBC Brown Boveri).

[81] Many thanks to Louis Galambos for the encouragement to address antitrust here.

Additionally, these vignette cases help differentiate between regionalization and globalization. Scholarship on globalization has traced the long arc of transnational interdependence and exchange and the role of sovereignty in shaping political geography.[82] Relatively less work has approached globalization through the perspectives of firms. But international business scholarship has found, similar to the conclusions drawn by Alan Rugman and his coauthors on multinationals, that global value chains are also clustered regionally rather than globally, with especially "positive correlations between trade in value-added and European standards for 'Factory Europe.'"[83] That globalization has primarily consisted of numerous regional developments puts into perspective the retreat from globalization that began after the 2008 Global Financial Crisis and was accelerated by the Covid-19 pandemic and the Russian invasion of Ukraine: In the 2020s, multinationals have largely re-regionalized out of necessity due to value chain disruptions rather than strategic business choices.[84] Just as the phenomenon of late twentieth-century globalization developed largely though the regionalization of European multinational firms, contemporary deglobalization may also unfold as a process of re-regionalization, raising the question of whether the region acts as the default unit of scale, strategy, and analysis for big business once national markets can no longer support their growth objectives and as national governments increasingly rely on them to solve their economic and social problems.

[82] See: Kevin O'Rourke and Jeffrey Williamson, *Globalization and History* (Cambridge, MA: MIT Press, 1999); John Agnew, *Globalization and Sovereignty: Beyond the Territoriality Trap* (Lanham, MD: Rowman & Littlefield, 2009); Dani Rodrik, *The Globalization Paradox: Democracy and the Future of the World Economy* (New York: W. W. Norton & Company, 2011).

[83] Blind et al., "Standards in the Global Value Chains of the European Single Market," 30.

[84] Geoffrey Jones and Valeria Giacomin, "Deglobalization and Alternative Futures," Harvard Business School Technical Note 322-088 (Cambridge, MA: Harvard Business School, March 10, 2022), 2.

4 Manufacturing the Single Market

The 1980s was a tumultuous decade for the European auto industry.[1] The second oil shock of 1979 caused yet another recession, driving down consumer demand especially for cars with poor fuel economy. National governments erected new protectionist trade barriers in response to the downturn and simultaneously intensified the global contest over emissions standards. Although car sales began to recover in 1984, European producers steadily lost market share to their Japanese competitors, whose production methods and export and foreign investment strategies had given them a strong foothold in the markets of the EEC. When the Single European Act was signed in 1986, European automakers faced both a new opportunity and a new challenge: a single European car market promised greater economies of scale and the chance to compete globally with producers from the US and Japan, but harmonization would also remove national protections and increase competition, upsetting the carefully orchestrated dominance of "national champions" in their domestic markets. In the words of the Volkswagen (VW) annual report from 1988, "[T]his development represents both a unique opportunity and a unique challenge … The harmonization of economic policy and technical standards, together with the abolition of border controls should help cut costs and stimulate economic growth. This will at the same time offer companies greater scope for innovation and investment, resulting in keener competition."[2] This tension between opportunity and challenge played out in debates among policymakers and carmakers alike over the following seven years as macroeconomic and geopolitical developments – like the fall of

[1] This chapter contains some analysis and tables first published in articles in *Business History Review* and *Business History* and reprinted here with the journals' permission: Grace Ballor, "Liberal Environmentalism: The Public-Private Production of European Emissions Standards," *Business History Review* 97, no. 3 (2023): 575–601; Grace Ballor, "Liberalisation or Protectionism for the Single Market? European Automakers and Japanese Competition, 1985–1999," *Business History* 65, no. 2 (2022): 302–328.

[2] Volkswagen, "Europe '92: A Totally New Dimension," *1988 Annual Report* (Wolfsburg: VW, 1988): 17.

the Berlin Wall in 1989 and opening of Eastern Europe in 1991 – fluxed the demand for passenger cars and the EEC worked to finalize new industrial, competition, and commercial policies for automobiles in a growing Single European Market. For its part, the Bayerische Motoren Werke (BMW), described how "European industry developed, at an early date, a vision of a politically and economically united free Europe. It prepared itself for this market, the largest in the world, with increasing dynamism. That is why the word 'Eurosclerosis' is no longer heard."[3]

Not only did Europe's manufacturing strength still dominate the agendas of regional policymakers in the 1980s, but of all productive industries, it was auto manufacturing that claimed the most symbolic and strategic value for the economies of EEC member states with its forward linkages to raw materials like steel and backward linkages to finished high-end goods like dashboard electronics.[4] In France, Italy, and Britain, flagship car producers had underpinned both growth and modernization since the early twentieth century. Even Spain, Sweden, and smaller countries sought to earn a place on the international economic stage by developing domestic auto industries. But nowhere was car production more important than in the postwar Federal Republic of Germany (FRG), home to the highest concentration of carmakers in the EEC, which spanned the full range of market segments and production systems – from volume producers of economy cars to small, specialty producers of luxury vehicles.[5] Germany's "Big Three" epitomized this spectrum: VW, the industrial darling of Lower Saxony whose Third Reich origins and *Wirtschaftswunder* success transformed it from the maker of the "people's car" to the largest global auto group, contrasted sharply with BMW, a small, boutique brand, offering German engineering to elite networks of enthusiast drivers, while Daimler-Benz occupied the space in between.

This chapter examines the response of car manufacturers to market integration through the cases of BMW and VW.[6] It finds despite their

3 BMW, "Upturn for Europe," 1989 *Annual Report* (Munich: BMW, 1989): 15.

4 European Parliament: Committee on External Economic Relations (rapporteur Mr. R.E. Filippi), "Report on Imports of Japanese Cars into the EEC," Document 1-997/82, December 15, 1982 ["Filippi Report"], AEI. For more on postwar motorization in Europe, see: Tony Judt, *Postwar: A History of Europe since 1945* (New York: Penguin Books, 2006); Kristin Ross, *Fast Cars, Clean Bodies: Decolonization and the Reordering of French Culture*. (Cambridge, MA: MIT Press, 1996).

5 In the 1980s, Germany produced one third of all new cars registered in the European Economic Community.

6 While this chapter discusses the larger auto industry as context, its analysis focuses primarily on the passenger car industry.

differences, these car companies embraced the opportunities afforded by the Single Market, contributed to the standardization discussed in Chapter 2 through their widespread supply and value chains, and mobilized their regional interest associations to mitigate the challenges of market integration by shaping regional policies in their favor.[7] VW's expansion was production oriented, and it paired its "volume and diversity" strategy with a Sloanian approach to managing its growing family of brands.[8] Conversely, BMW's internationalization was distribution oriented: it took a "quality" approach to profit and relied on a highly-skilled work force and huge network of specialty suppliers.[9] This contrast and the debates that took place within regional interest associations demonstrate how different automakers navigated the changing European business environment in the 1980s and 1990s. A comparison of their business strategies also shows how European multinationals used the regional internal market as a springboard from which to globalize and contributed to repositioning Europe in the global economy.

Differences in strategy between BMW and VW emerged in large part from their leadership. During the 1992 Program, both firms were chaired by equally charismatic CEOs, whose distinct approaches left permanent imprints on each company and determined their respective places in the emergent single car market. Eberhard von Kuenheim, a mechanical engineer from Stuttgart whose work in the auto industry began "by accident," caught the attention of the industrialist Herbert Quandt, who had rescued BMW from bankruptcy in the late 1960s and was named chairman of the still floundering company in 1970.[10] Over the course of his 23-year tenure, von Kuenheim oversaw the firm's embrace of a quality profit strategy and re-centered the company's focus on performance engineering as its market niche. By contrast, Carl Hahn was a salesman. After beginning his international career at the European

[7] For more analysis on the regionalization of car industries, see: Jorge Carrillo, Yannick Lung, and Rob van Tulder, eds. *Cars, Carriers of Regionalism?* (Hampshire: Palgrave MacMillan, 2004): Chapters 3 and 4, pp. 42–74.

[8] Some have argued that of all European producers VW was best prepared to take advantage of the Single Market, whereas BMW's success in an integrated Europe required more adjustments. For more on this, see: Roland Stephen, *Vehicle of Influence: Building a European Car Market* (Ann Arbor: University of Michigan Press, 2000): 24.

[9] For more on the various profit strategies employed across the European auto industry in the 1980s and 1990s, see: Michael Freyssenet, Koichi Shimizu, and Giuseppe Volpato, eds., *Globalization or Regionalization of the European Car Industry?* (New York: Palgrave Macmillan, 2003), Conclusion, pp. 241–260. On VW's particular strategies, see: Ulrich Jürgens, "VW at the Turning Point: Success and Crisis of a German Product Concept," *Actes du GERPISA*, no. 10 (1992): 91–108.

[10] Grace Ballor, Interview with Peter Tracey. Audio recording. Munich, October 24, 2016.

Productivity Agency in the context of the Marshall Plan, he grew the fledgling Volkswagen of America distributing company into one of the cornerstones of the Group's foreign sales subsidiaries; a subsequent leadership role at Continental AG then landed him the job as VW Group chairman in Wolfsburg in 1983.[11] Under his leadership, VW expanded rapidly, especially within Europe, and acquired SEAT (the Spanish state-owned company Sociedad Española de Automóviles de Turismo, S.A.) and Skoda in former Czechoslovakia to become a giant, multi-brand group. The two CEOs knew each other well; von Kuenheim described his "good connection" to Hahn during their respective chairmanships, their productive cooperation in regional industry associations in which they worked to coordinate the positions of European producers, and the candid conversations they have shared since they both retired in 1992 as the Single Market Program was declared complete and the EU was created.[12] For VW and BMW, the development of company strategies for the internal market were thus inextricably linked to the careers of these two executives, and their contrasting leadership styles and interpersonal connections reveal the complex dynamics of the industry en route to 1992.

To contextualize the managerial approaches and business strategies of von Kuenheim and Hahn within the evolution of the Single Market, this chapter begins by surveying the crises and competition that preceded the 1992 Program. It then discusses debates between firms, commissioners, and member states in the 1980s and 1990s about the policy framework for an internal car market – including the development of stricter common European emissions standards and a collective approach to the trade imbalance with Japan. Against this backdrop and as Eastern Europe also opened following the Soviet collapse, von Kuenheim and Hahn navigated their companies through the rising tide of global competition and the new opportunities and challenges created by an expanding internal market.

"Crisis" and Competition

Across Western Europe, the postwar boom of the 1950s characterized by "miraculous" economic growth was driven in large part by the car

[11] Famously, Hahn contracted the storied Manhattan-based ad agency Doyle Dane Bernbach to market VW "Beetles" to skeptical American drivers in the 1950s and 1960s. Campaigns like "Think Small" and "Lemon" propelled VW to success in the American market and made the creatives at Doyle Dane Bernbach advertising legends, as depicted on the popular television series *Mad Men*, AMC 2007–2015.

[12] Grace Ballor, Interview with Eberhard von Kuenheim. Audio recording. Munich, October 24, 2016.

industry. Among the economic consequences of the war in West Germany was the build up of industrial capacity, which primed the country for high-volume production.[13] Factories like Volkswagen's plant in Wolfsburg and BMW's motorcycle and engine works in Munich that had been coopted into the war effort of the late 1930s progressively returned to consumer-facing manufacturing in the aftermath of conflict. In fits and starts, under British and American occupation and then in the new Coal and Steel Community, these producers found new footing in a changing economic landscape. Rising income levels across Western Europe fueled middle-class demand for passenger cars, which, in turn, gave rise to suburbanization and the reorganization of societies. Demand-driven growth in the industry created a virtuous cycle of new middle-class jobs for employees who then became customers. During the 1950s and early 1960s, the demand for passenger cars grew at an average annual rate of 6 percent as many European households purchased their first vehicles.

American producers like Ford and General Motors (GM) built on their decades of experience in European markets to capitalize on the growing postwar car market in the region. Ford not only operated on six continents by the late 1950s, but it also showed itself to be even "more European than the Europeans" by mastering the EEC's new common market to such a degree that European officials decried American investment in the region as an industrial takeover requiring urgent collective solutions.[14] Despite the competition between the Community's "national champions" and the European subsidiaries of American producers, demand for cars in Europe remained strong enough to support growth for most producers in the EEC during the early and mid-1960s.

The rapid increase of motorization resulted in negative knock-on effects, however. Not only did more cars on the road mean more accidents, but air quality quickly worsened in areas with highest traffic.[15]

[13] Tamás Vonyó, *The Economic Consequences of the War: West Germany's Growth Miracle after 1945* (Cambridge: Cambridge University Press, 2018).

[14] On Ford's international expansion, see: Mira Wilkins and Frank Ernest Hill, *American Business Abroad: Ford on Six Continents* (Cambridge: Cambridge University Press, 2011); Hubert Bonin, Yannick Lung, and Stephen Tolliday, eds. *Ford, 1903–2003: The European History* (Paris: PLAGE, 2003). In 1980, the European Parliament noted the "irony that the most 'European' vehicle firms are Ford and General Motors." See: European Parliament: Committee on Economic and Monetary Affairs, rapporteur Mr. A. Bonaccini, "Report on the European Automobile Industry," December 15, 1980. Document 1-673/80, ["Bonaccini Report I"], AEI: 23.

[15] On standards and safety, see: Alice Milor, "Whose Business Is Road Safety?: From a Fragmented to an Integrated Approach in France and Europe (1972–1998)," *Transfers* 9, no. 3 (2019): 41–60; Marine Mougen-Toursel, "Demande de sécurité des véhicules et normes automobiles depuis les années 1960," in *L'Atelier du Centre de recherches historiques* 2 (2008).

As road safety and air quality became issues of high political salience and entered the realm of "noisy politics," regulators in the US, Japan, and Europe implemented new legislation for passenger cars.[16] The US passed a series of legislative measures, including the Clean Air Act of 1963, which provided research funding for emissions abating technologies and the Vehicle Air Pollution and Control Act of 1965. After the Environmental Protection Agency (EPA) was created, the US also introduced controversial amendments to the Clean Air Act in 1970, enabling the federal government to develop environmental regulations for industrial and vehicular emissions.[17] These rules affected both domestic producers and firms exporting goods into the US market. Similarly, severe air pollution in the 1960s had motivated the Japanese government to regulate car emissions as well.[18] In 1966, it became the first country in the world to introduce carbon monoxide emissions controls for automobiles. It also introduced lead-free petrol and supported the development of new engine technologies to reduce pollution.[19]

Collective coordination of auto safety and environmental standards had a longer history in Europe, although the region was slower to make collective progress than its single-state counterparts. The UN World Forum for Harmonization of Vehicle Regulations (WP 29), part of the UN Economic Commission on Europe (UNECE) framework, issued its

[16] For more on "quiet" vs. "noisy" politics, see: Pepper Culpepper, *Quiet Politics and Business Power: Corporate Control in Europe and Japan* (Cambridge; New York: Cambridge University Press, 2011). On the power of weak interests to bring issues like environmental regulation to the political agenda, see: Gunnar Trumbull, *Strength in Numbers: The Political Power of Weak Interests* (Cambridge, MA: Harvard University Press, 2012).

[17] In 2022, the US Supreme Court was poised to roll back this federal authority and potentially reverse decades of environmental legislation. See: Adam Liptak, "Supreme Court Considers Limiting EPA's Ability to Address Climate Change," *The New York Times*, February 28, 2022. For more on the history of US emissions policy, see: James E. Krier and Edmund Ursin, *Pollution and Policy: A Case Essay on California and Federal Experience with Motor Vehicle Air Pollution 1940–1975* (Berkeley: University of California Press, 1977).

[18] European Parliament: Committee on Economic and Monetary Affairs and Industrial Policy, "The Automobile Industry in the Community," (1985). Document A6170: AEI: 96.

[19] By 1978, Japan's emissions control standards had far surpassed any Western regulation, national or international. European Parliament, "The Automobile Industry in the Community: Evidence Given on the European Automobile Industry for the Hearing Organized by the Committee on Economic and Monetary Affairs and Industrial Policy," October 28–29, 1985, Economic Series no. 7, 12-1985, AEI; European Parliament, Committee on Economic and Monetary Affairs and Industrial Policy, "Bonaccini Report I," December 1980, 19. For more on Japanese emissions standards, see: David Bauner, "International Private and Public Reinforcing Dependencies for the Innovation of Automotive Emission Control Systems in Japan and USA," *Transportation Research Part A: Policy and Practice* 45, no. 5 (2011): 375–388.

first provisions on vehicle emissions in 1958 to which most European countries indicated an intention to conform with some reasonable delay.[20] As postwar growth began to slow, the US and Japan started setting stricter emissions regulations, and competition intensified in the shrinking car market, European governments implemented their own national regulations for passenger cars. West Germany adopted a car emissions law in 1968 to take effect in 1970, and France followed soon after with legislation limiting the carbon monoxide content of car exhaust and regulating the composition of exhaust gases from gasoline-fueled cars in two stages, by 1971 and 1972 respectively.[21] The result was a patchwork of disparate national approaches that threatened to make regional economies of scale extremely costly for producers already squeezed by the economic downturn. Furthermore, different national standards would undermine the EEC's efforts to create a common market and frustrated the efforts of European producers to expand across the region.

Amid rising competition over international emissions standards, economic downturn beginning in the late 1960s and 1970s brought an end to the "trente glorieuses," especially for carmakers. Auto sales in the FRG started to slump already in 1966, as the consumer market for passenger cars in the country underwent a major structural change from the booming growth of first-time purchases to the much slower growth rate of replacement buying. This shift in domestic consumer demand forced VW to reevaluate both its Fordist model of production, for which it relied on cheap labor and assembly lines, as well as its corporate structure of a central managerial core managing a wider periphery across the Americas and in South Africa.[22] Its acquisition of Audi in 1965 had achieved some diversification, but further restructuring was needed as sales declined across the VW Group. BMW's problems began even earlier than VW's, and its solutions proved more elusive. When von Kuenheim became chairman in January 1970, the company had been

[20] The UNECE emissions guidelines were adopted as recommended standards, rather than required regulations. For all of their relative easiness to develop, spared from the problems of intergovernmental bargaining, voluntary standards lacked effective enforcement mechanisms, which rendered them mostly toothless.

[21] Commission of the European Communities: "Proposition d'une directive du conseil concernant le rapprochement des législations des Etats membres relatives aux émissions de gaz pollutants en provenance des moteurs à allumage commandé équipant les véhicules à moteur," (1969), 1. Document COM(69)939, Vol. 1969/0163, Florence, HAEU.

[22] For a global history of Fordist production, see: Stefan Link, *Forging Global Fordism: Nazi Germany, Soviet Russia, and the Contest over the Industrial Order* (Princeton, NJ: Princeton University Press, 2020).

teetering on the verge of bankruptcy for over a decade. Weak motorcycle sales, the failure of its economy Isetta model, and the similarly unpopular launch of its larger sedans, and increasing competition all threatened to end the producer that had gotten its start equipping the wartime German *Luftwaffe*. After Herbert Quandt saved the company from a fire sale to Daimler in the late 1960s, introduced the 700 series, and acquired the small producer Glas, von Kuenheim was faced with the difficult task of identifying BMW's niche in a tightening European market. He charted a path forward that "made no competition to Ford and GM" and steered his company "away from mass production and away from Volkswagen by focusing instead on specialty cars."[23]

The oil shock of 1973 fundamentally changed both international competition and policymaking for the car industry.[24] Not only did the ensuing recession see the rate of new demand for cars drop to just 2.5 percent, but severe restrictions of the global supply of petroleum drove up the commodity's prices, causing the demand for large, gas-guzzling cars to fall sharply. American carmakers were hardest hit by this shift in consumer preferences, since their models tended to be larger and heavier than those produced by Japanese and European manufacturers, and "down-sizing" was a slow process requiring considerable investment. The consumers financially positioned to make new purchases demanded much more of their passenger cars than ever before, prioritizing greater fuel efficiency and advanced technologies. Japanese manufacturers utilizing the methods of lean production and flexible specialization were best positioned to respond quickly to changing consumer preferences.[25] Not only were their production methods more cost effective, but the lightweight, fuel-efficient models they produced became all the more attractive to American and European consumers, helping them to capture larger shares of markets on both sides of the Atlantic. In this global contest, European manufacturers faced a compounding disadvantage: for carmakers across the EEC, the production cost per unit had risen significantly with the wage increases and implementation of new social

[23] Grace Ballor, Interview with Eberhard von Kuenheim. Audio recording. Munich, October 24, 2016.

[24] It also changed the dynamics of the macroeconomy and motivated further integration in the European Community. See: Elisabetta Bini, Giuliano Garavini, and Federico Romero, eds., *Oil Shock: The 1973 Crisis and Its Economic Legacy*. (London: I.B. Tauris, 2016); Laurent Warlouzet, *Governing Europe in a Globalizing World: Neoliberalism and Its Alternatives following the 1973 Oil Crisis*, 1st ed. (New York; London: Routledge, 2018).

[25] Flexible specialization, whereby a firm's competitive strategy is oriented around diversification, innovation, and production speed, allowed firms to manufacture a diverse product line very quickly.

programs in the 1970s. Moreover, according to studies by the International Motor Vehicle Program at the Massachusetts Institute of Technology, European firms required twice as many hours to assemble a car as their Japanese competitors with automated factory lines.[26] Under such circumstances, the European industry as a whole struggled to compete.

Economic recovery in the late 1970s remained weak for many European carmakers. By then, the market had reached a saturation point, and even replacement purchases were deferred amid the downturn.[27] Demand for new cars across the region flatlined at just 0.5 percent. While there were 500 cars per 1000 inhabitants in the US in 1980, the EEC had only 300, and narrow cobblestone streets and dense urban centers in Western Europe made it unlikely for that number to grow much higher.[28] As Davignon put it: "everybody would like to have a Cadillac, yes, but was it made for European roads? The answer was no. … the big mistake of the US producers – and of the Europeans – was to believe that the cars could be identical on both continents."[29] High disposable income in the US made its export market a possible solution to the problem of declining demand in Europe, just as it had been for VW in the 1960s when Hahn introduced Americans to the classic Beetle. But the 1979 oil crisis caused further market contraction and permanently changed consumer preferences. US buyers faced the same economic constraints as their European counterparts, causing competition to further tighten between American, European, and Japanese producers. Moreover, the US's much more stringent emissions standards made it a difficult export market for European producers whose manufacturing and model ranges had largely been tailored to meet domestic norms.

Some European companies fared better than others in this new global business environment, and the balance of trade in vehicles for EEC countries varied greatly along national lines as a result. While the crises of the 1970s had zeroed out any export gains West Germany might have otherwise made between 1965 to 1985, it remained the largest net exporter of automobiles in the mid-1980s. VW led the way with its second generation of models, like the Golf launched in 1974, which

[26] Daniel T. Jones, "From Protection to Global Players: Corporate Strategy and the European Auto Industry," in *Corporate and Industry Strategies for Europe: Adaptations to the European Single Market in a Global Industrial Environment*, ed. Lars-Gunnar Mattsson and Bengt Stymne (New York: Elsevier, 1991). For more on Japanese productivity, see: Michael Cusumano, "Manufacturing Innovation: Lessons from the Japanese Auto Industry," *MIT Sloan Management Review* (Fall 1988).

[27] Gérard Lafay, Colette Herzog, et al., *Commerce international: La fin des avantages acquis* (Paris: Economica, 1989).

[28] European Parliament, "Bonaccini Report I," 14–15.

[29] Grace Ballor, Interview with Étienne Davignon, Audio recording. Brussels, June 16, 2016.

Table 4.1 *Balance of trade in cars, 1965–1986 (Measured in thousands)*

	FRG	France	Britain	Italy	Sweden	Japan	US
1965	1145	405	568	204	−114	88	−458
1970	1299	1084	532	240	66	706	−1728
1975	706	956	67	283	−35	1782	−1434
1980	847	846	−504	−396	16	4199	−2499
1985	1484	551	−864	−396	18	5099	−3694
1986	1298	562	−884	−199	29	5465	−4018

Table 4.1 Data adapted from the US Motor Vehicle Manufacturer Association and the French Chambre syndicale des constructeurs automobiles, as cited in: Sachwald, "De la libéralisation au néo-protectionnisme," 710.
Source: Ballor, G. (2022). Liberalisation or protectionism for the single market? European automakers and Japanese competition, 1985–1999. Business History, 65(2), 302–328. Reprinted by permission of Taylor & Francis Ltd.

was designed to capture the attention of those buyers looking to replace their family cars and work commute vehicles with a modest and fuel-economical upgrade. The launch of the Golf also marked the first time VW succeeded in "wresting the advance in production technology from the Japanese."[30] State interventions just kept the French industry afloat while revenues for its PSA Group and Renault declined sharply.[31] The situation was worse in Sweden, Britain, and Italy, where exports fell steeply during the 1970s and never recovered, as shown in Table 4.1. By 1980, Italy became a net importer of Japanese economy cars when even its flagship producer FIAT could not compete with foreign imports. But it was Britain that experienced the most dramatic shift in the EEC, nearly trebling its net imports by the 1980s.

By contrast, Japan increased its balance of trade in autos significantly. Not only had auto exports been a core growth strategy of its neomercantilist political economy, but the innovative production methods used by Japanese producers enabled them to manufacture more cost effectively and more quickly than any other carmakers in the world.[32] Moreover, the lightweight-fuel-efficient models they produced became all the more attractive to European customers in the wake of the

[30] Volkswagen, "1987: Fifty Million Volkswagens," *1986 Annual Report* (Wolfsburg: VW, 1986): 56.

[31] For a detailed analysis of the French approach to competition with Japan, see Alice Milor, "Ownership Matters: French Governments and Automotive Industrialists Facing the Japanese Challenge, 1974–1986," *Business History Review* (published ahead of print September 13, 2022), accessed November 4, 2022.

[32] For more analysis of Japanese industrial policy and an explanation of the Japanese 'miracle,' see: Chalmers Johnson, *MITI and the Japanese Miracle: The Growth of Industrial Policy, 1925–1975* (Stanford: Stanford University Press, 1982).

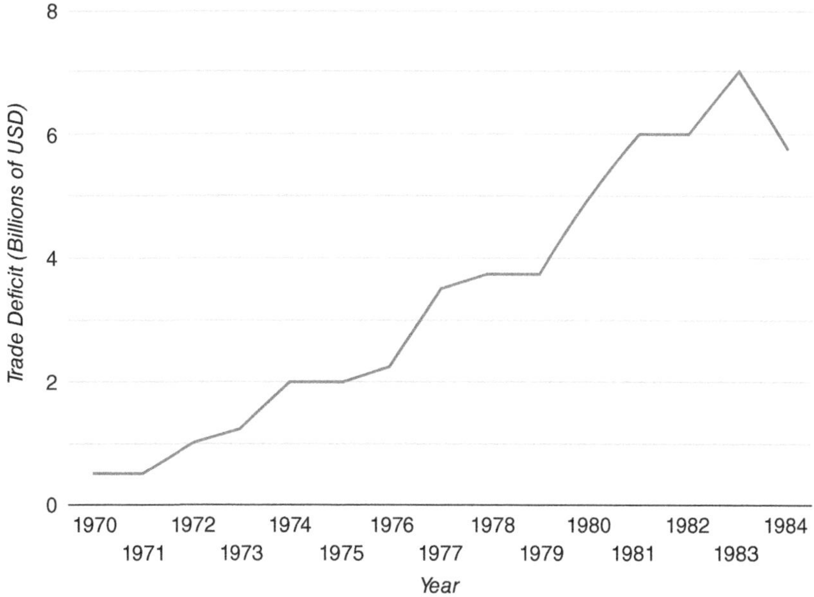

Figure 4.1 EEC trade deficit with Japan, 1970–1984. Adapted from IMF data published by: Bertoldi, "Forty Years of EU–Japan Economic Relations," 186.
Source: Ballor, G. (2022). Liberalisation or protectionism for the single market? European automakers and Japanese competition, 1985–1999. Business History, 65(2), 302–328. Reprinted by permission of Taylor & Francis Ltd.

oil shocks helping them to capture increasing market share. By the early 1980s, this surge of auto exports, along with those of Japan's booming high-tech industry, resulted in a growing trade deficit between the EEC and Japan, as shown in Figure 4.1. Between 1970 and 1984, the total value of Japanese exports to the EEC multiplied by a factor of ten, more than double the rate of imports.[33] Japan had emerged from the rubble of war an industrial dynamo, while Europe, the birthplace of the automobile, experienced relative industrial decline. That Japanese manufacturers could produce vehicles with just half the labor hours of their European competitors exacerbated the European industry's relative decline.[34] By the 1980s,

[33] Moreno Bertoldi, "Forty Years of EU–Japan Economic Relations: Were They Driven by Trade and Exchange Rate Concerns?" in *EU–Japan Relations, 1970–2012: From Confrontation to Global Partnership*, ed. Jörn Keck, Dimitri Vanoverbeke, and Franz Waldenberger (London: Routledge, 2013): 186.

[34] This is according to studies conducted by the International Motor Vehicle Program at the Massachusetts Institute of Technology. For more, see: Daniel T. Jones, Daniel Roos, and James P. Womack, *The Machine That Changed the World: The Story of Lean Production*. (New York: Harper Perennial, 1991).

European automakers collectively laid off more than 400,000 employees – almost one quarter of the sector's total employment – reflecting both increased manufacturing productivity and reduced demand for European cars. And with nearly 10% of all jobs in the EEC either directly or indirectly dependent on the motor vehicle sector and high unemployment a primary policy concern of the Commission, as explained in Chapter 1, the decline of the European auto industry was not taken lightly.[35]

Debating Market Solutions

The decline of the European auto industry relative to foreign competition became a chief concern for EEC policymakers in the early 1980s.[36] The EEC had recognized the importance of the car industry earlier in its articulation of a Community industrial policy in the Colonna Report of 1970 and in the Davignon Plan from 1978. The Commission had also authored several directives aimed at strengthening carmaking in the region, including two foundational pieces of legislation on EEC type approval and common exhaust emissions.[37] These efforts proved moderately successful: As of 1979, forty-four directives had been approved for the harmonization of car standards, instilling confidence in the liberal German cabinet member Martin Bangemann that with just three more directives the fully harmonized "Eurocar" would become a reality.[38] Such optimism reflected both the attendant shortcomings of early EEC political economy described in Chapter 1 and the shortsightedness of policymakers who presumed that the Treaty of Rome would "spontaneously create a single market" and that full liberalization would result in

[35] Hitoshi Suzuki, "The New Politics of Trade: EU–Japan," *Journal of European Integration* 39, no. 7 (2017): 876.

[36] That these debates about creating a single European car market intensified in the early 1980s and were rooted in finding solutions to the threat of globalization challenges two of the narratives discussed in Chapter 1: first, the view that integration was largely a product of interstate bargaining; second, the perception that the launch of the 1992 Program was "sudden" and "unexpected" in 1985. In fact, the plan to create an internal car market formalized by the SEA was the culmination of years of reports, discussions, and negotiations involving European institutions and industry leaders.

[37] These directives were 70/156/EEC on type approval, implementing mutual recognition for autos across the Community, and 70/220/EEC on emissions.

[38] For more on the debate about creating a "Eurocar," see: Marine Moguen-Toursel, "Emergence and Transfer of Vehicle Safety Standards: Why We Still Do Not Have Global Standards," *Enterprises et histoire* 1, no. 51 (2008): 88–102. Bangemann would go on to become a commissioner himself during the Delors presidency, in which he was instrumental in the negotiations around the EC's emissions scheme and its Elements of Consensus agreement with Japan. See: Grace Ballor, "Liberalisation or Protectionism for the Single Market? European Automakers and Japanese Competition, 1985–1999," *Business History* 65, no. 2 (2022): 302–328.

prosperity.[39] In the wake of the second oil shock and as global competition intensified, it became clear that further interventions were needed – not just to integrate auto industries in the region, but to ensure their survival. The major economic importance of the car industry also came into sharper focus with GDP and employment in jeopardy, and the institutions of the EEC increasingly saw the industry as the "keystone of the European industrial structure."[40] The European Parliament and Commission debated how to bolster European industry against foreign competition while mitigating the "recurrent national temptation to seek national solutions." Such discussions reflected the wider shift described in Chapter 2: Legislative harmonization and technical standardization became chief priorities, as did the need for a common position on Japanese imports and investment.

In December 1980, the Parliament's Committee on Economic and Monetary Affairs drafted a report on the auto industry, expressing concerns about the decline of European producers in previous years relative to their Japanese competitors and the ways national governments in the EEC had undermined multilateralism by seeking unilateral solutions. Rapporteur Aldo Bonaccini communicated the Committee's anxieties about how "certain developing countries such as Brazil, Mexico, and South Korea, [we]re creating the nucleus for what could well be major industries of the future," and laying foundations for the development of a "world car," a vehicle with imminently interchangeable parts meeting the highest global standards such that it could compete on any market.[41] Fear of nationalism met fear of globalization, with the social fabric of the Community hanging in the balance through the "potential loss of jobs" and economic dynamism. The Committee stressed the urgency for its counterparts at the Commission to make five major interventions: the elimination of technical barriers to trade, allowing "smaller specialist firms to flourish and thereby create jobs and contribute the the competitiveness of the entire industry"; a common research and development program; encouraging concentrations as a way to end fragmentation in the regional industry; consultation of social partners to ensure that changes implemented included support for workers; and the common market needed to be "afforded adequate protection" from Japanese competition.

[39] European Parliament: Committee on External Economic Relations, rapporteur Mr. R. E. Filippi, "Report on Imports of Japanese Cars into the EEC," Document 1-997/82, December 15, 1982. ["Filippi Report"] AEI: 10.

[40] European Parliament, "Filippi Report," 10.

[41] European Parliament, "Bonaccini Report I," 6–10.

Although the Bonaccini Report of 1980 did not itself produce a new industrial policy, the Commission and Council did take up the Parliament's plea to address the trade imbalance with Japan. First, the Commission conducted a detailed study on the future of European automaking in 1981, in which it outlined challenges the industry faced and the need for collective intervention.[42] Then, at the GATT negotiations in 1982, the Council sought recourse through Article 23, which provided for consultations between parties in the event of an imbalance of trade benefits resulting from one side failing to carry out its obligations. Initially, these negotiations proved as unsuccessful as the consultative meetings in Geneva held the year before.[43] Out of growing concern for the industry and perceiving a time of "imponderable" uncertainty given the "profound changes in the world economic situation," the Parliament's Committee on External Trade Policy authored a 1982 report on Japanese imports.[44] The Filippi Report, also named for its rapporteur, echoed Bonaccini's insistence on the need for a new common industrial policy, cooperation among European producers, coordinated research and development, and the completion of a single car market by removing obstacles to intra-Community trade. But its focus was on the imperative of temporary limitations on foreign competition in the EEC. It called for acceptance of the fact that "the period of restructuring needed to restore the competitive position of the European car industry must be accompanied by appropriate safeguard measures."[45] The policy dichotomy of simultaneous internal liberalization and external protectionism was taking shape.[46]

When the volume of Japanese auto imports peaked again in 1983, Bonaccini penned yet another report on the state of the industry for his Parliamentary Committee.[47] This time, the Committee asked the Commission to respond expediently to the "poor financial performances," of firms in the "still fragmented" market, experiencing a

42 European Commission, "Structure et perspectives d'avenir de l'industrie automobile européenne 1981," (COM (81)3 1 7final), INV 0015/2019 no. 8 (1977–1983), Florence, HAEU.

43 European Parliament, "Filippi Report," 25. 44 Ibid., 9. 45 Ibid., 27–29.

46 Many accounts locate the development of EC-wide protections for the European automobile industry and the development of a "Fortress Europe" in the late 1980s and early 1990s, as discussed in Chapter 1. In fact, the European Parliament's trade committee called for such protections a decade earlier at the start of the 1980s.

47 European Parliament: Committee on Economic and Monetary Affairs, "Report on the State of the European Automobile Industry," Document 1-1505/83, March 12, 1984. ["Bonaccini Report II"] AEI. It is important to note that these Parliamentary Committee reports predated the Stuttgart Declaration, in which the Council treated market integration as a low priority compared with its other social and political objectives and the goal of a common foreign policy.

"sustained offensive by Japanese exports."[48] It warned against the "intensification of protectionist measures" including unilateral environmental protections, and appealed for solutions to the "rapid technological changes and sharp fall in employment."[49] According to the Committee, only a realistic Community strategy that coordinated research and development, took a global approach to environmental, safety, and energy regulations, and was predicated on common competition and external trade policies would preserve the industry and the societies dependent on it.[50] Cross-border mergers were offered as a way to mitigate fragmentation and rectify imbalances between the strength of British and German industries and weakness of Italian producers, for example. In these three reports, all of which predated the SEA, the Parliament laid out a program to grow the European auto industry through industrial policies as well as a theory of the case for market protectionism. The EEC also made a voluntary export restraint (VER) agreement with Japan in 1983 after the US's 1981 VER pushed Japanese producers to "dump" their goods on European markets.[51]

Carmakers were equally proponents of cooperation and consolidation across the EEC. Those like Volvo and Renault with membership in the ERT joined with other industrial corporations like Siemens, Nestlé, and Philips to advocate for European research and development and increased business across the EEC and appeal for greater regional integration.[52] The transnational BIA of automakers in the EEC, the Committee of Common Market Automobile Constructors (CCMC), also met regularly with the Commission with appeals for collective solutions to fragmentation and global competition.[53] In the CCMC, Hahn and von Kuenheim found a forum for their intersecting corporate interests and a direct means of engaging with regional policymakers.

In 1984, the EEC's VER with Japan finally decreased the trade deficit by 15 percent. While this was seen as a small victory for those concerned about the persistent trade imbalance, it was quickly overshadowed by the growing problem of market fragmentation caused by divergent national emissions standards. Under pressure from both its green parties and its leading carmakers, Germany became the strictest regulator of auto

[48] European Parliament, "Bonaccini Report II," 6. [49] Ibid., 6. [50] Ibid., 7–13.

[51] Gregory S. Kurey, "GATT and the VRA: Japanese Automobile Imports and Trade Protectionism," *Dickinson Journal of International Law* (*Penn State International Law Review*) 5, no. 1 (1986): 51–80.

[52] See Chapter 2 for more on the ERT.

[53] For a history of the CCMC and its membership, see: Ballor, "Liberalization or Protectionism," 5–6.

emissions in the EEC in the mid-1980s.[54] When the US issued more stringent emissions rules requiring catalytic converters to be installed in a majority of vehicles, called "US83" for their implementation deadline, the German government moved quickly to align its national policies with those of its firms' largest overseas export market and announced plans to mandate the use of catalytic converters in passenger cars by 1986.[55] These devices, designed to reduce toxic gases and pollutants from internal combustion engines through redox reactions, were extremely costly and compromised fuel economy, however, and they required a wholesale switch to unleaded gasoline. The German government reasoned that its automakers could absorb the change because leading producers like VW and BMW had already begun to integrate catalytic converters into their latest models, and suppliers like Bosch were prepared for a large-scale rollout of the new technology. Meanwhile, specialist producers like BMW and Daimler-Benz publicly welcomed stricter emissions standards, giving the domestic government confidence that its approach would give its auto industry a comparative advantage over competitors. But even profitable German carmakers like Mercedes expressed concern about the high cost of the devices, prompting the German government to offer fiscal incentives to entice German customers to buy "clean cars."[56]

A debate erupted in the Commission about whether this German fiscal scheme was a violation of the Community's common commercial policy and how the EEC should move forward together, given the divergent approaches of other member states and their national champion firms. Italian and French producers resisted proposals for new, stricter standards since their profit margins were too narrow to accommodate the

[54] For more on international vehicle emissions standards, see: Grace Ballor and Mattias Näsman, "The Car Industry and Climate Change: The Historical Political Economy of a Green Transition," in *Climate Change and Business: Historical Perspectives*, ed. Teresa da Silva Lopes, Paul Duguid, and Robert Fredona (London; New York: Routledge, 2025): chapter 2.

[55] The actual cost of catalytic converters to producers varied widely, with volume producers expecting a 4–7% increase in the total production cost per vehicle and smaller manufacturers facing even higher costs, according to Näsman, "The Political Economy of Emissions Standards," 247. For more on Bosch's position, see: Samuel Klebaner and Sigfrido Ramírez Pérez, "Managing Technical Changes from the Scales of Legal Regulation: German Clean Cars Against the European Pollutant Emissions Regulations in the 1980s," Managem*ent & Organizational History* 14, no. 4 (2019): 450–451.

[56] Much to BMW's surprise, the German government offered incentives to diesel-fueled cars in addition to those with catalytic converters and powered by unleaded gas. See: BMW, "Varied Development on Foreign Markets," *1985 Annual Report* (Munich: BMW, 1985): 14.

additional cost per car fitted with a catalytic converter.[57] British carmakers had bet on lean-burn diesel engines, which were cheap and improved fuel economy but met only the lowest emissions standards.[58] After extensive legal review, which tested whether the German proposal adhered to or violated the Treaty of Rome's Article 92 on state aid, Germany was forced to drop both its proposal to adopt US83 standards and its corresponding incentive scheme.[59] In the wake of this debate and in an effort to move forward with a collective approach to car emissions, the Commission issued two new common measures related to octane levels and fuel economy.[60] More importantly, it struck a compromise through the "Luxembourg Agreement" of 1985, which developed a three-tiered Clean Car Directive to introduce common emissions limits and catalytic converters in stages according to engine size.[61] By setting standards less stringent than the German proposal, the Commission pragmatically prioritized market integration over environmental protections.[62]

European producers expressed wide ranging opinions of the new emissions directive. French and Italian carmakers viewed even the compromise as a threat to their profitability. The CCMC, meant to express the shared views of manufacturers in the EEC, became a megaphone for the French position with M. Perrin-Pelletier of Peugeot as its spokesman on the subject. He argued that the directive would "increase the cost of cars and their maintenance" and "cause a divergence in emissions standards in Western Europe, both within and outside the Community. … All this implies a further step away from one unified car market in Western

[57] European Parliament, "Bonaccini Report I," 19.

[58] For more on the member state debates about lean-burn engines and catalytic converters, see: Roland, *Vehicle of Influence*, chapter 4, pp. 85–110.

[59] While Commissioner for competition (DG IV) Peter Sutherland found no violation of Article 92, industry Commissioner Karl-Heinz Narjes determined that Germany's requirement of catalytic converters and fiscal incentive would give its own domestic industry an undue advantage since German producers had invested most in the new technologies. Germany unsuccessfully appealed this decision on the basis that the cost of a catalytic converter far exceeded the proposed fiscal incentive.

[60] European Commission, "Octane Level Set for Lead-Free Petrol," October 17, 1984, PSP-405, Florence, HAEU.

[61] The Luxembourg Agreement was struck in June 1985, one of the most consequential months in integration history, when the Commission presented its white paper on the Single Market to the Council's Intergovernmental Conference in Milan in preparation for the SEA to be signed that October.

[62] I developed this argument about the prioritization of market integration over environmental protections in: Grace Ballor, "Liberal Environmentalism: The Public-Private Production of European Emissions Standards," *Business History Review* 97, no. 3 (2023): 575–601.

Europe."[63] He dismissed the directive as a political decision rather than a necessary one, since "the causal link between acid rain or forest damage and emissions from motor vehicles is not proven."[64] Better fuel economy was the obviously superior solution in this Francophone expression of the transnational industry group's position.

Despite membership in the CCMC, German producers broke with their counterparts on the emissions issue. VW, which found Germany's unilateral approach "unsettling," applauded the EEC's Clean Car Directive as a "major step" toward common standards, which promised to reduce barriers to trade between member states. Not only did VW support market integration, but it recognized its own comparative advantage over regional competitors since it had already retooled its production according to US83 standards. European consumers increasingly wanted 'greener' models as well. After the uncertainty surrounding the Commission's debate kept consumers from buying cars "until the European authorities had reached an agreement about new emissions standards," West German customers increased their purchases of Volkswagens with catalytic converters by 47.2 percent in 1986 alone.[65] BMW also welcomed the EEC's move beyond unilateralism, which required manufacturers "to offer cars both with progressive and conventional exhaust technology," thereby increasing costs and hurting consumers.[66] Amid the Commission debate, the EEC had seen a 9 percent decrease in new registrations in Germany and a similar decline in markets with strictest environmental protections including Switzerland, Sweden, and Austria.[67] But it saw "the aim to preserve the European market by means of a uniform solution" as a means of securing customers across the region.[68] When Denmark bucked consensus to block the Luxembourg Agreement and the EEC was again without a common approach to emissions, BMW called for an return to collective negotiations for regional standards.[69] Ultimately, as I have argued elsewhere, the desire to complete

[63] European Parliament, "The Automobile Industry in the EC," 3. [64] Ibid., 2.

[65] Volkswagen, "West German Market Unsettled in First Half," *1985 Annual Report* (Wolfsburg: VW, 1985): 11; Volkswagen, "Audi AG: The New Audi 80 Was Well Received by the Market," *1986 Annual Report* (Wolfsburg: VW, 1986): 63.

[66] BMW, "Political Background for the German Automobile Industry," *1986 Annual Report* (Munich: BMW, 1986): 11.

[67] BMW, "Varied Development on Foreign Markets," *1985 Annual Report* (Munich: BMW, 1985): 14.

[68] BMW, "German Automobile Industry – All Set for the Car with Low Emission Levels," *1985 Annual Report* (Munich: BMW, 1985): 10; BMW, "Political Background for the German Automobile Industry," *1986 Annual Report* (Munich: BMW, 1986): 11.

[69] Before the SEA reforms, policy approval required unanimity among member states. Thinking the Luxembourg Agreement did not go far enough, Denmark withheld its

the Single Market motivated the Commission and the European auto industry alike to pursue "liberal environmentalism," an embrace of stricter common emissions standards in order to ensure the integrity of the internal market and the global competitiveness of European cars.[70]

In October 1985, the European Council signed the SEA, reforming the intergovernmental structure of the Community for the first time since the Treaty of Rome. The introduction of qualified majority voting (QMV) did away with the previous requirement of unanimity and empowered the Commission to move quickly with the Single Market Program it had outlined for the Council in the White Paper on Completing the Internal Market earlier that summer.[71] The white paper committed the Community to integration, which it defined in broad terms of economic openness and regulatory harmonization. As such, it made very few mentions of the auto industry aside from a modest table on "The Removal of Technical Barriers" in the Motor Vehicle Sector and a timeline for approximating laws regulating passenger cars.[72]

To fill this gap, the Parliamentary Committee on Economic and Monetary Affairs and Industrial Policy, which had been tasked with developing specific policy recommendations for the car industry, undertook an extensive review of "The Automobile Industry in the European Community."[73] The review surveyed academics, trade unions, suppliers, importers, consumer advocates, environmental groups, producers, and business associations based in the EEC – as well as foreign companies and associations with interests in European markets, like Saab, Ford, General Motors, Toyota, and the Japan Automobile Manufacturers Association (JAMA) – on three thematic pillars of issues: the economic and industrial implications of the Commission's efforts to implement a "Clean Car" directive on emissions standards; remaining barriers to a common market in cars; and implications for the structure of the Community auto industry due to increased internationalization.[74] The wide range of responses illuminated the ways stakeholders viewed the

consent, blocking the deal until 1987. On BMW's position, see: BMW, *1986 Annual Report*.

70 Ballor, "Liberal Environmentalism." For an earlier use of this term, see: Steven Bernstein, *The Compromise of Liberal Envrionmentalism*. (New York: Columbia University Press, 2001).

71 Commission of the European Communities, "Completing the Internal Market: A White Paper from the Commission to the Council," Milan, June 28–29, 1985.

72 European Commission, "Completing the Internal Market," 15.

73 The SEA had also augmented the powers of the Parliament and assigned it a larger role in developing Community policy. European Parliament, "The Automobile Industry in the EC," foreword.

74 European Parliament, "The Automobile Industry in the EC," foreword.

prospect of a single car market and helped the Committee identify four main challenges the European auto industry faced in the mid 1980s: overcapacity, fragmentation, Japanese penetration, and competitiveness. These four issues would drive both Commission policy and firm strategy over the course of the 1992 Program.

Strategies for a Single Car Market

Business support for the Single Market was not monolithic, even among firms in the same industry. Shortly after the 1992 Program was launched, the CCMC drafted a white paper to the Commission, raising concerns about the possible consequences of the SEA on their industry.[75] Like other BIAs, carmakers in the group worried that "the opening of the Community market will operate above all to the advantage of foreign companies" in much the same way the nascent EEC and its customs union had been a boon to American industrial firms in the 1950s and 1960s.[76] Collectively, members of the CCMC thought the SEA had formalized free market principles that would render European automakers all the more vulnerable to outside competition once the market was complete and protections were removed. It was no coincidence that Umberto Agnelli of FIAT spearheaded the white paper, since it was he who had appeared before the Parliamentary Committee just months before, arguing that the decline of the European auto industry was "largely because of the penetration of Japanese manufacturers," and demanding that transplants – cars made in the EEC by foreign companies – have at least 80 percent locally-produced content so as to contribute to rather than exploit European economies.[77]

Even though they were signatories of the white paper, VW and BMW expressed much different views outside of the forum of the CCMC. VW had already established a partnership with Nissan in Japan by the time the SEA was signed, and Hahn cheered progress toward uniform technical standards, even advocating for the EEC's adoption of US norms so that transatlantic harmonization could facilitate its creation of a "world car."[78] von Kuenheim also welcomed "the creation of a common European internal market with free and uniform trade," and insisted that

[75] European Parliament, "Livre blanc du Comité des constructeurs automobiles du marché européen," (December 1986), PE2–16864/16878, Florence, HAEU.

[76] European Commission, "1992: The Impact on the Outside World, part of The European Community in a Changing World: Speech by Willy De Clercq EC-Commissioner for External Relations and Commercial Policy," KM-257. (Buenos Aires, August 2, 1988), HAEU: 1.

[77] European Parliament, "The Automobile Industry in the EC," 90.

[78] Ibid., 43.

open trade was essential "both among its members and with others."[79] That the Federal Republic of Germany was the only EEC member state not to impose bilateral restrictions on Japanese auto imports and investment reflected the interests of German producers in "free access to all markets of the world" and their rejection of protectionism by both the EEC and Japan, from whom they demanded reciprocal market access.

As the Commission worked to implement the nearly 300 directives required to complete the internal market and to incorporate the Parliamentary Committee's findings, carmakers adjusted their strategies to reflect the changing business environment. Under the leadership of Hahn and von Kuenheim, VW and BMW took different approaches to international expansion and reorganization of production in the context of market integration: VW's internationalization strategy revolved around its production, while BMW internationalized its distribution networks. Their interests converged on the issue of common technical and environmental standards, and they worked together to develop consensus for the European auto industry on competition with Japan. For all of their differences, VW and BMW followed the same trend observed in Chapter 3: They regionalized in the context of the 1992 Program. This Europeanization and the foundation they laid in the EEC in the 1980s and 1990s positioned them to globalize by the turn of the millennium.[80]

Among Europe's volume producers in the 1980s, VW inhabited a middling position between those highly dependent on one national market like FIAT, Peugeot, and Renault, and those whose interests were diversely spread across the region like General Motors Europe. The geography of its sales distribution thus more closely resembled those of American multinational producers in Europe than those of its European counterparts. Because of its concomitant strength in the West German market and its export-orientation, VW occupied a central place in the German political economy of the late twentieth century, thanks to its geographically diverse portfolio, commitment to quality production, and investment in new technologies. Such market diversity also allowed VW to weather the economic downturn of the mid-1980s quite well; even as the growth in world trade declined precipitously in 1985 and 1986, VW beat its previous output record and restored its production

[79] BMW, "The Automobile Industry: Driving Force of the World Economy," *1987 Annual Report* (Munich: BMW, 1986): 7.

[80] The auto industry significantly restructured in the late twentieth and early twenty-first centuries. See: David Bailey, Alex de Ruyter, Jonathan Michie, and Peter Tyler, "Global Restructuring and the Auto Industry," *Cambridge Journal of Regions, Economy and Society* 3, no. 3 (2010): 311–318.

capacity to levels not achieved since before the second oil shock six years earlier.[81]

Most of this increase came from its Western European business in Italy, France, Britain, Spain, and Austria, while its markets in Nigeria, Mexico, Argentina, and South Africa had slumped amid an "extremely difficult economic situation," leading to plant closures and "considerable losses."[82] The failure of the Austral Plan in Argentina, long delivery delays in Brazil, a declining overall market in Mexico, a drastic drop in the price of oil in Nigeria, and the poor performance of the Group's assembly plant in Westmoreland, Pennsylvania all prompted VW to deglobalize in favor of regionalization.[83] It sold the US assembly plant, divested from South Africa, and partnered with Ford in order to sustain its Latin American business through a joint venture in Brazil called Autolatina.[84] As a result, the geography of its plan for "optimizing worldwide manufacturing" increasingly resembled a map of the European continent. Progressively between 1980 and 1987, the language it used to describe its operations shifted from "global" to "European." It also began to refer to its market forecast explicitly in terms of the EEC, attributing rising demand and economic growth in the late 1980s to "the prospect of a Single European Market."[85] VW did continue to produce cars in Mexico, Brazil, and South Africa during the late 1980s, and it also formed a manufacturing partnership in Shanghai when China began to open its economy. But in 1992, a full 85 percent of its total production was completed in the European region.[86]

On Hahn's third day as chairman of VW in 1982, he and his colleague W. P. Schmidt began to discuss the possibility of acquiring a producer in another Western European country to anchor Hahn's chief "Strategie der Europäisierung," his goal of Europeanizing the company.[87] Research on Alfa Romeo dissuaded Hahn from pursuing its acquisition, but a

[81] Volkswagen, "Social Rate of Growth on the World Economy," *1985 Annual Report* (Wolfsburg: VW, 1985): 9.

[82] Volkswagen, "Substantial Growth in North America; Differing Trends in Other Regions," *1985 Annual Report* (Wolfsburg: VW, 1985): 14.

[83] Much of Bernhard Rieger's book on Volkswagen deals with VW's early history and its efforts to expand globally in the 1950s and 1960s. See: Rieger, *The People's Car: A Global History of the Volkswagen Beetle* (Cambridge, MA: Harvard University Press, 2013).

[84] Volkswagen, "Structural Improvements within the Group," *1987 Annual Report* (Wolfsburg: VW, 1987): 11.

[85] Volkswagen, "World Economy Still Exhibiting Upward Trend," *1988 Annual Report* (Wolfsburg: VW, 1988): 10.

[86] Volkswagen, *1992 Annual Report* (Wolfsburg: VW, 1988): 25-46.

[87] Carl Hahn, *Meine Jahre mit Volkswagen* (Dresden: Signum, 2005): 138–141. Throughout his memoire, Hahn describes his goal of Europeanizing the company, especially by establishing production and capturing market share in Western Europe in

chance meeting with Juan Antonio Antoñanzas, the head of SEAT, showed promise. Hahn launched assembly of the Passat model in Spain in 1983 and production of the Polo in 1984 through partnerships with SEAT. Then, after Spain and Portugal had emerged from military dictatorships, both countries joined the EEC in 1986. Portugal's smaller market and weaker economy attracted less foreign investment early on, but Spain quickly became a popular destination for international capital.[88] Hahn saw Spain's membership in the EEC as investment insurance, and he made plans to move forward with VW's purchase of a 51 percent stake in SEAT, to which King Juan Carlos and Queen Sofía gave their blessing.[89] This acquisition allowed the VW Group to strengthen its position in the lower model ranges, thus balancing out Audi's focus on the luxury market and Volkswagen's middle range line – a true "multi-marque" strategy.[90] That SEAT finally turned a profit in 1988 after an eleven-year string of losses provided "clear proof that the right strategic decisions ha[d] been taken" in acquiring the company.[91] Such success, underpinned by Spain's surging growth rate and booming sales market, warranted the Group's commitment to invest another 6 million Deutsche marks in SEAT in the following years to build a new, modern assembly plant in preparation for the coming Single European Market.[92] VW representatives wrote with pride – and some naiveté – about having helped link Spain to Europe with anecdotes about "German dictionaries on Spanish desks" at SEAT and "German colleagues learning to speak Castilian;" this mutual dependence was, they explained, "a step towards the European Community of 1992," and SEAT was the "European idea already being put into practice."[93]

VW radically transformed its production methods during the 1980s through automation, modernization, and rationalization. New German plants at Kassel, Emden, and Brunswick set a model for other plants in

the 1980s and then moving into Eastern Europe in the 1990s. These strategies paved the way, in his words, for the eventual globalization of the VW Group.

88 In the late 1980s and early 1990s, both VW and BMW partnered with Ford Europe in Portugal to develop a "PeopleMover."

89 Volkswagen, "Investment in SEAT," *1985 Annual Report* (Wolfsburg: VW, 1985): 13.

90 Volkswagen, "Europe'92 – A Totally New Dimension," *1988 Annual Report* (Wolfsburg: VW, 1988): 17

91 Volkswagen, "A Profit for the First Time in Eleven Years," *1988 Annual Report* (Wolfsburg: VW, 1988): 62.

92 Volkswagen, "SEAT prepares for the Single European Market through Targeted Expansion," *1991 Annual Report* (Wolfsburg: VW, 1991): 38.

93 Volkswagen, "A Piece of Unity – With No Politics Involved," *1987 Annual Report* (Wolfsburg: VW, 1987): 75.

the Group to incorporate the latest technologies.[94] From clamping and welding robots to automated gearbox assembly to computer aided design (CAD), VW saw automation as the best way to rationalize its production. By 1988, 2,626 industrial robots were in use across its production plants, most of which it had also self-produced. These efforts replaced human labor and required huge capital injections, which were offset by further reducing the Group's workforce, thereby undercutting the EEC's objective to create "durable [industrial] jobs" described in Chapter 1. Along with implementing flexible specialization and just-in-time manufacturing models, this lean approach to rationalization helped VW remain competitive against Japanese manufacturers, even if it came at a cost to jobs.[95]

The acquisition of SEAT, which was finalized just as the 50 millionth Volkswagen car rolled off the assembly line, also launched the VW Group's strategy of "interlinked production," augmenting its total manufacturing capacity. Although its production networks reflected its purchasing approach of "global sourcing," only a fraction of component and spare parts, assemblies, and CKD kits were actually completed outside the EEC. In Europe, VW's interlinked production strategy was further strengthened through the Group's joint ventures in Comecon countries. It had purchased around 50 million Deutsche marks per year of parts from the region since the mid-1970s and signed a general agreement with Hungary in 1986, which allowed for the expansion of existing supply links there.[96] Soon, VW also began procuring engines from an East German plant in Chemnitz, Hahn's hometown.[97] It also augmented its production capacity by partnering with other European carmakers: It joined forces with Renault to manufacture gearboxes for their Polo, Golf, R14 and R15 models and partnered with Daimler-Benz in co-ownership of the DAUG electrical research company.[98] By the late 1980s, VW's multi-layered manufacturing spanned the region. The enlarged VW Group restructured its sales and distribution to suit the new business environment of the Single Market. By centralizing its sales and service in the region and creating a direct dealer system of importers

[94] In 1992, VW boasted that the Kassel plant was the largest catalytic converter factory in the world.

[95] Volkswagen, "Advanced Production Technology Strengthens Competitive Position," *1990 Annual Report* (Wolfsburg: VW, 1990): 39.

[96] Volkswagen, "Opening Up New Markets," *1986 Annual Report* (Wolfsburg: VW, 1986): 10.

[97] Rich Lyons, Interview with Carl Hahn. Video broadcast. Berkeley Haas, October 26, 2011.

[98] European Parliament, "The Automobile Industry in the EC," 67.

for VW, Audi, and SEAT models into Italy, France, and Spain, it made concrete its claim that "[o]ur 'domestic market' today is not just West Germany, but the whole of Europe."[99] Aiming to "make full use of the opportunities offered by the Single European Market" it also built the Europcar rental fleet, complete with cooperation agreements with European airlines, travel agents, and credit card companies.[100]

While VW expanded its production in the enlarged EEC through acquisitions and partnerships, BMW focused first on growing its distribution networks. Its specialty niche and quality profit model made the company reliant on export markets, especially in the EEC.[101] But its approach to foreign distribution in the 1960s had been to sell through local importers.[102] Early in his career as CEO, von Kuenheim had recognized two problems with such a model: first, that "importers made the money, rather than our company," and second, that the producer had no means by which to guarantee quality service for the life of the vehicle.[103] As one dealer in France quipped: "BMW drivers expect not only a perfect product, but also perfect service."[104] von Kuenheim resolved to build a "European Delivery Plan" to centralize all sales and service, and by the mid-1980s, BMW had cultivated a network of 4,400 authorized dealers worldwide, which sold 90 percent of all exported vehicles.[105] These SMEs served as the backbone of the company's sales operation and, because they were integrated into a centralized network, played a crucial role in ensuring the brand's uniform image across the region, from the Netherlands to Austria.[106] National import taxes and nontariff barriers sometimes tripled the landed consumer cost of an imported BMW, however, motivating von Kuenheim to be a vocal

[99] Volkswagen, "Europe'92 – A Totally New Dimension," *1988 Annual Report* (Wolfsburg: VW, 1988): 18.

[100] Volkswagen, "Europcar International SA," *1992 Annual Report* (Wolfsburg: VW, 1992): 27.

[101] BMW, "Studium des Exportmarktes und Erhöhung der Rabattstaffel für Exporte," UA 230: BMW Archive, Munich, Germany.

[102] BMW, "Vertriebssystem Europa," UR 8772/1: BMW Archive, Munich, Germany.

[103] Grace Ballor, Interview with Eberhard von Kuenheim. Audio recording. Munich, October 24, 2016.

[104] BMW, "A BMW Dealer in France," *1986 Annual Report* (Munich: BMW, 1986): 30.

[105] "Letter from BMW Aktiengesellschaft (Bullock and Schweickhardt) to the BMW Concessionaires (Mr. Morris-Marsham) in London," UA 824: BMW Archive, Munich, Germany; BMW, "Demand Differed from One Market to Another," *1987 Annual Report* (Munich: BMW, 1986): 9.

[106] BMW, "BMW Sales Organization Geared to Customers," *1992 Annual Report* (Munich: BMW, 1992): 42.

proponent of tax harmonization and the general liberal principles of market integration.[107]

When demand for BMWs declined in the Gulf States of the Middle East amid falling oil prices and high import duties and taxes in Thailand, Malaysia, Indonesia, and Latin America blocked exports there, BMW redoubled its investment in European sales. It did find some success in Japan, where it claimed a modest 2 percent share of the domestic market despite import protections. Lüder Paysen, the managing director of BMW Japan called this figure "peanuts," but the *Financial Times* called BMW's rising sales there the "best thing to happen to Japan in a long time."[108] While other producers eked out single digit sales – five for Chrysler, eight for Ferrari – BMW sold 11,000 cars, and quickly claimed the largest share of any European producer. Still, the vast majority of its sales were concentrated in the EEC, and it was there that it focused its resources toward further growth. By the late 1980s, it had fulfilled the "European mission" of regional exports it had outlined in 1980.[109]

By the mid-1980s, BMW had fully embraced the unique market segment von Kuenheim had outlined when he designed his strategy to keep the company from filing bankruptcy in the 1970s. Its niche was not in the supreme luxury of Lamborghini and Maserati, but in "business-class" cars designed to attract the discerning taste of Europe's corporate executives who fancied themselves skilled drivers. "German engineering" wrapped in sleek curves, outfitted with the latest technology and zipping through the Italian countryside for pleasure – as one splashy magazine spread promised.[110] The sporty, high-performance 3-series, featuring 6-cylinder engines, the latest dashboard technology, and meticulous design, anchored its its model range until the 7-series took the lead and the 12-cylinder 850i coupe dazzled the 53rd International Motor Show in Frankfurt.[111] As it Europeanized its sales, BMW remained focused on its "concentration on the upper market segment."[112]

Sales growth in the EEC motivated BMW to Europeanize its manufacturing, too. It had internationalized beyond the EEC in the 1950s and

[107] BMW, "EG-Richtlinie zur Harmonisierung der Umsatzsteuern," Document UR 860/1: BMW Archive, Munich, Germany.

[108] "The Management Page," *Financial Times*, Monday, July 8, 1985.

[109] BMW, "Anzeige Institutionelle Werbung: The European Mission," April 25, 1980. UR 1027/1: BMW Archive, Munich, Germany.

[110] BMW, "Werbekampagnen Europa – Advertising," Document UR 1027/1: BMW Archive, Munich, Germany.

[111] Throughout the 1980s, BMW was the largest producer of 6-cylinder engines in Europe, producing 70 percent of all engines in the category.

[112] BMW, "Business Prospects," *1987 Annual Report* (Munich: BMW, 1987): 12.

1960s, especially in South Africa, but production there paled in comparison to its European manufacturing volume.[113] As a means of scaling production and maintaining tight quality control, BMW embraced "system sourcing," by which it subcontracted much of its component part production to an elaborate web of suppliers, most of which were *Mittelstand* focused on producing a single specialized part under contract.[114] By the mid-1980s, BMW sourced parts from more than 1,200 such suppliers across Europe and nearly 5,000 subcontractors, about half of which were located in Germany and the other half split evenly between Western and Eastern Europe.[115] One historical account estimates that in the 1980s and 1990s, these suppliers and subcontractors were responsible for fully two thirds of the work of producing BMW cars.[116] Thanks to new technologies, it utilized Computer Aided Manufacturing (CAM) systems to coordinate and harmonize production across its vast supply network.[117] Over time and through very gradual changes, the "Bavarian company" von Kuenheim originally joined had become a "German company" and then a "European company."[118]

As they expanded their production and distribution networks across the region, both VW and BMW stressed the need for the EEC and its member states to invest in improved, interconnected transportation networks. BMW's creation of a 24-hour spare parts service throughout the EEC fulfilled by new supra-regional supply centers only increased its reliance on intercontinental rail and roadways. von Kuenheim had asked the German government to invest in rail infrastructure since the late 1970s.[119] As the 1992 Program incentivized expansion across the internal market, BMW pushed for an EEC-wide interlinking transport system to ensure the success of widespread production and distribution with a just-in-time model, and its executives collected and contributed to

[113] For more on BMW's early overseas expansion, see: Annika Biss, *Die Internationalisier ung der Bayerischen Motoren Werke AG: Vom reinen Exportgeschäft zur Gründung eigener T ochtergesellschaften im Ausland 1945–1981* (Berlin: De Gruyter, 2017).

[114] BMW, "Möglichkeiten Industrieller Kooperationen," 1979. UR 4850-1, BMW Archive, Munich, Germany.

[115] Manfred Grunert and Florian Triebel, *Das Unternehmen BMW seit 1916* (München: Bayerische Motoren Werke, 2006): 196; Grace Ballor, Interview with Eberhard von Kuenheim. Audio recording. Munich, October 24, 2016.

[116] Grunert and Triebel, *Das Unternehmen BMW seit 1916*, 189.

[117] BMW, "New Logistic Systems," *1986 Annual Report* (Munich: BMW, 1986): 19.

[118] Grace Ballor, Interview with Eberhard von Kuenheim. Audio recording. Munich, October 24, 2016.

[119] BMW, "Die Bedeutung Leistungsfähiger Internationaler Verkehrs Wege fur die Bayerische Wirtschaft," UR 4850-1: BMW Archive, Munich, Germany.

countless maps of European transit lines.[120] That the VW Group amassed a network of 35,120 suppliers in the region by 1987 also motivated it to appeal for EEC investment in interconnected transportation infrastructure. In fact, in the early 1990s, it was the largest customer of European railways, thanks to its interlinked supply network. Carmaker appeals for EEC transport networks echoed those of other industry groups like the ERT, which also saw the "Missing Links" between member state economies as a major impediment to full market integration.[121] The Commission, in turn, facilitated joint projects with carmakers in the EEC to prepare for fully open borders, as described in Chapter 1. Both VW and BMW contributed to DRIVE, which tackled traffic guidance and management at a regional level, and PROMETHEUS, aimed to design a European traffic system to "make private transport still safer, more economical, more comfortable, and less detrimental to the environment."[122]

One of VW's chief aims during this phase of expansion was to implement modular construction methods and homogenize its platforms. By combining vehicle components to form complex assemblies, integrating the dashboard, air conditioner, steering column, and pedals into a single cockpit module, for example, it could cut assembly times sharply.[123] Even more importantly, VW homogenized its platforms. Just as it had done in the 1970s when it built the Golf I and Audi 50 models on the same A1 platform, it aimed to expand its range of models – from the low end Siriaco to the award-winning Passat, the sporty Cortado to the luxury Audi 80 – while reducing its total number of platforms.[124] This approach relied on the interchangeability of components. By producing fewer part types in larger volumes, VW could cut costs and control quality.

[120] BMW, "Europäischer Verkehrsverbund - Herausforderung der Zukunft," UU 1430/10, BMW Archive, Munich, Germany.

[121] European Commission, "Meeting between the Commission and the Roundtable of European Industrialists 14 June 1985," PSP-385, Florence, HAEU. For more on business influence on EEC transport policy, see: Marco te Broommelstroet and Tobias Nowak, "How a Court, a Commissioner and a Lobby Group Brought European Transport Policy to Life in 1985," *GeoJournal* 72 (2008): 33–44.

[122] Volkswagen, "Expenditure on Research and Development," *1988 Annual Report* (Wolfsburg: VW, 1988): 16.

[123] Volkswagen, "Breaking New Ground in the Production of the New Golf," *1991 Annual Report* (Wolfsburg: VW, 1991): 21.

[124] Ludger Pries, "Volkswagen: Accelerating from a Multinational to a Transnational Automobile Company," in Michel Freyssenet, Koichi Shimizu, and Giuseppe Volpato, eds., *Globalization or Regionalization of the European Car Industry?* (Palgrave Macmillan, 2003): 60; Volkswagen, "50 Years of Volkswagen," *1988 Annual Report* (Wolfsburg: VW, 1988): 40.

As all of its vehicles became dependent on the same component parts, VW had to ensure that "[e]verywhere in the world Volkswagen quality is based on the same standards, aims, and principles, and even if the instruments differ according to local conditions, standards do not."[125] Similarly, BMW's system-sourced network produced the huge quantities of genuine parts and accessories that supplied both its new car manufacturing and its sales and service centers across the EEC. As BMW models became more sophisticated, the range of genuine parts it required soared from 70,000 unique components to over 100,000 by 1992. Each of these parts had special requirements and exacting technical standards, requiring the parent company to be in close cooperation with its suppliers to ensure quality control. In the words of Commissioner Étienne Davignon cited in Chapter 2, multinational manufacturers like BMW and VW contributed to a central objective of the Commission's 1992 Program by standardizing production systems and enforcing uniform technical standards across their supply chains.[126] Inadvertently, corporate strategy had dovetailed with the Single Market objectives of the Commission.

In addition to standardizing products and production across their own supply chains, VW and BMW led the way in implementing technical emissions standards for cars in Europe. Despite the failure of the Luxembourg Agreement in 1985 and the subsequent lack of concrete regional norms for environmental protection, both companies proceeded to incorporate catalytic converters into the cars they sold across the EEC. By the end of 1987, all petrol-fueled Audi and VW models were fitted with catalytic converters as a standard, and within two years the company had produced its first diesel engine equipped with a catalytic converter. VW even developed an LT 50 turbo-diesel, which it dubbed the "Environment Specialist" and an "eco" version of its ever-popular Golf.[127] Its Golf III earned accolades as "Car of the Year" and "Best Car in the World" by marketing the way it exceeded the emissions standards of EEC, Germany, and the US.[128]

125 Volkswagen, "Quality Knows No Limits," *1987 Annual Report* (Wolfsburg: VW, 1987): 36.

126 Grace Ballor, Interview with Étienne Davignon. Audio recording. Munich, June 16, 2016.

127 Volkswagen, "Systematic Use of Ney Key Technologies in Production," *1988 Annual Report* (Wolfsburg: VW, 1988): 53; Volkswagen, "Manoeuvrable, Fast, and Fully-Equipped – the VW 'Environment Specialist," *1989 Annual Report* (Wolfsburg: VW, 1989): 56.

128 Volkswagen, "Volkswagen Wins Numerous Awards," *1991 Annual Report* (Wolfsburg: VW, 1991): 20; Volkswagen, "The Golf III – An All-Around Success," *1992 Annual Report* (Wolfsburg: VW, 1992): 18.

VW claimed it was "not content to rest on [its] laurels" by addressing exhaust pollution alone.[129] In successive annual reports, press releases, and marketing materials, and letters from Hahn – all of which read rather ironically in the wake of the 2016 "Dieselgate" scandal – VW projected an image of principled environmentalism and painstakingly described its "exemplary environmental protection activities" as efforts to minimize pollution in its production process as much as in its products, from switching to water-based paints to using recycled plastics, improving its waste-water treatment to purifying the air around its plants.[130] When it realized that sponsorships had the highest rate of return on marketing investment, VW sponsored the UN's Environment and Development Conference in Rio de Janeiro in 1992, supplying the UN with more than 150 "low-pollution" cars emblazoned with the UN Conference on Environment and Development (UNCED) logo.[131] BMW was less overt in its public relations campaign of environmentalism, although it did run ads with eco-promises like "60mph at 0mpg."[132] But it recognized consumer demand for low-emission technologies and ensured that all of the cutting edge 6-cylinder diesel engines it produced in Steyr, Austria included catalytic converters.[133] Some of the 1 billion Deutsche marks it invested in its Technik Research headquarters in Munich funded its experimentation with hydrogen-fueled engines, which it saw as the future of green motorization.[134] By the time the European Commission finally agreed on uniform emissions standards to be implemented in stages by the end of the 1992 Program, BMW and VW had already exceeded them. By the late 1980s, both VW and BMW were turning impressive annual profits, thanks in part to their ability to satisfy consumers and regulators with low emission technologies and high emissions standards. The VW Group had captured the low, middle, and high segments of the market with its family of three brands. And for both VW and BMW, sales were bolstered by their ability to satisfy consumers and regulators by

[129] Volkswagen, "Environmental World Première – the New VW Catalyst Diesel," *1989 Annual Report* (Wolfsburg: VW, 1989): 54.

[130] Volkswagen, "Progressive Environmental Technology," *1988 Annual Report* (Wolfsburg: VW, 1988): 55.

[131] Volkswagen, "Culture, Sport, and a Concern for the Environment – All Three Supported by Volkswagen," *1991 Annual Report* (Wolfsburg: VW, 1988): 27.

[132] BMW, "Advertising," UR 1027/1, BMW Archive, Munich, Germany.

[133] Eberhard von Kuenheim, "Vorsitzender des Vorstands der BMW AG," UR 4850-1 (1979), BMW Archive, Munich, Germany: 3.

[134] On cars and climate change, see: Grace Ballor and Mattias Näsman, "Cars and Climate Change: The Historical Political Economy of a Green Transition," in Teresa da Silva Lopes, Paul Duguid, and Robert Fredona, eds., *Business and Climate Change* (London and New York: Routledge, 2025): chapter 2.

including low emission technologies. But they still faced tough competition from Japanese producers, who continued to increase their shares of European markets, especially after the Plaza Accord devalued the yen against the US dollar and pushed Japanese exports into the EEC.[135]

The signing of the Single European Act in 1986 dramatically changed the landscape for foreign producers in the EEC. On the one hand, it promised the same internal trade liberalization it afforded local automakers, meaning that any vehicle approved for sale by one member state could be sold without additional tariffs or barriers in the markets of other member states; on the other hand, foreign producers in the US and Japan saw in the SEA and the 1992 Program the threat of a "Fortress Europe" – internal liberalization for EEC carmakers, but high external barriers for foreign manufacturers.[136] Nissan and Toyota quickly adapted to this threat through foreign direct investment, since per GATT rules "transplant" vehicles produced by a Japanese company in Europe should be considered European goods and move freely between member states. Alongside the Japanese-made cars that continued to flow into EEC markets, Nissan, Toyota, Honda, and Mitsubishi increased their local production, mostly in the UK, where they began making cars that would qualify as "European" products.

European member states and producers responded to Japanese competition and investment in divergent ways. Because BMW and VW had both embraced flexible specialization and just-in-time production, and because of their export orientation, they did not feel threatened by Japanese exports or investment. VW reinforced its view that "free trade is the key to expansion"; "it [wa]s vital for the automobile industry that the world upholds free trade and does not lapse deeper into protectionism."[137] von Kuenheim, too, believed that all import restrictions "will have to be eliminated by 1993 when the single European market comes into being."[138] As the European company with the largest share of the Japanese market, BMW insisted on reciprocity: "not only must the EEC

[135] At a Group of Five (G5) meeting in New York in 1985, the US convinced Japan and Germany to let the dollar depreciate against their currencies. The resulting Plaza Accord caused the exchange rate of the dollar to the yen to decline by more than 50%. This pushed Japanese exports into the EEC since their cars had suddenly become so much more expensive in the US.

[136] Jörn Keck, "1987-1990: Keeping Relations on an Even Keel," in Jörn Keck, Dimitri Vanoverbeke and Franz Waldenberger, eds. *EU–Japan Relations, 1970-2012: From Confrontation to Global Partnership* (London: Routledge, 2013): 81.

[137] Volkswagen, "Free Trade Is the Key to Expansion," *1985 Annual Report* (Wolfsburg: VW, 1985): 28.

[138] BMW, "Import Barriers Provoke the Construction of Additional Production Plants: Excess Capacities Increase," *1988 Annual Report* (Munich: BMW, 1988): 16.

market be free of internal trade barriers, but also the EEC's trade with other countries must not be hampered by protectionism. Just as the Federal Republic offers all foreign car manufacturers free access to its market, the German automobile industry needs to be able to export freely to the world's markets."[139]

Automakers most dependent on their domestic markets, like FIAT in Italy and Renault in France, appealed for national protections against Japanese imports. Even in Britain, which welcomed early foreign investment by Nissan, sought a "gentleman's agreement" on export restraints when the Japanese share of the British market reached 10 percent.[140] Concerned producers with membership in the CCMC pushed the group to adopt a common position on Japanese competition and advocated for quotas to be set on Japanese imports even beyond the opening of the Single Market in 1993. Speaking to the Commission in 1989, CCMC president Umberto Agnelli argued that while the industry "supports Free Trade," "it wishes to have a reasonable period of transition before the further opening of the European frontiers and corresponding opening of the Japanese market."[141] Agnelli also pushed the Commission to set a threshold of 80 percent local content for a Japanese transplant to qualify as a European product.[142] While some members agreed to allow Japanese transplants as long as export restrictions were implemented, PSA Group Chairman Jacques Calvet vehemently opposed categorizing Japanese transplants as European products under any circumstances. He also called the United Kingdom "a Japanese aircraft carrier moored off the northwest coast of Europe" for having invited in the "Trojan horses" of Nissan, Honda, and Toyota.[143] Bitter fights between chairmen on the CCMC ultimately rendered consensus impossible. Because of the CCMC's unanimity rule, the dispute over Japanese transplants resulted in an impasse, and the association dissolved in 1990.

[139] BMW, "Political Background for the German Automobile Industry," *1986 Annual Report* (Munich: BMW, 1986): 12.

[140] Stephen Roland, *Vehicle of Influence: Building a European Car Market* (Ann Arbor: University of Michigan Press, 2000): 56.

[141] "CCMC Letter to Commissioner Martin Bangemann," October 4, 1989, FL-714, Florence, HAEU: 2.

[142] BMW, "Import Barriers Provoke the Construction of Additional Production Plants: Excess Capacities Increase," *1988 Annual Report* (Munich: BMW, 1988): 16.

[143] Diana T. Kurylko, "No Fear: Europe's Makers Put Away Protectionism as Japanese Import Quotas Run Out," *Automotive News*, July 1, 1999; Albrecht Rothacker, "The EC and Japan: From Mutual Neglect to Trade Conflicts and Beyond," in *Europe's Cold War Relations: The EC Towards a Global Role*, ed. Ulrich Krotz, Kiran Klaus Patel, and Federico Romero (London: Bloomsbury, 2020): 112–113.

BMW, which had remained relatively neutral during the disputes about Japanese transplants, was tasked with developing a new organization for the region's industry. After some months of deliberation, BMW assembled several leading European automakers, many of which had been members of the CCMC, to form the European Auto Manufacturers Association (referred to by its French acronym, ACEA) in February 1991. The ACEA was designed to be a forum in which member companies could discuss shared challenges and take collective decisions through a new qualified majority voting mechanism with a 75 percent threshold.[144] Unlike the CCMC, the ACEA welcomed European subsidiaries of American companies. Ford Europe joined immediately, and, together with VW, formed the core of the ACEA's new position. The new group was much more functional than its predecessor from the outset, not only because of its improved structure, but also because the disputes of previous years found de facto resolution when Calvet refused to join the new ACEA. With Calvet out of the way – at least until the PSA Group rejoined its peers on the ACEA in 1993 – this group of European automakers had a more unified position from which to articulate collective concerns to the Commission, and they focused their attention on securing export restraints. As the CCMC discussed its common position, VW increasingly saw Japanese cars as a threat to its SEAT business in Spain and aligned itself with those producers calling for import quotas.[145]

Pressure from the ACEA and member state governments compelled Commission President Jacques Delors to exclude autos from a global trade agreement with Japan signed in 1991 and Commissioner for External Trade Andriessen to broker a secretive agreement with his counterparts at MITI. This "Elements of Consensus" (EOC) agreement restricted Japanese car imports into five key EEC markets – France, Italy, Spain, Portugal, and the UK – until 1999.[146] The agreement made no explicit mention of transplants, leaving the door open for some member states to reject local production by Japanese carmakers, prompting the Japanese trade minister M. Nakao to write a bristling letter to the Commission: "let me call your attention to your commitment in the 'Elements of Consensus' that Japanese investment or sales of its products

[144] "Interview with Ms. Innike Herreman," Brussels, December 1993, MID-102, Florence, HAEU.

[145] For more on VW's shifting position in this debate and how the EOC fit within EC–Japan relations more broadly, see: Thomas Bourke, "EC–Japan Relation, 1985–1993: The Impact of Foreign Direct Investment on Regional Political Integration," PhD dissertation, European University Institute, Florence, Italy, 1995.

[146] On the Elements of Consensus, see: Ballor, "Liberalization or Protectionism."

in the Community shall not be restricted."[147] Because the EOC was negotiated privately and unpublished in the *Official Journal of the European Communities* to keep member states from disputing its articles in the Court of Justice, the Commission had the ability to make a unilateral determination about transplants.[148] It decided that "if transplants increase, direct imports must decrease."[149] The European car industry was thus sheltered against Japanese competition throughout the 1990s by a Community-wide commercial policy, thus liberalizing the European auto market while erecting barriers to Japanese manufacturers. In the end, the feared Japanese takeover of the Single European car Market was "the Revolution [that] did not happen;" the instability of the yen meant that Japanese sales did not reach the maximum levels allowed by the Elements of Consensus agreement.[150]

Expansion in Europe and Beyond

The political upheavals in Eastern Europe beginning in late 1989 threw open the doors to a new world of possibilities for Western producers that had previously been caught behind the Iron Curtain. In the fall of the Berlin Wall, carmakers, like the banks and retailers described in Chapters 5 and 6, immediately recognized the potential for new dimensions for European integration.[151] If the EEC would invest in the transition to free market economies there, firms like BMW could provide the "finance, technology, know-how, courage, solidarity, and business acumen" required to transform the region into a fitting addition to the "pan-European" market.[152] The unification of Germany was the first priority, of course, which BMW preempted by setting up a service network in the GDR as early as December 1989, with the promise of further investment "if rapid progress is made towards a free market economy." German unification would shift the entire continent's center

147 "Réponse de M. Nakao à M. Andriessen: Voitures japonaises: Déclarations 'conclusives' version finale," July 31, 1991, FL-713, HAEU.

148 For another interpretation of the EOC, see: Alice Milor, "Non-Documents for Big Decisions: The Commission and the EEC–Japan Automotive Agreement," *JCMS: Journal of Common Market Studies* 62, no. 6 (2024): 1654–1671.

149 Le Cabinet du Président: Francois Lamoreaux, "Note pour le président: Voitures japonaises: Déclarations "'conclusives,'" Brussels, July 31, 1991, FL-713, HAEU.

150 Tomasso Pardi, "La Révolution qui n'a pas eu lieu: Les constructeurs japonais en Europe (1970–2010)," PhD dissertation, EHESS, Paris, 2011.

151 BMW, "The World Economy and the Automobile Industry," *1989 Annual Report* (Munich: BMW, 1989): 14.

152 BMW, "Integration in the West – Opening in the East," *1989 Annual Report* (Munich: BMW, 1989): 15.

of economic gravity: Once straddling the periphery, Germany would become the new economic core of an enlarged Europe, and German manufacturers like VW and BMW could hardly contain their enthusiasm.

At VW, Hahn made no secret of his hope that Soviet Bloc states would quickly embrace a market economy, which his board saw as "superior to every conceivable alternative when it comes to offering the prerequisites for political, economic, and social progress."[153] In advocating for a new kind of "European solidarity" that supported the transition of Eastern European countries to capitalism, VW was also shifting its production center of gravity eastward and reconstituting its Group's "home base." Because of the relatively high cost of labor in Europe compared with Japan, the opening of Eastern Europe also promised to level the playing field between volume producers like VW and their Japanese competitors. Economic change had its challenges to be sure, but VW was encouraged by signs of growth in Hungary, Poland, and Czechoslovakia and their efforts to establish closer links with the EEC. In this pivotal moment of 1989, VW articulated its tandem mission of playing its part in the "realization of the Single European Market" and constructing for itself a correspondent "European house."

VW's most significant move in Eastern Europe came in 1990 when a nascent cooperation with Czech carmaker Skoda paved the way for its acquisition as the Group's fourth independent brand. Hahn led the take over of 31 percent of Skoda's capital stock in April 1990, with plans to assume management the following year and increase its stake to 70 percent by 1995.[154] Using SEAT's assimilation as a guide, VW was confident that it could integrate Skoda into the group as a second strong producer of economy cars – like the Favorit model – to meet the "pent-up consumer demand" in the repressed markets of Eastern Europe.[155] But this acquisition did not only give VW access to a new consumer base; it also offered the company a "flexible, highly skilled, well-trained workforce" at close proximity to the Group's headquarters and near to its interlinked supply chain. VW presented its investment in Eastern Europe to the public in much the same way that it had touted its entrance into

[153] Volkswagen, "Management Report: Volkswagen AG and Volkswagen Group: Development in the Current Year and Prospects," *1989 Annual Report* (Wolfsburg: VW, 1989): 17.

[154] Volkswagen, "Management Report: Volkswagen AG and Volkswagen Group: Development in the Current Year and Prospects," *1990 Annual Report* (Wolfsburg: VW, 1990): 24.

[155] Volkswagen, "World Automobile Industry Faced with Declining Demand and Tougher Competition," *1990 Annual Report* (Wolfsburg: VW, 1990): 17.

Spain: as an "immense benefit for both sides," "furthering Czechoslovakia's economic development."[156] With plans to invest 9.5 million Deutsche marks in the following decade for capacity increases, new engine production facilities, the building of a sales network, and a roadmap for integrating the Czech supplier industry into the VW Group's supply chains, the Skoda deal certainly promised gains, although more for the parent company than for anyone else.[157] Indeed already in 1992, Skoda had "surpassed all expectations" by already turning a profit, strengthening the Group's bid for additional investment financing from the International Finance Corporation, European Investment Bank (EIB), and European Bank for Reconstruction and Development (EBRD).[158] Like many other Western European multinationals that entered Eastern Europe in the early 1990s, VW discovered consumers in those markets required financing support to be able to purchase cars. As part of its rollout of financial products like Eurobonds and credit cards under its new VAG Bank and VAG Leasing companies, it opened a financial services division to develop lending programs specifically aimed at potential buyers in East Germany, Hungary, Poland, and the new Czech Republic, thereby growing its sales in those markets and establishing financial services as part of its global revenue strategy.[159]

The reunification of the two Germanies in October 1990 provided growth opportunities for BMW, too. While its upmarket models were too expensive for most East German consumers just emerging from forty years of communism, its motorcycle range sold well almost immediately.[160] German reunification also enabled BMW to reopen its former Eisenach factory. Given its market segment and volume approach, German reunification gave VW an even larger boost. Alongside its acquisition of Skoda, VW worked with the privatization agency Treuhandanstalt to expedite the transition of formerly state-owned enterprises in East Germany, opened a Polo assembly plant near

[156] Volkswagen, "SKODA – The Fourth Independent Marque in the Volkswagen Group," *1990 Annual Report* (Wolfsburg: VW, 1990): 11.

[157] Volkswagen, "Management Report: Volkswagen AG and Volkswagen Group: Economic Trend in the Fiscal Year 1990," *1990 Annual Report* (Wolfsburg: VW, 1990): 12.

[158] Volkswagen, "Skoda: Major Improvements and Key Figures," *1992 Annual Report* (Wolfsburg: VW, 1992): 41.

[159] Volkswagen, "Financial Services – An Important Means of Sales Promotion," *1991 Annual Report* (Wolfsburg: VW, 1991): 50.

[160] BMW, "Business at BMW Still Satisfactory in 1990," *1990 Annual Report* (Munich: BMW, 1990): 10. Despite low income levels across the Bloc, BMW did celebrate its sale of 2,500 cars in Eastern Europe in 1990. See page 12.

Zwickau in 1990, and set up two new companies to assemble and produce vehicles. It saw itself as contributing "to the process of rebuilding the economy in Germany's new federal states."[161] In a symbolic gesture of the role the German state saw private enterprise playing in the unification process, Chancellor Helmut Kohl laid the foundation stone of a new plant in Mosel together with Hahn.[162] VW also worked with the Slovakian government to cooperate with Bratislavské Automobilové Závody (BAZ) in 1991 to produce gearboxes for the Group's interlinked supply system, and soon controlled 80 percent of the new company Volkswagen Bratislava, spol. s.r.o.[163] These efforts made VW the largest private investor in former Bloc states. With four independent brands and 16 percent share of the EEC market, VW declared itself "a truly European manufacturer."[164]

As the VW Group consolidated its twenty-two German and fifty-one foreign companies in 1990 and expanded its European operations from Barcelona to Bratislava, it recognized the importance of international training experiences for its employees. The "Haus Rhode" Center established in the late 1960s to train Volkswagen staff had operated as a kind of elite social club for VW management, but the Group's growth and widespread internationalization required more comprehensive and inclusive programs. A new European Volkswagen Group Works Council, created at the European Parliament in 1992, represented 90 percent of employees across the four brands. Through partnerships with foreign universities, the Group also worked to recruit elite graduates, and it launched exchange programs for young trainees across Western and Eastern Europe. An agreement with the French Ministry of Vocational Education in 1991, made in light of the Single Market and "with a view to harmonization of the varying education systems in Europe," brought forty-eight French apprentices to VW headquarters for a three-week vocational training course.[165] Since women comprised an increasing

161 Volkswagen, "Volkswagen by Far the Largest Investor Helping to Rebuild Saxony's Economy," *1991 Annual Report* (Wolfsburg: VW, 1991): 11.

162 In light of the EC's common Competition Policy, the Federal German government had sold its 20 percent holding in the voting capital stock of VW through an international banking consortium in 1988. Still, because VW loomed large in the German economy, it retained a close connection to the domestic government.

163 Volkswagen, "Management Report: Volkswagen AG and Volkswagen Group: Development in the Current Year and Prospects," *1990 Annual Report* (Wolfsburg: VW, 1990): 24; Volkswagen, "Volkswagen Bratislava, spol. s.r.o.," *1990 Annual Report* (Wolfsburg: VW, 1990): 29.

164 Volkswagen, "Skoda – The Fourth Independent Marque in the Volkswagen Group," *1990 Annual Report* (Wolfsburg: VW, 1990): 11.

165 Volkswagen, "International Exchanges for Young People," *1990 Annual Report* (Wolfsburg: VW, 1991): 223.

percentage of the Group's labor force, personnel policy changes were also needed. The monthly discussion groups centered on "women's information" and family accommodations, and flexible working hours became hallmarks of the new policy, even if these early steps were superficial relative to the deep-rooted problems of unequal treatment and gender pay gaps among VW employees.[166] BMW, too, implemented skilled apprenticeships in the late 1980s, recording about 13 percent participation by women, who – to the apparent surprise of corporate management – mostly "chose classic male occupations, such as toolmakers, power plant electronics technicians, or sheet metal workers."[167] These employee training programs epitomized the cultural, educational, linguistic, and social diversity of the European region and also the inherent challenges of integration.

Any fanfare there might have been at BMW and VW about the completion of the Single Market at the end of 1992 was eclipsed by the concurrent economic downturn. German reunification and the opening of the East proved to be a painful process, compounded by the rhythm of business cycles. A recession clouded the economic forecast for 1992 and 1993. What is more, there were exchange rate problems in the European Monetary System (EMS), which complicated international trade. All of this caused BMW management to adopt a sober approach to the end of the 1992 Program and the new European Union's plans for further integration: "1992's currency turbulences showed the way to economic and monetary union, which was started by the Maastricht agreements, is far more difficult than the creation of a single European market."[168] The Single Market had been received with "great expectations"; "in contrast, the plans for political union and a common currency met with great restraint."[169]

1992 marked the end of one era for BMW and VW and the beginning of another. Its dynamic chairmen both retired just as the last directives to complete the Single Market were being implemented and with the Maastricht Treaty negotiations already underway. If the hallmark of the 1980s was Europeanization, the 1990s were defined by increasing globalization.

166 Volkswagen, "Volkswagen Group Undergoing Radical Changes," *1989 Annual Report* (Wolfsburg: VW, 1989): 35. The 1991 Annual Report tokenizes female employees, especially in its depiction of a lone woman cupping the cheeks of her five male colleagues. See page 24.

167 BMW, "Education Schemes are Investments in the Future," *1988 Annual Report* (Munich: BMW, 1988): 71.

168 BMW, "Economic Weakness in Europe," *1992 Annual Report* (Munich: BMW, 1992): 35.

169 Ibid.

Before retiring, Hahn described Europe as "the base for worldwide operations" at VW.[170] Ferdinand Piëch, the Audi chairman who replaced Hahn as chairman of VW, built on Hahn's legacy by using the Group's European home base as a springboard from which to globalize. He found that China's "increased receptiveness to free-market principles ... made the country an attractive partner in the economic sector."[171] The Group's joint venture in China, the Shanghai-Volkswagen Automotive Company, Ltd., which Hahn had worked to grow through small agreements in the 1980s,[172] became a channel through which to access the Chinese economy as it began to open in the 1990s, and VW quickly became the largest passenger car manufacturer in the Peoples' Republic of China.[173] Likewise, the consultancy office and importer, Yanese, it had opened in Japan in the late 1980s became a platform from which to launch a robust import business there, especially as Japanese officials conceded to European demands for reciprocal market access in the wake of the Elements of Consensus disputes.[174] Not only had the Group's Mexican factory made a strategic export base for its Golf, Vento, and A3 models in the US market, but the North American Free Trade Agreement (NAFTA), which took effect in 1994, made an even stronger case for North America as a site for cost-effective production and access to a huge consumer market in all market segments. By the end of the 1990s, VW was operating in nearly two dozen countries. It had also further differentiated its multitiered approach with the acquisition of luxury carmakers Bentley, Bugatti, and Lamborghini.

When he succeeded von Kuenheim, Bernd Pischetsrieder articulated a new global strategy for BMW. The auspices of the NAFTA agreement motivated BMW to break ground on a new plant in Spartanburg, North Carolina in 1993, intended to serve as the company's anchor in the US. Of this expansion, Pischetsrieder explained: "We will no longer be building any fully integrated production plants here in Germany, and Spartanburg is probably not the last plant that we will be establishing in

[170] Volkswagen, "Dr. Carl H. Hahn: Letter to Stockholders," *1991 Annual Report* (Wolfsburg: VW, 1991): 6.
[171] Volkswagen, "*The Future Has Already Begun*," *1989 Annual Report* (Wolfsburg: VW, 1989): 84.
[172] Hahn, *Meine Jahre mit Volkswagen*, 156–157.
[173] For more on European producers in China and Chinese producers in Europe, see the ongoing work of Yuan Jia-Zheng.
[174] Volkswagen, "Asia: Shanghai-Volkswagen Automotive Company, Ltd.," *1987 Annual Report* (Wolfsburg: VW, 1987): 59; Volkswagen, "Nissan Assembly in Japan," *1989 Annual Report* (Wolfsburg: VW, 1989): 74. SEAT partnered with Suzuki in 1992 to produce a compact car, pending approval from the European Commission.

a foreign country."[175] In fact, he went on to develop a *Weltbebauungsplan* for global manufacturing, predicated on the dual production of one world car model paired with one designed specifically for Europe. BMW's most significant step toward global expansion in this period was its acquisition of the British Rover Group of producers like Land Rover, Mini, and Austin-Healy in 1994. This attempt at "going global" proved unsuccessful in the end, with BMW forced to break up the group and sell some of its brands by the end of the decade. But the acquisition was a key part of the way European producers like BMW and VW strove to grow the European base they had built in the 1980s into global operations in the 1990s.

Conclusions

From the crises of the 1970s to global expansion in the 1990s, the European auto industry underwent a dramatic transformation. Central to this transformation was the EEC's 1992 Program, which harmonized legislation, established common norms and standards, and created an internal car market in the region. Carmakers experienced the Single Market differently, largely because of their unique national origins, market segments, production methods, and profit strategies.[176] Some saw internal liberalization as a threat to their state protections; others supported liberalization that exceeded the Commission's original vision for an integrated European market.

Together, the cases of BMW and VW illuminate the ways different European automakers responded to the process of market integration. While BMW, led by von Kuenheim, focused its production on performance vehicles engineered in Germany and produced through a network of suppliers and subcontractors, it internationalized its sales and service network to reach every corner of the European Community and its trading partners in the region. As a volume producer, VW sought expansion through the building of a multinational family of four major brands. Its homogenized and modular platforms required centralized control of component parts manufacturing at such large volumes that the VW

[175] Quoted from the translation by Andrea Eckardt and Matthias Klemm: "The Internationalization of a Premium Automobile Producer: The BMW Group and the Case of Rover," in *Globalization or Regionalization of the American and Asian Car Industry?*, ed. Michel Freyssenet, Koichi Shimizu, and Giuseppe Volpato (London: Palgrave Macmillan, 2003): 177.

[176] Mira Wilkins reflected on the connections between corporations and their contexts in: "Multinational Enterprises and the Varieties of Capitalism," *Business History Review* 84, no. 4 (2010): 638–645.

Group became a force for technical standardization. Because of their export orientations, both companies embraced the new technologies of catalytic converters to reduce emissions much more readily than their European counterparts, giving them a competitive advantage. They also took a comparatively open approach to debates in the industry association and European Commission about restricting Japanese imports and investment, neutrality that positioned von Kuenheim to constitute a new transnational BIA for the industry in Munich in 1991.

Building on the analysis and methodology developed in Chapter 3, this history of the Europeanization of car manufacturers reflects the effects of regional integration on business strategy. The case of automakers in the EEC also situates the making of the Single Market in its larger, global context. Like French, Italian, and British producers, BMW and VW were faced with the challenge of foreign competition, and in the Single European car Market they found the growth opportunities and supportive industrial and commercial policies required to remain competitive. But by the mid-1990s – unlike some of their counterparts – they had not only weathered the storm but had become some of the largest and most profitable car companies in the world, financially and operationally prepared to launch their own global offensive.[177]

In contrast to Volkswagen and BMW, the French merchant bank Paribas was not an early supporter of regional market integration. Its chairmen instead expressed ambivalence about the 1992 Program and skepticism about European banking integration, especially through its membership in national and transnational BIAs. Yet as Chapter 5 shows, Paribas played a pivotal role in regional economic transformation across Europe in the late twentieth century, thereby shaping the contours of the internal market.

[177] In their introduction and conclusion, Freyssenet, Shimizu, and Volpato lay out a framework to test the assumptions that globalization is linear and irreversible. See: *Globalization or Regionalization of the European Car Industry?* (New York: Palgrave Macmillan, 2003).

5 Financing Economic Transformations

The Single Market Program seemed to change relatively little for the storied French bank Paribas in the 1980s. Not only did the 1992 Program target industrial manufacturing as explained in Chapter 1, but internal market integration did not initially change the business environment much for an already very international bank. Founded in 1872 as a banque d'affaires or merchant bank facilitating commercial loans and investments, the Banque de Paris et des Pays-Bas had long been a "bank for Europe," its companies, and its industries since its inception, according to historian Eric Bussière.[1] The bank leveraged its international connections, primacy in French finance, and adaptability to survive the economic turmoil of the twentieth century, from two world wars to economic shocks, rising economic nationalism to large geographies of the bank's earlier business becoming part of the Soviet and socialist world. From the 1950s to 1990s, the bank reinforced its merchant bank expertise, specializing in mergers and acquisitions and cross-border transactions, focused on the chemical and pharmaceutical, consumer goods, electronics, defense and aerospace industries.[2] Over the same period, it also multiplied its "intrinsic worth" "by 5.7 and size by 22."[3] Bank chairman André Levy-Lang expected the Single Market to "allow Paribas to affirm its vocation as the European banque d'affaires."[4] But Levy-Lang also recognized that balance sheet problems, a tightening capital market, and widespread economic turmoil in the early 1980s motivated the bank to "reorganize, innovate, and concentrate" on the commercial lending activities where the bank was successful and look

[1] Eric Bussière, *Paribas 1872–1992: Europe and the World* (Antwerp: Fonds Mercator, 1992).

[2] "Paribas Credentials," Paribas, Dinan, 1AH-33, BNP Paribas archive (hereafter BNPPA).

[3] Bussière, *Paribas*, 304.

[4] André Levy-Lang, "Speech at the Conseil de Surveillance de la Banque, 8 February 1991: Preparation for the Council of 21 March," Paribas, Dinan, 100AH/1000, BNPPA.

for new opportunities, afforded by the potential widening, although not the deepening of the Single Market and its attendant regulatory challenges.[5]

Drawing on archival sources from Paribas as well as published statements from bank chairmen Jean-Yves Haberer, Michel François-Poncet, and André Lévy-Lang, this chapter examines Paribas in the European economy of the 1980s and 1990s, the evolution of the bank's business strategy amid the macroeconomic changes of market integration and market openings, and the bank's perspectives on the Single Market and banking regulation in European economic governance. If carmakers like Volkswagen and BMW expressed enthusiasm about the business opportunities of the Single Market Program for their supply chains, production, and distribution and even supported the EEC's efforts to develop environmental regulations, merchant banks like Paribas seemed rather ambivalent and even directly opposed to the regulatory and social dimensions of market integration through their lobbying efforts and business interest associations. In the early 1990s, the opening of Central and Eastern Europe presented new investment and growth opportunities making Paribas much more interested in business opportunities in Central and Eastern Europe, the "CEE," than in the business environment of the EEC and its Single Market.

This chapter first establishes Paribas' standing in European and global markets until the 1980s and discusses the bank's nationalization and subsequent privatization in the mid-1980s when it adopted its position of relative market ambivalence. It then examines Paribas' role in the formation of the transnational banking BIAs and clubs that developed collective positions on various aspects of regional economic integration toward "1992." The subsequent section examines collective bank mobilization against European regulation like the Second Banking Directive and its related legislation. Finally, this chapter shows the active role of Paribas in the economic transformations of Central and Eastern European former Soviet Bloc countries in the early 1990s and its interest in growth markets outside the Western European core including countries in Scandinavia, which it anticipated would soon join the Single Market. Ultimately, this chapter finds Paribas' regional business shaped the real economy of the region beyond the internal market, even as its political activity reflected ambivalence qua skepticism about the 1992 Program.

[5] André Levy-Lang, "Speech at the Conseil de Surveillance de la Banque, 8 February 1991: Preparation for the Council of 21 March," Paribas, Dinan, 100AH/1000, BNPPA.

Paribas in Europe and the World

As a uniquely international merchant bank since its inception, Paribas had always done business internationally, from issuing Cuban Treasury bonds in 1878 and Argentine and Portuguese bonds in 1886 to bond issues in Russia, Morocco, and the Ottoman Empire in 1914, from participating in the creation of the American South African Investment Company in 1958 and creating partnerships with other European banks in Germany (SEDI), Spain (CEFISA), and Italy (SFIDI) in the postwar period to opening branches in Oman, Bahrain, Japan, Indonesia, and the Philippines in the early 1970s.[6] The bank's total global presence shrank, however, amid the economic challenges and widespread nationalist protectionism following the oil shocks of 1973 and 1979. It was in this moment economic and financial historian François Caron argued banks like Paribas "must look to the spirit of the 1870s [when Paribas was founded] for inspiration" to break with nationalism and "establish the New Europe."[7]

Paribas had faced some global competition during the 1960s and 1970s, including from foreign banks based in the US, who saw the EEC's common market in the 1970s as what financial historian Richard Sylla called a "godsend," given strict domestic banking regulations.[8] In addition to the push factor of regulation, strong demand from US-based industrial firms for familiar financial institutions in Europe pulled US-based banks to the EEC. From 1963, when US manufacturers demanded US-based capital in Europe, to 1974, when the US government implemented protectionist banking policies that prevented continued activity abroad, American banks – led by Citibank, J. P. Morgan, Chase Manhattan, and Bank of America – operated in Europe.[9] This "invasion did not lead to conquest" as happened in other sectors, but rather to "assimilation," pressuring European banks like Paribas to adopt similar structures and strategies as their American competitors.[10] Indeed, Paribas had established its own activities in the US in the late twentieth century. But in the recession of

[6] Bussière, *Paribas*, 255–301. On Paribas' European partnerships, see: Grace Ballor, "Agents of Integration: Multinational Firms and the European Union," PhD dissertation, UCLA, 2018: Chapter 5, pp. 141–175.

[7] François Caron, "Introduction," in Bussière, *Paribas*, 15.

[8] Richard Sylla, "United States Banks and Europe: Strategy and Attitudes," in *European Banks and the American Challenge: Competition and Cooperation in International Banking under Bretton Woods*, ed. Stefano Battilossi and Youssef Cassis (Oxford; New York: Oxford University Press, 2002): 54–55.

[9] Sylla, "United States Banks and Europe," 55.

[10] Ibid., 69.

the early 1980s, revenue from its business in New York, through which it lent to the Morgan Stanley Group, Inc., declined sharply, reflecting the widespread economic downturn across the global economy and the changing economic geography of merchant and investment banking.[11]

The strategic and voluntary restructuring of French banks like Paribas amid economic change and global competition the 1960s and 1970s was quickly replaced by forced nationalization in the 1980s. In 1982, soon after American banks were compelled to leave Europe, the socialist French government of François Mitterrand nationalized banks, including the Banque de Paris et des Pays-Bas.[12] During its nationalization, the bank was formally renamed Paribas and restructured into six departments, focused on international markets, export finance, capital markets, and industrial finance. Mitterrand largely abandoned his socialist policies by 1985, however, paving the way for Paribas to be quickly reprivatized in January 1987, following the parliamentary victory of Jacques Chirac and just as the Single European Act was about to introduce the institutional reforms needed to make completing the internal market possible. Jean-Yves Haberer, chairman of Paribas during its nationalization from 1982–1986, expressed his support for "the [progressive] building of Europe" since the Second World War, but he argued it was the "signing of the Single [European] Act in 1985 that returned Paribas to its original culture and led it to forge a more specifically European policy."[13] For Haberer, then, the 1992 Program was restorative, a path back to an earlier business environment for the bank. Haberer also explained Paribas significantly expanded its "European networks" during the 1970s and early 1980s, when doing business in other parts of the world was impeded both by military conflicts like the Yom Kippur War, as well as economic challenges like oil shocks and stagflation.

Given Paribas' adaptive dexterity and global activities developed during the turbulences of the twentieth century, the bank did not look to regional policymakers for solutions in the 1980s as manufacturers like those discussed in Chapter 4 did. Indeed, to some financial institutions like Paribas, which had already achieved economies of scale through early internationalization, the 1992 Program did not offer the scalar benefits

[11] Charles T. Spinner, "Memorandum to Jacques Rinino and Everett Schenck," July 17, 1990. Paribas, Dinan, 1AH-33, BNPPA. It was during this period, too, that Paribas unsuccessfully partnered with the Warburg and Chicago-based investment bank A. G. Becker to develop business in the US. This joint venture was ultimately sold to Merrill Lynch.

[12] David Cobham, "The Nationalisation of the Banks in Mitterand's France: Rationalisations and Reasons," *Journal of Public Policy* 4, no. 4 (1984): 351–358.

[13] Jean-Yves Haberer, "1970–1992," in Bussière, *Paribas*, 217.

manufacturers and industrial firms needed from an integrated internal market. Nor did policymakers seem to have banks very much in mind when designing the Single Market. In its treatment of services, the White Paper on Completing the Internal Market presented banking as a "traditional service," along with insurance and transport, and Articles 101–107 outlined the liberalization of financial services, which, "if properly mobilized, [could] play a key supporting role for industry and commerce."[14] In the view of the Commission, banking in the internal market was ancillary to the manufacturing activity policymakers were really after.

The Board of Paribas did turn their attention to the 1992 Program in January 1989, when the second Delors Commission made clear its intentions to pursue EMU and more stringent regulation of firms in the internal market. These developments made the board wonder how the bank could best adapt to the changing business environment: "Should Paribas develop a commercial banking network across Europe? Which products would be most conducive to a multinational approach? Should the bank have a European approach to asset management? Should it become a transnational merchant bank? Should it have a European IT base?" Paribas' international portfolio changed markedly in the 1990s when the opening of Eastern Europe created new opportunities for the bank. As was the case with other European multinationals discussed in Chapter 3, the bank's definitions of "Western" and "Eastern Europe" were not consistent over time. In the 1990s, for example, the bank's "Europe Department" did not include France, and its "International Department" was responsible for all business outside of "Europe," without defining "Europe" or its borders. The bank's management described the region only as "a situation very complex, thus we find in this geographic zone, and in the same time zone: the headquarters, London, which is the most important financial capital, and five other branches, more than a quarter of subsidiaries having an important activity, notably Brussels and Geneva."[15] Additionally, historians collating the bank's self reported data have sometimes imposed their own presents back onto the past by merging the categories of Western and Eastern Europe already in the 1950s to reflect the seeming linear and teleological progression of regional integration this book refutes.[16] Also of note is the evolution of the distribution of Paribas' areas of activity over

[14] European Commission, "White Paper on Completing the Internal Market," Article 100.

[15] Paribas Documents de Sociétés, 1991, Paribas, Dinan, 100AH/1000, BNPPA.

[16] Not only have I, myself, been guilty of this in earlier work, but so has much of the literature on regionalization discussed in Chapter 3.

time. From the late nineteenth to mid-twentieth centuries, Paribas inverted the distribution of its lending between public services (65% of its business in 1880 but just 1.5% by 1969) and industry (40–50% of its portfolio by 1990 up from just 10% in 1919), while also increasing its lending to banks and financial companies.[17] Its attention to industrial lending in the twentieth century reflects the bank's rootedness in the real economy. Likewise, the broad regionalization of its activities in the 1980s and 1990s reflects the ways Paribas returned to its historical networks of "concentric circles" in rings that reached the "edges of Europe" and eventually "covered the whole continent," as described by Eric Bussière.[18] Importantly, though, these circles did not fully map onto the Single Market, revealing Paribas' relative market ambivalence and different regional geography, especially after the opening of Eastern Europe.

Insofar as Paribas did adapt its business strategy to the 1992 Program, it did so through an announcement in 1990 of plans to create "a European investment capital network," aimed at acquiring 5–50 percent stakes in companies – including small and medium sized enterprises – needing financing.[19] The bank first created a Dutch industrial holding company, Paribas Deelnemingen, in 1990 along with plans to create similar entities, "distinct from the banking activity of Paribas" in Germany, and the new EEC member states of Spain and Portugal.[20] Was this investment capital network motivated by the Single Market Program, or by the bank's strategy of refocusing its growth plans on its "home" region after decades of difficulty in other markets? Its regional business strategy took further shape a few weeks later when it established a new Portuguese investment and consulting company, Copapor, the mission of which was "halfway between those of the new Hungarian financial services company created last June [Magyar Paribas]," discussed later in this chapter, "and the establishment of European industrial holding companies decided this summer [Paribas Deelmingen NV]."[21] Much like Paribas' international industrial investment firm Compagnie Belge de Participations Paribas (Cobepa) shown in the

[17] This data comes from Bussière, *Paribas*, 307. [18] Bussière, *Paribas*, 56

[19] "Paribas veut développer un réseau européen de capital-développement," *Les Echos* September 12, 1990, Paribas, Dinan, 1AH-33, BNPPA.

[20] "Paribas a constitué un holding aux Pays-Bas," *AGEFI*, September 12, 1990, Paribas, Dinan, 1AH-33, BNPPA.

[21] Paribas, "La Banque Paribas cree au portugal une societe d'investissement et de conseil Copapor," *La Correspondance économique*, September 21, 1990, Paribas, Dinan, 1AH-33, BNPPA.

organigram in Figure 5.1, Copapor was designed "to play an active role in the advising of European mergers and acquisitions and in the program of privatizations in Portugal."[22] As a model for facilitating economic transformations in Europe through privatization, Copapor would give Paribas "a [strategic] presence in all 12 capitals of the EEC."[23] In 1991, Paribas went further when it considered developing its business in Portugal, encouraged by the country's "dynamism," EEC membership and "European convergence" especially in the "principal subject of privatization," the rhythm of which was, however, "slow."[24] As the following sections show, Paribas' role in economic transformation through privatization intensified in the 1990s when it worked to be a leading merchant bank both within and outside the EEC and to adapt to and work to influence common banking regulation together with its counterpart banks through European banking associations and clubs. Additionally, Paribas contributed to the development of banking norms and standards through its extensive network of branches, partnerships, and subsidiaries, some of which are shown in Figure 5.1.[25]

Banking BIAs and Clubs

Some banks had taken early interest in regional economic integration. Already in 1946, even before the creation of the UNECE, a network of economic and intellectual elites formed the Ligue européenne de coopération economique, or European League for Economic Cooperation (ELEC), which supported for regional banking integration and became one of the strongest forces advocating for a single capital market in the context of the Treaty of Rome.[26] Several Paribas bankers maintained seats in ELEC, putting them in close proximity to other lead

[22] Paribas, "La Banque Paribas cree au portugal une societe d'investissement et de conseil Copapor," La Correspondance économique, September 21, 1990, Paribas, Dinan, 1AH-33, BNPPA. Copeba was founded in 1957 and was initially a partner of Paribas. By 1991, Paribas owned 60 percent of its shares.

[23] Paribas, "La Banque Paribas cree au portugal une societe d'investissement et de conseil Copapor," *La Correspondance économique*, September 21, 1990, Paribas, Dinan, 1AH-33, BNPPA.

[24] "Compte-rendu de la reunion Portugal 'risques-pays' du 27/06/91"; "Lettre de lisbonne – IV/90 – octobre-décembre 1990)," Paribas, Dinan, 1AH-33, BNPPA.

[25] Drawing adapted from: Paribas Conseil de surveillance (Paribas Supervisory Board), Séance du 15 novembre 1990 (Meeting of November 15, 1990), III. Les filiales européennes (European subsidiaries), Paribas, Dinan, 100AH/1000, BNPPA. With many thanks to Rasmus Salén for the visualization.

[26] Michel Dumoulin and Anne-Myriam Dutrieue, *La Ligue européenne de coopération économique, 1946–1981: Un groupe d'étude et de pression dans la construction européenne* (Bern: Peter Lang, 1993).

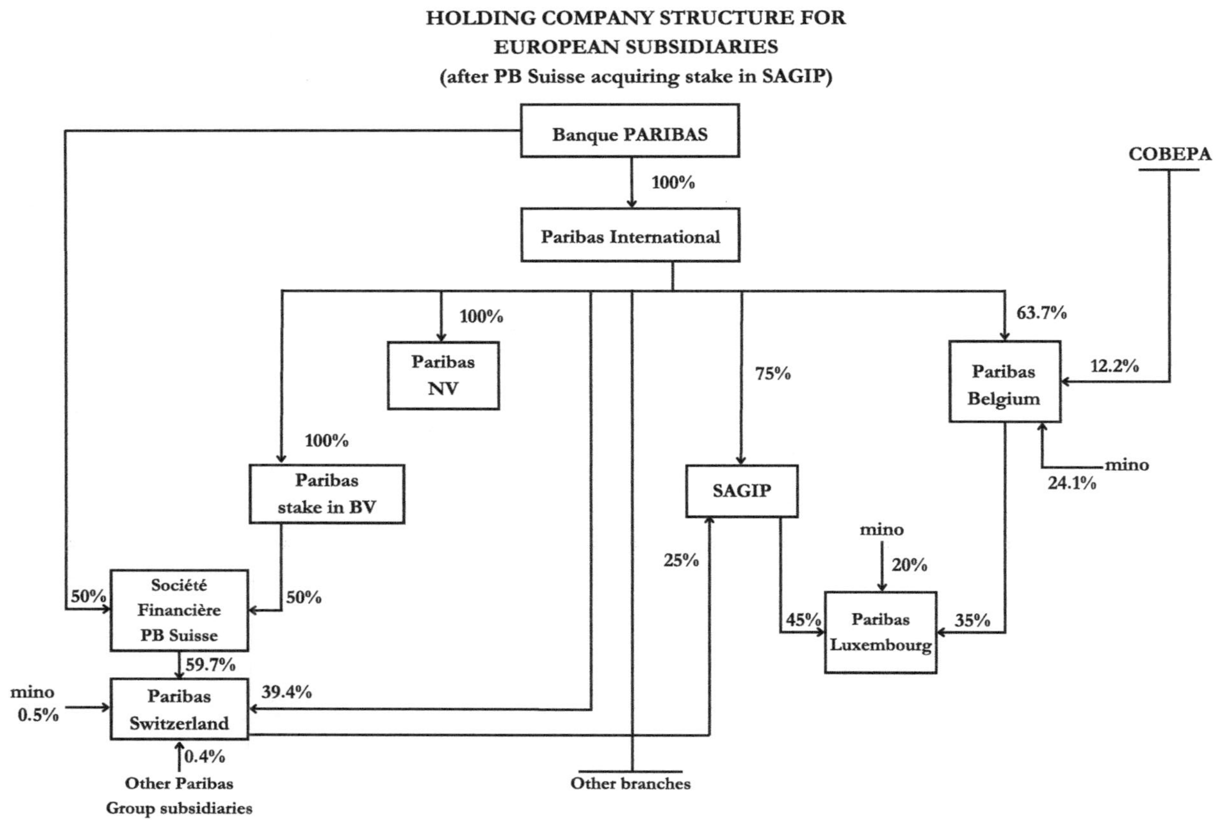

Figure 5.1 Structure of Paribas' European subsidiaries in 1990.

bankers from firms across the region, and following the creation of the EEC, to regional policymakers as well. Most notably and most important for understanding Paribas' role in this association was the presence of Bernard de Margerie, Chairman of the bank and Deputy Director General responsible for the bank's foreign investments in the 1970s.[27] de Margerie, like so many other bankers, including Herman Abs, chairman of Deutsche Bank in the same period, maintained positions as both private banking executive staff and as senior officials of ELEC.

Furthermore, as with firms in many sectors, European banks had developed national banking associations to lobby domestic governments in the late nineteenth and early twentieth century.[28] The creation of supranational institutions in the EEC in the late 1950s motivated national banking associations across the region to join together in 1960 to form the European Banking Federation (EBF) to submit collective comments and proposals to the Commission about policies for a common banking market. Consequently, by the 1960s, several types of European banking associations had formed to influence regional economic integration in the common market. But as historian Alexis Drach has shown through cases of British and French commercial banks, the banking sector did not lobby for financial integration in Europe out of ambivalence about the value of a common banking market, fear of increased regulation, and a higher prioritization of global and domestic issues, especially for the French banks that had experienced nationalization in the 1980s.[29] These banks and their BIAs like the EBF, Drach argued, became "reluctant Europeans," only when Commission policy on liberalization aligned with their interests, the horizontal dimensions of regional integration expanded to include the possibility of new member states and their economies, and the competitive and regulatory circumstances changed to make Europe a good business opportunity for European banks.[30]

In addition to banking associations to share information and influence policymaking, European banks also formed banking clubs between the late 1950s and the 1970s. Again, Alexis Drach has shown how many large European commercial banks formed and joined clubs like the

[27] Hubert Bonin, *Le monde des banquiers francais au XXe siècle* (Paris: Broché, 2000): 114.

[28] Sabine Pitteloud and Grace Ballor, "The Rise and Fall of Private Advocacy Forums from 1945 to the Twenty-first Century," *Socio-Economic Review*, 2025.

[29] Alexis Drach, "Reluctant Europeans? British and French Commercial Banks and the Common Market in Banking (1977–1992)," *Enterprise & Society* 21, no. 3 (2020): 768–98.

[30] Drach, "Relucant Europeans?" 796.

European Banking Industry Committee (EBIC), Europartners, and Associated Banks of Europe Corporation (ABECOR) to create a form of competitive "European champions," much like the buying clubs described in Chapter 6.[31] Also like commercial buying clubs, banking clubs served as forums for information exchange between their members as much as organizations to influence policymaking.[32] While the value of these clubs had diminished by the 1980s, they persisted during the Single Market Program as groups of banks worked to adapt to the changing business environment of global competition, national regulations, and regional market integration. Clubs like ABECOR also nurtured partnerships between its members. In 1988, BNP and Dresdner Bank proposed a partnership, which Dresdner chairman Wolfgang Röller explained was a strategy driven by "Europe 1992."[33] Wolfgang Kartte, president of the German Federal Bureau of Cartels, critiqued the proposed partnership on the same grounds his office opposed a similar proposal between the Allianz insurance company and Dresdner Bank, saying "we do not want the companies to merge" for the sake of customers and users.[34] In publishing an interview with Kartte, German newspaper *Der Spiegel* printed an image of Kraken, whose tentacles tangled around the logos of Bayer, Allianz, and Dresdner Bank, above their coverage of Kartte's investigation of "whether these spider webs of financial and personal entanglements have also spread to other sectors," including the automotive industry.[35] Similarly, the French Communist Party (PCF) criticized the proposed partnership between BNP and Dresdner as a symptom of how the Maastricht Treaty "would further distance the seats of power from citizens," since its promise of an "open economy with free competition actually means increased domination of financial markets, and therefore of multinational corporations, over the fundamental choices of the people."[36] Only a referendum on Maastricht could uphold the democracy the PCF argued was needed to "resolve the major problems

[31] Alexis Drach, "An Early Form of European Champions? Banking Clubs between European Integration and Global Banking (1960s–1990s)," *Business History* 66, no. 1 (2022): 287–310.

[32] Hélène Michel, "Businesseurope au-delà du 'lobbying': Le travail d'intégration européenne d'une organisation patronale," *Critique internationale* 59, no. 2 (2013): 133–155.

[33] Wolfgang Röller, "Réunion á Francfort, le 16 mai 1988," Paribas, Dinan, 50AH-46, BNPPA.

[34] "Interview of Wolfgang Kartte," *Der Spiegel* April 8, 1992, Paribas, Dinan, 50AH-54, BNPPA.

[35] Ibid.

[36] PCF, "Maastricht et Nous: Tract du parti communiste français (PCF) de 1992," Paribas, Dinan, 50AH-54, BNPPA.

of our time: employment, the environment, training, cooperation, [and] transparency. Decision making must be brought closer to citizens, neighborhoods, municipalities, and businesses … This is the complete opposite of the Maastricht Treaty."[37] Ultimately, the Commission did not find this partnership as problematic as Kartte or the PCF and prioritized the development of European banking over competition policy in approving their joint ventures in Central and Eastern Europe in 1991.[38]

With the encouragement of the same commissioners (especially Davignon) who established other peak sectoral BIAs like the ERT and Big Twelve Round Table on High Tech, representatives from some banks and some of the industrial corporations in the ERT formed the Association pour l'union monétaire de l'Europe, or Association for Monetary Union of Europe (AMUE) in 1987 to advocate for the achievement of a regional monetary union in the Single Market.[39] As a member of the AMUE, Paribas, too, supported the benefits of easy capital transfers, homogeneous banking regulations, and the region's greater resilience to exogenous threats. The AMUE remained active in its appeals and even consultation on matters of monetary union through the late 1980s and 1990s and provided frequent comments on draft agreements for the European monetary union, achieved by the end of the century.[40] As Aleksandra Komornicka has shown, however, the AMUE's rapid expansion to include many diverse member perspectives frustrated the development of consensus positions on technical aspects of regional economic integration like EMU.[41]

The Threat and Recourse of European Banking Regulation in the Single Market

For banks like Paribas, the Single Market Program promised new European banking regulations, which presented both an operational threat and also an opportunity for recourse amid disputes with

[37] PCF, "Maastricht et Nous: Tract du parti communiste français (PCF) de 1992," Paribas, Dinan, 50AH-54, BNPPA.

[38] European Commission, "Commission Decision of 28 August 1991 on règlement CEE no.4064/89 sur les concentrations a propos de la Banque Nationale de Paris et Dresdner Bank)," 1991, https://ec.europa.eu/competition/mergers/cases/decisions/m124_fr.pdf.

[39] Association pour l'union monétaire de l'Europe, "Répertoire numérique": http://www.archivesnationales.culture.gouv.fr/chan/chan/AP-pdf/109-AS.pdf.

[40] Harold James, *Making the European Monetary Union:* (Cambridge, MA: Belknap Press, 2014); Emmanuel Mourlon-Druol, *A Europe Made of Money: The Emergence of the European Monetary System.* (Ithaca, NY: Cornell University Press, 2012).

[41] Aleksandra Komornicka, "Stable Support, Scant Initiative: European Business Associations and Economic and Monetary Union, 1946–1992," *Business History* 67, no. 4 (2025): 1021–1042.

competitors. Common legislation could just as easily constrain bank activity as it could be marshalled against rivals. In 1977, the European Council had approved a Banking Directive to harmonize banking supervision and create a single banking market.[42] This first Banking Directive coordinated banking laws across EEC member states for credit institutions and bank branches across borders, harmonized licensing procedures, and defined the responsibility for supervision and relationships with third countries. It also established a framework for further common banking legislation.

In the 1985 White Paper on Completing the Internal Market, the Commission already anticipated the need for a second banking directive to be drafted in 1987 and approved by the Council in 1989.[43] Indeed, by early 1989, it was clear the internal market would require further banking legislation, largely to overcome market failures, so the Commission drafted a Second Banking Directive to regulate banking licenses and set capital requirements and continued to propose further directives aimed at the sector over the following year.[44] Reflecting its relation to the internal market, this Second Banking Directive had an implementation deadline of December 31, 1992.[45] In 1989, the Council approved two more directives to harmonize banking regulation by recognizing the capacity of banking authorities of member states to carry out mutual supervision.[46] These additional directives also established a solvency ratio for credit risk and capital adequacy requirements for financial institutions, per the "supervised freedom" of the "Cooke Ratio" of capital requirements set at the Bank for International Settlements (BIS) with the Basel Capital Accord in 1988 after the banking crises of the previous decades, to be implemented across the EEC by the internal market

[42] First Council Directive 77/780 of December 12, 1977 on the Coordination of Laws, Regulations and Administrative Provisions Relating to the Taking Up and Pursuit of the Business of Credit Institutions, Art. 1, 1977 OJ. (L 322) 30.

[43] European Commission, "White Paper on Completing the Internal Market," 25.

[44] Catherine Schenck and Emmanuel Mourlon-Druol, "Banking Regulation and Supervision," in *The Oxford Handbook of Banking and Financial History*, ed. Youssef Cassis, Richard Grossman, and Catherine R. Schenck (Oxford: New York: Oxford University Press, 2016): 396; Second Council Directive 89/646/EEC of December 15, 1989 on the coordination of laws, regulations and administrative provisions relating to the taking up and pursuit of the business of credit institutions and amending Directive 77/780/EEC.

[45] On the Second Banking Directive, see René Smits, "The European Community's Second Banking Directive," in *Current Legal Issues Facing Central Banks, Vol. IV*, ed. Robert C. Effros (International Monetary Fund, 1997): Chapter 6, pp. 83–104.

[46] Council Directive 89/647 of December 18, 1989 on a Solvency Ratio for Credit Institutions, 1989 OJ. (L 386) 14, as amended; Council Directive 89/299 on the Own Funds of Credit Institutions, 1989 O J. (L 124) 16.

completion deadline.[47] The Cooke Ratio required banks to hold 8 percent of risk-weighted assets in reserve.

The board of the Association française des banques (AFB), a national business interest association for banks of which Paribas was a member, met frequently in 1989 and 1990 to discuss these Council directives on banking regulation and supervision, especially the Commission's ongoing work to implement the efforts of a committee led by Hungarian-Belgian banker Alexandre Lamfalussy on an "Investment Services Directive" to apply the Basel Cooke Ratio for solvency and risk management requirements on investment institutions in addition to retail banks, subjects the AFB euphemistically filed under "European Questions."[48] In a December 1989 draft letter to Commissioner Leon Brittan, the AFB reminded him it had already warned the Commission's Director General for Financial Institutions Geoffrey Fitchew in June 1989 against "overly hasty proposal for a directive" and had suggested a "period of observation" "to evaluate the practicality of any proposals."[49] Now six months later, the AFB appealed to Brittan for an "integrated supervisory regulation," with uniform "position risk" weights across banks, subsidiaries of banks, and independent investment firms."[50] "Account must always be taken," they argued, "of the size and diversity of a firm's business and also of the level of supervision and control to which it was already subjected," lest Commission regulation become overly burdensome for French banks.[51] This conservative position seemingly advocated for the concerns of the smallest and least competitive French banks, despite the AFB's diverse membership, reflecting widespread opposition among French banks in the ABF to the EEC's stricter banking regulations.

The AFB acknowledged its recommendations would require a "substantial revision of the Solvency Ratio Directive" and "substantial revision of the recommendations of the Basel Committee."[52] Its suggestion of more integrated regulation, the AFB argued, would address market

[47] On banking supervision and the Basel Committee, see the many works of Alexis Drach, including: Alexis Drach, "Supervisors against Regulation? The Basel Committee and Country Risk before the International Debt Crisis (1976–1982)," *Financial History Review* 27, no. 2 (2020): 210–233; Alexis Drach, Liberté surveillée: Supervision bancaire et globalisation financière au Comité de Bâle, 1974–1988, (Rennes: Presses Universitaires de Rennes, 2022).

[48] J.-P. Mattout, "Handwritten note to Madame Jolly," December 10, 1990, Paribas, Dinan, 1AH-228, BNPPA. Lamfalussy led the BIS in Basel before joining the Delors Commission, where he played a key role in EMU.

[49] Association française des banques, "Letter to Sir Leon Brittan," December 4, 1989, Paribas, Dinan, 1AH-228, BNPPA.

[50] Ibid. [51] Ibid. [52] Ibid.

risk as well as the credit risk covered by the Council's 1989 Directives. The AFB proposed the short term, interim solution of considering banks that have fulfilled the Solvency Ratio Directive "to have made sufficient provision against market risk," as required by the Second Banking Directive and Investment Services Directive.[53] In an association meeting held just a week after writing to Brittan, the AFB critiqued the Commission's planned legislation as an unfitting extension of the Cooke Ratio, a conflation of banks and nonbanks, and a distortion of competition between EEC and non-EEC banks, which it argued contradicted the objectives of the Single Market Program.[54] To strengthen its case against European banking risk regulations, the national AFB cited the interests of the transnational EBF in its broad appeal to the Commission for more harmonized and flexible banking regulation in the Single Market.

Additionally, the AFB discussed a 1988 recommendation for proposed regulation on issues like payments systems in the internal market and new electronic payments technologies, which the Delors Commission designed to "extend the financial protection of consumers," as part of its "social turn."[55] This proposed regulation drew criticism from the AFB, which blamed the 1985 White Paper on Completing the Internal Market for initiating the Commission's communications to the Council in 1987 on the interoperability of payment cards within the EEC by the internal market deadline of December 31, 1992.[56] The ABF thought such retail issues "put the Commission [too much] under the influence of consumer organizations" and social stakeholders.[57] It subsequently established a "European committee to study and draft a report on these proposals," and suggested a five-to-ten-year prospective study of the needs of French banks regarding electronic payments.[58] The AFB also

[53] Association française des banques, "Letter to Sir Leon Brittan," December 4, 1989, Paribas, Dinan, 1AH-228, BNPPA.

[54] Association française des banques, "Proposition de directive européenne concernant les services d'investissement dans le domaine des valeurs mobilières," December 12, 1989, Paribas, Dinan, 1AH-228, BNPPA.

[55] "Recommendation de la Commission du 17 novembre 1988 concernant les systèmes de paiement et en particulier les relations entre titulaires et émmetteurs de cartes 88/590/ CEE," *Journal officiel des communautés européennes*, no. L 317/55.

[56] Association française des banques, "Les paiments dans le marche interieur europeen," December 11, 1990, 1AH-228, BNPPA; Official Journal of the European Communities, "Recommendation by the Commission regarding the system of payments, especially relations between carholders and issuers," November 17, 1988 (88/590/CEE).

[57] Association française des banques, "Code de meilleure pratique en europe pour les cartes," December 12, 1989, Paribas, Dinan, 1AH-228, BNPPA.

[58] Association française des banques: "Observations de l'association française des banques: projet de LIVRE VERT sur le développement des systèmes de paiement européens," August 3, 1990. Paribas, Dinan, 1AH-228, BNPPA.

followed the positions of three European credit industry federations, the Group of EEC Cooperative Banks, the EBF, and the Group of Savings Banks of the EEC, which created an inter-federation working group to monitor the consumer credit protectionism of the Commission. This group both developed best practices "containing the minimum consumer protections for certain types of electronic payments" and "questioned the Commission's legal "right to intervene in questions of consumer protection in the domain of payment systems."[59] Ultimately, the AFB's resistance to Commission consumer credit protections resembles the ways the commercial firms discussed in Chapter 6 mobilized against the threat of the social Single Market.

In addition to the ABF's collective response to proposed legislation on solvency ratios, the management board of Paribas, including honorary president Michel François-Poncet and bank chairman André Levy-Lang, met in 1990 to discuss what EEC enforcement of the Cooke Ratio would mean for the bank. Levy-Lang argued the bank's declining income in 1990 "is explained as much by structural factors like interest rate positions as by economic factors such as commercial credit risks."[60] Even so, the Board recognized the bank's need to consolidate, given the "already very European" organization of Paribas' large industrial clients and the possible "major crises" on the horizon, especially in global energy markets.[61] Increased European regulation in the Single Market exacerbated the challenging global economic environment of the late 1980s, in which the "Euro-marché" emerged an otherwise bright spot of relatively high growth.[62]

While the ABF rejected proposals for European banking regulation and the consumer-oriented dimensions of integrated payments systems, it also viewed the EEC and its economic governance served as a forum for the arbitration of disputes between banks. In November 1990, the board of the AFB drafted "Elements for a complaint to the European Commission" regarding its proposals, in which it seemed to relish "the honor" of "calling the attention of the Commission to violations of articles 90, 92, and 93 of the Treaty of Rome" resulting from the

59 Association française des banques, "Observations de l'association française des banques: projet livre vert sur le développement des systèmes de paiement européenns," August 3, 1990, Paribas, Dinan, 1AH-228, BNPPA.

60 Conseil de surveillance, "Séance du 20 septembre 1990," Paribas, Dinan, 1AH-1000, BNPPA.

61 Ibid.

62 "Rapport de gestion de la banque: les activites de la banque paribas et de ses filiales en 1989," Paribas, Dinan, 100AH-999, BNPPA.

measures of tax relief offered by the French state to savings accounts issues by Crédit Mutuel.[63] The AFB insisted the EEC uphold the competition policies of the Treaty and argued: "By granting Crédit Mutuel the privilege of distributing tax free savings accounts, the French state is introducing discrimination, not only against competing French banks, but also against all common market banks, which will not be able to offer products as competitive."[64] AFB asked the Commission to "declare the incompatibility of this state aid with the premise of Article 92 of the Treaty and bring all related legal consequences to bear," and "to order the French state to suspend its aid to Crédit Mutuel in the form of tax exemptions."[65] For members of the AFB, then, the stricter state aid prohibitions implemented for the completion of the internal market offered a mechanism for reducing selective state support and ensuring fair competition between French banks.

Beyond the Internal Market

Paribas chairmen participated in the AMUE and the activities of the AFB regarding European banking regulation, but the changing business environment of the internal market did not on its own seem to shape the bank's business strategy. Instead, "Europe's long 1989" and the opening of new markets seemingly presented new opportunities for the bank and motivated strategy change.[66] While "helping Eastern Europe out of the red," as an advertisement in *The Economist* put it, by facilitating liberalization and privatization promised significant profits, an interest in doing business in Eastern Europe in the early 1990s set Paribas apart from other global counterparts.[67] On a trip to New York in 1990 to meet with the chairmen of the NY Fed, Chase Manhattan Bank, Chemical Bank, Morgan Stanley, and Rogers and Wells, the members of the bank's board noted that while the international group had discussed Eastern Europe, "there was little real interest" in the subject. At least Paribas' leadership interested in Soviet Bloc countries

[63] Association française des banques, "Plainte de lAFB aupres de la commission des communautes europeennes relative aux mesures de fiscalisation du livret bleu reservees par l'etat francais au credit mutuel," Paribas, Dinan, 1AH-228, BNPPA.

[64] Ibid.: 24. [65] Ibid.: 27.

[66] Christopher Bickerton, "Europe's Long 1989," *Contemporary European History*, published online: February 18, 2025, 1–18.

[67] Price Waterhouse East European Services advertisement in *The Economist*, September 21, 1991, Paribas, Dinan, 1AH-33, BNPPA.

could rest assured "no competition would come from American banks, at least for the moment."[68]

The opening of Bloc states to the West began early, with flows of trade and investment intensifying already in the 1970s.[69] By late 1989, after some years of Mikhail Gorbachev's glastnost and perestroika and subsequent political weakening of the Soviet Union, and following widespread liberal democratic revolutions of the "Autumn of Nations," the EEC extended an aid program to Poland and Hungary: Assistance for Restructuring their Economies (PHARE), which was eventually extended to thirteen former socialist republics and Balkan countries to promote legislative convergence as well as economic and social cohesion.[70] The European Council's extension of this aid as a "pre-accession instrument" revealed its intention to prepare those countries for eventual EEC membership already in 1989. Poland and Hungary were identified as first recipients of this aid because of their longstanding historical ties with the West, early anti-Soviet resistance, and rapid economic and political transformation already in the late 1980s. In addition to the EEC's interest, that openness attracted the attention of Bretton Woods institutions like the World Bank and International Monetary Fund (IMF) as well as foreign private investment from multinationals. The IMF's intentions were laid bare quite early in its framing of socialist economies as the "Wild, Wild East," where the "Russian far East could be to the twenty-first century what the American West was to the nineteenth," and where the next billionaires would soon emerge after the injection of sufficient capital "and plenty of nerve."[71]

Such expectations fueled the "shock therapy" approach to economic transformation that destabilized societies through rapid privatization and liberalization, in which Paribas played a leading role.[72] It also motivated Paribas to seize the unparalleled new business opportunity of the "process of transition to a market economy" and push to privatize state owned companies, especially in the countries most advanced in reform: Poland,

[68] Paribas, "Note sur les entretiens a New York les 19 et 20.7.90," Paribas, Dinan, 1AH-33, BNPPA.

[69] Aleksandra Komornicka, *Poland and European East-West Cooperation in the 1970s The Opening Up* (London: Routledge, 2023).

[70] Council Regulation (EEC) No 3906/89 of December 18, 1989 on economic aid to the Republic of Hungary and the Polish People's Republic.

[71] Paribas tracked the IMF's position in its visits to Eastern Europe between 1988 and 1991.

[72] Kristen Ghodsee and Mitchell A. Orenstein, *Taking Stock of Shock: Social Consequences of the 1989 Revolutions* (Oxford; New York: Oxford University Press, 2021).

Hungary, and Czechoslovakia, where GDP was 50 percent higher than that of Bulgaria, Romania, and Yugoslavia. In an advertisement in *The Economist* in 1991, ABB Asea Brown Boveri called this transformation "Europe's new industrial revolution," which Paribas explained would require unprecedented financing and investment from the private sector, since aid from the EEC and the European Bank for Reconstruction and Development (EBRD) were important, but insufficient "for an operation of this magnitude," in the words of French diplomat and former ambassador to the Soviet Union Henri Froment Meurice. Paribas was encouraged by early foreign investment by Pizza Hut, McDonalds, and Tampax in socialist economies, but watched the economics and politics of each state closely to plan its business strategy and expressed concern about the "insufficiently clear" rules for free enterprise in the region, where state seizures, rent hikes, and bartering practices left "whole areas open to doubt" for Western firms.[73]

On May 22, 1990, Paribas founded a subsidiary bank in Budapest, Hungary, called Magyar Paribas, of which Paribas would control 57 percent, while two Hungarian bankers, M. Robert de Balkany and M. Peter Medgyessy would jointly control the other 43 percent.[74] The new subsidiary bank's mission was simply to "participate in the restoration of the Hungarian economy," by responding to the "needs of Hungary and concentrating its activities as a banque d'affaires on the matter of privatization" by facilitating both direct and indirect investments and industrial operations.[75] Paribas offered its Hungarian subsidiary financial backing, experts and international banking clientele, and the specific sector knowledge it needed to be successful in its stated mission of privatizing and developing industries of "highest importance (transports, energy, and telecommunications)." By the time the Board of Magyar Paribas met in Budapest on June 25, 1991, they recognized "change in this part of Europe [would] be slow due to the "radical change of the political regime," and they acknowledged debates about of the speed of privatization in Hungary, as well as a trifecta of three political uncertainties: the problem of ethnic minorities, the difficulty normally encountered during such changes, and a lack of confidence among the people in major economic and political

[73] E.M. King, "Note a lattention de M. François-Poncet: re l'union soviétique," November 1990, Paribas, Dinan, 1AH-33, BNPPA.

[74] For Limousin's summary of Magyar Paribas' founding, see: "Note a l'attention de monsieur H. de Saint Amand, Europe, Conseil de la banque du 15 juin 1990," Paribas, Dinan, 1AH-1000, BNPPA.

[75] "La Vocation de Magyar Paribas S.A.," Paribas, Paris, DG/313, BNPPA.

transformation.[76] With much optimism and some naiveté, the Board cited the bank's role in postwar reconstruction in France as evidence of its credentials to facilitate economic transition in Hungary. At very least, it committed to "equip bankers in Hungary with the expertise they need" to facilitate privatization, especially of large industrial firms such as "Autoker, MAT, Magyar Kábelmüvek, Debreceni Baromfifeldolgozo" and more.[77] While Paribas focused on privatization and economic transformation, other Western banks like Credit Lyonnais prepared bond issuances for the National Bank of Hungary.[78] Magyar Paribas attracted Western companies interested in investing in Hungary, including the French subsidiary of the American appliance manufacturer Hoover, for which Magyar Paribas developed a three-stage plan for market entry, identified a possible distributor in the local Skala Corp. and arranged visits to facilitate its manufacturing investment.[79]

Paribas' Deputy Director Jean-Pierre Magné was intrigued by proposals for elaborate consumer retail projects in transitional Hungary. The first was put forward by Multi Land, SARL, founded by Cooperative Corporation Csopak in August 1991 to "satisfy expanding demands on bakery products" by establishing thirty to forty bakery factories across Hungary for distribution across its forty-seven restaurants and pubs and commercial clients. Multi Land approached Paribas' Hungarian subsidiary, Magyar Paribas, to ask for 10 million forints of capital to acquire French bakery machines and acquire/rent real estate for its production. Magné expressed his desire for French firms to use the services of Magyar Paribas to develop business in Hungary, however, and referred Multi Land to export-import consulting firm Co-Nexus Kalmar for support.[80] Likewise, in spring 1992, Paribas analyzed a proposed drugstore/bakery/brasserie project in Budapest, newly opened to foreign investment and private enterprise after the collapse of the Soviet Bloc. With its Canadian inspired business model and successful location on the Avenue Champs Elysées in Paris, the drugstore Publicis promised Hungarian workers hundreds of new jobs and consumers a huge range of nonstop services in one location, from an 80-seat restaurant and 450-seat

[76] Proces verbal du conseil d'administration de Magyar Paribas, S.A., held June 25, 1991 in Budapest, Paribas, Paris, DG/313, BNPPA: 2.
[77] Ibid.
[78] Tom Priday, "Letter to Michel François-Poncet," October 21, 1993, Paribas, Dinan, 1AH-240, BNPPA.
[79] "Letter from B. François to J. P. Magné, 1 octobre 1990," Paribas, Dinan, 11AH-738, BNPPA. Likewise, the Whirlpool company looked to Magyar Paribas for support in establishing manufacturing in Czechoslovakia.
[80] Jean-Pierre Magné, "Lettre de Banque Magyar Paribas á Madame Margrit Racz," November 19, 1991. Paribas, Dinan, 11AH740, BNPPA.

cinema to a convenience store (with tobacco shop, newsstand, and photo/printing office) and pharmacy.[81] French bank network Crédit Lyonnais was already working with Publicis to capitalize the project, but Paribas saw opportunities to get involved by offering forecasting services and cash investment products. However, profitability in Hungary had been negative in 1987 and 1988, reached equilibrium in 1989, and then declined again in 1990, resulting in insufficient returns to justify Paribas' involvement in this ambitious project. Both the Multi Land bakeries and Publicis retail center proposals reflected frenetic optimism by economists and multinationals alike about a rapid transition to capitalism in formerly socialist economies. Indeed, in 1990 Peter Medgyessy aimed to use Magyar Paribas as a base from which to engage the "two target markets" of Czechoslovakia and the Soviet Union.[82] And Michel François-Poncet's participation in IMF meetings in Washington in Spring 1993, along with the chairman of Inter-Europa Bank, underscored Paribas' role in economic transformation. By 1994, however, the *Financial Times* lamented the slowing of Hungarian economic development as a "hare becom[ing] a tortoise," despite "almost half of the privatization in Hungary [having been] accomplished," since "47% of state property had been privatized."[83]

As Levy-Lang noted in a meeting of the parent company's board in early 1991, the opening of the Soviet Bloc, combined with the "perspective of the single market," marked a new period of possibility for the bank, in which Paribas could affirm its original vocation as a European merchant bank.[84] Indeed, in May 1991, Paribas representative Michel Piquet made a three day trip to Poland to report back to the bank on "The Direction of Central and Eastern Europe," much like the early market research trip undertaken by Pierre-Olivier Beckers-Vieujant described in Chapter 6.[85] Piquet found "shock therapy," the rapid liberalization, marketization, and transformation of planned economies,

[81] "Premier contact de l'Agence George V avec la société les Drugstores Publicis," April 23, 1992. Paribas, Dinan, 11AH740, BNPPA.

[82] Peter Medgyessy, "Conceptions stratégiques de Magyar Paribas SA: rapport á soumettre á l'assemblée générale du 24 octobre 1990 á Budapest," Paribas, Dinan, 1AH-240, BNPPA.

[83] Nicholas Denton and Virginia Marsh, "The Hare Becomes a Tortoise," *The Financial Times*, November 11, 1994, Paribas, Dinan, 1AH-240, BNPPA; State Holding Co., "New Privatization Syreategy in Hungary: Accelerating Privatization," Paribas, Dinan, 1AH-240, BNPPA.

[84] André Levy-Lang, "Speech at the Conseil de Surveillance de la Banque, 8 February 1991: Preparation for the Council of 21 March," Paribas, Dinan, 100AH/1000, BNPPA.

[85] Michel Piquet, "Direction de l'europe centrale et orientale," May 29, 1991. Paribas, Dinan, 1AH-33, BNPPA.

which had been administered according to the "precepts of the IMF," had reduced inflation (spectacularly), liberated prices, and allowed for internal conversion to the Polish Zloty.[86] He also found, however, that economic equilibrium would "continue to have a high social cost," with unemployment already at 7.2 percent.[87] Economic aid – from the Club of Paris, IMF, World Bank, European Investment Bank (EIB), EBRD, and EEC, whose PHARE program contributed exponentially more international aid to Poland than any other entity – could help restructure the economy, develop infrastructure, and "stimulate the process of privatization," however.[88] In fact, according to Piquet, such international aid had restored Poland's dynamism and "entrepreneurial spirit" already. In his view, "[t]he [Polish] Parliament's expected adoption of a long-awaited law liberalizing foreign investments" could further liberalize and open the Polish market of 39 million people. Perhaps most importantly, Piquet underscored the fact that Paribas could not stay away from the important Polish market, both because Poland was a key market in the "chain" of Eastern European countries the bank had identified for investment and because its competitors were already there: Germans and Anglo-Saxons, sure, but also French competitors like Crédit Lyonnais and Société Générale. Paribas would need to think quickly, Piquet warned, about the opportunity to build on its long-standing interest in Poland, since the early twentieth-century creation of the Banque Franco-Polonaise, and establish its own presence in Warsaw.[89]

By the time Paribas merged with BNP in 1998, it had established nearly a dozen subsidiary banks in former Soviet Bloc states of Central and Eastern Europe. Still in the twenty-first century, the majority of the Central and Eastern European financial sector remained under the control of Western banks.[90] Consequently, while Paribas' networks facilitated the inflow of capital into countries in need of development and to the integration of markets in the region, they also contributed to the persistence of inequalities between European economies.

[86] An annex Piquet provided on "The Economic Situation in Poland" explained inflation had reached 12 percent in January 1991 before falling to 2.6 percent that April.

[87] Michel Piquet, "Direction de l'europe centrale et orientale," May 1991. Paribas, Dinan, 1AH-33:, BNPPA.

[88] Ibid. On the Club of Paris, see the work of historian Svan van Mourik.

[89] Michel Piquet, "Direction de l'europe centrale et orientale," May 29, 1991. Paribas, Dinan, 1AH-33, BNPPA; Paribas, Franco Polonaise: 4DFOM/221/583.

[90] Ivan T. Berend, *An Economic History of Twentieth Century Europe* (Cambridge: Cambridge University Press, 2006).

Beyond the opening of Eastern Europe, the potential membership of Nordic EFTA member countries in the EU and its Single Market also created new opportunities for merchant banks like Paribas or the Wallenberg Group, which noted "Swedish harmonization with EC regulation" when "assuming an acceptance of its membership application to EC" and a likely rapid abolition of Sweden's "foreign ownership clause."[91] Already in 1984, Paribas had decided to "implant itself" in Scandinavia and develop its merchant and investment banking activities there. But the simultaneous arrival of too many other foreign banks, coupled with strict domestic regulation, forced the bank to rapidly close its operations in Sweden, Finland, and Norway, while it maintained a presence in the marginally more promising market of Denmark, and while its "longtime partner" Cobepa maintained contacts in all four countries.[92] Paribas did keep its Stockholm office open, however, in case future opportunities arose. The developments of the early 1990s convinced Paribas to return to Scandinavia, primarily to facilitate privatization, mergers, and acquisitions in economies in transition. Chairman Michel François-Poncet claimed in 1991 that Paribas' extensive privatization experience, including its own privatization in 1986, positioned the bank to "assist in the privatization program now underway in Sweden."[93]

In Sweden in 1991, center-right parties nominated state-owned companies like Swedish Steel, Swedish food company Procordia (of which Volvo was the largest shareholder), and Nordbanken bank for privatization.[94] Swedish politicians wanted to close the "widening investment gap" between outgoing capital and incoming investment. While Swedish companies had increased their investment in the EEC by a factor of 20 during the 1980s, business representatives from elsewhere in the region, like Sir Brian Corby of the CBI, said Sweden had been a "hostile environment for foreign investors" which had given the impression of "Fortress Sweden."[95] Swedish politicians, some of whom cultivated homegrown neoliberalism according to historian Jenny Andersson, recognized the GDP and employment contributions of the foreign firms in Sweden, like German Siemens, Dutch Philips, American IBM and

91 Lars Nord, "The Wallenberg Group – Meeting in Stockholm 08.08.91," Paribas, Dinan, 1AH-33, BNPPA.

92 "Paribas en europe du nord," January 1990, Paribas, Dinan, 100AH-999, BNPPA.

93 "Letter to M. Per Westerberg, Swedish Minister of Industry and Commerce," December 11, 1991, Paribas, Dinan, 1AH-33, BNPPA.

94 "Swedish Privatizations," January 17, 1991. Paribas, Dinan, 1AH-33, BNPPA.

95 Robert Taylor, "Swedish Investment Looks Inward," ADE News, August 14, 1991. Paribas, Dinan, 1AH-33, BNPPA.

General Motors (after its 1989 acquisition of Saab-Scania), and Swiss Brown-Boveri through its merger with Asea.[96] Swedish bankers expected "EC integration" would catalyze a new "stage of consolidation" within Swedish industry, "as the appetite for major foreign acquisitions to a large degree has been satisfied."[97] Tax reform "eased the tax burden of foreign companies," but most attractive to foreign firms was Sweden's application to join the EEC in summer 1991 and its linking of the Swedish Krona to the ECU. That the ruling Social Democrats also promised to prioritize competition instead of the prevailing local monopolies and change company laws to allow foreign firms to own more than 40 percent of Swedish subsidiaries further encouraged foreign investment.[98]

Paribas' Stockholm office became the gateway to renewed business in Scandinavia. Its deputy there, Lars Nord, appealed to Michel François-Poncet in 1991 to upgrade investment banking activities in Stockholm.[99] Nord asked for upgrades after client firms began seeking the Stockholm Office's expertise in intra-European and inter-Nordic mergers and acquisitions.[100] He described deeper integration as a potential regulatory challenge for the bank, but wider integration – especially the likely accession of Scandinavian countries – as a major business opportunity, especially since increased regional competition would accelerate mergers and acquisitions as industrial firms worked to achieve regional economies of scale. Moreover, Nord noted, Paribas could enjoy great returns from increased investment in its Scandinavian business, since it could be among the first and best positioned European banks to capitalize on both the opening of markets typically closed to foreign investment and the integration of those economies with the larger European internal market.[101] At meetings in Stockholm with members of Scandinavian banks, the chairmen of Paribas discussed mergers in light of the internal market, including a merger of Nordic bank SEB and insurer Skandia, planned for 1992 but opposed by Pehr Gyllenhammar,

[96] Jenny Andersson, "Neoliberalism from Within: The Business Fund and the Struggle for Market Ideology in Sweden," *Contemporary European History*, published online: January 28, 2025, 1–17.

[97] Lars Nord, "Svenska Handelsbanken Sphere – Industrivärden – Meeting in Stockholm, 09.08.91," Paribas, Dinan, 1AH-33, BNPPA.

[98] Robert Taylor, "Swedish Investment Looks Inward," ADE News, August 14, 1991. Paribas, Dinan, 1AH-33, BNPPA.

[99] Lars Nord, "Memo to Michel François-Poncet re: Upgrading of Investment Banking Activities at the Stockholm Office," 1991, Paribas, Dinan, 1AH-33, BNPPA.

[100] Ibid. [101] Ibid.

former chairman of Volvo and then vice chairman of SEB.[102] The Swedish Minister of Industry, Per Westerberg, and Head of Planning for the Swedish privatization program, Hans Lundgren, expressed interest in Paribas' privatization expertise, especially on the issue of Volvo's "rumored plans to increase ownership in Procordia to balance the unprofitable car division," the high cost of which "would create a cash negative position for Volvo," unacceptable given Volvo's primacy in the Swedish economy.[103] Paribas' Privatization Unit was well positioned, Lars Nord argued, to lend its expertise.[104] The bank's Capital Markets Group consulted on the privatization of Swedish Telecom in 1991, in which it recommended the "strategy of creating an international group of long-term core shareholders."[105]

For its economic primacy, shareholding in other firms, partnerships with other European carmakers, and connections to the Swedish state, Volvo loomed large in Paribas' operations in Sweden. In April 1991, Paribas banker Philippe Dulac reported to Michel François-Poncet and André Levy-Lang on his lunch meeting with Louis Schweitzer, then executive and later chairman of Renault, about Renault's relationship with Volvo, following a 1989 partnership deal between the two carmakers to give Volvo better access to the European market amid rising local labor costs.[106] Schweitzer explained to Dulac how Renault and Volvo were working on "common components" for heavy vehicles like trucks and also for intercompatibility in automobiles.[107] Eventually, Schweitzer envisioned a total merger of Régie Renault and AB Volvo, or at least a merger of their automotive divisions, until which time "the main challenge is to bring the spirit of cooperation down to the middle layer of average decision makers."[108] Schweitzer approached Dulac to consult on these merger plans, and Dulac reminded his bosses of the business opportunity for Paribas if the bank could "be associated with" this

102 Lars Nord, "Svenska Handelsbanken Sphere – Industrivärden – Meeting in Stockholm, 09.08.91," Paribas, Dinan, 1AH-33, BNPPA.

103 Lars Nord, "Swedish Privatizations," November 28, 1991, Paribas, Dinan, 1AH-33, BNPPA.

104 Lars Nord, "Notes de Stockholm, 7–9 août – 17 août 1991," August 20, 1991, Paribas, Dinan, 1AH-33, BNPPA.

105 Henrik Wallgren, "Memo on Telecom-Paribas Meeting in Stockholm 8 August 1991," August 9, 1991, Paribas, Dinan, 1AH-33, BNPPA.

106 Christian Daroutier, "Brief Update on Volvo Group," Paribas, Dinan, 1AH-33, BNPPA.

107 Philippe Dulac, "Dejeuner avec Louis Schweitzer," April 12, 1991, Paribas, Dinan, 1AH-33, BNPPA.

108 Ibid.: 2.

project.[109] This episode sheds additional light on the dynamics of car manufacturing in the Single Market described in Chapter 4 and the role of merchant banks like Paribas in cultivating the "European champions" the Commission envisioned in its plan for the internal market as discussed in Chapter 1.

Paribas did upgrade its Stockholm office in the 1990s, from which it facilitated mergers, acquisitions, privatizations, and the restructuring of Scandinavian economies as their democratic publics weighed membership in the EEC and EU. In the early 1990s, it also considered developing its business in Ireland, the new Czech Republic, and especially Austria, where potential industrial clients were numerous and there were many ongoing privatization projects, but which was "overbanked" and in need of "further privatization."[110] Economist Pierre Bruneau de la Salle noted Austria's potential, especially after the country met the Maastricht Treaty convergence criteria of price, exchange rate, and interest rate stability, a 3 percent annual deficit relative to GDP, and a 60 percent ratio of sovereign debt to GDP, but said the country needed to "further reduce the role of the state in the economy" to prepare to join the rest of Europe.[111] Clearly, demand for Paribas' expertise would continue through the decade, during which Austria, Sweden, and Finland joined the EU in 1995, as part of the fourth enlargement. Eight former socialist states in Central and Eastern Europe, including Hungary and Poland, joined in the fifth enlargement in 2004.

Conclusions

While the 1992 Program did not shape Paribas' business strategy to the degree it did for the auto manufacturers discussed in Chapter 4 or for the bank's clients, it did motivate the bank to develop Pan-European industrial holding companies, to participate in both national and transnational BIAs in opposition to European banking regulations and in support of competition policies much like the commercial BIAs described in Chapter 6, and to seize new business opportunities in markets beyond the EEC, especially in states that could soon become part of the Single internal Market like those in Central and Eastern and Northern Europe. Paribas' role in financing regional investment, facilitating privatization,

[109] Philippe Dulac, "Dejeuner avec Louis Schweitzer," April 12, 1991, Paribas, Dinan, 1AH-33, BNPPA: 1.

[110] F. W. Pfeil, "Memo to M. François-Poncet re: Visit of Dr. Ernst Löschner on 18 May," May 12, 1994, Paribas, Dinan, 1AH-240, BNPPA.

[111] Monsieur P. Bruneau de la Salle, "Letter to Michel François-Poncet re: Autriche," December 15, 1993, Paribas, Dinan, 1AH-240, BNPPA.

mergers, and acquisitions across Europe in the 1980s and 1990s contributed to economic transformations in numerous ways.

Paribas enabled the creation of the large European multinationals the Commission hoped for in its plan for market integration, especially by financing mergers and acquisitions, but also by supporting industrial partnerships like that between Renault and Volvo. Additionally, as a merchant bank, Paribas was particularly well positioned to capitalize on the privatization movement of the early 1990s, from Portugal to Sweden, Hungary to Poland. It carried out the privatizations the European Commission did not require but strongly supported in its effort to achieve an integrated, cohesive, capitalist internal market.[112] This widespread sell off of SOEs fundamentally changed the relationship between states and markets across Europe and further insulated economies from democratic publics, as feared by the French Communist Party and as this book's Conclusion addresses. That Western banks like Paribas financed this process, along with the industrial development that followed, in what one international paper called a "French attack on Hungary," secured Western ownership of Eastern European assets and profits, thereby exacerbating inequity in the region.[113] But banks like Paribas also readied so-called peripheral economies to join the European core, Single European Market, and, in some cases, Economic and Monetary Union.

112 On privatization in the EEC, see: Mattia Ravano and Grace Ballor, "National Choices and European Rules: Privatization and the European Commission," presented at LMU Munich, 2025.

113 Rémy Arnaud, "Les francais à l'assaut de la hongrie," *l'Entreprise*, Friday, May 7, 1993, Paribas, Dinan, 1AH-240, BNPPA.

6 Commerce against the Social Single Market

Had you blinked, you would have missed the reaction of European commerce to the launch of the Single Market Program in 1985 or the Single European Act that made market-making possible in 1986. The sector remained highly localized throughout the twentieth century, and its few multinational firms internationalized before and outside of the internal market. Retailers and distributors based in the region did not neglect the potential implications of "1992" for their business when plans to complete the internal market were announced in the mid-1980s. Instead, the Commission's White Paper on Completing the Internal Market all but ignored the sector, save two small legislative measures on electronic payments and price transparency.[1] By 1988, however, as the Commission accelerated market integration and implemented its social dimensions, retailers and distributors alike scrambled to form regional cooperatives and peak interest associations, citing a need to "defend" themselves against the Single Market and its new regulations. These commercial companies were less worried about the capture of the internal market by foreign competition than their counterparts in manufacturing like Volkswagen and BMW, discussed in Chapter 4, and less ambivalent about the potential advantages of market integration than European banks like Paribas, covered in Chapter 5. By contrast, commercial firms regionalized out of a concern that market integration would incentivize consolidation among producers, thereby driving up prices, and that the social policies introduced by the European Commission in the late 1980s would directly threaten their consumer-oriented, labor-intensive business. Ironically, as this chapter argues, the response of creating regional cooperatives, intensifying regional investment, and forming regional business associations ultimately made

[1] European Commission, "Towards a Single Market in Distribution: Internal Trade in the Community, the Commercial Sector, and the Completion of the Internal Market," COM (91) 41 final, Brussels, March 11, 1991, p. 16.

European commerce more European, positioning firms in the sector to help realize not only the economic objectives of the Single Market Program but even its social dimensions.

Business ambivalence about the 1992 Program is especially clear in the response of food retailers, like the Belgian grocer Delhaize. This family company – born out of the nineteenth century retail revolution, turned leader in twentieth-century internationalization – was at the center of efforts by food commerce to respond to the Single Market Program and its "flanking" social and environmental policies.[2] Its executives were also closely involved in the creation of new regional collaborations and sectoral interest associations, both of which aimed to shore up corporate interests against the tide of a rapidly changing business environment. Evidence from Delhaize's company archive, interviews with company executives, and the records of interest associations in which its executives were key members, reveal that fears about industry consolidation and plans for a social market economy drove Delhaize and many other commercial firms to reorient their political activity defensively around the apparatus of regional governance in Brussels just as progress toward the Single Market motivated them to Europeanize their business strategies as well.

This chapter begins by tracing the development of European food retail during the postwar commercial revolutions of the 1950s to 1970s, when firms like Delhaize had to adapt their strategies to rising household income, evolving consumer behavior, and shifting residential geography. It then examines the approaches of European policymakers to developing an internal commercial market and a social Single Market in the 1980s. While firms like Delhaize did not initially respond to the Single Market Program in the mid-1980s, they mobilized swiftly in the late 1980s to prepare for the new business and regulatory environment of an integrated regional market governed by social and environmental protections. Together with other food retailers, Delhaize formed sectoral clubs and associations to defend its interests: buying clubs collectivized price negotiating power against producer consolidation and protected profit margins, while interest associations brought distributors and retailers together to influence European policymaking.[3] At the same time,

[2] Laurent Warlouzet, "A Flanking European Welfare State: The European Community's Social Dimension, from Brandt to Delors (1969–1993)," *Contemporary European History* 33, no. 1 (2024): 23–36.

[3] For more on sectoral social dialogue, see: Anne Dufresne and Christophe Degryse, *The European Sectoral Social Dialogue: Actors, Developments and Challenges* (Bern: Peter Lang, 2006).

Delhaize and other commercial firms saw in the opening of Eastern Europe a profitable business opportunity, and they expanded quickly into the markets of Poland, Hungary, and the new Czech Republic in the early 1990s. As a result, the case of Delhaize gives us purchase on the complexity of business responses to the Single Market – ranging from "setting the agenda" for the 1992 Program, to adapting their business strategies to EEC competition policy, to becoming "reluctant Europeans" – and it demonstrates the diverse paths to regionalization *for* and *against* the Single Market.[4]

The Evolution of European Commerce

Delhaize was born of the same nineteenth century industrialization, advent of mass production, and commercial revolutions that gave rise to department stores like Paris' famous Le Bon Marché and its growing bourgeois clientele.[5] Delhaize's expansionary success was also made possible by new technologies in food preservation, health, and safety. In 1867, accounting professor Jules Delhaize, together with his eight brothers and brother-in-law Jules Vieujant, formed *Delhaize Freres et Cie*, a modern grocery chain. The company revolutionized food retail in Europe with its innovative business model of multiple-branch distribution, focus on specialty items and exotic goods, and priority for excellent customer service. The family company enjoyed immediate success. By 1914, Delhaize operated 774 "Le Lion" stores in Belgium alone, with marketing designed to invoke and capitalize on the legacy of the Belgian crown.[6]

[4] For a discussion of this spectrum of business responses to regional integration, see the Introduction of this book. On the argument that business "set the agenda" for the Single Market, see: Maria Green Cowles, "Setting the Agenda for a New Europe: The ERT and EC 1992," *JCMS: Journal of Common Market Studies* 33, no. 4 (1995): 501–526; See also: Neil Rollings and Laurent Warlouzet, "Business History and European Integration: How EEC Competition Policy Affected Companies' Strategies," *Business History* 62, no. 5 (2020): 717–742; Alexis Drach, "Reluctant Europeans? British and French Commercial Banks and the Common Market in Banking (1977–1992)," *Enterprise & Society* 21, no. 3 (2020): 768–798; Alan MacKinlay, Helen Mercer, and Neil Rollings, "Reluctant Europeans? The Federation of British Industries and European Integration, 1945–63," *Business History* 42, no. 4 (2000): 91–116.

[5] Several retailers were founded during this period of the late nineteenth century, including Le Bon Marché in Paris. For a history of nineteenth-century retail in Germany, see: Paul Lerner, *The Consuming Temple: Jews, Department Stores, and the Consumer Revolution in Germany, 1880–1940* (Ithaca, NY: *Cornell University Press*, 2015).

[6] Emmanuel Collet, *Delhaize "Le lion", épiciers depuis 1867* (Brussels: Racine Lannoo, 2003): 36.

Two world wars and an intervening depression resulted in tremendous losses for Delhaize: Stores were bombed, supplier facilities and producer farms destroyed, shipping routes severed, and the company lost a sizeable group of Jewish employees from one Belgian area to Nazi concentration camps. Its customers suffered similar fates. When the war ended in the mid 1940s, Delhaize initially struggled to get its stores restocked, restaffed, and back open to the public. But the 1950s marked the beginning of a new chapter in the grocer's history, and Delhaize's postwar success reflected the wider transformation of the commercial revolution of the twentieth century.[7] Although many European countries rationed food supplies throughout the 1940s – Italy into the mid-1950s – the economic miracles of postwar reconstruction contributed to production booms, steep wage increases, rising household incomes, and new consumer demands. Newfound purchasing power, coupled with pent-up consumer demand after decades of conflict and decline, fueled consumption of the durable and consumer goods made readily available by advancements in the mass manufacturing of appliances and passenger vehicles.[8] Increased wages and new financial products enabled many middle-class households to afford their own cars, and consumer preferences for food products were transformed by the growing accessibility of home refrigerators, ovens, and washing machines.

Concurrent with these changes in production and consumption was a remaking of the economic geography of European commerce. As in the US, motorization begat suburbanization: Europeans increasingly moved to residential communities outside of urban centers, and retailers followed their customers to the suburbs. In addition to neighborhood chain stores, European food retailers also opened new hypermarkets

[7] For more on Delhaize's early history, see: Grace Ballor, "Agents of Integration: Multinational Firms and the European Union" PhD dissertation, UCLA, 2018: Chapter 6.

[8] There is a large literature on changes in postwar wages, living standards, and consumption. See, for example: Kristin Ross, *Fast Cars, Clean Bodies: Decolonization and the Reordering of French Culture* (Cambridge, MA: MIT Press, 1996); Victoria de Grazia, *Irresistible Empire: America's Advance through Twentieth-Century Europe* (Cambridge, MA: Harvard University Press, 2006). See also debates about the role of the US' Marshall Plan aid in the postwar economic miracles: Barry Eichengreen, *Europe's Postwar Recovery* (Cambridge: Cambridge University Press, 1995); J. Bradford DeLong and Barry Eichengreen, "The Marshall Plan: History's Most Successful Structural Adjustment Program," Working Paper, Working Paper Series (National Bureau of Economic Research, November 1991); Barry Eichengreen and Marc Uzan, "Marshall Plan: Economic Effects and Implications for Eastern Europe and the Former USSR," *Economic Policy* 7, no. 14 (1992): 13–75; Tamás Vonyó, *The Economic Consequences of the War: West Germany's Growth Miracle after 1945* (Cambridge: Cambridge University Press, 2018).

modeled after American super groceries.[9] The Mutual Security Agency, the successor of the Economic Cooperation Administration that administered the Marshall Plan from 1948 to 1951, and the International Association of Chain Stores (ICA) both hosted European retailers in Washington DC in the 1950s for business exchange programs, designed to facilitate knowledge transfers, build business connections, and encourage transatlantic and intra-European business cooperation.[10] Just a year after participating in an ICA meeting in 1956, Delhaize opened continental Europe's first hypermarket in the Brussels suburb of Flagey, which offered a wide range of produce, dry goods, and household items.[11] Their visit to the US also exposed Delhaize's leadership to a self-service retail model, which they quickly imported to their Belgian business for its labor efficiency.[12] Participation in US business exchanges also laid the foundation for Delhaize to invest in the US in the decades that followed.

As revolutions in manufacturing fueled economic growth and retail chains and hypermarkets spread through the suburbs of Western Europe in the late 1950s and 1960s to meet rising consumer demands, consumers across the region enjoyed access to diverse goods, more calories, and greater choice than ever before. This was especially true after the European customs union promised in the Treaty of Rome was completed in 1968, by which time household consumption had increased by 80 percent since the first Marshall Aid funds were dispersed in 1948 to facilitate European reconstruction after the Second World War.[13] Still, commercial supply chains remained relatively localized during this period due to the specificity of consumer tastes and differences in national health and safety regulation of food products. Companies like Delhaize were eager to expand, however. Not only did countries like Belgium offer only small domestic consumer markets, making "expansion

[9] For more on the shift from small shops to hypermarkets in France, see the ongoing work of Tristan Jacques. Hypermarkets are markets carrying extensive ranges of fresh and pantry food products, as well as home goods, personal care and even clothing items.

[10] Such programs continued well into the late twentieth century: In 1989, GEDIS advertised the "11eme voyage d'étude CBD aux Etas Unis, 13 jours à l'exploration de nouvelles tendances et technologies" to visit hypermarkets, supermarkets, and specialized food stores in New York, Ohio, and California. See: GEDIS B.14.2, Delhaize Corporate Archive (hereafter DEL).

[11] For more on the impact of these exchange programs on foreign investment, see: Grace Ballor, "From the 'American Challenge' to European Expansion: Transatlantic Economic Relations from the 1950s to the 1970s," *Relations internationales* 180, no. 4 (2019): 43–57.

[12] Collet, *Delhaize "Le lion,"* 86.

[13] Collet, *Delhaize*, 99.

outside Belgium essential for Delhaize," according to Gui de Vaucleroy, great grandson of one of the retailer's founders and Deputy Director during the 1990s, but new restrictions imposed amid the oil shock and stagflation crises of the 1970s further constrained domestic retail expansion.[14] In 1973, Belgian lawmakers passed the Ackerman Act, a "genuine padlock law" reminiscent of the country's earlier legislation to block chain store expansion in defense of SMEs, which set limits on the number of chain stores a retailer could operate.[15] France and the Netherlands enacted their own similar protections. As a result, retailers like Delhaize and the French grocery chain Carrefour could no longer grow within their home markets. Meanwhile, expansion into neighboring countries was also constrained by padlock laws and fierce competition. Only widespread int ernationalization offered a path to growth.

Delhaize initially considered expanding into nearby North Africa, but "religious problems" and cultural differences motivated its leadership to look for growth markets more like its native Belgium.[16] Eager to diversify its political risk during the ongoing Cold War, Delhaize made its first major international acquisition in 1974 in the US, where its executives had already established contacts during the ICA meetings two decades earlier and where regulation was lax relative to European markets.[17] Rather than risk greenfield investment, the family board of Delhaize resolved to acquire a small chain with a proven market but in need of capital. Food Town Stores, a new retailer with eighteen stores in North Carolina, seemed ideal because of its debt-free balance sheet and proximity to direct flights between nearby Washington DC and parent company headquarters in Belgium.[18] Most attractive was its 450 percent growth in revenue between 1967 and 1970, thanks to the bulk-buying strategy of its founder, Ralph Ketner.[19] Delhaize initially acquired 34.5 percent of Food Town and allowed Ketner to retain full managerial

[14] Grace Ballor, Interview with Gui de Vaucleroy, Audio recording. May 11, 2023.

[15] Collet, *Delhaize*, 136. Peter Heyrman also described this protectionist policy in his "Unlocking the Padlock: Retail and Public Policy in Belgium, 1930–1961," *Business History* 59, no. 3 (2017): 1049–1081. The earlier Belgian padlock law (1930–1961) had restricted chain stores to 400 meters square in areas with 50,000 residents or fewer.

[16] Grace Ballor, Interview with Gui de Vaucleroy, Audio recording. May 11, 2023.

[17] Grace Ballor, Interview with Pierre-Olivier Beckers-Vieujant, Audio recording. March 31, 2023.

[18] Grace Ballor, Interview with Gui de Vaucleroy, Audio recording. May 11, 2023.

[19] Ketner detailed his bulk-buying, low-price approach in: Ralph Ketner, Jason Lesley, and Mark Wineka, *Five Fast Pennies* (New York: Theodora, 1994). In many ways, Ketner's approach resembled the business models of Walmart (est. 1950) and Costco (est. 1976), although Food Town executives claim this legacy to be their own.

control.[20] By 1983 – when Food Town earned a reputation as the "fastest growing food chain in America" and its stock value growth outpaced that of the new technology company Microsoft 73 to 1 – Delhaize increased its stake to 50 percent and renamed its US subsidiary Food Lion to bring it in line with the Belgian brand's image.[21] While Delhaize's second US acquisition of Alterman Foods in 1979 was ultimately unsuccessful, Delhaize's US subsidiaries quickly became the Belgian parent company's most profitable assets, contributing up to 80 percent of the group's revenue.[22] Through simultaneous geographic expansion and vertical integration, Food Lion grew to operate 881 stores, nine distribution centers, and a truck fleet across South Carolina, Virginia, Florida, Tennessee, Georgia, Texas, Kentucky, Maryland, Delaware, West Virginia, and Pennsylvania.[23]

By the 1980s, consolidation characterized food commerce in parts of Western Europe as well. Not only had the restrictive padlock laws been lifted in Belgium and the Netherlands, but new technologies in communication and computing enabled distributors to manage supply chains digitally, providing valuable information for minimizing waste and maximizing efficiency. Retailers, too, began automating checkout counters, accepting digital payments from customers, and maintaining tight control of their inventories. Detailed sales information motivated high-volume retailers like Delhaize to exert greater control over product specifications and maximize higher profit margins by increasingly contracting producers to make "own label" goods, products bearing the retailer's brand, consequently blurring the lines between wholesale and retail commerce. These developments also created new labor, privacy, and competition challenges for regulators, even as they contributed to the rise of larger commercial firms.

After advising Portuguese grocer Jeronimo Martins in the early 1980s, Delhaize seized on a second opportunity for international expansion, this time within its own region. Its good working relationship with the firm, combined with the "attractive economic prospects of Portugal, which was undergoing transitions to democracy and capitalism to enter the EEC in 1986, made Delhaize look for a more capitalistic link between both companies."[24] In 1984, the partnership between Delhaize with

[20] Ketner maintained managerial control until his retirement in April 1991. Grace Ballor, Interview with Linda Ketner, Audio recording. April 26, 2019; Records of the North Carolina Business Hall of Fame.

[21] Collet, *Delhaize*, 169. Not only did the presence of another Food Town chain in Tennessee require Food Town to taken on a new name in order to enter that market, but the name change further consolidated the US firm under its Belgian parent.

[22] Grace Ballor, Interview with Pierre-Olivier Beckers-Vieujant, Audio recording. March 31, 2023.

[23] Food Lion, Inc., *Delhaize Annual Report 1992*, Harvard Baker Library, 36.

[24] Collet, *Delhaize*, 177.

40 percent ownership and Jeronimo Martins with 60 percent ownership opened the first store under the new brand Pingo Doce. Within just five years, Pingo Doce opened thirty-three points of sale and grew its sales to ESC 39 billion per year.[25] The partnership dissolved in 1992 over a dispute about whether to enter the hypermarket business: The Delhaize board did not support the hypermarket plan, but the sale of its shares of Pingo Doce proved very profitable anyway, and its experience in Portugal laid a foundation for later regional expansion.

Vertical integration accelerated the growth of large commercial companies in the UK, France, and West Germany and further increased their ability to implement new systems and managerial practices. Concentration occurred to a lesser extent in Denmark, the Benelux states, and the industrialized regions of Italy, where hypermarkets slowly claimed greater market share over smaller sellers. But the rate of change was slowest in Spain, Portugal, Greece, Ireland, and rural Italy, which strongly resisted retail concentration and where SMEs dominated markets throughout the 1980s.[26] Such national divergences resulted in commercial heterogeneity across the region. When European policymakers began to deliberate how to make a single, internal market in the early 1980s, they listed these structural differences in commerce among the primary obstacles to regional economic cohesion and development.[27]

Toward a Single Commercial Market

Despite provisions for the free circulation of goods in the EEC established in Articles 30 and 36, 95 and 96 of the Treaty of Rome, and even after the European Court of Justice's 1979 ruling in the *Cassis de Dijon* case introduced the principle of mutual recognition and provided for the free circulation of goods across the EEC's member states, European commerce remained nationally fragmented. Recognizing this, the Commission outlined in its White Paper on Completing the Internal Market aims to integrate member state markets by facilitating cross-border business. But the vast majority of articles in the 1985 White Paper and subsequent Single European Act focused on manufacturing and banking and paid little initial attention to the specific needs of integrating commerce beyond updates to the Common Agricultural

[25] Collet, *Delhaize*, 177.

[26] European Commission, "Towards a Single Market in Distribution: Internal Trade in the Community, the Commercial Sector, and the Completion of the Internal Market," COM(91) 41 final, Brussels, March 11, 1991, p. 3.

[27] See Chapter 1 on these debates.

Policy.[28] The Commission did issue a communication on "Community Legislation on Foodstuffs" in November 1985, in which it differentiated the aspects of market integration that required Community legislation from those that could be left to market forces.[29] Among the areas requiring European laws were: the protection of the health and safety of humans, per Article 36 of the Treaty of Rome, and fair trade, requiring proper labeling, quality control, and the protection of geographical indications for the provenance of specialty goods.[30] Consequently, the Commission needed to draft common policy in these areas during the 1992 Program.

When, very much at the instigation of then Commissioner for Industrial Affairs Étienne Davignon, the European Commission began meeting with industry groups like the Big Twelve Round Table, the ERT, and CCMC in the late 1970s, it also recognized the need for greater regional representation of the trade sector, which it saw as both fundamental to a robust European economy and problematically fragmented.[31] Some early international sectoral BIAs had been created in the postwar period, like the democratic Comité internationale des entreprises et succursales (International Association of Chainstores, CIES), which met regularly to discuss shared interests, and the Paris-based Centre des relations internationales pour le commerce de gros (Center for International Relations in Wholesale Trade), established in 1949 to bring commercial firms together around shared business and political interests. As the nascent Community worked to remove tariff barriers and create a customs union between its six member states in the 1950s and 1960s, existing national associations of wholesalers and retailers increasingly engaged with one another to form new regional associations, including the Groupement européen des maisons d'alimentation et d'approvisionnement à succursales (European Multiple Retailers' Association, GEMAS), created in Brussels in 1965. But Davignon

[28] See: European Commission, "Perspectives for the Common Agricultural Policy" Brussels, July 15, 1985, COM(85) 333 final.

[29] European Commission, "Completion of the Internal Market: Community Legislation on Foodstuffs," November 8, 1985.

[30] The protection of geographical indications was especially important for producers of specialty foods and beverages in countries like Italy and France, where localized traditions gave wines, cheeses, cured meats and other goods high export value. For analysis of how protection for geographical indications intersected with European market integration in the production and distribution of wine in France, Italy, and Germany, see the ongoing research of Dr. Lisbeth Matzer at LMU Munich.

[31] European Commission, "Habilitation dans le secteur du Commerce – nomination des membres du Comité du Commerce et de la Distribution," SEC(81)843, Vol. 1981/0038: Annex I.

wanted to bring sectoral leaders together in an even more concentrated way under the auspices of the Commission.[32] After what must have been a sufficiently convincing "experimental period of three years," during which two new regional interest associations were formed – the Confédération européenne du commerce de détail (European Confederation of Retail Trade, CECD) and the Federation of European Wholesale and International Trade Associations (FEWITA) – the Commission formalized the Committee on Commerce and Distribution (CCD) in May 1981.[33] This Committee aimed to facilitate the "constant improvement of living and working conditions and harmonious economic development," which the policy-makers in Brussels believed could be advanced through "close and permanent links with trade interests."[34] Karl-Heinz Narjes, commissioner for Competition from 1981 to 1985 and author of the Commission's decision, articulated the CCD's express purpose: providing the Commission with information about European commerce and the effects of regional policymaking on business in the sector.[35]

Representatives of the hotel, catering, advertising, and leasing industries were included in the CCD in addition to franchise firms and a wide variety of retailers and wholesalers. Of the forty-two members of the Committee installed in unpaid, two-year terms through a Commission approval process, more than half were designated for experts in the sector representing regional retail trading organizations. The other seats were allocated to representatives from national commercial organizations, to "those particularly qualified on matters of commerce and distribution, all heads or directors of companies," and to UNICE and the Permanent Chambers of Commerce and Industry, which were given one observer seat each.[36] By working closely with the Commission, the CCD aimed to

[32] The Bibliotheque Nationale Française maintains several texts on the CIES: https://data.bnf.fr/fr/12091164/comite_international_des_entreprises_a_succursales/.

[33] European Commission, "Further Delegation of Powers in Respect of Trade: Appointment of Members of the Committee on Commerce and Distribution," Brussels, May 26, 1981.

[34] Official Journal of the European Communities, Commission Decision of May 20, 1981, establishing a Committee on Commerce and Distribution (81/428/EEC), Preamble. van Ewijk dated the committee's origin to 1979, when European retailers became aware of the Commission's intention to focus on commerce in the region.

[35] European Commission, "Further Delegation of Powers in Respect of Trade: Appointment of Members of the Committee on Commerce and Distribution," Brussels, May 26, 1981.

[36] Articles 3 and 4, Commission Decision 81/428/EEC. The Official Journal was tasked with publishing a list of the Committee's members; European Commission, "Habilitation dans le secteur du Commerce – nomination des membres du Comité du Commerce et de la Distribution," SEC(81)843, Vol. 1981/0038. Note: The

facilitate the "constant improvement of living and working conditions and harmonious economic development," which policymakers in Brussels believed could be advanced through "close and permanent links with trade interests."[37]

While the CCD did provide the European Commission with information about commerce in the region, neither commercial firms nor policymakers perceived the committee to have made a meaningful change in the integration of European commerce in the early and mid-1980s. The launch of the Single Market Program motivated the CCD to pay greater attention to the changing European business environment, though, such that by 1989, the CCD had six permanent working groups focused on a wide range of issues including "commerce in view of 1992/ internal market," and fourteen subgroups addressing everything from competition and SMEs to "EC external policy-Fortress Europe-Article 115 EC Treaty" to the transport of goods through non-EEC countries.[38] The Commission, committed to ensuring that "the needs of commerce are properly reflected in all areas" of its work, also increasingly saw the CCD as a "valuable source of expert advice" on sectoral issues like the environment, consumer protection, means of payment and external trade.[39]

Biannual reports on progress toward the internal market in 1987 and 1988 revealed the need to accelerate the Single Market Program considerably to meet the 1992 deadline.[40] By late 1988, the qualified "majority voting rule [wa]s beginning to bite and the council work [became] faster."[41] And by 1989, the Council of Ministers recognized that the successful "Europeanization" of retail and distribution would be "indispensable to the efficient working of the market" and drafted new

Commission's decision to create the CCD was authored by competition Commissioner Karl-Heinz Narjes.

37 Official Journal of the European Communities, Commission Decision of May 20, 1981 establishing a Committee on Commerce and Distribution. (81/428/ EEC), Preamble.

38 Aad van Ewijk, "Approved Project with Revised Budget, 13 July 1990," GEDIS B.14.2, DEL: 2.

39 European Commission, "Towards a Single Market in Distribution: Internal Trade in the Community, the Commercial Sector, and the Completion of the Internal Market," COM(91) 41 final, Brussels, March 11, 1991, pp. 11, 4.

40 These reports included date on the achievement percentage of the 300 steps toward legislative harmonization required to complete the internal market. See, for example, European Commission, "Second report from the Commission of the European Communities on the completion of the internal market (18 May 1987)."

41 European Commission, "Completing the Internal Market: An Area without Internal Frontiers: The Progress Report Required by Article 8B of the Treaty," COM(88)650 final, Brussels, November 17, 1988.

directives for the sector.[42] It described the distribution and retailing of food as "one of the most important aspects of the common market," as much for its reflection of the health and wellbeing of citizens as for its tendency toward fragmentation through national regulation.[43] Not only did commerce account for about 17 percent of output and employment in the Community in the late 1980s, but European commerce was still partitioned along national lines because of structural fragmentation, a lack of regional retail multinationals, and the persistence of national distribution channels. In short, it quickly became clear that the success of the internal market was contingent in large part on the "international ization " or "regionalization" of European commerce and that "[s]-ustainable economic prosperity depends on a balanced development of productive and commercial activity."[44] The Council subsequently passed a resolution on commerce in November 1989 in which it asked the Commission to develop recommendations for ensuring that retail and distribution would fit into existing community policies and align with the objectives of the internal market.[45]

The Commission spent the following year consulting commercial business associations and trade federations, out of which it developed a plan to internationalize commerce in the region "Towards a Single Market in Distribution."[46] Beyond the work of the Single Market Program to harmonize member state legislation, the Commission aimed to not only to "improve understanding and awareness of the obstacles regional retailers and distributors uniquely faced" and remove existing issues, but also to "anticipate problems before they arise and to encourage self-regulation."[47] Following the logic of the New Approach described in Chapter 3, the Commission resolved only to draft formal

42 European Council, "Council Directive of 14 June 1989 on the Official Control of Foodstuffs," 89/397/EEC; Official Journal of the European Communities, "Council Resolution of 14 November 1989 on Internal Trade in the Context of the Internal Market," (89/C 297/02).

43 European Council, "Council Directive of 14 June 1989 on the Official Control of Foodstuffs," 89/397/EEC.

44 Official Journal of the European Communities, "Council Resolution of 14 November 1989 on Internal Trade in the Context of the Internal Market," (89/C 297/02). (This argument echoed the Commission's vision for the Single Market as described in Chapter 1.)

45 Official Journal of the European Communities, "Council Resolution of 14 November 1989 on Internal Trade in the Context of the Internal Market," (89/C 297/02).

46 European Commission, "Towards a Single Market in Distribution: Internal Trade in the Community, the Commercial Sector, and the Completion of the Internal Market," COM(91) 41 final, Brussels, March 11, 1991.

47 Ibid., Summary: 1–3.

proposals for directives and regulations as a last resort.[48] In the Commission's view, links between suppliers, retailers, and customers could facilitate the free movement of goods across member state borders. Further concentration was, they believed, a core element of this regionalization, since vertically integrated firms with subsidiaries in multiple member states were best positioned to capture and retain market share. The Commission's objective was to "assist the process" of "convergence in commercial structures," itself a "probable natural consequence of the evolution of the internal market."[49] It argued that "commercial development and internationalization will to a significant extent be carried forward *naturally* as businesses respond to the completion of the internal market." Seeing regionalization as a natural response to the 1992 Program streamlined the Community's role to providing quality information, removing any regulatory obstacles, and encouraging businesses to participate in its policies and programs.[50] In the context of the 1992 Program, transportation infrastructure became increasingly important for the completion of a Single commercial Market. To gain a clearer picture of European commerce and develop policies to promote integration in the sector, the Commission tasked the EEC's Statistical Office, Eurostat, with maintaining data on European commerce.[51] It also aimed to collect information on national regulations affecting commerce, all of which it planned to circulate back to the business community.

For European policymakers, firm size was key for market preparedness. In its communication on completing an internal market in commerce, the Commission viewed trade as not just a sector, but as a "process or function within the economy" and re-narrated the success of American, European, and East Asian economic prosperity as a function of commercial integration.[52] The Commission expected large firms to adapt well to the enlarged market and anticipated SMEs would need to engage in joint activities with other firms to prepare for the

[48] Chapters 1 and 3 described the logic of the "New Approach," which was central to the Commission's efforts to develop European standards.

[49] European Commission, "Towards a Single Market in Distribution: Internal Trade in the Community, the Commercial Sector, and the Completion of the Internal Market," COM(91) 41 final, Brussels, March 11, 1991, p. 10.

[50] Ibid.

[51] On December 17, 1990, the Commission informed the Council of its program to develop statistics for the service sector in document COM(90) 578.

[52] On market integration in the US and Europe, see: Michelle P. Egan, *Single Markets: Economic Integration in Europe and the United States* (Oxford: Oxford University Press, 2015); Craig Parsons, "The Extraordinary, Taken-for-Granted Achievement of Europe's Single Market," in *European Studies: Past, Present, Future*, ed. Erik Jones (Newcastle upon Tyne: Agenda Publishing, 2020). See also the ongoing ARENA project directed by Craig Parsons.

internal market. Article 85 of the Treaty of Rome prohibited agreements designed to restrict competition, but equally allowed for any arrangement "which contributes to improving the production or distribution of goods or to promoting technical or economic progress, while allowing consumers a full share of the resulting benefit, and which fulfills the other conditions of Article 85(3)," which already permitted joint activities like exclusive distribution and franchising.[53] As Chapter 1 explained, economies of scale were the primary tool of EEC industrial policy during the Single Market Program, but EEC competition policy prohibited the creation of purchasing cooperatives, even if the Commission believed that such structures "may also be an essential precondition for the development of new distributive channels, which may be regarded as a source of economic benefit" and "essential to creating a favorable economic environment for SMEs" since smaller firms tend to be more risk averse and lack the resources required for competitive internationaliza tion.[54] While the Commission encouraged collaboration among SMEs, it worried about the same behavior by large firms, who were also likely to pursue partnerships with similar companies for the purposes of "pooling their expertise in procurement, marketing, and other fields." The rise of multinational wholesale chains had further confirmed the potential for big business partnerships to run afoul of EEC competition rules.

Such findings required policymakers in the Commission to pay greater attention to commerce. The macroeconomic shift from manufacturing to services increased the sector's importance, and amid the challenges of German reunification and the Gulf War in 1990 and 1991, the Commission found only commerce was posting consistent gains.[55] To maximize the sector's contributions to regional growth and ensure its alignment with the economic and social objectives of 1992, the Commission strengthened its ties with the "consultative mechanism" of the CCD.[56] Policymakers tapped the CCD's working groups for input on how commerce viewed the internal market.[57] The Commission also

[53] European Commission, "Towards a Single Market in Distribution: Internal Trade in the Community, the Commercial Sector, and the Completion of the Internal Market," COM(91) 41 final, Brussels, March 11, 1991, p. 18; Commission Regulation 1983/83 and Regulation 4087/88, respectively.

[54] European Commission, "Towards a Single Market in Distribution: Internal Trade in the Community, the Commercial Sector, and the Completion of the Internal Market," COM(91) 41 final, Brussels, March 11, 1991, p. 18.

[55] GEDIS, "GEDIS November/December 1990 Meeting," GEDIS B.14.2, DEL.

[56] European Commission, "Towards a Single Market in Distribution: Internal Trade in the Community, the Commercial Sector, and the Completion of the Internal Market," COM(91) 41 final, Brussels, March 11, 1991, pp. 11, 4.

[57] van Ewijk, "Approved Project with Revised Budget," 2.

used the CCD as a platform from which to conduct an extensive survey to inform its design of regional vocational training programs like FORCE to boost European employment and living standards.[58] The collapse of the Soviet Union and opening of Eastern Europe made the goal of regional cohesion all the more challenging. But the Commission expected that through structural funds and by working closely with business associations it could even bring about "convergent prices" across the Community as the "single market grows toward maturity."[59]

Meanwhile, commercial organizations like GEDIS circulated encouragement to its members about how "big and diverse industrial multinationals [we]re again very advanced in putting in place winning strategies on internationalization, diversification, and the domination of supply chains and subsidiaries."[60] Distributors and retailers did adapt their structures to the new business environment of the market, largely to defend themselves against the "challenge" it presented.

Europeanizing against the Single Market

The Commission expected European companies to take considerable interest in the Single Market Program and its industrial, competition, and commercial policies. Wholesale distributors supplying retail chains did respond to "Europe 1992" in earnest, acquiring firms in second and third countries in preparation for the reality of a large internal market.[61] And sectoral trade and business associations began to discuss the internal market in the wake of the 1985 White Paper. The CIES dedicated a session of its 1986 meeting in Cannes to the topic of 1992, which was headlined by the former French president (1974–1981) Valéry Giscard d'Estaing, who spoke about "the union of Europe" as a "factor of security and stability in the Western world," presented integrated Europe as a "kind of continental state," and encouraged companies to prepare to

[58] European Commission, "Towards a Single Market in Distribution: Internal Trade in the Community, the Commercial Sector, and the Completion of the Internal Market," COM(91) 41 final, Brussels, March 11, 1991, p. 21. For more on these programs, see Chapter 1.

[59] European Commission, "Towards a Single Market in Distribution: Internal Trade in the Community, the Commercial Sector, and the Completion of the Internal Market," COM(91) 41 final, Brussels, March 11, 1991, p. 7.

[60] Remo Linda, "L'antitrust européen et les concurrances de la dernière génération: oligopolistique, globale, sauvage, civilisée, structurante, endogène, multiple," GEDIS B.14.2, DEL: 7, 13.

[61] Evidence of this comes from the response of retailers to Europe 1992 and feeling the need to catch up to distributors who had regionalized earlier. See: van Ewijk, "Approved Project with Revised Budget, 13 July 1990."

price goods in the European currency unit (ECU), already reflecting a view that one market needed one money.[62] Pierre Delhaize attended the CIES meeting in Cannes and took many pages of notes about presentations from d'Estaing and his peers in retail commerce.[63] But the Delhaize board made no mention of the Single Market Program in 1985 when the Commission introduced its plan, nor in 1986 when the Single European Act provided the institutional reform needed to complete the internal market by the ambitious deadline of December 1992. Only in June 1987, Delhaize executives made passing mention of having asked the company's special projects manager, Mr. D. Maeck, to study the implications of "European deregulation in 1992" for their business.[64] Because this study was not mentioned in any subsequent minutes of the board nor in the firm's annual reports, it is unclear whether it was ever completed, and there is no record of its conclusions shaping company strategy in late 1987 or early 1988.[65]

Delhaize's perception of the 1992 Program started to change in mid-1988, however, as did the views of several other European commercial firms. That was the year that the "great European 1992 talk, as far as we were concerned, had just begun," according to the chairman of the Italian food retailer Esselunga.[66] It was in 1988 that the pace of legislative harmonization across the EEC quickened thanks to the SEA's institutional reforms. As Chapter 1 described, it was also in 1988 that Paolo Cecchini completed his report on "The Cost of Non-Europe," the Delors Commission published its mid-term review on progress toward the internal market, and the Delors Report outlined a three-stage plan for Economic and Monetary Union. Half-way to 1992, European food retailers like Delhaize started paying attention to the Single Market and what they perceived to be its potential threats to their business: open borders, reorganized suppliers, harmonized monetary and tax systems,

[62] Valéry Giscard d'Estaing, "L'Union de l'europe, facteur de securite et stabilite du monde occidentale," March 10–11, 1986, B.6.9 1973-92 CIES, DEL; At the center of the European Monetary System created in 1979, was the ECU, the European currency unit, a weighted average of member state currencies. For work on the private use of and private market for ECUs, see ongoing joint work by Aleksandra Komornicka and Alexis Drach.

[63] Delhaize's notes on the event are in the file: B.6.9 1973-92 CIES, DEL.

[64] "Proces verbal du comite de direction du 9 juin 1987," PVCD 1987, DEL.

[65] Additionally, the company archive could not locate any records of a final report on 1992, nor could Gui de Vaucleroy or Pierre-Olivier Beckers recall its existence when interviewed for this book.

[66] Bernardo Capriotti (Esselunga), "Letter to Mr. Fritz Ahlquist (Ahold)," November 10, 1989, B.14.1, DEL.

transformed logic systems and digitized distribution systems.[67] Contrary to the Commission's competition policy objectives, these companies feared that the proposed reduction of financial and nonfinancial trade barriers would "stimulate manufacturers to centralize production facilities and encourage distributors to service larger geographical areas."[68] Consolidation among producers, they worried, would put retailers at a significant price disadvantage unless they developed a new strategy of their own.

To fend off these challenges, noncompeting food retailers formed buying clubs to collectively purchase goods and protect their margins. "It's very simple: everyone negotiates with everyone," quipped Jan Delveaux, lead buyer at the Belgian Grand Bazar Innovation Bon Marché (GIB Group).[69] Building on the precedent of Intergroup Trading, a club founded in the Netherlands in the interwar period, and Intercoop, a Danish buying club created in 1971, Delveaux spearheaded the creation of two early groups in mid-1988, including Eurogroup with Dutch Vendex Food and German ReWe.[70] At the same time, French Casino "wove a European spiderweb" with British Argyll and Dutch Ahold to create the European Retail Alliance at a meeting in Marrakech in summer 1988, which Harvard Business School's professor of retailing Walter J. Salmon said "could be the beginning of a chain which ultimately operates throughout the common market under a single trade name or at least acknowledges to consumers a common affiliation. Furthermore," Salmon continued, "the alliance enhances the influence of each constituent in dealing with suppliers who already operate throughout the common market and facilitates cooperation in such areas as the procurement of private label and the development of common systems."[71] The Casino-Argyll-Ahold alliance also soon developed Associated Marketing Services (AMS) to coordinate advertising activities across an even wider network including Italian La Rinascente and Swiss Migros.[72] The European Marketing Distribution (EMD), a purchasing organization still operating today, was formed shortly after, in 1989 in Switzerland.

67 R. de Kat (SHV Holdings), "International Buying," August 22, 1988, Groupement d'achats, B.14.1, DEL.
68 Delhaize Chairman's Office, "Joint Buying Organization," September 19, 1988, Groupement d'achats, B.14.1, DEL.
69 Marianne Hendrickx, "Vive la centrale," *Tendances*, September 7, 1989, Groupement d'achats, B.14.1, DEL.
70 Eurostat, "Retailing in the European Single Market," Brussels, Eurostat, 1993: 28.
71 Walter J. Salmon, "Multinational Retailing in the Nineties," September 1, 1989, B.6.9. Seminaires CIES (1973–1992), DEL.
72 "Les poupees russes de Casino," LSA September 15, 1989, Groupement d'achats, B.14.1, DEL.

In Fall 1988, Delhaize chairman Guy Beckers approached chairmen at several other Western European food retailers, including British Sainsbury's, French Carrefour, Italian Esselunga, and Dutch Makro, about creating their own club with the goal of "buying together in view of the 1992 EEC market."[73] Delhaize had to start its own club because it could not join the other existing ones, in which its closest competitors, Colruyt and Carrefour, were already participating.[74] To quell any skepticism and make a case for the group, Beckers assured his counterparts and appealed to their shared market concerns: "This is a European matter; we are not competing, our assortments and qualities are similar; with the other partners we could really reinforce each other to face the 1992 situation."[75] Through collaboration, they could meet the challenge of market integration. Several chairmen responded to the proposal with interest, prompting a first meeting of the group in Brussels in October 1988. They also exchanged "homework": unaudited company reports and manifestos on the importance, method, and means of collective purchasing. Ultimately, Sainsbury's and Esselunga joined Delhaize's new club, which offered the "young and small" Italian chain a chance to regionalize so "that the next generation will be able to make it grow and thrive."[76] de Vaucleroy remembered Delhaize's collaboration with Esselunga fondly, given the "wonderful contacts" the Belgians had at the Italian firm and the way the buying club was a "success for both companies."[77]

As they envisioned it, the new Groupement d'achats, or buying club, would include no more than one company from each EEC country, foster close connections between the lead buyers at each firm, and create a minimum joint structure complete with a pool of common funds. Its aim was to focus on "simple" core goods with long shelf lives and marketability to consumers across the EEC, the "obvious example" of which is a branded product with wide appeal like Nescafe. But, while goods from producers like Nestle, Unilever, and Coca Cola would suit a range of consumer markets, the rationalization and monopolization retailers anticipated with the Single Market would reduce the benefit of joint buying from big, powerful suppliers. Instead, the buying club planned to jointly source products from areas of the world where "it is

[73] Guy Beckers, "Letter to Mr. de Kat," August 11, 1988, Groupement d'achats, B.14.1, DEL. Beckers also tried to woo Ahold over to the new club.

[74] Grace Ballor, Interview with Gui de Vaucleroy, Audio recording. May 11, 2023.

[75] Guy Beckers, "Letter to Mr. Albert Heijn," December 1, 1988, B.14.1, DEL.

[76] Bernardo Capriotti (Esselunga), "Letter to Mr. Fritz Ahlquist (Ahold)," November 10, 1989, Groupement d'achats, B.14.1, DEL.

[77] Grace Ballor, Interview with Gui de Vaucleroy, Audio recording. May 11, 2023.

difficult to obtain specific quality standards," like South America and East Asia and where information sharing was most necessary.[78] Once they decided on goods they wanted to procure in common, a group of half a dozen retailers could have "considerable purchasing power" and even exploit new product ranges. Private label products promised the highest returns.[79] In cartel-like behavior, club members planned to fix group prices for their common goods, assured that the Single Market's common VAT tax would prevent price arbitrage and keep club members on equal footing in the widened consumer market of 1992.[80] As a result, consumers in Bari and Brussels would use the same toothpaste, eat the same canned tomatoes, and drink the same milk for nearly the same prices as consumers in Sussex and Sorrento.

Delhaize, Esselunga, and Sainsbury's considered inviting another member, preferably a small or medium sized family firm from either France or Germany, but they decided "not to make public announcements about the existence of the group" to attract new members, lest they draw unwanted attention from regulators for their cooperation.[81] The Commission was actually well aware of these groups, which it saw as "new types of wholesaler-like commercial firms"; and rather than questioning such collective procurement and price setting, it celebrated the Europeanization of the sector.[82] With no regulatory constraints, a "buying club fever" consumed European food retailers. By 1991, there were nine European buying associations.[83] That number doubled by 1993 when then eighteen associations including 133 member firms collectively purchased more than 20 percent of all food in the European market.[84] These

[78] Delhaize Chairman's Office, "Joint Buying Organization," September 19, 1988, Groupement d'achats, B.14.1, DEL.

[79] For more on private label goods, see: Liesbeth Colen et al., "Retail Alliances in the Agricultural and Food Supply Chain," Joint Research Center, European Commission (2020): 12.

[80] "Milan 1991 Meeting: Sainsbury, Esselunga, Delhaize "Le Lion," Groupement d'achats, B.14.1, DEL; Ingrid van Nuffel, "Le groupement d'achats," October 16, 1989, Groupement d'achats, B.14.1, DEL. For a business history of cartels, see: Susanna Fellman and Martin Shanahan, eds., *A History of Business Cartels: International Politics, National Policies and Anti-Competitive Behavior* (London: Routledge, 2022).

[81] "Meeting of 31 October 1989, Brussels," Groupement d'achats, B.14.1, DEL.

[82] European Commission, "Towards a Single Market in Distribution: Internal Trade in the Community, the Commercial Sector, and the Completion of the Internal Market," COM(91) 41 final, Brussels, March 11, 1991, p. 4.

[83] Philip Revzin, "Europe's Retailers Are Consolidating in Preparation for Post-1992 Market," *Wall Street Journal*, June 28, 1991, sec. International.

[84] Neil Wrigley, "Pan-European Alliances Lead the Way for the Retail Sector," *International Journal of Retail & Distribution Management* 21, no. 2 (1993): vii.

"distributors without borders" contributed to "segmented integration" by cooperating *against* the Single Market.[85]

Despite the Commission's regulatory leniency and the creation of so many regional purchasing associations, European buying "remained a myth."[86] Across the similar markets of France and Belgium, the GIB Group found that of the 300 products it surveyed for potential collective purchasing in its buying club, "only 5 were actually comparable."[87] Even with the principle of mutual recognition and legislative harmonization, persistent national differences in consumer preferences impeded collective buying; Delhaize's plums in wine vinegar did not appeal to Italian consumers, even if the group did find synergy across their ketchup purchases from Delmonte, canned peaches from a Greek supplier, and chocolate from Ferrero-Rocher.[88] Cracks formed in the clubs' relationships, too, with Sainsbury's sensing already in 1990 that Guy Beckers was "a little concerned about the progress – or lack of it – that we were making on the co-operative buying front."[89] Disintegration of the group including Ahold, Argyll, and Casino disappointed SVH Holding, which then made plans to sell off the stake it had acquired in Ahold when it hoped that buying club activities would boost the retailer's overall EEC market share, a meager 1.4 percent.[90] Many of the smallest clubs did not deliver the returns they promised, and, like the Groupement d'achats, ceased to function within just a few years of their creation.[91] That's not to say that regional buying clubs were ineffective. To the contrary, the gains from collective procurement were amplified by association size, incentivizing further consolidation in retail purchasing. Eventually, Delhaize and most other European food retailers joined either EMD or AMS, which became the two dominant buying clubs in the twenty-first century.[92] This defensive Europeanization against the Single Market

[85] "Distributors sans frontières," *Distribution aujourd'hui*, August–September 1989, Groupement d'achats, B.14.1, DEL.

[86] Marianne Hendrickx, "Vive la centrale," *Tendances*, September 7, 1989, Groupement d'achats, B.14.1, DEL.

[87] Ibid.

[88] "Milan 1991 Meeting: Sainsbury, Esselunga, Delhaize "Le Lion," Groupement d'achats, B.14.1, DEL.

[89] R. T. Vyner (Sainsbury's), "Letter from to G. Beckers (Delhaize), 25 June 1990," Groupement d'achats, B.14.1, DEL.

[90] "SHV Says 12% Ahold Stake May Be Sold After Talks Fail," *Wall Street Journal*, June 27, 1989; Marianne Hendrickx, "Vive la centrale," *Tendances*, September 7, 1989, Groupement d'achats, B.14.1, DEL.

[91] John A. Dawson and Masao Mukoyama, "The Increase in International Activity by Retailers," in *Strategic Issues in International Retailing*, ed. John A. Dawson, Roy Larke, and Masao Mukoyama (London: Routledge, 2006): 9.

[92] Collet, *Delhaize*, 207.

ironically contributed to the regional integration of retail and positioned retailers like Delhaize to become European and then global businesses.

Toward a Social Single Market

With a new mandate as Commission president, Jacques Delors turned the institution's attention in the late 1980s to the Single Market's "broader social, economic, and environmental objectives."[93] The efforts described in Chapter 1 to move toward a social single market coincided with dramatic social, economic, and political change in Europe and the world, resulting in mixed outcomes for the Social Charter's labor protections and Delors' legacy.[94] They were also influenced by the increasing capacity of the European Parliament and democratic interventions in regional economic policymaking.[95] Consequently, the Commission had to adapt quickly to changing circumstances even as it worked to adopt new directives on a wide variety of issues. That regional cohesion, labor rights, consumer protections, environmental regulation, "convergent prices" and their socioeconomic implications became progressively important as the "single market gr[ew] toward maturity" had significant implications for regional commerce.[96] The Delors Commission urged commerce to embrace its policy shift toward social cohesion and anticipated even greater reliance on the "consultative mechanism" of BIAs like the CCD and trade unions representing employees for policy input on how to achieve a more social single market.

93 Chapter 1 described the vision Jacques Delors and his commissioners outlined for the European economy, internal Single Market, and Economic and Monetary Union in this pivotal year. European Commission, "Towards a Single Market in Distribution: Internal Trade in the Community, the Commercial Sector, and the Completion of the Internal Market," COM(91) 41 final, Brussels, March 11, 1991, p. 4.

94 On the economic outcomes of the Social Charter, see: John T. Addison and W. Stanley Siebert, "The Social Charter of the European Community: Evolution and Controversies," *Industrial and Labor Relations Review* 44, no. 4 (1991): 597–625; and on the outcomes for Delors' reputation, see: Aurelie Dianara, "Jacques Delors Was the Gravedigger of 'Social Europe,'" accessed April 13, 2024, https://jacobin.com/2024/01/jacques-delors-obit-eu-neoliberal-turn.

95 This is clear in the work of Laurent Warlouzet on "The Role of the European Parliament in the Single Market Programme: The Cost of Non-Europe and the Car Emission Directive," *Journal of European Integration History* 27, no. 1 (2021): 21–36; and in the work of scholars publishing research with support of the European Parliament Research Service, including Liesbeth van de Grift and Koen van Zon. See their "The European Parliament and the Origins of Consumer Policy," European Parliament Think Tank, March 2024.

96 European Commission, "Towards a Single Market in Distribution: Internal Trade in the Community, the Commercial Sector, and the Completion of the Internal Market," COM(91) 41 final, Brussels, March 11, 1991, p. 7.

The Berlin Wall fell just weeks after the adoption of the Social Charter. As the Soviet Bloc and Union subsequently collapsed from 1989 to 1991, the EEC grappled with a united – although uneven – Germany, and contemplated potential membership for other former Bloc states, adding further urgency to the Community's treatment of commerce in the region for reasons of both economic integration and social cohesion.[97] In his contribution to the 33rd Annual Executive Congress of the CIES in September 1989, Walter J. Salmon argued regional cohesion was also essential for the success of multinational retail in Europe, since "[t]he foundation for international food retailing is the *similarity* of consumer lifestyles in the developed economies of the free world."[98] Perhaps equally crucial to cohesion in Salmon's view were business and "[t]rade associations [like the CIES] with tentacles that reach almost all corners of the globe and food processors and manufacturers that operate on an international basis help transfer the know-how of food distribution among countries," including "the universal product code, scanners, computers, and large, partially automated warehouses."[99] Since the Treaty of Rome and especially in the wake of the enlargements of the 1970s and 1980s, the Community supported economic cohesion and development across a growing number of diverse member states by creating a directorate general for regional policy, a European Regional Development Fund, and in 1991 a European Bank for Reconstruction and Development (EBRD). In the wake of the Soviet collapse, the EEC also launched technical assistance programs, including PHARE with the aim of preparing those emerging democracies and their economies for future EEC membership.[100]

But the Commission worried that structural funds and technical assistance could not sufficiently ensure the full development of commerce in strained regions nor economic and social cohesion across the continent. As a result, it continued to see business as an essential ally in reducing disparities not only across but also within member states, where

[97] On German reunification as a de facto enlargement, see: Helga Haftendorn, "German Unification and European Integration Are but Two Sides of One Coin: The FRG, Europe, and the Diplomacy of German Unification," in *Europe and the End of the Cold War*, ed. Frédéric Bozo, Marie-Pierre Rey, N. Piers Ludlow, Leopoldo Nuti (Bozo et al.) (London: Routledge, 2008).

[98] Walter J. Salmon, "Multinational Retailing in the Nineties," September 1, 1989, B.6.9. Seminaires CIES (1973–1992), DEL.

[99] Ibid. Salmon's description of commercial trade associations reflects the bestiary described in Chapter 1.

[100] The earliest step in the development of PHARE was "Council Regulation (EEC) No. 3906/89 on Economic Aid to Hungary and Poland," December 18, 1989.

long run asymmetrical development had stunted even national integration: "recent changes in Eastern Europe illustrate strikingly the failure of any productive system which is divorced from the discipline of the market, which alone ensures that the productive sector is responsive to the needs of the customer."[101] Not only did the Commission think former socialist states needed market economies, but it also wanted to "encourage the efforts of EEC commercial enterprises in relation to investment and training, and to support the efforts of new enterprises, and networks of federations of enterprises in Central Europe."[102] New EEC cohesion funds were intended to integrate SMEs from assisted regions into regional distribution and marketing networks.[103]

Together with EEC support for the economies of the former Soviet Bloc, the perception of new business opportunities motivated direct investment by Western European companies.[104] In mid-1990, the Beckers family, a branch of the Delhaize genealogy and controlling owners of the retailer since the 1860s, sent their son, Pierre-Olivier Beckers-Vieujant, just out of school "to Eastern Europe with a backpack on his back," instructed to survey the possibilities for his family's firm in Poland, Hungary, and Czechoslovakia, countries they realized were actually geographically closer to the parent company's headquarters than even some places in Western Europe like Southern Italy.[105] In February 1990, Pierre-Olivier had conducted a study for the board on business opportunities for Delhaize in the "Europe of tomorrow," in which he found of all Bloc states, these three countries were particularly appealing to Western European companies looking to invest in the East and seemingly "very likely to soon join the EU."[106] Poland had quickly become familiar to Western Europeans thanks to the exodus of Polish people streaming into Germany, France and the Low Countries in 1989 and 1990. Throughout the decades of Soviet control, Hungary

[101] European Commission, "Towards a Single Market in Distribution: Internal Trade in the Community, the Commercial Sector, and the Completion of the Internal Market," COM(91) 41 final, Brussels, March 11, 1991, p. 2.

[102] Ibid., p. 14.

[103] Ibid., p. 19; For a history of asymmetrical development in Europe, see: Ivan Berend, *Economic History of a Divided Europe: Four Diverse Regions in an Integrating Continent* (London: Routledge, 2020).

[104] For more on Delhaize's investments in Eastern Europe, see the dissertation from which this material is derived: Grace Ballor, "Agents of Integration: Multinational Firms and the European Union" PhD dissertation, UCLA, 2018: Chapter 6, pp. 176–220.

[105] Grace Ballor, Interview with Pierre-Olivier Beckers-Vieujant, Audio recording. Brussels, October 10, 2016; Grace Ballor, Interview with Pierre-Olivier Beckers-Vieujant, Audio recording. March 31, 2023.

[106] Grace Ballor, Interview with Pierre-Olivier Beckers-Vieujant, Audio recording. March 31, 2023.

had proven itself to be the most independent country in the Bloc, with a deeply ingrained rule of law and strong institutions. Czechoslovakia had a long history of close connections to Western Europe, particularly through the century-long Paris–Prague relationship. According to Delhaize's reports, the Velvet Revolution in December 1989 had primed Czechoslovakia for successful foreign investment.[107] Moreover, its strong economic foundations and robust institutions promised a rapid transition to capitalism, and its population of sixteen million seemed eager for new retail offerings.

Initially, Pierre-Olivier disappointed the family board, however, having returned to Brussels with the report that the few state-owned chains in operation in the three Eastern target markets were as backward in their business strategies as they were in their balance sheets.[108] Moreover, he could find no retailers in those markets that seemed to share Delhaize's values or key performance indicators. But within just months of his return to Brussels, Beckers-Vieujant was approached by two brothers, who had fled Czechoslovakia for Belgium just before Soviet occupation in the 1960s and whose small desserts and sauces company, Avita, had become part of the Delhaize specialty goods supply chain in Belgium. Having learned about Delhaize's interest in entering the markets of Eastern Europe, the Parik brothers pitched a Czech joint venture to the company's board, to which they would contribute their linguistic, cultural and culinary knowledge of their home country.[109] In 1991, Delhaize and the Parik brothers formed Delvita, conceptualized as a friendly neighborhood market, catering to the health-conscious upper middle class consumer with pent up demand for new and improved products.

To launch the Czech subsidiary, Delhaize purchased five existing state-owned grocery stores from the Czechoslovakian government and brought in a Belgium-based management team to launch the brand and create standards and practices consistent with the parent company's core strategies, while still being attentive to the unique preferences of Czech consumers. The primary supply-side goal was to offer a product range that went far beyond the limited line of roughly 400 items to which they had been restricted by the Soviet supply chain. In fact, Delhaize's commitment to expanding the product line in its Delvita stores originated in the disappointment Beckers-Vieujant had felt when he inventoried products in Czech stores as part of his investigative foray into the grocery

[107] Collet, *Delhaize*, 198–199

[108] Grace Ballor, Interview with Pierre-Olivier Beckers-Vieujant, Audio recording. October 10, 2016.

[109] Collet, *Delhaize*, 198-99.

market of Eastern Europe.[110] He found the product range to be so "austere and uninspiring" that he became all the more motivated to improve it through a retail partnership.[111] Delvita certainly accomplished that goal. With designs on becoming the premier supermarket chain in Prague and then extending its network to the rest of the country, the first few Delvita stores were large, modern, yet "rooted in the local culture."[112] Meanwhile, British Tesco also invested aggressively in former Bloc states.

The 1990s were a decade of explosive growth for Western retailers in Eastern and peripheral Europe. In 1991, Delhaize took a 51 percent stake in the Vassilopoulos family's thirteen Alfa-Beta supermarkets in Athens, which had just been awarded the prestigious title of "best all-around European supermarket by the International Food Retail Association.[113] Stiff competition prompted the head of the Vassilopoulos family to pursue an international partnership, and Delhaize promised optimization without the loss of character or quality. "In line with its strategy of decentralization and local empowerment," Delhaize left the local management in place and "sent four representatives to Alfa-Beta's Board of Directors."[114] In just eight years, Delhaize accelerated Alfa-Beta's growth from fifteen supermarkets and 36.3 billion Greek drachmae (GRD) in sales to fifty-three supermarkets and GRD 160 billion in sales.[115] Furthermore, within just two years of opening its first store in Prague, Delvita already employed 1,240 people, and by the end of the decade, that number topped 5,000. After the "Velvet Divorce" and separation of the Czech Republic and Slovakia, Delhaize increased its ownership stake of Delvita to 88.5 percent and opened two distribution centers to support its booming business, one in Prague (1996), described as the most modern distribution center in all of Europe, and one in Moravia (1998).[116] Local distribution enabled Delvita to continue its growth rate – fueling its entrance into Slovakia in 1998, and also to maintain quality control and cut costs. More importantly for the region, local distribution, resonant with the organizational logic of subsidiarity the company had practiced in its other foreign endeavors, meant that the investment of the Belgian group was much more integrative, than exploitative. In 1999, Delhaize became full owner of Delvita and subsequently doubled the subsidiary's size with the

[110] Grace Ballor, Interview with Pierre-Olivier Beckers-Vieujant, Audio recording. October 10, 2016.
[111] Ibid. [112] Collet, *Delhaize*, 198. [113] Collet, *Delhaize*, 201. [114] Ibid.
[115] Ibid.; In 2001, Alfa-Beta acquired another Greek retailer, Trofo, and became the second largest food retailer in Greece.
[116] Collet, *Delhaize*, 199.

acquisition of "39 Interkontakt stores in the Czech Republic and 11 in Slovakia."[117] Under then CEO Pierre-Olivier Beckers-Vieujant in the late 1990s and early 2000s, Delhaize worked to close the geographical gap between its successful subsidiaries in the Czech Republic and Greece and capture some of the markets in between using its well-established talent and supply chains.[118] It entered half a dozen southeast European countries, including Bulgaria, Serbia, and Romania, which became a one of the most lucrative markets by 2023 for the newly merged Ahold Delhaize, success bolstered by the EEC/EU's fifth enlargement.

For all their benefits, the commercial revolutions of the twentieth century, which incorporated new technologies into distribution and retail and increased efficiency and competitiveness, negatively affected regional employment. Automation reduced both the number of – and skill required – for entry level jobs, a large percentage of which were part-time or seasonal. The dearth of women advancing to management positions despite comprising a majority (70–80 percent) of entry level retail positions compounded the concerns for policymakers thinking about the social aspects of European commerce.[119] Concerned that the Single Market would only exacerbate the trends of competition, automation, and gender inequality, the Commission stressed the need to direct existing Community vocational training programs, originally designed for industry, to commerce at a regional level.[120] Only with vocational training programs could a humane Single Market be achieved.

The Commission organized a European Forum on Social Aspects of Retail Trade in 1990 and formed a Steering Group to inform the

117 Collet, *Delhaize*, 199.

118 Grace Ballor, Interview with Pierre-Olivier Beckers-Vieujant, Audio recording. March 31, 2023.

119 European Commission, "Towards a Single Market in Distribution: Internal Trade in the Community, the Commercial Sector, and the Completion of the Internal Market." COM(91) 41 final. Brussels, March 11, 1991, p. 20.

120 European Commission, "Towards a Single Market in Distribution: Internal Trade in the Community, the Commercial Sector, and the Completion of the Internal Market." COM(91) 41 final. Brussels, March 11, 1991, p. 20. The COMETT, EUROFORM, EUROTECNET, and TELEMATIQUE programs developed in the 1980s addressed technological change through technical training; LINGUA and ERASMUS offered support for language acquisition and university exchanges; LEADER addressed rural development; PETRA provided targeted training for young workers and IRIS and NOW were initiatives aimed at women's advancement; and DELTA and FORCE aimed to advance the continuing education of management and employees within firms. See: European Commission, "Towards a Single Market in Distribution: Internal Trade in the Community, the Commercial Sector, and the Completion of the Internal Market." COM(91) 41 final, Brussels, March 11, 1991, p. 20; "EuroCommerce and Euro-Fiet [sic] Agreement on Fundamental Rights and Principles at Work, Brussels 6 August 1999," University of Minnesota: Human Rights Library.

Commission's proposals on employment and working conditions in retailing. There were similar developments in wholesale: FEWITA and the European Federation of Cleaning Industries Trade Unions (EUROFIET) worked together to develop vocational training programs.[121] A 1987 Commission working group on training the managers of SMEs created an initiative in December 1988 on "Preparing SMEs for 1992 – Experimental Training Schemes," on how to help managers "define strategies for their enterprises in the European context" and out of which the Commission subsequently launched a vocational training program (FORCE) as part of the Social Charter.[122] While FORCE was intended to help train employees in all industries, the Commission implemented it first in the retail sector, which it used as a pilot for a future Community-wide labor policy. An extensive survey in 1991 would determine which skill needs the training program would address.[123]

SMEs were the intended beneficiaries of several of the Commission's commercial business development programs in the early 1990s. Beyond the general interest of promoting cross border business described in Chapter 1, and given the new objectives of the Social Charter, the Commission recognized the specific needs of SMEs in the areas of scalar competition and technological innovation. Supporting the technological capacity of European retailers was a key priority for the Commission. Drawing comparisons with commerce in the US and Japan, it argued that "technical change is reinforcing the internal markets of our main industrial competitors in a manner which European efforts have not so far succeeded in matching."[124] The Commission had previously supported EAN standards for computer readable barcode numbering, and created new programs like the Strategic Program for Innovation and Technology Transfer (SPRINT), Trade Electronic Data Interchange Systems (TEDIS), and Electronic Data Interchange (EDI) in the late 1980s and early 1990s, which aimed to help commercial firms across EEC member states embrace new technologies and benefit from the internal market. The introduction of point-of-sale systems (POSs) generated a large

[121] European Commission, "Towards a Single Market in Distribution: Internal Trade in the Community, the Commercial Sector, and the Completion of the Internal Market," COM(91) 41 final, Brussels, March 11, 1991, p. 12.

[122] European Commission, "Report on the Activities of the Commission of the European Communities in the Field of Education, Training and Youth during 1990," Brussels January 24, 1992, SEC(91) 2409 final, p. 83–84.

[123] European Commission, "Towards a Single Market in Distribution: Internal Trade in the Community, the Commercial Sector, and the Completion of the Internal Market," COM(91) 41 final, Brussels, March 11, 1991, p. 21.

[124] Ibid., p. 9.

amount of data, which many small firms were unequipped to manage, much less optimize. Moreover, stock keeping units (SKUs) and POSs enabled firms to utilize the new tool of "Direct Product Profitability" (DPP) to analyze profit per item as well as turnover and sell-through, thereby generating data to help retailers improve profitability and minimize waste. This information was also of Community interest, according to the Commission, since it could facilitate cross-border business and standardization.[125]

In addition to managerial and vocational training programs, the Commission also worked to harmonize rules for matters related to public health, protection of consumers, fairness of commercial transactions, and environmental protections. Food retail was a primary target of these efforts, since food products are the primary consumer goods of all Europeans and have the greatest impact on health. To assess the potential risks of food products to consumer health and safety, the EEC consulted standards set by the World Health Organization and the UN Food and Agriculture Organization's Codex Alimentarius Commission.[126] During the second Delors Commission, the institution drafted eight directives on food production, retail, and distribution. Some of these aimed to harmonize technical specifications across member states by requiring domestic governments to report to Brussels on their food safety standards. The Commission's strategy "essentially consist[ed] in combining the adoption of harmonized rules at Community level … with the principle of mutual recognition of national regulation and standards."[127] Council Directive 79/112/EEC of December 18, 1978 had already addressed the harmonization of food product labeling, but in the late 1980s and early 1990s, the Commission developed specific requirements with consumer protection in mind including nutritional labeling.[128] The Court of Justice also intervened on the regulation of food products. A case on milk substitutes upheld the *Cassis de Dijon* ruling, while deciding that only public health concerns could prohibit the marketing and

125 European Commission, "Towards a Single Market in Distribution: Internal Trade in the Community, the Commercial Sector, and the Completion of the Internal Market," COM(91) 41 final, Brussels, March 11, 1991, p. 23.

126 The international Codex Alimentarius Commission was created in the 1960s to protect consumer health and safety with regard to food products. The US also created a system for "hazard analysis and critical control points" or HACCP. On the US case see: Ashton Merck, "The Fox Guarding the Henhouse: Coregulation and Consumer Protection in Food Safety, 1946–2002," PhD Dissertation, Duke University, 2020.

127 Official Journal of the European Communities, "Communication on the Free Movement of Foodstuffs within the Community," 89/C 271/03, Vol. 32, (October 24, 1989): Summary.

128 In late 1988, the Commission sent the Council two proposals for Directives concerning nutritional labeling of foodstuffs.

importing of a food product. And in twenty-five further cases between 1979 and 1989, the ECJ forbade the use of hormones in food, regulated the fat content in cheese, and controlled the distillation of table wine.[129]

Still, the Commission resolved to use its regulatory power to go further by developing new socially oriented directives on the content of food products and rules for food labeling, designed to inform consumers, to give certain products special designation, and to protect geographic indications and appellations of origin for heritage products like wine, spirits, and cheese.[130] A June 1989 directive subjected foodstuffs to regular inspections for both domestic consumption and export, narrowing the *Cassis de Dijon* ruling from a decade before.[131] Also in 1989, Carlo Ripa di Meana, the commissioner for Environmental Policy in the second Delors Commission, proposed to create a European ecological label like Germany's "Blue Angel" to indicate the environmental impact of products from production to disposal.[132] In his view, a single common label would guard the internal market against the "fragmentation" of many national ecological labels.[133] And Commissioner for Agriculture Ray MacSharry, who joined the Commission in 1989, drafted a directive to regulate spreadable fats like butter and margarine through the adoption of product specifications.[134] In May 1990, the Commission announced its Action Plan for consumer protection policy, specifically targeting "doorstep-selling" not protected by the older Council directive on consumer protection, and it announced its intention to develop new rules for remote transactions through telemarketing and digital advertising by television.[135] Meanwhile, as part of the Commission's growing commitment to developing Community environmental policy, German environmental minister Klaus Töpfer proposed new measures to require commercial and industrial firms to

[129] These included cases on beer purity (CEE 178/84), misleading wine marketing (CEE/788/79), and hormones in food (CEE/88/164).

[130] There were simultaneous discussions at the GATT about designations of geographic origin, urged by producers, especially in in Italy and France, whose competitive advantage was rooted in the concept of terroir.

[131] European Council, "Council Directive of 14 June 1989 on the Official Control of Foodstuffs," 89/397/EEC; *Cassis de Dijon* (OJ No. C 256, 30. 10. 1980, p. 2).

[132] The proposed label, a daisy encircled by twelve stars like the EEC and EU flags, continues to appear on a voluntary basis on certain product categories circulating in the EEA.

[133] "La Commission propose un label ecologique europeen," GEDIS B.14.2, 1991, DEL.

[134] "La Commission propose un reglementation CEE sur les matieres grasses jaunes," GEDIS B.14.2, 1991, DEL.

[135] Council Directive 85/577/EEC of December 20, 1985 aimed to protect the consumer in respect of contracts negotiated away from business premises.

recycle packaging waste.[136] Building on Directive 85/339/EEC on liquid container packaging, the Commission drafted "A Community Strategy for Waste Management" in 1989, that would require distributers and retailers to be responsible for recycling packaging waste.

While the Commission claimed to be "examining ways to ensure that the [commercial] sector [wa]s properly prepared for the challenge of the internal market," retailers and distributors organized themselves against the social Single Market and collectively mobilized against the implementation of these "flanking policies."[137] Commerce clarified that it was "in favor of liberalization of trade" and "abolishing existing trade barriers," but against social initiatives that undermined the market.[138]

Commerce against the Social Single Market

In the late 1980s and early 1990s, as the second Delors Commission developed its Social Charter, regional policymakers implemented new social and environmental regulations to guarantee food product safety, enforce labeling and packaging requirements, and monitor hiring and labor practices. While the first half of the 1992 Program had all but ignored retail and distribution, it was in this shift toward a social Single Market that the Commission issued two directives and a communication aimed at regulating the commercial sector.

In response, commercial business associations reorganized their political activities against the social Single Market. GEMAS was reconstituted in early 1989 as the Groupement européen des entreprises de distribution intégrée (GEDIS) (The European Group of Integrated Distribution Companies) with "the double role of informing its members of developments at the European level and to represent their interests before different European institutions."[139] As was the case for many private advocacy forums and BIAs, GEDIS was a multiplication of other efforts: "the representatives of GEDIS are already present in many committees

136 On environmental policy, see the works of Jan-Henrik Meyer.

137 European Commission, "Towards a Single Market in Distribution: Internal Trade in the Community, the Commercial Sector, and the Completion of the Internal Market," COM(91) 41 final, Brussels, March 11, 1991, p. 10.

138 "Draft Minutes: CECD/FEWITA Circulaire no. 54/48," May 15, 1990, GEDIS B.14.2, DEL.

139 "Commerce: Le GEDIS a le double role d'informer ses membres et de representer leurs interets devant les insitutions europeennes," Saturday, January 28, 1989, no. 4943 (nouvelle série), GEDIS B.14.2, DEL.

of the European Commission."[140] As association president, Guy Beckers invited Commissioners Ray MacSharry, Karel van Miert, Christiane Scrivener, and António Cardoso e Cunha to attend a cocktail and "private dinner offered by the members of the Board of GEDIS to selected representatives of both European institutions and private organizations," organized in February 1989 to launch GEDIS.[141] National business associations like the British Retailers Association expressed support for and interest in joining the new GEDIS "to ensure maximum use of all our resources in our representations to the [European] Commission."[142]

Other commercial organizations adapted similarly to the Social Single Market. In a sign of just how much "Europe" and its boundaries had changed and just how reactive commercial companies had become to developments in European policy, the thirty-fourth annual congress of the CIES was held in Berlin in summer 1990, where the CIES developed its own resolutions on packaging waste to counter those of the Commission. This marked a much more active stance toward European policymaking for the CIES than the organization had taken in Cannes just a few years prior during the launch of the Single Market Program. In the view of the CIES, consumers – not retailers – should be responsible for recycling packaging, demanding a broad campaign to educate the public about recycling to prepare consumers for the responsibility.[143] According to Delhaize's management in October 1989, the Commission's initiative to require retailers to recycle packaging waste was "premature and too ambitious, and we would like it not to come into effect."[144] Meanwhile, GEDIS continued to express doubt about whether recycling was actually "the most environmentally effective way of recovering packaging material," and a newly formed European Retail

[140] "Commerce: Le GEDIS a le double role d'informer ses membres et de representer leurs interets devant les insitutions europeennes," Saturday, January 28, 1989, no. 4943 (nouvelle série), GEDIS B.14.2, DEL. On the redundant multiplication of private advocacy forums, see Sabine Pitteloud and Grace Ballor, "The Rise and Fall of Private Advocacy Forums from 1945 to the Twenty-First Century," *Socio-Economic Review*, 2025.

[141] Guy Beckers, "Letter to Mr. R. MacSharry," Brussels, January 4, 1989, GEDIS B.14.2, DEL; Guy Beckers, "Letter to Monsieur Karl [sic] van Miert," Brussels, January 4, 1989, GEDIS B.14.2, DEL; Guy Beckers, "Letter to Madame C. Scrivener," Brussels, January 3, 1989, GEDIS B.14.2, DEL; Guy Beckers, "Letter to Monsieur A. Cardoso e Cunha," Brussels, January 3, 1989, GEDIS B.14.2, DEL

[142] Nigel Matthews, "Letter to Guy Beckers," October 7, 1988, GEDIS B.14.2, DEL.

[143] CIES, "Emballage et Environnement: Resolutions adoptées par le conseil d'administration du CIES," Berlin, June 10, 1990, DEL: B.6.9 Seminaires CIES (1973–1992).

[144] Dominique Raquez (Attaché to the Sales Manager) and Ph. Stroobant (Membre of the Board and Manager), "Letter to M. Thyssen," Brussels, October 25, 1989, GEDIS B.14.2, DEL.

Working Group on Environment announced its decision to "counter-attack" environmental efforts by the Commission, which would hurt business, and by national governments, which they argued would result in detrimental "market fragmentation."[145] To the Commission's suggestion that retailers should bear responsibility for recycling glass, metal, carboard, and plastic packaging waste, the industry replied: "It is not for the trade to act as the dustbin of Europe[!]"[146]

As it noticed investor support for environmental initiatives, and the ways "the European citizen is becoming more aware that pollution does not stop at national frontiers," Delhaize became more pragmatic and eventually described "the environment [a]s everybody's business" in 1991.[147] After conducting analysis on the European framework directive on packaging, Delhaize established a public–private partnership with the Flemish government to share the burden of recycling with municipalities and consumers. Delhaize chairman and GEDIS president, Guy Beckers also encouraged his peers in the association to "adopt a positive attitude on the matter of the environment."[148] By 1993, Delhaize touted its own Environmental Committee's efforts to implement "the most environmentally friendly policy possible," by offering its customers reusable shopping bags "to reduce the consumption of raw materials," encouraging the "quest for lightweight, practical, easy to handle, non-dangerous packaging," reusing bottles within its own brand wine production, recycling cardboard, paper, and plastic within its business and for its distributors, and earning a "Greenstar" trophy for eliminating chlorofluorocarbons in its refrigeration.[149]

The adoption of the Social Charter marked a decisive turning point in the way regional retailers viewed and approached the internal market. Already in early 1989, GEDIS was suspicious of the new Delors Commission, missing the liberal Commissioners Cockfield and Sutherland; they worried MacSharry and other new commissioners from

[145] "Revised Position of European Commerce on the Outline Proposal for a Directive on Packaging Waste," April 23, 1991, GEDIS B.14.2, DEL; "Summary Report of the Meting of the European Retail Trade Working Group on Environment," Brussels, October 16, 1989, GEDIS B.14.2, DEL.

[146] "Explanatory Memorandum on the Proposed Draft Directive on Environmental Packaging," GEDIS B.14.2, DEL.

[147] Delhaize Annual Report 1991, 23. "Policy Statement of the European Retail Trade with Regard to Retailing and the Environment," October 16, 1989, GEDIS B.14.2, DEL.

[148] "Proces Verbal de la réunion du consil d'administration du 29 mai 1989 à Bruxelles," GEDIS, B.14.2, DEL:4.

[149] Delhaize Annual Report 1993, 22–23.

France and Spain were likely to be more activist and protectionist.[150] In addition to the labor regulations proposed by the Charter, the new Commission also started to produce directives aimed at the protection of consumers and the environment. Distributors in GEDIS were outraged. They had supported the Commission's earlier efforts to ensure food quality and protect the geographical indications of food products. But they wholly rejected the Commission's "recipe legislation" to create "Euro-sausages," "Euro-jam," and "Euro-honey," which they argued was "incompatible with the White Paper," and they decried the potential for heavy-handed environmentalism to jeopardize business.[151] Such "agro-alimentaire" had no place in a competitive international market. GEDIS argued that labeling provided sufficient protection to consumers, who were free to make their own choices, and that policy intervention in the precise ingredients of each food product would constrain both economic and cultural development. "This is why we need to intervene!" they rallied, as they prepared a collective, dissenting position to the Commission.[152]

GEDIS expressed additional frustration at the Commission's suggestion that products should bear multiple trade descriptions at the same time, since policymakers did not seem to acknowledge the additional costs this would create for producers, which would then inevitably be passed down to consumers.[153] In April 1990, GEDIS penned its own "balance sheet of the Single Market of 1992," including a "preview of the Social Economy," a challenge to European enterprises.[154] GEDIS also worked to gather information on European policymaking, which it circulated amongst its membership by producing bulletins of information on the Commission's proposals for ecological labeling, social protections for employees, vocational training programs, VAT and excise taxes, and more.[155] GEDIS closely monitored Commissioner Karel Van Miert's initiatives on consumer concerns like marketing and cosmetic product

[150] "Retour à la législation-recette: l'échance 1992 pourra-t-elle être respectée?" GEDIS B.14.2, DEL.

[151] "Projet: Prise de position du commerce européen sur la libre circulation des denrées alimentaires dans la CE," 1989, GEDIS B.14.2, DEL: 2; "Droit Alimentaire," 1991, GEDIS B.14.2, DEL; GEDIS, "Retour à la législation-recette: l'échance 1992 pourra-t-elle être respectée?" GEDIS B.14.2, DEL.

[152] "GEDIS November/December 1990 Meeting," GEDIS B.14.2, DEL.

[153] Official Journal of the European Communities, "Communication on the Free Movement of Foodstuffs within the Community," 89/C 271/03, Vol. 32 (October 24, 1989): Trade Description.

[154] "Bulletin d'information n.4/90," Brussels, April 1990, GEDIS B.14.2, DEL.

[155] "Bulletin d'information n.9/90," November/December 1990, GEDIS B.14.2, DEL. GEDIS also worried about the Commission's 1989 discussions on customs services after 1992. See: Official Journal of the European Communities, "Déclaration des

ingredients, as well as efforts by the Bureau européen des unions de consommateurs (European Consumer Organisation, BEUC) to propose new consumer protections. And it launched forceful "counterinfluence" campaigns in response.[156]

Additionally, GEDIS worked with the other major regional interest associations, CECD and FEWITA, to draft a common position on the elements of the Social Charter focused on labor. Of particular objection for retailers and distributors were the Charter's requirement that all conditions of employment must be written clearly in the contract document, restricting the flexibility of employers and the means by which women would be further integrated into the European labor market as the Charter promised. Furthermore, GEDIS worried about the Commission's intentions to restrict store openings on Sundays for reasons of labor protection.[157] CECD, FEWITA, and GEDIS formed a working group on such "social questions," which expressed concern in April 1990 that the Commission's policies on "atypical work" like seasonal and part-time employment would distort labor market competition and ultimately undermine the Commission's very intentions and that Sunday closures would hurt both their revenues and the living standards of consumers.[158] Such labor regulation concerns were especially acute in the early 1990s in the newly open former Bloc states of Central and Eastern Europe, where socialism had strictly controlled store opening hours and societies were reluctant to embrace the longer working hours expected by Western retailers.[159]

By 1990, there was no longer any doubt in the minds of European retailers "that the completion of the internal market in 1992 will be a fact."[160] With certainty that the nearly 300 legislative proposals outlined in the 1985 White Paper were just the first of many European rules to govern business in the Single Market, executives with representation in regional retail associations made a case for increasing their presence – and influence – in Brussels. Aad van Ewijk of the Dutch food retailer Ahold prepared a GEDIS document on "The Brussels Representation of Commerce and Distribution," a manifesto of sorts advocating for more

répresentants des gouvernements des États membres, réunis au sein du Conseil, sur la persistance du rôle des services douaniers aprés 1992," 90/C/262/03.

156 "Bulletin de Participation – á la reunion du Conseil d'administration de GEDIS le 30 Novembre 1990," GEDIS B.14.2, DEL.

157 GEDIS, "Bulletin d'information n.8/89," Brussels, December 1989, GEDIS B.14.2, DEL.

158 "Preuve écrite da la relation de travail," GEDIS B.14.2, DEL.

159 Grace Ballor, Interview with Pierre-Olivier Beckers-Vieujant, Audio recording. March 31, 2023.

160 Aad van Ewijk, "Approved Project with Revised Budget, 13 July 1990," GEDIS B.14.2, DEL.

representation of retailers in the policymaking of the Community. While European industrialists had successfully secured influence with the Commission through the ERT and had increased its UNICE staff to maintain close contact with policymakers in Brussels,[161] retailers like van Ewijk expressed anxiety about their relative lack of influence on regional policymaking and embarrassment about their comparatively modest coordination and facilities. Despite the fact that commerce accounted for more than 10 percent of employment and 12 percent of added value in the EEC in 1990, van Ewijk regretted that it had taken "many years to convince the European Commission that the opinion of this sector should be taken into account when formulating policy."[162] Now that they had "reached a position where … the Commission no longer neglects this sector but asks for its opinion on really every subject" through its new director general XXIII for Enterprise Policy, Commerce, and Tourism, Heinrich von Moltke, who "s[aw] them as respected interlocutors," it was time to restructure regional representation to augment the sector's influence in Brussels.[163]

Throughout the early 1990s, various members of all three regional commercial associations made concerted efforts to bring their organizations in closer alignment "for maximum efficiency for the defense of our specific interests and the harmonious development of our forms of commerce in Europe."[164] van Ewijk suggested that GEDIS, CECD, and FEWITA should invest in a shared office in Brussels, giving them easy access to one another for the purposes of information sharing and to regional policymakers for exerting "daily" influence.[165] The Administrative Council of GEDIS echoed van Ewijk's appeal in their November 1990 meeting, in which they made the case that CECD and GEDIS should collaborate since shared knowledge could improve the market and lobbying positions of all their members.[166] That the Council was already using language like "European commerce, represented by CECD/FEWITA/GEDIS," in its communications seemed further evidence of the need to merge into one organization so they could speak

[161] As van Ewijk noted, UNICE "excluded the food industry, which had an independent organization (CIAA) representing its interests." See: van Ewijk, "Approved Project with Revised Budget," GEDIS B.14.2, DEL: 1.

[162] van Ewijk, "Approved Project with Revised Budget," GEDIS B.14.2, DEL: 2.

[163] Ibid.

[164] "Conseil d'Administration de GEDIS – Réunion du mercredi 12 septembre 1990," Paris, August 24, 1990. GEDIS B.14.2, DEL.

[165] van Ewijk, "Approved Project with Revised Budget," GEDIS B.14.2, DEL: 2; Grace Ballor, Interview with Gui de Vaucleroy, Audio recording. May 11, 2023.

[166] Ibid.

with one voice to the Commission.[167] Others, like GEDIS President (1990–1993) and Chairman of Casino France Charles Urbain, were more ambitious and argued that GEDIS and CECD should merge to create a European Retail Round Table (ERRT) to influence regional policymaking most effectively, mirroring the regional organizations of their industrialist counterparts.[168] An ERRT could even collaborate with the ERT, Urbain suggested. In May 1991, the European Commerce alliance wrote a "Letter to Industry," in which it appealed to the ERT to forge a "united front" between industry and trade "vis-à-vis the European Commission," the DG XI of which "seems to be dead set" on implementing new rules on packaging waste; European commerce argued it would "be wise to put forward more flexible proposals to achieve practicable solutions and to adopt an even more positive approach vis-à-vis the European Commission."[169]

As the internal market completion deadline approached, PMS Marketing Consultants BV recognized the business opportunity of publishing "a European magazine to fill the information gap between Legislators and the [Common Market's Food and Distribution] Industry," tentatively titled "Euro Supermarket," the sample first issue of which discussed the nearly "200 restrictive regulations still in force within the bisquit [sic]/chocolate/beer/softdrink and pastry segments of the food industry!!!" and the "far reaching" subjects European legislators were dealing with, including labelling, packaging, and standards.[170] PMS Marketing Consultants' research showed that 88.89 percent of food production companies surveyed were interested in an industry publication focused on "EC 1992." Armed with PMS' market research, the alliance of CECD, FEWITA, and GEDIS ultimately decided to produce and circulate their own *Commerce Newsletter* with articles written in English, French, and German. Some articles directly criticized regional policymakers, like the piece published in November 1991 on "The Commission [going] in a Bad Direction," for proposing new social

[167] "Bulletin de Participation – á la reunion du Conseil d'administration de GEDIS le 30 Novembre 1990," GEDIS B.14.2, DEL.

[168] Denise Larking Coste, Secretary General of the International Center for Companies of the Food Trade and Industry (CIES), "Letter to Mr. Nigel F. Matthews, Company Secretary at Sainsbury PLC on the European Retail Roundtable," August 29, 1990, GEDIS B.14.2, DEL; Charles Urbain, "Letter to GEDIS Members," Paris, July 16, 1991, GEDIS B.14.2, DEL.

[169] Katrin Recke, "Letter to Industry," Brussels, May 22, 1991, GEDIS B.14.2, DEL.

[170] D.R. Klawer, PMS Marketing Consultants BV, "Letter to GEDIS, M. Thyssen," Leiden, September 27, 1989, GEDIS B.14.2, DEL.

and environmental policies.[171] Interestingly, the *Newsletter* also published a critique of the CE Marking described in Chapter 2, which it argued was "superfluous and confusing for consumers."[172] The alliance dedicated space in its newsletter to authors like Commissioner António Cardoso e Cunha, who published a sympathetic piece in 1991 on "1992, A Challenge for Commerce," trying to convince European commerce that the success of the Single Market depended on the "speed and efficacy with which companies will adapt to its changes."[173] He moreover recognized that the erasure of internal borders had required companies to restructure and change their investment policies and endorsed the "Europeanization" of commercial associations. Other smaller "circulaires" published by the alliance criticized national protectionism for hurting consumers and producers alike and undermining competition and looked to Eastern Europe as a place of new commercial opportunities.[174] Such publications helped BIAs develop common positions on the Single Market and European policymaking.

In January 1993, as the newly completed Single Market laid the foundation for the new EU to pursue economic and monetary union. After much debate about whether the interests of retailers and distributors were "in opposition" or aligned, GEDIS and CECD and FEWITA merged to create EuroCommerce, a single consolidated interest association representing distributors and retailers in food commerce.[175] At the time of its creation, it represented 4.3 million enterprises, with an increasing focus on the many SMEs that comprised the sector. According to the first association president, Albert Heijn of Ahold, the association's mandate was "defending the interests of commerce in Brussels," especially in "the domain of environmental and social policy."[176] For retailers like Delhaize, "Europe" – synonymous with the Single Market – had liberated companies from restrictive padlock laws of the 1970s and liberalized commerce by abrogating exclusivity for branded products like Martini vermouth and cigarettes. Market policies also allowed Delhaize to win a lawsuit against winemakers and wine cooperatives, ultimately enabling the retailer to buy wine in bulk and

171 "La Commission européenne dans la mauvais direction," *Commerce Newsletter*, November 12, 1991, GEDIS B.14.2, DEL.

172 "Nouvelles Breves," *Commerce Newsletter*, November 12, 1991, GEDIS B.14.2, DEL.

173 Antonio Cardoso e Cunha, "1992: un défi pour le commerce," Commerce Newsletter, November 1991, GEDIS B.14.2, DEL.

174 Circulaire no. 181, Brussels, December 1991. GEDIS B.14.2, DEL.

175 GEDIS, "Proces Verbal de la réunion du consil d'administration du 29 mai 1989 à Bruxelles," 2–3.

176 *Commerce Newsletter*, November 1991.

bottle it in house resulting in enormous profits. In the face of social market policies, however, EuroCommerce had to defend the lucrative liberalized market from the imposition of new regulatory restrictions.[177] To that end, the association's leadership met two to four times per year throughout the 1990s and organized a regular annual conference, the Journée Européenne du Commerce, or European Retail Day, featuring talks by Commission officials like Heinrich von Moltke, who later became the director general for DG XXIII for entrepreneurship and small and medium enterprises.[178] At one meeting in November 1993, EuroCommerce aimed "to study the implications for commerce of the activities of the EU in general and more specifically the current proposals in substance and social policy of consumers."[179] It remained explicitly wary of the Social Charter and actively opposed proposals for European environmental directives on recycling commercial packaging waste. Ironically, by creating a single European interest association among producers, distributors, and retailers, EuroCommerce brought commercial firms of all sizes, national origins, and market segments together around a shared skepticism of the social Single Market.

For its part, Delhaize saw "pooling resources together ... to defend common interests as immensely important," and "never questioned whether we should be a member of EuroCommerce."[180] What Delhaize did question "relatively rapidly, [however,] was whether EuroCommerce was in a position to defend or promote ... the interests of large European retailers," with such a large and diverse membership, ranging from multinational retailers like IKEA to small textile stores in Southern Italy.[181] As the association grew larger and more diverse, it lacked cohesion, and, consequently, policy influence. "This is why, relatively quickly, we founded, on the side, the European Retail Round Table," Pierre-Olivier Beckers-Vieujant explained.[182] "Working

[177] Grace Ballor, Interview with Gui de Vaucleroy, Audio recording. May 11, 2023.
[178] EuroCommerce, "4ème Journée Européenne du Commerce," Brussels, November 2–3, 1993, GEDIS B.14.2, DEL.
[179] Ibid.
[180] Grace Ballor, Interview with Pierre-Olivier Beckers-Vieujant, Audio recording. March 31, 2023.
[181] Ibid.
[182] Ibid. While the ERRT's first entry on the lobby-tracking EU Transparency Register was May 29, 2012, archival documents indicate its members first met in the 1990s, and Pierre-Olivier Beckers-Vieujant was included in ERRT meetings in 1999 when he became Chairman of Delhaize. A 1998 report by the Danish Ministry for Industry mentions an ERRT publication from 1996, called "The Business of Adding Value: European Retail and Distribution," indicating the organization had been formally created at least by then. See: Betaenkning fra Butiksstrukturkommissionen, "Butikker og forbrugere nu og i fremtiden," 1998: www.betænkninger.dk/wp-content/uploads/2021/02/1353.pdf.

[together] on a regular basis … and having substantial meetings with key people [in the Commission] was very beneficial: we could convince them that what we were asking in most cases was beneficial to everyone – consumers in particular – and it was not just a way for us to make big, short-term profits."[183] "Absolutely" the ERRT was more beneficial for Delhaize than EuroCommerce, so "we had a tendency to go directly to the policymakers in Brussels."[184] By the early 2000s, EuroCommerce had to restructure to better reflect the needs and interests of large multinational retailers, or risk losing their membership altogether.

In the twenty-first century, EuroCommerce became the leading regional commercial association, both through consolidation and through cooperation with the many other commercial trade associations in Europe shown in the organigrams in Figures 6.1 and 6.2. Throughout the 1990s, it followed the activities of EUROCHAMBRES, the Association of European Chambers of Commerce, closely, especially on the internal market and the opening of Eastern Europe.[185] While J. Joubert of the Comité de liaison des associations européennes du commerce de détail (Liaison Committee of European Retail Associations, CLD) had proposed cooperation with GEDIS "against the 1992 challenge" and Guy Beckers welcomed further discussion with Joubert, the CLD was not included in European commercial alliances.[186] But in 2019, EuroCommerce "joined forces" with the ERRT to "create a stronger and more united retail organization [under the name EuroCommerce] to safeguard and promote the sector's interests on a European stage."[187] As ERRT president and former Delhaize chairman, Frans Muller noted at the time: Commerce employed more Europeans than any other sector, giving it a fundamental importance to the European economy and society.[188]

Conclusions

In addition to their cartelization and political mobilization, European commercial companies also capitalized on opportunities to expand their

[183] Grace Ballor, Interview with Pierre-Olivier Beckers-Vieujant, Audio recording. March 31, 2023.
[184] Ibid.
[185] "European Conference on Transborder Regions," Circulaire no. 145, August 24, 1991, GEDIS B.14.2, DEL.
[186] J. Joubert, "Letter to Guy Beckers," Brussels, December 16, 1988; G. Beckers, "Letter to J. Joubert," Brussels, January 9, 1989, B.14.2 GEDIS, DEL.
[187] Ibid.
[188] EuroCommerce, "Press Release: EuroCommerce and the European Retail Round Table to Join Forces," Brussels, November 7, 2019.

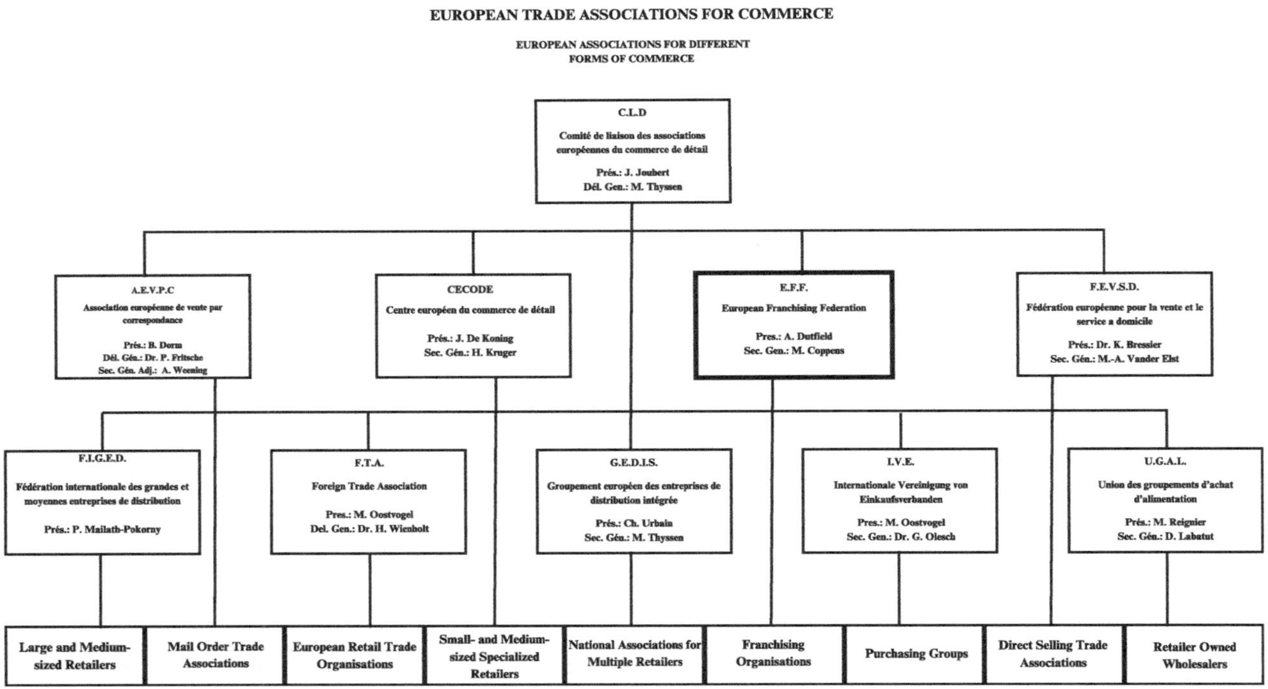

Figure 6.1 European trade associations for commerce within the CLD. Organigramme adapted from Delhaize archive document (in GEDIS B.14.2, DEL), thanks to Rasmus Salén.

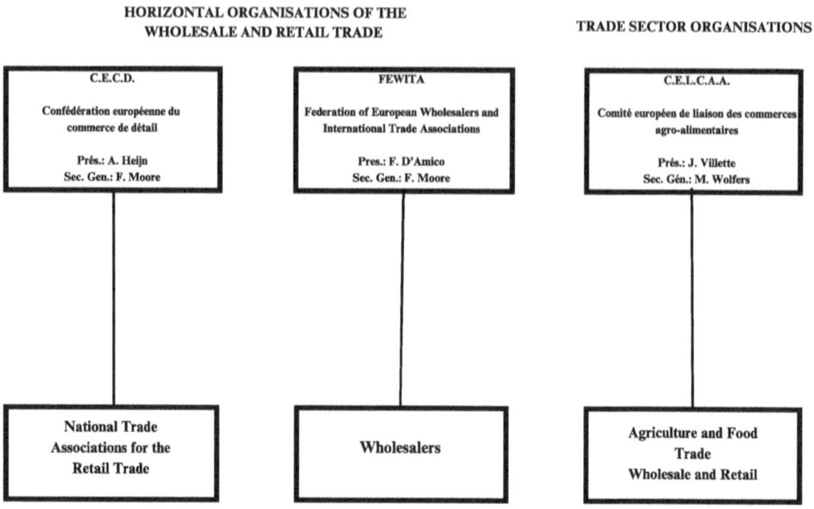

Figure 6.2 European trade associations for commerce outside of the CLD. Organigramme adapted from Delhaize archive document (in GEDIS B.14.2, DEL), thanks to Rasmus Salén.

business in the region, especially in the wake of the Soviet collapse. This multi-faceted regionalization gave European multinational retailers the financial and experiential confidence in the late 1990s and early 2000s to use Europe as a springboard from which to expand beyond their regional "home" market into farther-flung emerging global markets. British Tesco, which was described as having ambitions on every continent, and its CEO Terry Leahy, who could reportedly "turn anything to gold," opened chains across Thailand and Malaysia.[189] In this period, Carrefour entered North Africa and South America. With the mantra "to grow is to survive," believing "economies in Asia were going to explode," "blinded by its previous international successes," and compelled by peer pressure from its European competitors and fellow ERRT members who were also expanding globally, Delhaize made "an important experiment in Asian markets" with acquisitions in Thailand, Singapore and operated Super Indo in Indonesia in 1997 and 1998.[190] Some of these ventures were initially successful, while others struggled

[189] James Thompson, "The Unassuming Empire-Builder," *The Independent*, February 26, 2011.

[190] Grace Ballor, Interview with Gui de Vaucleroy, Audio recording. May 11, 2023; Grace Ballor, Interview with Pierre-Olivier Beckers-Vieujant, Audio recording. March 31, 2023.

from the start. Already by the 2010s, most of these multinationals were divesting from their global assets to refocus on Europe. Not only did it prove difficult to coordinate supply and distribution so far away from their core businesses, and not only were those markets more susceptible to instability caused by financial crises and political risks, but European retailers operating outside of the EEC, EU, and EEA also did not have the benefits of the Single Market or the infrastructure of BIAs through which to share information, form partnerships, and influence policymaking. Delhaize learned that while it seemed "strategic to think global," the success of its business required "acting local," just as local contacts had provided the foundation for its other international expansions.[191] As part of its return to Europe, Delhaize merged with the Dutch food retail multinational Ahold in 2016 to form Royal Ahold Delhaize, one of Europe's largest commercial firms, with subsidiaries across the EU and a persistently lucrative group of assets in the US, thanks to vertically integrated supply and distribution.

As this chapter has shown, commercial companies reacted much later to the Single Market Program than their counterparts in manufacturing and banking. While they initially felt marginalized by the Commission's early interest in and cooperation with industry, changes to the regional business environment motivated retailers like Delhaize to establish regional buying clubs to protect their profits in a new internal market. Furthermore, when faced with the "challenge" of the Commission's new social and environmental policies in the late 1980s and early 1990s, they created new BIAs to defend themselves against the challenge of the social Single Market. Paradoxically, European commerce became more European in its defensive opposition to the Single Market, a position they then used to globalize. It is therefore in the case of commerce and the social Single Market that the tensions between capitalism and democracy, further discussed in the Conclusion, become most clear.

[191] Grace Ballor, Interview with Gui de Vaucleroy, Audio recording. May 11, 2023.

Conclusion
Capitalism and Democracy

In 2012, Jacques Delors reflected: "In addition to its benefits – freedom of movement for people, goods, services and capital – the single market also increases the interdependence among national economies and fuels the feeling that we need 'to act together.' That is especially important today when, in each of our countries' grass-roots opinions, the globalisation process is frightening people and populism is gaining ground, urging countries to turn in on themselves. That is why elected governments have a tendency to assign priority to purely national interests, forgetting the benefits of shared sovereignty. This interdependence in the market is a kind of plinth, a base which, even if the climate were to deteriorate in the future, would still make it possible to keep the construction of Europe alive."[1]

Thus far, however, the twenty-first century has not upheld Delors' optimism about the ability of the Single Market to stave off the corrosive forces of globalization, populism, and nationalism and maintain the integrity of the union. Indeed, his hope in 2012 that the Single Market could be the bedrock of European democracy had already been outmoded by Hungary's reelection of a populist autocrat in Viktor Orbán in 2010 and further tested a few years later by Britain's referendum on membership in the European Union. In Britain, as in so many other places, globalization and immigration had "frightened" people through job losses and rising inequality, causing Britain, ultimately, to "turn in on" itself in Delors' words and succumb to populist politics, although not authoritarianism.[2] Still, the referendum was itself a democratic exercise made possible by Article 50 of the Treaty on European Union, but in which only two thirds of Britons participated, while those citizens who had lived outside the UK for more than fifteen years and who may have been greater beneficiaries of integration and thus more inclined to "Remain"

[1] Jacques Delors, "The Single Market: Cornerstone of the EU." *Notre Europe*, November 22, 2012.

[2] Sara B. Hobolt, "The Brexit Vote: A Divided Nation, a Divided Continent," *Journal of European Public Policy* 23, no. 9 (2016): 1259–1277.

were excluded from voting. While no other EU member states have yet made the same choice – largely dissuaded by Britain's economic and political struggles since its departure – European publics have progressively chosen the very nationalist populism Delors warned against and hoped the benefits and interdependence of the Single Market would overcome.

The role of multinational enterprises in the making of the Single Market and shaping its policy contours uncovered in this book demands a close consideration of the relationship of democracy and capitalism in the EU. Has the capitalism at the core of the Single Market undermined democracy in Europe and contributed to the "democratic deficit"? If Europe "rescued the nation state" in the 1950s as Alan Milward argued, did it subsequently hollow out the democratic nation state by economic means in the 1980s and 1990s, reflecting Dani Rodrik's "trilemma" between global capitalism, democracy, and national sovereignty?[3] What does contemporary Europe tell us about whether and how an economic system of uneven capital accumulation "predicated on atomized individuals" can be reconciled with the democratic promise of equity in political power?[4] This Conclusion brings the historical evidence presented in the previous chapters to bear on such questions. To do so, it reviews thinking about the relationship of capitalism and democracy in the "long twentieth century" and engages seriously with Europe's discontents and the social consequences of firm-led market integration.[5] Ultimately, by engaging with both the democratic critics of capitalism and the capitalist critics of democracy, it synthesizes the book's arguments that the making of the Single European Market was a capitalist project with strong, but insufficient, social dimensions to sustain European democracy without significant reform.

Questions about capitalism and democracy underpinned the twentieth-century competition between economic, social, and political systems, which equally motivated and served as the backdrop of regional market integration in Europe. The early twentieth-century work of "Geneva School" neoliberals to encase markets from democratic intervention created a framework with which globalists critiqued the kind of regional cooperation institutionalized in Western Europe in the aftermath of the Second World War.[6] As explained in the Introduction to this

[3] Alan S. Milward, *The European Rescue of the Nation-State*, 2nd ed. (London; New York: Routledge, 2000); Dani Rodrik, "How Far Will International Economic Integration Go?" *Journal of Economic Perspectives* 14, no. 1 (February 1, 2000): 177–186.

[4] Trevor Jackson, "Never Too Much," *The New York Review*, January 16, 2025.

[5] Giovanni Arrighi periodized the history of capitalism into seven "long centuries" in his *The Long Twentieth Century: Money, Power, and the Origins of Our Times* (London: Verso, 2010).

[6] Quinn Slobodian, *Globalists: The End of Empire and the Birth of Neoliberalism* (Cambridge, MA: Harvard University Press, 2018); Quinn Slobodian and Dieter Plehwe, "Neoliberals

book, however, the earliest regional international organizations of the UNECE, Western Union, Council of Europe, and European Payments Union were formed to reconstruct the region after war and born out of a transatlantic desire to insulate Western Europe against Soviet influence and aggression in the East. But the Coal and Steel Community reflected a Western European commitment – largely under American pressure – to a capitalist organization of economies and societies, on the foundation of which the common and single markets were built and of which many European and American multinationals were enthusiastic supporters.[7] In the second half of the century, the ideological Cold War further pitted Friedrich Hayek's socialism and "serfdom" on the one hand against Milton Friedman's "capitalism and freedom" on the other, with non-aligned states and trade across the Iron Curtain occupying the economic, political, and social space in between.[8] That both teacher and student professed liberal orthodoxy from Chicago reflects the mirror effect of their focus on two sides of the same debate.

Already in 1944, Hayek critiqued economic planning and argued: "If capitalism means here a competitive system based on free disposal over private property, it is far more important to realize that only within this system is democracy possible. When it becomes dominated by a collectivist creed, democracy will inevitably destroy itself." Despite his defenses of individual liberty, Hayek went on to dismiss the "fetish" of democracy, which he described as "essentially a means, a utilitarian device for safeguarding internal peace and individual freedom. As such it is by no means infallible or certain … – and it is at least conceivable that under the government of a very homogenous and doctrinaire majority democratic government might be as oppressive as the worst dictatorship."[9] Friedman followed with his own demo-skepticism in the 1980s, critical of the rise and fall of Keynesian state interventionism, emboldened by his work with the "Chicago Boys" in Pinochet's Chile the decade before, and excited by so many new opportunities to "crack up capitalism" by zoning the global economy away from democracy.[10] According to Friedman,

against Europe," in *Mutant Neoliberalism: Market Rule and Political Ruptures*, ed. William Callison and Zachary Manfredi (New York: Fordham University Press, 2019), 89–111.

7 On US multinationals in Europe, see: Janick Marina Schaufelbuehl, *Crusading for Globalization: US Multinationals and Their Opponents since 1945* (Philadelphia: University of Pennsylvania Press, 2025).

8 Milton Friedman and Rose D. Friedman, *Capitalism and Freedom* (Chicago: University of Chicago Press, 1982); Friedrich A. Hayek, *The Road to Serfdom*. (New York: George Routledge and Sons, 1944).

9 Hayek, *The Road to Serfdom*, 73–74.

10 Quinn Slobodian, *Crack-Up Capitalism: Market Radicals and the Dream of a World Without Democracy* (New York: Metropolitan Books, 2023).

"history suggests only that capitalism is a necessary [but not sufficient] condition for political freedom." And the economic coordination required for social organization can be achieved either forcefully through coercion or voluntarily through the marketplace, a "free private enterprise exchange economy – what we have been calling competitive capitalism."[11] For Friedman as for Hayek, market economies and individual economic liberty were inextricably linked, mutually reinforcing, even codependent. Democracy, however, was a mere trend, not even necessarily preferrable to dictatorship.

Even orthodox and neoliberal thinkers embraced democracy after the events described in Chapter 5, when Francis Fukuyama proclaimed the "end of history" and triumph of liberal democracy, and the new European Union developed democracy as a clear criterion for membership with the implementation of the Copenhagen Criteria established by the Council in 1993. In 2023, the *Financial Times*' Martin Wolf lamented *The Crisis of Democratic Capitalism*, which he attributed to the failure of market economies to deliver on the needs of societies, prompting publics to embrace populist politics and succumb to antidemocratic forces, as happened in 2016 with the tandem Brexit referendum result in Britain and election of Donald J. Trump in the US.[12] Insofar as it is informed by history, Wolf's book connects the political trust required for democracy to function to economic outcomes, a relationship with origins in the economic transformation of the First Industrial Revolution and reverberations in the political upheaval of the French Revolution. Imbued with nostalgia, it presents "democratic recession" as evidence of the frailty of the world order that made Wolf himself a privileged elite. He borrowed this term from political scientist Larry Diamond, who connected economic downturn to the decline of "freedom," a claim with which Steven Levitsky and Lucan Way later took issue before Levitsky and his colleague Daniel Ziblatt typologized exactly *How Democracies Die*: often after economic crises, which can equally topple autocracies.[13] Economic reform is urgently needed in the twenty-first century, Wolf argued, to ensure market capitalism can deliver on its promises and stave off deeper slide into authoritarianism. Indeed, as historians have shown, Europe has no monopoly on the "pathologies of democratic capitalism," which prevail in the US as well.[14] Such

[11] Friedman and Friedman, *Capitalism and Freedom*, 10–13.

[12] Martin Wolf, *The Crisis of Democratic Capitalism*, 1st ed. (London: Allen Lane, 2023).

[13] Larry Diamond, *The Spirit of Democracy: The Struggle to Build Free Societies throughout the World* (New York: MacMillan, 2008); Steven Levitsky and Lucan A. Way, "The Myth of Democratic Recession," *Journal of Democracy* 26, no. 1 (2015): 45–58; Steven Levitsky and Daniel Ziblatt, *How Democracies Die* (New York: Crown, 2018).

[14] Sidney M. Milkis and Scott C. Miller, eds., *Can Democracy and Capitalism Be Reconciled?* 1st ed. (New York: Oxford University Press, 2025).

convergence undermines some of the EU's claims to be pioneering a new relationship of capitalism and democracy and shows transatlantic comparisons to reflect what Peter Baldwin, echoing Sigmund Freud, called the "narcissism of minor differences."[15]

Heterodox thinkers and critical theorists have also attended to the shortcomings of capitalism and their threats to democracy but have argued more for systemic reform than economic policy innovation. German sociologist and career critic of capitalism Wolfgang Streeck exposed the myth of the postwar "settlement of social-democratic capitalism," which he described as a "shotgun marriage."[16] For Streeck, like Marx, capitalism contains the "seeds of its own destruction," made obvious in the "structural crises" of the 1970s, also discussed by Robert Brenner.[17] In Streeck's view, those crises were exacerbated by the structural shift from "tax states" to "debt states," giving rise to the financial system Susan Strange called *Casino Capitalism* and the neoliberal epoch.[18] Streeck pointed to the 1980s – the decade characterized by the neoliberal policy hallmarks of privatization, liberalization, and deregulation – as the pivotal period when the national democracies that had redistributed the "proceeds of the capitalist market economy downward ... provided for rising standards of living among ordinary people, and thereby procured legitimacy for the capitalist market economy" succumbed to the globalization of international trade agreements that helped capital "outgrow national borders" and ultimately weakened the power of labor by redistributing gains "from the bottom to the top."[19] In the wake of the 2008 Global Financial Crisis, Streeck argued, the EU evolved from a collection of "debt states" into a "European Consolidation State," a transformation with "fundamental implications for both domestic democracy and international order."[20] For critical theorists Magnus Ryner and Alan Cafruny, too, the crises of the early twenty-first century exposed the limitations and contradictions of the EU, seemingly no better than the problems of globalization.[21]

Others have examined the material dimensions of capitalism and democracy in Europe by calculating the economic and social

[15] Peter Baldwin, *The Narcissism of Minor Differences: How America and Europe Are Alike. An Essay in Numbers* (Oxford; New York: Oxford University Press, 2009).

[16] Wolfgang Streeck, *How Will Capitalism End? Essays on a Failing System* (New York: Verso, 2016), ebook version: 4.

[17] Robert Brenner, *The Economics of Global Turbulence: The Advanced Capitalist Economies from Long Boom to Long Downturn, 1945–2005* (London: Verso, 2006).

[18] Susan Strange, *Casino Capitalism* (Oxford: B. Blackwell, 1986).

[19] Streeck, *How Will Capitalism End?* 22. [20] Streeck, *How Will Capitalism End?* 113.

[21] Magnus Ryner and Alan Cafruny, *The European Union and Global Capitalism: Origins, Development, Crisis* (London: Red Globe Press, 2016).

consequences of regional market and political integration in the 1990s. Even before the Single Market was completed, economist Richard Baldwin revised Paolo Cecchini's "Costs of Non-Europe" discussed in Chapter 1 by modeling not just Cecchini's calculation of 2.5–6.5 percent one-time, short-run gains from market integration, but the long-term innovation, productivity, and investment "growth effects of 1992."[22] His "back of the envelope calculations" using "new" theories of growth and approaches to calculating factors "supposedly impossible to measure" found the Single Market "might add between 0.2 and 0.9 percentage points to the EC's long term growth rate," which would mean "Europe's real income would triple in an average person's lifetime rather than doubling" as was the case before the 1992 Program.[23] Delors' second term (1989–1993) was plagued by economic recession, however. Cecchini's projected 2.5–6.5 percent one-time, short-run gains from market integration had not yet materialized, despite the market having been declared complete. After the new EU posted negative growth rates in 1993, Delors issued a "White Paper on Growth, Competitiveness, and Employment" to introduce a "new development model" to "take advantage of the internal market" and "simultaneously address all aspects of the current economic crisis – sluggish growth, low inflation, lack of competitiveness, labor market inflexibility," and 10.5 percent unemployment.[24] For Delors, the EU's economic problems in the early 1990s could be relativized in relation to a global index. For economist Paul Krugman, this reflected Delors' "dangerous obsession with competitiveness" and unwillingness to address the EU's real problems in the 1990s, as he saw them: the incompatibility of the European welfare model with economic growth and the challenge of preserving the EMS amid the high costs of German reunification.[25]

Despite the recessionary late 1980s and early 1990s, retrospective reports by European institutions and national foundations from the twenty-first century found market integration ultimately boosted intra-European trade by a factor of five, raised European GDP by 8.5 percent, and boosted employment by at least 1.4 percent.[26] But many of these

[22] Richard Baldwin, Pierre-Andre Chiappori, and Anthony Venables, "The Growth Effects of 1992," *Economic Policy* 4, no. 9 (1989): 247–281.

[23] Baldwin et al., "The Growth Effects of 1992," 249.

[24] European Commission, "White Paper on Growth, Competitiveness, and Employment," COM(93)700 final, Brussels, December 5, 1993.

[25] Paul Krugman, "Competitiveness: A Dangerous Obsession," *Foreign Affairs* 73, no. 2 (1994): 28–44.

[26] Jan in 't Veld, "Quantifying the Economic Effects of the Single Market in a Structural Macromodel," European Commission Discussion Paper 094, February 2019; Affari

studies fail to disentangle vertical market integration from horizontal enlargement, despite the accession of sixteen new member states (a 160 percent increase in size) since the launch of the Single Market Program. In short, only when taken together with enlargement and only after considerable time did market integration address some of the economic and social problems of the 1970s and early 1980s by achieving economic growth and creating jobs.

Predictably, the market produced winners and losers. Economists like Baldwin expected the internal market to inflict high social costs, since the anticipated rate of industry consolidation would come as "bad news for those in contracting regions" likely to experience deindustrialization, a loss of jobs, and economic downturn in the wake of market integration.[27] Political scientist Catherine de Vries has studied the electoral consequences of such "loss," finding that economic hardship, even with environmental causes, inclines voters toward the nationalism and authoritarianism of the "far right."[28] Further revisions of Baldwin and Cecchini more than three decades after the 1992 Program found the Single Market's effect on GDP growth was actually a much higher 12–22 percent, largely because of increasing horizontal integration during the 1990s and early 2000s. These gains were distributed unevenly across member states, with disproportionate benefits for member states on the European "periphery," where the radical economic transformation of "Shock Therapy" was coupled with distribution of EU regional development and cohesion funds, which have worked to redistribute resources and facilitate economic development across the Single Market area.[29] Those gains aside, sociologists and political scientists have uncovered how "the consequences of neoliberal capitalism in Eastern Europe" like rising inequality and economic crises paved the way for populism and authoritarianism, especially in former Soviet Bloc states like the now

Europei, "25 Years of the Single Market: Factsheet," 2018: www.affarieuropei.gov.it/media/3973/25-years-of-the-eu-single-market-factsheet.pdf.

[27] Baldwin et al., "The Growth Effects of 1992," 261.

[28] See her European Research Council project "Narratives of Loss: Unravelling the Origins of Support for Socially Conservative Political Agendas," 2020–2025, the team of which produced the following case study: Simone Cremaschi, Nicola Bariletto, and Catherine E. De Vries, "Without Roots: The Political Consequences of Collective Economic Shocks," *American Political Science Review*. Published online 2025: 1–20.

[29] Jonne Lehtimäki and David Sondermann, "Baldwin versus Cecchini Revisited: The Growth Impact of the European Single Market," *Empirical Economics* 63, no. 2 (August 1, 2022): 603–635; Ivan T. Berend, *Economic History of a Divided Europe: Four Diverse Regions in an Integrating Continent* (London: Routledge, 2020). On "Shock Therapy," see: Naomi Klein, *The Shock Doctrine: The Rise of Disaster Capitalism*, 1st ed. (New York: Metropolitan Books, 2007).

"illiberal democracies" of Hungary and Poland.[30] Multinational enterprises, like the ones discussed in this book, contributed to the productivity, investment, and growth gains of market integration as well as to the negative social consequences of neoliberal capitalism in Europe. Some benefitted considerably from liberalization and access to large labor and consumer markets. In part, Jacques Delors' Social Charter and vocational training programs described in Chapters 1 and 6 and which skeptics have criticized for being inherently neoliberal, aimed to remedy the labor, consumer, and environmental problems often blamed on capitalism and the Market, as have regional and cohesion policies.[31] As shown in Chapters 5 and 6, that firms like BNP, Delhaize, and their business interest associations opposed the Social Charter reveals the social Single Market to have been more a threat than a boon to big business.

Jacques Delors' death in late 2023 occasioned many eulogies cum analyses of his storied career as Commission president, most of which addressed the tensions between neoliberal and social Europe and Delors' role in both sides of regional integration. Scholars like Aurélie Andry, who had already called "social Europe the road not taken," critiqued Delors as the "gravedigger of social Europe" for betraying his erstwhile trade unionism and "build[ing] a new European order in thrall to free-market dogmas;" others remembered Delors' commitment to rebuilding Europe's economy, albeit through liberalization and by empowering big business, as a fundamentally social achievement, and one that likely did safeguard democracy in the region, even if only temporarily until macroeconomic change and the arbitrage on which multinationals rely resulted in deindustrialization, job losses, and communities starved for resources.[32] Eric Bussière chronicled Delors' long career to find more

[30] Kristen Ghodsee and Mitchell Orenstein, *Taking Stock of Shock: Social Consequences of the 1989 Revolutions* (Oxford; New York: Oxford University Press, 2021); Sheri Berman, "The Consequences of Neoliberal Capitalism in Eastern Europe," *Social Europe*, September 6, 2021. See also the work of Cas Mudde: "The Populist Zeitgeist," *Government and Opposition* 39, no. 4 (January 2004): 541–563; "Populism in Europe: An Illiberal Democratic Response to Undemocratic Liberalism (The Government and Opposition/Leonard Schapiro Lecture 2019)," *Government and Opposition* 56, no. 4 (2021): 577–597.

[31] For more on these tensions, see: Laurent Warlouzet, *Europe contre europe: Entre liberté, solidarité, et puissance* (Paris: CNRS Editions, 2022).

[32] Aurélie Dianara, "Jacques Delors Was the Gravedigger of 'Social Europe,'" *Jacobin*, January 8, 2024; Aurélie Dianara Andry, *Social Europe, the Road Not Taken: The Left and European Integration in the Long 1970s*, Oxford Studies in Modern European History, 1st ed. (Oxford; New York: Oxford University Press, 2022); Laurent Warlouzet, "The EEC/EU as an Evolving Compromise between French Dirigism and German Ordoliberalism (1957–1995)," *JCMS: Journal of Common Market Studies* 57, no. 1 (2019): 77–93.

nuance in his complex vision for Europe and the challenges he faced in implementing it.[33] Indeed, supporters of Delors recognize the ways European governance has always been an "evolving compromise," as Laurent Warlouzet has described it, between divergent national approaches and ideologies, many of which opposed Delors' efforts to create a social Single Market.[34] Nor was the EEC/EU alone in having to find compromises between approaches to economic thinking in the late twentieth century: In tracing *The Rise and Fall of the Neoliberal Order*, historian Gary Gerstle identified compromises in American economics and politics that resemble those made in Europe in the 1980s and 1990s.[35] In the wake of economic crises, Gerstle explains, US Attorney General Robert Bork traded strict enforcement of antitrust legislation for the economic and social benefits of jobs and cheap goods provided by big business. The Delors Commission similarly prioritized employment and consumer choice in the wake of crises and similarly saw the economies of scale promised by big business as the answer to Europe's economic and social problems in the late twentieth century. Historical counterfactuals can be useful here: Would democracy in Europe have succumbed to authoritarian nationalism far sooner and on a wider scale if the Single Market Program had not addressed the challenges of the 1970s? Still, if the social balance sheet of Delors' presidency and his efforts to create a European "capitalism with a human face" have had such mixed results, what lessons might history offer for future reform?[36]

My narrative has shown how European policymakers pursued market integration in the 1980s to resolve the social and economic problems of the 1970s and saw big business as allies in the process of market making. Through granular business cases, I examined the pivotal period between the crises of the 1970s and peak neoliberalism of the 1990s when European economies, societies, and governance evolved from the so-called postwar "golden age of capitalism," featuring high growth rates and in which labor and trade unions still played a political role, to the crises of the twenty-first century, which precipitated "democratic

[33] Eric Bussière, *L'Europe de Jacques Delors: Gestation et mise en œuvre d'un projet* (Paris: Presses de l'Université Paris-Sorbonne, 2024).

[34] Laurent Warlouzet, "The EEC/EU as an Evolving Compromise between French Dirigism and German Ordoliberalism (1957–1995)"; *Governing Europe in a Globalizing World: Neoliberalism and Its Alternatives Following the 1973 Oil Crisis*, 1st ed., Routledge Studies on Government and the European Union (New York; London: Routledge, 2017).

[35] Gary Gerstle, *The Rise and Fall of the Neoliberal Order: America and the World in the Free Market Era* (Oxford: Oxford University Press, 2022).

[36] Samuel Brittan, *Capitalism with a Human Face* (London: Edward Elgar Publishing, 1995).

recession."[37] Chapter 1 showed how the Delors Commission looked to big business to deliver the growth Europe needed both to emerge from the economic and social crises of the 1970s and remain globally competitive. I find policymakers saw the stagflation and high unemployment of the 1970s as circumstantial, rather than structural, as the consequences of economic shocks, not as the crisis of accumulation. Chapter 1 also uncovered the paradoxes of the Commission's view of big business as an ally in market making and its commitment to competition policy, as is also echoed in Chapter 3. This history highlighted a shortcoming of the Single Market: the attempt to recapture the industrial economy of postwar reconstruction without fully attending to structural changes in the global economy, requiring the European Commission to continue to work on making the Single Market "deeper and fairer" in the 2010s and 2020s by removing barriers to the free movement of services, modernizing standards, facilitating access to finance, and strengthening the digital internal market.[38] However problematic in the long term, that flaw did prolong investment in the kinds of "durable" industrial jobs desired by the Council in its Copenhagen Summit in 1982 and described in Chapter 4. Efforts to recapture the industrial economy of the postwar boom delayed the democratic consequences of what World Economic Forum founder Klaus Schwab has called the "Fourth Industrial Revolution" but did not prepare the EU for competition in an increasingly tech driven service economy. Economist Mariana Mazzucato has argued how crucial the investment of "entrepreneurial states" is to economic and energy transitions, the development of new technologies and industries, and "earthshots" to mitigate the consequences of climate change.[39] Yet, as Chapter 1 explained, national industrial policy is restricted by the state aid prohibitions agreed in the Treaty of Rome, and the EU lacks clear legal competence in common industrial policy.[40]

[37] On labor in postwar capitalism, see: Grace Ballor and Sabine Pitteloud, "Introduction: Capitalism and Global Governance in Business History," *Business History Review* 97, no. 3 (2023): 459–479.

[38] European Commission, "The Single Market in a Changing World: A Unique Asset in Need of Political Commitment," COM(2018) 772 final. Reports by Enrico Letta and Mario Draghi in 2024 underscored the need to finally complete the internal market for Europe to remain globally competitive against the resurgent industrial policy of China and the US.

[39] Mariana Mazzucato, *The Entrepreneurial State: Debunking Public vs. Private Sector Myths* (London: Demos, 2011); *Mission Economy: A Moonshot Guide to Changing Capitalism* (New York: Harper Business, 2021).

[40] See publications by many colleagues at LUISS on industrial policy, the dissertation of David Irion on research policy, and the joint work of Rasmus Salén and Grace Ballor on the history of business forums and European research, technology, and industrial policy.

This book has uncovered the role of multinational enterprises in the making of the Single European market by uncovering both firm strategies in the new business environment of an internal market as well as firm mobilization against to various dimensions of market governance. Chapter 2 studied the public–private coproduction of common standards in the Single Market, which closed the Commission's expertise gap, gave business another channel of influence, and facilitated multinational economies of scale, especially in the production of goods. Chapter 3 made the argument for using a case study methodology for understanding regional business strategy of multinationals across the Single Market, deployed by Chapters 4, 5, and 6 to examine the cases of auto manufacturing, merchant banking, and food commerce in Europe in the 1980s and 1990s. Together, these case studies add a new, granular perspective to European political economy, not focused on the theoretical framework of capitalism, but on the business strategies that constitute its praxis. They also demonstrated the very different ways multinationals approached market integration and the Commission's efforts to establish market regulations for the benefit of consumers, workers, and the environment, with automakers most enthusiastic about the industrial focus of the market's design, banks more interested in the new opportunities of market enlargement and its regulation than in deeper market integration, and commerce mobilizing against the threats of producer consolidation and the social dimensions of the Single Market.

Consequently, this business history of the Single European Market has provincialized European market integration by situating it in its global and macroeconomic context; pluralized the actors involved in market integration beyond nation states and supranational institutions; problematized big business influence, especially over small and medium sized enterprises and social stakeholders like consumer advocacy groups, trade unions, and the environment; and politicized the market's social and political consequences in relation to capitalism and democracy. Its treatment of transnational business interest associations in manufacturing, banking, and services also explains how big business influence on European policymaking has inspired the creation of many activist watchdog organizations, like the Corporate Europe Observancy, which tracks and problematizes corporate lobbying.

At the urging of the Council and by working with the Parliament, policymakers in the Commission in the 1980s and 1990s aimed to build a robust and competitive market as the core of a Social Europe that improved the lives of Europeans with greater consumer choice, lower prices, labor and consumer protections, and the "greener perspective" of environmental regulation.[41] Did market making as a way out of the economic and social problems of the 1970s reflect the fundamental neoliberalism of European integration and its corrosion of state sovereignty from the top down, or did the "Bocconi Boys go to Brussels" and bring neoliberalism with them?[42] While socialists and labor groups initially endorsed the aims of "Europe 1992" to harmonize living standards across the EEC, they quickly doubted the Single Market's ability to deliver the benefits it promised without causing further social harm, especially in light of the recessionary context into which the Single Market was born in the early 1990s.[43] Their fears were confirmed in the early 2000s when multinational investment in "peripheral" economies in the region provided some jobs and goods but the repatriation of profits to "core" economies exacerbated regional inequalities. Technology and knowledge transfers proved no match for structural asymmetries. Such dynamics, which also increased total European GDP and the redistributive resources of the EU, became undeniable after the global financial, sovereign debt, and euro crises, by which time geographies of GDP across the EU easily mapped onto electoral distributions of Euro-support and Euroskepticism. Already in 2003, a report by experts including André Sapir and Jean Pisani-Ferry found economic performance in the EU's integrated market to be "mixed: While macroeconomic stability has considerably improved during the 1990s and a strong emphasis on cohesion has been preserved, the EU system has failed to deliver a satisfactory growth performance."[44] "Such underperformance," they argued, was a threat to the very European model, to democracy, and to the social demand for cohesion in light of globalization and competition, first with the US in the postwar period, then Japan in the 1980s, and China by the twenty-first century. Without more economic growth, in their view, Europeans would have no choice but to turn against Europe.

[41] On compromises between German ordoliberalism and the social market economy, see: Mathieu Dubois, *L'économie sociale de marché à la conquête de l'Europe: La diplomatie allemande et le modèle européen (1953–1993)* (Rennes: Presses universitaires de Rennes, 2024).

[42] Oddný Helgadóttir, "The Bocconi Boys Go to Brussels: Italian Economic Ideas, Professional Networks and European Austerity," *Journal of European Public Policy* 23, no. 3 (2016): 392–409. For more on "European varieties of neoliberalism," see the special issue of *Contemporary European History* edited by Mattia Ravano and Grace Ballor.

[43] Henry Neuberger, "The Economics of 1992: A Report Commissioned by the British Labour Group of Euro-MPS," HAEU: HW-37.

[44] André Sapir et al., "An Agenda for a Growing Europe. Making the EU Economic System Deliver." Report of an Independent High-Level Study Group established on the Initiative of the President of the European Commission, 2003.

Efforts to complete a digital Single Market and reform the Eurozone after sovereign debt crises seem to have had little effect in the 2010s.[45] Further pandemic, economic, and security crises in the early 2020s motivated national and European officials to outline plans for reforming the EU to include capital market integration and a single market for defense. In his 2024 commissioned by the European Council, Enrico Letta tempered the usual growth paradigm by insisting Europe needed "Much More Than a Market," a constellation of flanking social, economic, and environmental policies to make the market competitive, human, and sustainable.[46] Just months later in his landmark report on "The Future of European Competitiveness" requested by Commission President Ursula von der Leyen, Mario Draghi echoed arguments made by many orthodox thinkers before him, including Delors in 1993: Only more business-led growth could preserve democracy in Europe and help the EU survive competition, especially in high tech, with the US and China, whose rise has rendered the European social market model obsolete and which already dominates the industries of the future. He argued if the EU cannot deliver "prosperity, equity, freedom, peace, and democracy in a sustainable environment … it will have lost its reason for being."[47] Subsequent implementation of Draghi's competitiveness agenda aimed to deregulate the Single Market, dismantling many of the social and environmental protections put in place to moderate the market and giving big business all the more room to exert policy and market influence over their small- and medium-sized counterparts and the European demos.

These proposals reflect the centripetal and centrifugal dynamics of European cooperation and integration: at various times in the twentieth century, cooperation has been motivated by endogenous desires for federalism, peace, and prosperity, while at other times, European states and societies cooperated in response to exogenous pressures and shocks. As the newly reelected US President Trump prepared to launch a global trade war in early 2025, he claimed because "the European Union was formed in order to screw the United States," higher tariffs on EU goods

45 Among these efforts was Mario Monti's proposal of "A New Strategy for the Single Market at the Service of Europe's Economy and Society," European Commission, May 8, 2010.

46 Enrico Letta, "Much More Than a Market," April 2024. Letta's report was commissioned by the European Council. For more analysis of these reports, see: Daniel Gros, "The Draghi and Letta Reports: Overloaded Messages and Limited Impact," *JCMS: Journal of Common Market Studies*, first published online July 2025.

47 Mario Draghi, "The Future of European Competitiveness: Part A," European Commission, September 2024: 5.

were more than justified both to punish erstwhile allies for not putting "America first" and to reshore manufacturing to the predominantly service economy of the US, despite few possible productivity gains and already low US unemployment.[48] But as this book has shown, not only does regional economic integration in Europe have a much longer history than Trump and his political base realize, but early regional market integration occurred under direct American pressure and directly benefitted US multinationals. Furthermore, the Single European Market at the economic core of the EU belongs to the broader histories of market liberalization and globalization that characterize the twentieth-century "pax Americana."[49] However ahistorical, Trump's antagonism toward the EU reflects the EEC's "relaunching" of its economic project in the 1980s and 1990s, laying the foundation for the EU's subsequent economic "threat" to the fragility of the US economy in the twenty-first century as a liberal, democratic, and regulatory power, subsequent American backlash against Europe, and the political resonance of Trump's nationalist policies, paradoxically more likely to harm the same working class Americans who elected a billionaire autocrat than to undermine the large and diversified Single European Market with many other trade partners. Still, without reform to sufficiently meet the needs of European societies in light of demographic, economic, technological, and climate change, the EU and its member states remain vulnerable to the populism, autocracy and cronyism roiling the US since 2016 and all too obvious on the inaugural dais in 2025.

According to the European Parliament Research Service, while European regional and cohesion policies have been chief policy tools to ameliorate the negative consequences of European capitalism since the 1950s, a lack of coordination with other EU policies have allowed inequities to persist, which has weakened democracy in some parts of Europe even as capitalism has meanwhile strengthened, and big business remains both underregulated and highly influential.[50] That Euroskepticism continues to spread, including across the Western European "core" and EEC founding members of France, Germany, and the Benelux

[48] Furthermore, European economies had already similarly exploited the productivity gains of technologies to move away from manufacturing into services, resulting in few possible manufacturing movements from Europe to the US.

[49] Daniel J. Sargent, "Pax Americana: Sketches for an Undiplomatic History," *Diplomatic History* 42, no. 3 (June 1, 2018): 357–376.

[50] Lenka Jančová, Christa Kammerhofer-Schlegel, and Marco Centrone, "The Future of EU Cohesion: Scenarios and Their Impacts on Regional Inequalities," European Parliament Research Service, European Added Value Unit PE 762.854 (December 2024).

countries – and that the European Parliament itself lurched to the political right in its 2024 elections – both seems to disprove Delors' view of the Single Market as a "plinth" of European interdependence and reinforces concerns that significant further reform is needed to reconcile the capitalism at the core of the EU and its Market with democracy in contemporary Europe.[51] The history of big business in the making of the Single European Market reveals longrun increases in economic growth, consumer choice, and industrial jobs, even when complemented by some social and environmental protections, to be important but insufficient to meet the needs of European democratic societies, as the "polycrisis" and crisis politics of the twenty-first century have equally made so clear.

[51] The distinction between capitalism as an economic and political system and markets as forums for exchange is helpfully illuminated in John Cassidy's *Capitalism and Its Critics: A History from the Industrial Revolution to AI* (New York: Allen Lane, 2025).

Appendix European Commission Directorates General 1985–1992

DG I: External Relations
DG II: Economic and Financial Affairs
DG III: Internal Market and Industrial Affairs (Task Force Small and Medium-sized Enterprises)
DG IV: Competition
DG V: Employment, Industrial Relations, and Social Affairs (initially Education)
DG VI: Agriculture
DG VII: Transport
DG VIII: Development
DG IX: Personnel and Administration
DG X: Information, Communication, and Culture
DG XI: Environment, Consumer Protection, and Nuclear Safety
DG XII: Science, Research, and Development (Joint Research Center)
DG XIII: Telecommunications, Information Industries, and Innovation
DG XIV: Fisheries
DG XV: Financial Institutions and Company Law (initially Taxation)
DG XVI: Regional Policy
DG XVII: Energy
DG XVIII: Credit and Investments
DG XIX: Budgets
DG XX: Financial Control
DG XXI: Customs Union and Indirect Taxation
DG XXII: Coordination of Structural Policies
DG XXIII: Enterprise Policy, Distributive Trades, Tourism and Social Economy/Cooperatives

Acknowledgments

This book could not have been written without the support of many esteemed colleagues, patient editors, generous granting institutions, excellent archivists, willing interviewees, multidisciplinary communities of scholars, and loving friends and family.

Editors at Cambridge University Press so generously supported this book from early writing through production. This book exists thanks to the early interest and patient attention of Michael Watson and the constant support of Geoffrey Jones, Louis Galambos, and Susie Pak, whose guidance and encouragement shaped the manuscript from the abstractions of early ideas to the materiality of communicated argument you read now. Two anonymous readers offered helpful comments on the book's framing and scope. Rosa Martin, Lisa Carter, and Hariharan Jayamoorthy kindly ensured the book's elements were in order for publication.

While this book differs substantively from my doctoral dissertation, I am indebted to many at the University of California Los Angeles who shaped my early development there as a researcher and teacher. A research assistantship at UCLA's Center for 17th- and 18th-Century Studies afforded me the opportunity to refine my research skills by supporting the work of David Sabean, Margaret Jacob, Joseph Bristow, and Felicity Nussbaum. I remain grateful to Peter Baldwin, Robert Brenner, Caroline Ford, Lynn Hunt, Margaret Jacob, Muriel McClendon, Robin D. G. Kelly, Teofilo Ruiz, David Sabean, and Peter Stacey, from whom I learned to teach and whose reading seminars laid my foundations in European and economic history, and to Stefania Tutino for her generous mentorship and model of tenacity. Ivan Berend graciously took me on as his last doctoral student and taught me how to read well and write often. He remains the kindest, most resilient person I have ever known, and I will forever endeavor to rise to the challenge of his example. He and Katalin Radics have become cherished family. Naomi Lamoreaux generously agreed to serve on my committee despite having moved from Westwood to New Haven just before I started my dissertation, and she offered excellent comments on my work even from afar. Her career bridging economics and history continues to be an inspiration. John Agnew was the ideal external reader of my work, for his innovative approach to political geography and his mastery of scholarship across disciplines. In addition to being a thoughtful discussant and source of great encouragement, Mary Yeager introduced me to the field of business history and to the Business History Conference (BHC) and European Business History Association. I am grateful to the BHC for the opportunity to join the Doctoral Colloquium in 2018, where Edward Balleisen, Daniel Raff, and Teresa da Silva Lopes encouraged me to pursue research on multinationals in European integration, and for later opportunities to serve on the BHC's Emerging Scholars Committee, Board of Trustees, and Program Committee with Stephen Mihm and Ai Hisano.

Ideas for this book in its current form took shape at the European University Institute, where I benefitted intellectually from the vibrancy of the institute, the mentorship of Youssef Cassis and Federico Romero, and from friendships with my Max Weber colleagues, especially Claire Bright, Madeleine Dungy, James Lee, Benoît Maréchaux, Bilyana Petrova, Christopher Roberts, Athina Sachoulidou, Christos Tsakas, Aydin Yildirim, and Eva Zschirnt, among many others. I hope they see in this book reflections of conversations over lunches at Piatti e Fagotti and coffees in the giardini of the Villa Paola, Villa Schifanoia, and Villa Salviati. My formation as a scholar and historian of contemporary Europe has also been shaped by other colleagues I first met in Florence and continue to value as interlocutors and collaborators, including Aurélie Andry, Eric Bussière, David Coen, Alexis Drach, Johanna Gautier, Aleksandra Komornicka, Ulrich Krotz, Piers Ludlow, Emmanuel Mourlon-Druol, Neil Rollings, Angela Romano, Arlo Poleti, Glenda Sluga, Corinna Unger, and Laurent Warlouzet. A joint fellowship at the Graduate Institute, Geneva brought me across the Alps and afforded me meaningful exchanges with many scholars I admire, including the late Mohamed Mahmoud Ould Mohamedou, Gopalan Balachandran, Carolyn Biltoft, Damian Clavel, Fernanda Conforto de Oliveira, Emmanuel Dalle-Mulle, Cédric Dupont, Rui Esteves, Amalia Ribi Forclaz, Michael Goebel, André Liebich, Davide Rodogno, Nathan Sussman, Nadya Wells, and Ryan Whitaker.

It was at Harvard Business School (HBS) during the eerily quiet months of the "third wave" of the Covid-19 pandemic when I started writing this manuscript, the framework of which bears the marks of the business case method I honed at HBS. HBS is also home to the *Business History Review*, which published two pilot articles of this book, sections and tables of which are reprinted in Chapters 2 and 4 with the journal's generous permission. Twice-weekly Covid testing kept Geoffrey Jones and I in the dynamic MBA classroom of "Entrepreneurship and Global Capitalism" for most of the fall 2020 semester, and new technologies like Zoom kept the Business History Initiative seminar and events running, during which I greatly valued exchanges with Rawi Abdelal, Kristin Fabbe, Matthias Fibiger, Walter Friedman, Tom Nicholas, Sophus Reinert, Meg Rithmire, Charlotte Robertson, and Marlous van Waijenburg. MaryAnn Hart and Gerry McDonough, Laura Gossett and Jacob Brady, John Boonstra and Meredith Leich, Lizzy Comuzzi and Jono Jaquette, Brigid McMahan and Brian Sennett, and Liz and Tom Buoni turned the loneliness of the pandemic into shared backyard joy in Cambridge, Massachusetts.

Bocconi colleagues in Milan supported the later stages of my writing process with encouragement and stimulating conversation, especially Guido Alfani, Carlo Altomonte, Amelia Campagni, Italo Colantone, Andrea Colli, Catherine de Vries, Mattia Fochesato, Vincenzo Galasso, Valeria Giacomin, Giulia Giupponi, Daniel Gros, Marlene Jugl, Alexandros Kentikelenis, Lanny Martin, Valentina Mele, Mario Monti, Sienna Nordquist, Gianmarco Ottaviano, Zachary Parolin, Mattia Ravano, Sonia Schifano, Eleanor Spaventa, Romain Svartzman, Tamás Vonyó, and Scott Williamson. The Bocconi Lab for European Studies and Institute for European Policymaking offered forums for meaningful intellectual exchange. Perhaps most of all in Milan, I must thank the students of my "History of European Integration," "Global History of Capitalism and Governance," and "Future of Europe" courses, whose probing questions and enthusiastic engagement with these topics inspired and energized my writing. A consolidated teaching schedule gave me the time required to focus on archival research and intensive writing each spring after being motivated and energized by my students each fall. This allowed me to consult archives in 2022 and 2023 and finish editing and indexing from a fellowship at the Ludwig Maximilian University of Munich (LMU) in Spring 2024, where I greatly benefitted from interlocutors like Victor Jaeschke, Lisbeth Matzer, Stephen Milder, Kiran Klaus Patel, Maté Rigo, Thomas Süsler-Rohringer, Martin Schulze-Wessel, Philipp Ther, Benjamin Thomas, Jared Warren, Andreas Wirsching, and other excellent fellows and colleagues of the Project House Europe and the Center for Advanced Studies on Universalism and Particularism in Contemporary European History.

Any contributions this book may make are the fruit of access to the archival materials of corporations and political institutions, made possible equally by commitments to transparency as material support for research travel. Evidence supporting this book was made accessible by archivists Annika Biss at BMW; Jean-Charles Bouguet, Marie Laperdrix, Pierre de Longuemar, Roger Nougaret, Marie-Eve Rakuzin at Paribas; Emmanuel Collet at Delhaize; Philip Wilkin at the Archive of European Integration; Laura Linard at the Harvard Baker Library; the helpful staff of the Archive of the European Commission, including Lamia El Abdellaoui, María Francisca Ciudad Rodriguez, and Flore Plisnier; and Dieter Schlenker and the wonderful team at the Historical Archives of the European Union. This book was also greatly enriched by the inclusion of interviews with executives and policymakers who generously shared their time and experience, especially Pierre-Olivier Beckers-Vieujant, Étienne Davignon, Peter Tracey, Eberhard von Kuenheim, and Gui de Vaucleroy.

Several centers across the University of California supported my early research in corporate archives and at the Historical Archives of the European Union. A grant from the Foundation Jean Monnet pour l'Europe in Lausanne, Switzerland allowed me to consult the Foundation's files, with the support of Vincent Bezençon, Gilles Grin, and Natalie Troisfontaines among others, and to build a network of equally kind and impressive Swiss colleagues, including Thomas David, Pierre Eichenberger, Stephanie Ginalski, Janick Marina Schaufelbuehl, and Sabine Pitteloud, a treasured collaborator and dear friend. A Junior Faculty Research Award from Bocconi made possible trips to the Paribas archive in Dinan, France and the Historical Archives of the European Commission in Brussels. I annotated enthusiastically in these archives, but I wrote best in public libraries: sometimes under the frescoed ceilings of Italy's Biblioteca nazionale, and during holiday closures and ever hotter summers, inside the thick stone walls of France's Bibliothèque nationale.

I am deeply indebted to the research assistants who supported my writing and revisions. Elizabeth Anastasi and Jessica Boutchie lent this book's early drafting the same attention to detail that has now made both of them successful lawyers. This book's final form owes much to Rasmus Salén, an excellent emerging scholar and valued collaborator, who matched his meticulous work on the references and index of this book with boundless patience and good cheer.

Participants at numerous conferences and workshops provided feedback on presentations of parts of this book, including the American Historical Association, Business History Conference, Council for European Studies (special thanks to Daniel Kinderman, Thomas Paster, and Dennie Oude Nijhuis), European Business History Association, European Union Studies Association, and World Economic History Congress, and many events at the European University Institute, Institute for European

Policymaking, and the universities across North America and Europe that kindly invited me to present my work. For their valuable comments on various chapters and excerpts of the manuscript, this book owes much to Catherine de Vries, Christakis Georgiou, Neil Rollings, Sabine Pitteloud, JoAnne Yates and Craig Murphy, Laurent Warlouzet, and Mira Wilkins. Trevor Jackson's invaluable comments helped me identify and develop this book's core contributions; he is the most humane scholar I know, a clear and incisive thinker, a true and longsuffering friend in the in-between spaces, and a cracking wit, especially by email and sometimes even by voice message.

For their friendship and moral support, I am deeply grateful to Kelly McCormick and Maia Woolner, who first taught me how to be an expat and welcomed me into their homes in Tokyo and Paris; Elizabeth Comuzzi, Sarina Kuersteiner, and the Sheet Meet writing group; Samuel Keeley for his enduring friendship – from writing sessions at UCLA's Charles E. Young Research Library (YRL) and meditation breaks with Marv to a decade-long correspondence across time and space; and my lifelong friend Sarah Dischinger, whose adventurous spirit and determination have inspired me since we were young. Many family members have provided endless encouragement and support, especially Shannon, Kim, Vonda, Steve, Carroll, LuAnn, John, Norma, Jim, Sarah, Claire, James, Margaux, Julien, Marion, Dan, and so many Hardys and Sauers.

This book is dedicated to Dan and Max, who are my home anywhere and everywhere. They patiently tolerated my habit of "working in inappropriate places," and they sustained, encouraged, and motivated me through feverishly productive writing retreats, often in rural France, and equally through the struggles we have experienced in our uncannily adopted country, where we learned with enough moxie, *tutto è possibile, anche dove c'è sempre l'impossibile.*

Bibliography

Archives

The Archive of European Integration (AEI)
Historical Archives of the European Commission (HAEC)
Les archives historiques de BNP Paribas (BNPPA)
BMW Archive (BMW)
Centre virtuel de la connaissance sur l'Europe (CVCE)
Delhaize Corporate Archive (DEL)
Fondation Jean Monnet Pour L'Europe (FJME)
Historical Archives of the European Union (HAEU)

Annual Reports

"Annual Report 1991: Telefónica de España," Annual Report, 1992. www.telefonica.com/en/shareholders-investors/financial-reports/historical-archive-annual-reports/1991/.

BMW. 1985–1992 Annual Report. Munich: BMW, 1985–1992.

Food Lion, Inc., *Delhaize Annual Report 1992*. Harvard Baker Library.

Volkswagen. 1985–1992 Annual Report. Wolfsburg: VW, 1985–1992.

Interviews

Ballor, Grace. Interview with Eberhard von Kuenheim. Audio recording. Munich, October 24, 2016.

Interview with Etienne Davignon. Audio recording. Brussels, June 16, 2016.

Interview with Gui de Vaucleroy. Audio recording. May 11, 2023.

Interview with Linda Ketner. Audio recording. April 26, 2019.

Interview with Peter Tracey. Audio recording. Milan, April 1, 2023.

Interview with Pierre-Olivier Beckers-Vieujant. Audio recording. March 31, 2023.

Interview with Pierre-Olivier Beckers-Vieujant. Audio recording. October 10, 2016.

Lyons, Rich. Interview with Carl Hahn. Video broadcast. Berkeley Haas, October 26, 2011.

Published EEC/EU Documents

Bangemann, Martin. "Yes to the Community's Industrial Policy." Commission of the European Communities: Monthly Newsletter on the Single Internal Market, April 4, 1992.

Brittan, Leon. "Competition Policy Report, 26 July 1989." P/89/44 European Commission.

Cecchini, Paolo. "Research on the Cost of Non-Europe, Basic Findings. The Completion of the Internal Market: A Survey of European Industry's Perceptions of the Likely Effects." Vols. 1–16. Luxembourg: Office for Official Publications of the European Communities, 1988.

Colen, Liesbeth et al. "Retail Alliances in the Agricultural and Food Supply Chain." Joint Research Center, European Commission, 2020.

Commission Européenne. "Lettre mensuelle sur l'Europe sans frontières." Juin 1990. Extrait du discours prononcé à Rotterdam, le 6 avril 1990.

Commission of the European Communities and European Parliament, eds. *Forum on the European Automobile Industry, Brussels, Palais Des Congrès, 1 March 1994: Written Proceedings*. Brussels/Luxembourg, 1994.

Commission of the European Communities. "European Economy: 1998 Broad Economic Policy Guidelines." Directorate General for Economic and Financial Affairs, 1998.

"1989 Annual Report: ESPRIT - European Strategic Programme for Research and Development in Information Technology." 1989, EUR 12626. Brussels: Commission for the European Communities, 1990.

"Commission Decision of 28 August 1991 on règlement CEE no.4064/89 sur les concentrations a propos de la Banque Nationale de Paris et Dresdner Bank)." 1991. https://ec.europa.eu/competition/mergers/cases/decisions/m124_fr.pdf

"Communication on the Free Movement of Foodstuffs within the Community." 89/C 271/03, Vol. 32, October 24, 1989.

"Completing of the Internal Market: Progress Report on the 1st of April 1989." Memo 89/16.

"Completing the Internal Market: An Area without Internal Frontiers: The Progress Report Required by Article 8B of the Treaty." COM(88)650 final, Brussels, November 17, 1988.

"Completion of the Internal Market: Community Legislation on Foodstuffs." November 8, 1985.

"Council Directive of 14 June 1989 on the Official Control of Foodstuffs." 89/397/EEC.

Decision of 20 May 1981 establishing a Committee on Commerce and Distribution. Official Journal of the European Communities, 81/428/EEC.

"Europe's Pharmaceutical Industry: An Innovation Profile." EIMS Publication no. 32 (August 1996), Directorate-General XIII.

"Further Delegation of Powers in Respect of Trade: Appointment of Members of the Committee on Commerce and Distribution." Brussels, May 26, 1981.

"Habilitation dans le secteur du Commerce – nomination des membres du Comité du Commerce et de la Distribution." SEC(81)843, Vol. 1981/0038.

"Low Voltage Directive." 73/23/EEC. Brussels, 19 February 1973.

"Perspectives for the Common Agricultural Policy." COM(85) 333 final, July 15, 1985.

"Programme de recherche et d'action sur le developpement du marche de l'emploi." 1982.

Proposal for a Council Regulation (EEC) Concerning the Affixing and Use of the CE Mark of Conformity on Industrial Products. COM(91)145 final, May 17, 1991.

"Recommendation by the Commission regarding the system of payments, especially relations between carholders and issuers." November 17, 1988 (88/590/CEE).

"Recommendation de la Commission du 17 novembre 1988 concernant les systèmes de paiement et en particulier les relations entre titulaires et émmetteurs de cartes 88/590/CEE." *Journal officiel des communautés européennes*, no. L 317/55.

"Second report from the Commission of the European Communities on the Completion of the Internal Market." May 18, 1987.

"The Thrust of Commission Policy: Statement by Jacques Delors, President of the Commission, to the European Parliament." Strasbourg: Bulletin of the European Communities, January 14–15, 1985.

Together since 1957: 35 Years of Eurobarometer: European Integration as Seen by Public Opinion in the Member States of the European Union. 2009.

"Towards a Single Market in Distribution: Internal Trade in the Community, the Commercial Sector, and the Completion of the Internal Market." COM (91) 41 final, Brussels, March 11, 1991.

"Une perspective européenne: Intervention de Gaston Thorn, Lors d'un dejeuner, Causerie organise par la chambre de commerce de Bruxelles." April 1984.

"White Paper from the Commission to the European Council on Completing the Internal Market." COM(85)310 final, Milan, June 28–29, 1985.

"White Paper on Growth, Competitiveness, and Employment." COM(93)700 final, Brussels, December 5, 1993.

Council of the European Communities. "Ad hoc Committee for Institutional Affairs Report to the European Council (Brussels, 29-30 March 1985) [Dooge Report]." March 29, 1985.

"Council Decision of 25 November 1983 Concerning a Plan for the Transnational Development of Supporting Infrastructure for Innovation and Technology Transfer." Official Journal of the European Communities, 83/624/EEC.

"Council Directive on Laying Down a Procedure for the Provision of Information in the Field of Technical Standards and Regulations." Directive 83/189/EEC. Official Journal of the European Communities, March 28, 1983.

"Council Resolution of 14 November 1989 on Internal Trade in the Context of the Internal Market." 89/C 297/02.

"Council Resolution of 7 May 1985 on a New Approach to Technical Harmonization of Standards." (85/C 136/01) Official Journal of the European Communities.

Directive 77/780 of 12 December 1977 on the Coordination of Laws, Regulations and Administrative Provisions Relating to the Taking Up and Pursuit of the Business of Credit Institutions, Art. 1, 1977 OJ. (L 322).

Directive 89/299 on the Own Funds of Credit Institutions, 1989 O J. (L 124).
Directive 89/647 of 18 December 1989 on a Solvency Ratio for Credit Institutions, 1989 OJ. (L 386).
"Joint Declaration: Ministerial Meeting between EFTA Countries and the EC and Its Member States." Luxembourg, April 9, 1984.
Regulation (EEC) No. 3906/89 of 18 December 1989 on economic aid to the Republic of Hungary and the Polish People's Republic.
"Single European Act." Luxembourg, Office for the Official Publication of the European Communities, 1986.
"The Treaty Establishing the European Community (Treaty of Rome)." March 25, 1957, Rome, Italy.
Council of the European Union. "Council Directive 2001/86/EC of 8 October 2001 supplementing the Statute for a European company with regard to the involvement of employees." OJ L 294, 10.11.2001.
"Council Regulation (EC) No. 2157/2001 of 8 October 2001 on the Statute for a European company (SE)." OJ L 294, 10.11.2001.
Delors, Jacques. "1992: The Social Dimension – Address at the Trades Union Congress, Bournemouth 8 September 1988."
"Speech at Bruges, 17 October 1989." Speech 89/73.
Devantier, Alexandra. "Appointment of the Commission: Parliament's Role before 1995." European Parliament: Briefing.
European Commission, Directorate General for Internal Market, Industry, Entrepreneurship, and SMEs. "CE Marking." Accessed May 2021.
European Council. "Fontainebleau Summit." 1984.
"Hanover European Council." June 27–28, 1988, Bulletin of the European Communities, No. 6/1988.
"The Presidency's Conclusions on the Proceedings of the European Council, Copenhagen, 3–4 December 1982." 1982.
"Solemn Declaration on European Union." Stuttgart, June 19, 1983.
"Treaty on European Union." OJ C 191, 29.7.1992.
European Court of Justice. Judgement of February 20, 1979: Case 120/78.
"Cassis de Dijon."[RS1] OJ No. C 256, 30.10.1980.
Eurostat. "Retailing in the European Single Market." Brussels, Eurostat, 1993.
Genscher, Hans-Dietrich, and Emilio Colombo. "Draft European Act Submitted by the Governments of the FRG and Italy (6 November 1981)." *Bulletin of the European Communities*. November 1981, no. 11. Luxembourg: Office for Official Publications of the European Communities.
Löffler, Klaus. "More of a Heavyweight Than It Looks: The European Parliament's Role in Setting Up the Internal Market." Commission of the European Communities: Monthly Newsletter on the Single Internal Market, April 4, 1992.
Nicholas, Florence. Common Standards for Enterprises. Luxembourg: Office for Official Publications of the European Communities, 1995.
Official Journal of the European Communities. "Communication on the Free Movement of Foodstuffs within the Community." 89/C 271/03, Vol. 32, (October 24, 1989): Communication, A.
Official Journal of the European Communities. "Déclaration des répresentants des gouvernements des États membres, réunis au sein du Conseil, sur la persistance du rôle des services douaniers aprés 1992." 90/C/262/03.

Steinherr, Alfred. "The Great Depression: A Repeat in the 1980s? Economic Papers No. 10, November 1982." EU Commission – Working Document, 1982.

Published/Secondary Sources

Addison, John T., and W. Stanley Siebert. "The Social Charter of the European Community: Evolution and Controversies." *Industrial and Labor Relations Review* 44, no. 4 (1991): 597–625.

Affari Europei. "25 Years of the Single Market: Factsheet." 2018. www.affarieuropei.gov.it/media/3973/25-years-of-the-eu-single-market-factsheet.pdf

Aharoni, Yair. "Book Review: The Regional Multinationals MNEs and Global Strategic Management." *International Business Review* 14, no. 4 (August 2006): 439–446.

Ahrens, Ralf. "The Importance of Being European: Airbus and West German Industrial Policy from the 1960s to the 1980s." *Journal of Modern European History* 18, no. 1 (February 1, 2020): 63–78.

Albors-Llorens, Albertina, Catherine Barnard, and Brigitte Leucht, eds. *Cassis de Dijon: 40 Years On.* Oxford: Hart Publishing, 2021.

Álvaro-Moya, Adoración. "Networking Capability Building in the Multinational Enterprise: ITT and the Spanish Adventure (1924–1945)." *Business History* 57, no. 7 (October 3, 2015): 1082–1111.

Anderson, Perry. The Breakaway: Goodbye Europe." *London Review of Books*, January 21, 2021.

"The European Coup." *London Review of Books*, December 17, 2020.

"Ever Closer Union?" *London Review of Books*, January 7, 2021.

The New Old World. London: Verso, 2009.

Andersson, Jenny. "Neoliberalism from Within: The Business Fund and the Struggle for Market Ideology in Sweden." *Contemporary European History*, January 28, 2025: 1–17.

Andry, Aurélie Dianara. "Jacques Delors Was the Gravedigger of 'Social Europe'" *Jacobin*, January 8, 2024.

Social Europe, the Road Not Taken: The Left and European Integration in the Long 1970s, Oxford Studies in Modern European History. 1st ed. Oxford; New York: Oxford University Press, 2022.

Arrighi, Giovanni. *The Long Twentieth Century: Money, Power, and the Origins of Our Times*. London: Verso, 2010.

Association pour l'union monétaire de l'Europe. "Répertoire numérique." www.archivesnationales.culture.gouv.fr/chan/chan/AP-pdf/109-AS.pdf

Bähr, Johannes, Paul Erker, and James Amery Underwood. *Bosch: History of a Global Enterprise.* 1st ed. Munich: Verlag C.H. Beck, 2015.

Bailey, David, Alex de Ruyter, Jonathan Michie, and P. Tyler. "Global Restructuring and the Auto Industry." *Cambridge Journal of Regions, Economy and Society* 3, no. 3 (November 1, 2010): 311–318.

Bair, Jennifer. "Corporations at the United Nations: Echoes of the New International Economic Order?" *Humanity: An International Journal of Human Rights, Humanitarianism, and Development* 6, no. 1 (2015): 159–171.

Balassa, Bela. *The Theory of Economic Integration*. Homewood, IL, USA: RD Irwin, 1961.

Baldwin, Peter. *The Narcissism of Minor Differences: How America and Europe Are Alike: An Essay in Numbers*. Oxford; New York: Oxford University Press, 2009.

Baldwin, Richard, Pierre-Andre Chiappori, and Anthony Venables. "The Growth Effects of 1992." *Economic Policy* 4, no. 9 (1989): 247–281.

Ballor, Grace, and Sabine Pitteloud "Introduction: Capitalism and Global Governance in Business History." *Business History Review* 97, no. 3 (2023): 459–479.

"The Rise and Fall of Private Advocacy Forums from 1945 to the Twenty-first Century." *Socio-Economic Review*, 2025. https://doi.org/10.1093/ser/mwaf056

Ballor, Grace. "Agents of Integration: Multinational Firms and the European Union." *Enterprise & Society* 21, no. 4 (2020): 886–892.

"Agents of Integration: Multinational Firms and the European Union." PhD dissertation, University of California Los Angeles, 2018.

"From the 'American Challenge' to European expansion: Transatlantic economic relations from the 1950s to the 1970s." *Relations Internationales* 180, no. 4 (2019): 43–57.

"Business Eurosceptics: British Industry on Economic and Monetary Union, 1978–1999." *Business History* (2026).

"CE Marking, Business, and European Market Integration." *Business History Review* 96, no. 1 (2022): 77–108.

"Europe between Nationalism and Neoliberalism." In Cemil Aydin et al., "Rethinking Nationalism." *The American Historical Review* 127, no. 1 (2022): 311–371.

"Liberal Environmentalism: The Public-Private Production of European Emissions Standards." *Business History Review* 97, no. 3. (2023).

"Liberalisation or Protectionism for the Single Market? European Automakers and Japanese Competition, 1985–1999." *Business History* 65, no. 2 (2022): 302–328

Banalieva, Elitsa R., and Michael D. Santoro. "Local, Regional, or Global? Geographic Orientation and Relative Financial Performance of Emerging Market Multinational Enterprises." *European Management Journal, Is International Business Strategy Global or Regional?* 27, no. 5 (2009): 344–355.

Bartlett, Christopher A., and Ashish Nanda. "Ingvar Kamprad and IKEA." Harvard Business School Case 9-390-132, May 7, 1990.

Basosi, Duccio, Giulano Garavini, and Massimiliano Trentin, eds. *Counter-shock: The Oil Counter-Revolution of the 1980s*. London; New York: I. B. Tauris, 2018.

Berend, Ivan. *Economic History of a Divided Europe: Four Diverse Regions in an Integrating Continent*. Routledge, 2020.

An Economic History of Twentieth Century Europe. London: Cambridge University Press, 2006.

Europe in Crisis: Bolt from the Blue? London: Routledge, 2012.

The History of European Integration: A New Perspective. 1st ed. London; New York: Routledge, 2016.

From the Soviet Bloc to the European Union: The Economic and Social Transformation of Central and Eastern Europe since 1973. Cambridge: Cambridge University Press, 2009.

Berle, Adolf. *Power Without Property: A New Development in American Political Economy*. New York: Harcourt, Brace & Co., 1959.

Bernstein, Steven. *The Compromise of Liberal Envrionmentalism*. New York: Columbia University Press, 2001.

Berman, Sheri. "The Consequences of Neoliberal Capitalism in Eastern Europe." *Social Europe*, September 6, 2021.

Besen, Stanley M., and Joseph Farrell. "Choosing How to Compete: Strategies and Tactics in Standardization." *Journal of Economic Perspectives* 8, no. 2 (1994): 117–131.

Bibby, Andrew. "The Boss Who Gave Away the Business." *Financial Times*, January 24, 2006.

Bickerton, Christopher. "Europe's Long 1989." *Contemporary European History*, February 18, 2025, 1–18.

Bini, Elisabetta, Giuliano Garavini, and Federico Romero, eds. *Oil Shock: The 1973 Crisis and Its Economic Legacy*. London: I.B. Tauris, 2016.

Biss, Annika. *Die Internationalisierung der Bayerischen Motoren Werke AG. Die Internationalisierung der Bayerischen Motoren Werke AG*. Berlin: De Gruyter Oldenbourg, 2017.

Blind, Knut, Axel Magelsdorf, Crispin Niebel, and Florian Ramel. "Standards in the Global Value Chains of the European Single Market." *Review of International Political Economy* 25, no. 1 (2017): 28-48.

Bonin, Hubert. *Le monde des banquiers français au XXe siècle*. Paris: Broché, 2000.

Bonin, Hubert, Yannick Lung, and Stephen Tolliday, eds. *Ford, 1903–2003: The European History*. Paris: PLAGE, 2003.

Bourke, Thomas. "EC–Japan Relation, 1985–1993: The Impact of Foreign Direct Investment on Regional Political Integration." PhD dissertation, European University Institute, 1995.

Boynton, Andrew, and Mark R. Eaker. "Abb Asea Brown Boveri (a): The Merger." UVA-BP-0323. Rochester, NY, October 21, 2008. https://papers.ssrn.com/abstract=907785

Bradford, Anu. *The Brussels Effect: How the European Union Rules the World*. New York: Oxford University Press, 2020.

Brenner, Robert. *The Economics of Global Turbulence: The Advanced Capitalist Economies from Long Boom to Long Downturn, 1945–2005*. London: Verso, 2006.

Brittan, Leon. *European Competition Policy: Keeping the Playing Field Level*. Brussels: Center for European Policy Studies, 1992.

Brittan, Samuel. *Capitalism with a Human Face*. London: Edward Elgar, 1995.

Buckley, Peter J. "Business History and International Business." *Business History* 51, no. 3 (2009): 307–333.

"Historical Research Approaches to the Analysis of Internationalisation." *Management International Review* 56, no. 6 (2016): 879–900.

"The Role of History in International Business: Evidence, Research Practices, Methods and Theory." *British Journal of Management* 32, no. 3 (2021): 797–811.

Bürbaumer, Benjamin. "TNC Competitiveness in the Formation of the Single Market: The Role of European Business Revisited," *New Political Economy* (2020): 1–15.

Burgelman, Robert A. "Bridging History and Reductionism: A Key Role for Longitudinal Qualitative Research." *Journal of International Business Studies* 42, no. 5 (2011): 591–601.

Burr, Wolfgang, and Britta Fischmann. Review of the Regional Multinationals, MNEs and "Global" Strategic Management, by Alan M. Rugman. *MIR: Management International Review* 48, no. 1 (2008): 137–140.

Busch, Lawrence. *Standards, Recipes for Reality*. Cambridge, MA: MIT Press, 2011.

Bussière, Éric. "EU Industrial Policy: Lessons from the Experience of the 1960s to the 1990s." In Jean-Christophe Defraigne et al., eds., *EU Industrial Policy in the Multipolar Economy*. Edward Elgar Publishing, 2022, 159–172.

L'Europe de Jacques Delors: Gestation et mise en œuvre d'un projet. Paris: Presses de l'Université Paris-Sorbonne, 2024.

Paribas 1872–1992: Europe and the World. Antwerp: Fonds Mercator, 1992.

et al., eds. *Milieux économiques et intégration européenne au XXe siècle: La relance des années quatre-vingt (1979–1992)*. Paris: Comité pour l'Histoire économique et financière, 2008.

Bussière, Éric, Michel Dumoulin, and Sylvain Schirmann. *Europe organisée, Europe du libre-échange?: Fin XIXe siécle - années 1960*. Bern: Peter Lang, 2006.

Bussière, Éric, Piers Ludlow, Federico Romero, Dieter Schlenker, Vincent Dujardin, and Antonio Varsori. *The European Commission 1986–2000: History and Memories of an Institution*. Luxembourg: Publications Office of the European Union, 2019.

Büthe, Tim, and Walter Mattli. *The New Global Rulers: The Privatization of Regulation in the World Economy*. Princeton: Princeton University Press, 2011.

Carrillo, Jorge, Yannick Lung, and Rob van Tulder, eds. *Cars, Carriers of Regionalism?* London: Palgrave Macmillan, 2004.

Carroll, William K. *The Making of a Transnational Capitalist Class: Corporate Power in the 21st Century*. Illustrated ed. London; New York: Zed Books, 2010.

Cassidy, John. *Capitalism and Its Critics: A History from the Industrial Revolution to AI*. New York: Allen Lane, 2025.

Cassis, Youssef. *Big Business: The European Experience in the Twentieth Century*. Oxford: Oxford University Press, 1999.

Catalan Vidal, Jordi. "The Stagflation Crisis and the European Automotive Industry, 1973–85." *Business History* 59, no. 1 (January 2, 2017): 4–34.

Cecchini, Paolo, Alex Jacquemin, and Michael Catinat. *The European Challenge, 1992: The Benefits of a Single Market*. Hampshire: Aldershot, 1992.

CEN/ELEC. "About CEN." Accessed February 2, 2021. www.cencenelec.eu/about-cen/

Centre on Transnational Corporations, ed. *The Triad in Foreign Direct Investment*. World Investment Report 1991. New York: United Nations, 1991.

Charue-Duboc, Florence. "Repositioning of European Chemicals Groups and Changes in Innovation Management: The Case of the French Chemical industry. The Global Chemical Industry in the Age of the Petrochemical Revolution." Cambridge University Press, 2007. https://hal.science/hal-00263318/document

Chase, Kerry A. *Trading Blocs: States, Firms, and Regions in the World Economy.* Ann Arbor: University of Michigan Press, 2005.

Clavin, Patricia. *Securing the World Economy: The Reinvention of the League of Nations, 1920–1946.* Oxford: Oxford University, 2013.

Clavin, Patricia, and Madeleine Lynch Dungy. "Trade, Law, and the Global Order of 1919." *Diplomatic History* 44, no. 4 (2020): 554–579.

Clavin, Patricia, and Glenda Sluga, eds. *Internationalisms: A Twentieth Century History.* Cambridge: Cambridge University Press, 2016.

Clifton, Judith, Francisco Comín, and Daniel Díaz-Fuentes. "From National Monopoly to Multinational Corporation: How Regulation Shaped the Road towards Telecommunications Internationalisation." *Business History* 53, no. 5 (August 2011): 761–781.

Cobham, David. "The Nationalisation of the Banks in Mitterand's France: Rationalisations and Reasons." *Journal of Public Policy* 4, no. 4 (1984): 351–358.

Cockfield, Arthur. *The European Union: Creating the Single Market.* Chichester: Wiley Chancery Law, 1994.

Coen, David, Alexander Katsaitis, and Matia Vannoni, *Business Lobbying in the European Union.* Oxford: Oxford University Press, 2021.

Coen, David. "The European Business Interest and the Nation State: Large Firms Lobbying in the European Union and Member States." *Journal of Public Policy* 18, no. 1 (1998): 75–100.

"The Evolution of the Large Firm as a Political Actor in the European Union." *Journal of European Public Policy* 4, no. 1 (1997): 91–108.

Coen, David, and J. J. Richardson, eds. *Lobbying the European Union: Institutions, Actors, and Issues.* Oxford; New York: Oxford University Press, 2009.

Colantone, Italo, and Piero Stanig. "Global Competition and Brexit," *American Political Science Review* 112, no. 2 (May 2018): 201–218.

Colantone, Italo, Gianmarco I. P. Ottaviano, and Piero Stanig. "The Backlash of Globalization." SSRN Scholarly Paper. Rochester, NY, September 3, 2021.

Collet, Emmanuel. *Delhaize "Le lion," épiciers depuis 1867.* Brussels: Racine Lannoo, 2003.

Collis, David J., Elizabeth Johnson. "Smashing the Cube: Corporate Transformation at Ciba-Geigy Ltd." HBS Case 9795041 (1995).

Corea, Gamani. "Unctad and the New International Economic Order." *International Affairs (Royal Institute of International Affairs 1944–)* 53, no. 2 (1977): 177–187.

Cosgrove Twitchett, Carol, ed. *Harmonization in the European Economic Community.* London: Palgrave Macmillan, 1981.

Cowles, Maria Green. "Setting the Agenda for a New Europe: The ERT and EC 1992." *JCMS: Journal of Common Market Studies* 33, no. 4 (1995): 501–526.

Cremaschi, Simone, Nicola Bariletto, and Catherine E. De Vries. "Without Roots: The Political Consequences of Collective Economic Shocks." *OSF*, December 6, 2023.

Culpepper, Pepper D. *Quiet Politics and Business Power: Corporate Control in Europe and Japan.* Cambridge; New York: Cambridge University Press, 2011.

Curhan, Joan P., William H. Davidson, and Rajan Suri. *Tracing the Multinationals: A Sourcebook on U.S.-based Enterprises.* Cambridge, MA: Ballinger, 1977.

Cusumano, Michael. "Manufacturing Innovation: Lessons from the Japanese Auto Industry," *MIT Sloan Management Review* (Fall 1988).

Czychon, Christoph. *Regional and Global Multinationals: An Examination of Theory and Empirical Evidence from European MNEs.* MIR Edition. Wiesbaden: Springer Gabler, 2021.

Danish Ministry for Industry. "Butikker og forbrugere nu og i fremtiden." *Betaenkning fra Butiksstrukturkommissionen*, 1998. www.betænkninger.dk/wp-content/uploads/2021/02/1353.pdf

Darmer, Michael, and Laurens Kuyper, eds. *Industry and the European Union: Analyzing Policies for Business.* Northhampton, MA: Edward Elgar, 2000.

da Silva Lopes, Teresa. *Global Brands: The Evolution of Multinationals in Alcoholic Beverages.* Cambridge: Cambridge University Press, 2007.

et al. "Organizational Innovation in the Multinational Enterprise: Internalization Theory and Business History." *Journal of International Business Studies* 50, no. 8 (2019): 1338–1358.

David, Thomas, and Pierre Eichenberger. "Business and Diplomacy in the Twentieth Century: A Corporatist View." *Diplomatica* 2 (2020): 48–56.

"'A World Parliament of Business?' The International Chamber of Commerce and Its Presidents in the Twentieth Century." *Business History* 65, no. 2 (2022): 1–24.

Davies, William. "Martin Wolf: The Business-Lounge Intellectual." *New Statesman*, January 14, 2023.

This Is Not Normal: The Collapse of Liberal Britain. London: Verso, 2020.

Dawson, John A., and Masao Mukoyama. "The Increase in International Activity by Retailers." In John A. Dawson, Roy Larke, and Masao Mukoyama, eds., *Strategic Issues in International Retailing.* London: Routledge, 2006.

de Grazia, Victoria. *Irresistible Empire: America's Advance through Twentieth-Century Europe.* Cambridge, MA: Harvard University Press, 2006.

Dehousse, Renaud, and Joseph H. H. Weiler. "The Legal Dimension." In William Wallace, ed., *The Dynamics of European Integration.* London: Pinter Publishers, 1990: 242–259.

Dekker, Wisse. "Europe 1990 An Agenda for Action." *European Management Journal* 3, no. 1 (1985): 5–10.

DeLong, Bradford J. and Barry Eichengreen. "The Marshall Plan: History's Most Successful Structural Adjustment Program." Working Paper, Working Paper Series. *National Bureau of Economic Research*, November 1991.

Delors, Jacques. "The Single Market: Cornerstone of the EU." *Notre Europe*, November 22, 2012.

"Une strategie efficace pour une France non frileuse." *French Politics and Society* (1987).

Delors, Jacques, and Louis J. Arnaud. *Mémoires*. Plon, 2003.

Dermine, Paul. *The New Economic Governance of the Eurozone: A Rule of Law Analysis*. Cambridge Studies in European Law and Policy. Cambridge: Cambridge University Press, 2022.

Diamond, Larry. *The Spirit of Democracy: The Struggle to Build Free Societies throughout the World*. New York, NY: Henry Holt, 2008.

Drach, Alexis. "An Early Form of European Champions? Banking Clubs between European Integration and Global Banking (1960s–1990s)." *Business History* 66, no. 1 (2022): 287–310.

"The Forgotten Currency: The European Currency Unit Private Market and European Integration." Paper presentation at the World Economic History Congress (WEHC) 2022. Aubervilliers, France, 2022.

Liberté surveillée: Supervision bancaire et globalisation financière au Comité de Bâle, 1974–1988. Rennes: Presses Universitaires de Rennes, 2022.

"Reluctant Europeans? British and French Commercial Banks and the Common Market in Banking (1977–1992)." *Enterprise & Society* 21, no. 3 (2020): 768–798

"Supervisors against Regulation? The Basel Committee and Country Risk before the International Debt Crisis (1976–1982)." *Financial History Review* 27, no. 2 (2020): 210–233.

Dubois, Mathieu. *L'économie sociale de marché à la conquête de l'Europe: La diplomatie allemande et le modèle européen (1953–1993)*. Rennes: Presses universitaires de Rennes, 2024.

Dufresne, Anne, and Christophe Degryse. *The European Sectoral Social Dialogue: Actors, Developments and Challenges*. Bern: Peter Lang, 2006.

Dumke, Rolf H. "The Political Economy of German Economic Unification: Tariffs, Trade and Politics of the Zollverein Era." *The Journal of Economic History* 38, no. 1 (1978): 277–278.

Dumoulin, Michel, and Anne-Myriam Dutrieue. *La Ligue européenne de coopération économique, 1946–1981: Un groupe d'étude et de pression dans la construction européenne*. Bern: Peter Lang, 1993.

Dumoulin, Michel, Élisabeth Palmero, Vincent Dujardin, Éric Bussière, Piers Ludlow, and Jan Willem Brouwer. *The European Commission 1973–86: History and Memories of an Institution*. Luxembourg: Publications Office of the European Union, 2014.

Dungy, Madeleine Lynch. *Order and Rivalry: Rewriting the Rules of International Trade after the First World War*. Cambridge: Cambridge University Press, 2023.

Dür, Andreas, David Marshall, and Patrick Bernhagen. *The Political Influence of Business in the European Union*. Ann Arbor: University of Michigan Press, 2019.

Eckardt, Andrea, and Matthias Klemm. *BMW: Wirtschaftswoche*. 1995.

Egan, Michelle. "Bandwagon or Barriers? The Role of Standards in the European and American Marketplace." *University of Pittsburgh: Center for West European Studies*, Working Paper No. 1 (1997).

Single Markets: Economic Integration in Europe and the United States. Oxford: Oxford University Press, 2015.

Egan, Michelle, and Jacques Pelkmans. "Fixing European Standards: Moving Beyond the Green Paper," *CEPS Working Document* no. 65/ CEPS Standards Programme Paper no. 3, (May 1992).

Eichenberger, Pierre, Neil Rollings, and Janick Marina Schaufelbuehl. "The Brokers of Globalization: Towards a History of Business Associations in the International Arena." *Business History* 65, no. 2 (2023): 217–234.

Eichengreen, Barry. *Europe's Postwar Recovery*. Cambridge: Cambridge University Press, 1995.

Eichengreen, Barry, and Marc Uzan. "Marshall Plan: Economic Effects and Implications for Eastern Europe and the Former USSR." *Economic Policy* 7, no. 14 (1992): 13–75.

Emerson, Michael, Daniel Gros, and Alexander Italianer. *One Market, One Money: An Evaluation of the Potential Benefits and Costs of Forming an Economic and Monetary Union*. Oxford; New York: Oxford University Press, 1992.

EuroCommerce. "Press Release: EuroCommerce and the European Retail Round Table to join forces." Brussels, November 7, 2019.

European Voice. "Belgium's Driving Force." *Politico*, March 26, 1997. www.politico.eu/article/belgiums-driving-force/

Evans, Geoffrey, and Anand Menon. *Brexit and British Politics*. Hoboken, NJ: John Wiley & Sons, 2017.

"EU Referendum: CBI Warns of UK Exit 'Serious Shock.'" *BBC News*. April 14, 2016.

"EU Referendum: More than 1,280 Business Leaders Sign Letter." *BBC News*. June 22, 2016.

"EuroCommerce and Euro-Fiet [sic] Agreement on Fundamental Rights and Principles at Work, Brussels 6 August 1999." University of Minnesota: Human Rights Library, 1999.

Farrell, Joseph, and Garth Saloner. "Converters, Compatibility, and the Control of Interfaces." *The Journal of Industrial Economics* (1992): 9–35.

Fastnacht, Kathrin, et al. "The Emergence of a Global Player: The Internationalization of the Bosch Group." *Journal of Bosch History*, n.d.

Fellman, Susanna, and Martin Shanahan, eds. *A History of Business Cartels: International Politics, National Policies and Anti-Competitive Behavior*. London: Routledge, 2022.

Filippaios, Fragkiskos, and Ruth Rama. "Globalisation or Regionalisation? The Strategies of the World's Largest Food and Beverage MNEs." *European Management Journal* 26, no. 1 (2008): 59–72.

Fitzgerald, Robert. *The Rise of the Global Company: Multinationals and the Making of the Modern World*. Reprint ed. Cambridge: Cambridge University Press, 2016.

Fligstein, Neil, and Alec Stone Sweet. "Constructing Polities and Markets: An Institutionalist Account of European Integration." *American Journal of Sociology* 107, no. 5 (March 1, 2002): 1206–1243.

Fligstein, Neil, and Iona Mara-Drita. "How to Make a Market: Reflections on the Attempt to Create a Single Market in the European Union." *American Journal of Sociology* 102, no. 1 (1996): 1–33.

Frankel, Karen. "The Politics of Standards and the EC." *Communications of the ACM* 33, no. 7(1990).

Fredona, Robert, and Sophus A. Reinert. "Leviathan and Kraken: States, Corporations, and Political Economy." *History and Theory* 59, no. 2 (2020): 167–187.

Freyssenet, Michel, Koichi Shimizu, and Giuseppe Volpato, eds. *Globalization or Regionalization of the American and Asian Car Industry?* London: Palgrave Macmillan, 2003.

Friedman, Milton, and Rose D. Friedman. *Capitalism and Freedom.* Chicago: University of Chicago Press, 1982.

Friedman, Thomas L. *The World Is Flat: A Brief History of the Twenty-First Century.* 3rd ed. New York: Picador, 2007.

Frigant, Vincent, and Martin Zumpe. "Regionalisation or Globalisation of Automotive Production Networks? Lessons from Import Patterns of Four European Countries." *Growth and Change* 48, no. 4 (2017): 661–681.

Fukuyama, Francis. *The End of History and the Last Man.* New York: Simon & Schuster, 2006.

"The End of History?" *The National Interest* 16 (1989): 3–18.

Funk, Jeffrey L. *Global Competition Between and Within Standards.* London: Palgrave Macmillan, 2001.

Garavini, Giuliano. *After Empires: European Integration, Decolonization, and the Challenge from the Global South, 1957–1986.* Oxford: University Press, 2012.

The Rise and Fall of OPEC in the Twentieth Century. Oxford: Oxford University Press, 2019.

Garrett, Geoffrey. "International Cooperation and Institutional Choice: The European Community's Internal Market." *International Organization* 46, no. 2 (1992): 533–560.

Gehlen, Boris, Christian Marx, and Alfred Reckendrees. "Ambivalences of Nationality—Economic Nationalism, Nationality of the Company, Nationalism as Strategy: An Introduction." *Journal of Modern European History* 18, no. 1 (2020): 16–27.

Geisler Asmussen, Christian. "Local, Regional, or Global? Quantifying MNE Geographic Scope." *Journal of International Business Studies* 40, no. 7 (2009): 1192–1205.

Georgiou, Christakis. *Les grandes firmes françaises et l'Union Européenne: Economie politique de la construction du capitalisme européen intégré, de l'Acte Unique à la crise de la zone euro.* Vulaines sur Seine: Editions du Croquant, 2017.

Gerstle, Gary. *The Rise and Fall of the Neoliberal Order: America and the World in the Free Market Era.* Oxford; New York: Oxford University Press, 2022.

Ghodsee, Kristen, and Mitchell Orenstein. *Taking Stock of Shock: Social Consequences of the 1989 Revolutions.* Oxford; New York: Oxford University Press, 2021.

Ghoshal, Sumantra, and Christopher A. Bartlett. "The Multinational Corporation as an Interorganizational Network." *The Academy of Management Review* 15, no. 4 (1990): 603–625.

Goodfader, Joel. "European Unity: Pursuing the Vision: An Interview with Viscount Etienne Davignon." *Harvard Internatinal Review* 6, no. 1 (1983): 11–13.

Greenhouse, Steven. "Merger Mania Strikes Europe as Barrier-Free Market Nears." *The New York Times*, August 26, 1988, sec. Business. www.nytimes.com/1988/08/26/business/merger-mania-strikes-europe-as-barrier free-market-nears.html

Greenwood, Justin. *Interest Representation in the European Union*. 4th ed. London: Palgrave, 2017.

Grin, Gilles. *The Battle of the Single European Market: Achievements and Economic Thought, 1985–2000*. London: Kegan Paul, 2003.

Gros, Daniel. "The Draghi and Letta Reports: Overloaded Messages and Limited Impact." *JCMS: Journal of Common Market Studies*. https://doi.org/10.1111/jcms.70012

"One Market, One Money: A Mistaken Argument (Post Factum)?" *Center for European Policy Studies*, no. 2017/05, February 16, 2017.

Grunert, Manfred, and Florian Triebel. *BMW since 1916*. BMW Dimensions 5. München: BMW Group Mobile Tradition, 2006.

Guillen, Mauro F., and Esteban Garcia-Canal. "How to Conquer New Markets with Old Skills." *Harvard Business Review*, November 2010.

Haas, Ernst B. *The Uniting of Europe: Political, Social, and Economic Forces, 1950–1957*. Notre Dame: University of Notre Dame Press, 2004.

Haftendorn, Helga. "German Unification and European Integration Are but Two Sides of One Coin: The FRG, Europe, and the Diplomacy of German Unification." In Frédéric Bozo, Marie-Pierre Rey, N. Piers Ludlow, Leopoldo Nuti, eds., *Europe and the End of the Cold War*. London: Routledge, 2008: 135–147.

Hahn, Carl. *Meine Jahre mit Volkswagen*. Dresden: Signum, 2005.

Hall, Peter A. and David Soskice. *Varieties of Capitalism*. Oxford University Press, 2001.

Hamdani, Khalil, and Lorraine Ruffing. *United Nations Centre on Transnational Corporations: Corporate Conduct and the Public Interest*. London: Routledge, 2015.

Hanson, Brian T. "What Happened to Fortress Europe? External Trade Policy Liberalization in the European Union." *International Organization* 52, no. 1 (1998): 55–85.

Hayek, Friedrich A. *The Road to Serfdom*. New York: George Routledge and Sons, 1944.

Helgadóttir, Oddný. "The Bocconi Boys Go to Brussels: Italian Economic Ideas, Professional Networks and European Austerity." *Journal of European Public Policy* 23, no. 3 (2016): 392–409.

Henderson, W. O. "The German Zollverein and the European Economic Community." *Zeitschrift Für Die Gesamte Staatswissenschaft / Journal of Institutional and Theoretical Economics* 137, no. 3 (1981): 491–507.

Hewitt, Liane. "Monopoly Menace: The Rise and Fall of Cartel Capitalism in Western Europe, 1918–1957." PhD dissertation, Princeton University, 2023.

"The World in Blocs: Leo Amery, the British Empire and Regionalist Anti-Internationalism, 1903–1947." *Journal of Global History* 18, no. 2 (2023): 236–258.

Higgins, David M. *Brands, Geographical Origin, and the Global Economy: A History from the Nineteenth Century to the Present*. Cambridge: Cambridge University Press, 2018.

Hobolt, Sara B. "The Brexit Vote: A Divided Nation, a Divided Continent." *Journal of European Public Policy* 23, no. 9 (October 20, 2016): 1259–1277.

Hodson, Dermot. "Jacques Delors: Vision, Revisionism, and the Design of EMU." In Kenneth Dyson and Ivo Maes, eds., *Architects of the Euro: Intellectuals in the Making of European Monetary Union*. Oxford: Oxford University Press, 2016: 212–232.

Hooghe, Liesbet and Gary Marks, *Multi-Level Governance and European Integration*. Lanham, MD: Rowman & Littlefield Publishers, 2001.

Hudson, Raymond, Eike W. Schamp, and Ash Amin, eds. *Towards a New Map of Automobile Manufacturing in Europe? New Production Concepts and Spatial Restructuring*. Berlin; New York: Springer, 1995.

in 't Veld, Jan. "Quantifying the Economic Effects of the Single Market in a Structural Macromodel." European Commission Discussion Paper 094, February 2019.

Jabko, Nicolas. *Playing the Market: A Political Strategy for Uniting Europe, 1985–2005*. Cornell Studies in Political Economy. Ithaca: Cornell University Press, 2006.

Jackson, Trevor. *Impunity and Capitalism: The Afterlives of European Financial Crises, 1690–1830*. Cambridge: Cambridge University Press, 2022.

Jackson, Trevor. "Never Too Much," *The New York Review*, January 16, 2025.

James, Harold. *Making the European Monetary Union*. Cambridge, MA: Belknap Press, 2014.

Jensen-Eriksen, Niklas. "Creating Clubs and Giants: How Competition Policies Influenced the Strategy and Structure of Nordic Pulp and Paper Industry, 1970–2000." *Business History* 62, no. 5 (July 3, 2020): 763–781.

"Industrial Diplomacy and Economic Integration: The Origins of All-European Paper Cartels, 1959–72," *Journal of Contemporary History* 46, no. 1 (January 1, 2011): 179–202.

Johansson, Ulf. "IKEA: The Making of a Global Giant." In John A. Dawson and Masao Mukoyama, eds., *Global Strategies in Retailing: Asian and European Experiences*. Routledge Studies in International Business and the World Economy. Abingdon, Oxon; New York: Routledge, 2014: 137–145.

Johnson, Chalmers. *MITI and the Japanese Miracle: The Growth of Industrial Policy, 1925–1975*. Stanford: Stanford University Press, 1982.

Jones, Daniel T., Daniel Roos, and James P. Womack. *The Machine That Changed the World: The Story of Lean Production*. New York: Harper Perennial, 1991.

Jones, Geoffrey. *Deeply Responsible Business: A Global History of Values-Driven Leadership*. Cambridge, MA: Harvard University Press, 2023.

Multinationals and Global Capitalism: From the Nineteenth to the Twenty-First Century. Oxford; New York: Oxford University Press, 2005.

"Nationality and Multinationals in Historical Perspective." Harvard Business School Working Paper 00-052 (June 2006).

Jones, Geoffrey, and Peter Miskell. "European Integration and Corporate Restructuring: The Strategy of Unilever, c.1957–c.1991." *The Economic History Review* 58, no. 1 (2005): 113–139.

Jones, Geoffrey, and Tarun Khanna. "Bringing History (back) into International Business." *Journal of International Business Studies* 37, no. 4 (2006): 453–468.

Jones, Geoffrey, and Valeria Giacomin. "Deglobalization and Alternative Futures." Harvard Business School Technical Note 322-088. Cambridge, MA: Harvard Business School, March 10, 2022.

Jonsson, Anna, and Nicolai J Foss. "International Expansion through Flexible Replication: Learning from the Internationalization Experience of IKEA." *Journal of International Business Studies* 42, no. 9 (December 2011): 1085–1088.

Judt, Tony. *Postwar: A History of Europe since 1945*. New York: Penguin Books, 2006.

Jullien, Bernard, Tommaso Pardi, and Sigfrido M. Ramírez Pérez. "The EU's Government of Automobiles: From 'Harmonization' to Deep Incompleteness." In *The EU's Government of Industries: Markets, Institutions, and Politics*. London: Routledge, 2014: Chapter 2, pp. 57–83.

Jürgens, Ulrich. "VW at the Turning Point: Success and Crisis of a German Product Concept." *Actes du GERPISA* 10 (1992): 91–108.

Kaiser, Wolfram, and J. W. Schot. *Writing the Rules for Europe: Experts, Cartels, and International Organizations*. Making Europe: Technology and Transformations, 1850–2000. Houndmills, Basingstoke, Hampshire: Palgrave Macmillan, 2014.

Keck, Jörn, Dimitri Vanoverbeke, and Franz Waldenberger, eds. *EU-Japan Relations, 1970–2012: From Confrontation to Global Partnership*. London: Routledge, 2013.

Ketner, Ralph, Jason Lesley, and Mark Wineka. *Five Fast Pennies*. Theodora, 1994.

Kindleberger, Charles P. "Standards as Public, Collective, and Private Goods." *Kyklos* 36 (1983): 377–396.

Klebaner, Samuel, and Sigfrido Ramírez Pérez. "The European Automotive Industry: A Strategic Sector in Search of a New Industrial Policy." In Jean-Christophe Defraigne et al., eds., *EU Industrial Policy in the Multipolar Economy*. Cheltenham: Edward Elgar Publishing, 2022: 304–331.

"Managing Technical Changes from the Scales of Legal Regulation: German Clean Cars Against the European Pollutant Emissions Regulations in the 1980s." *Management & Organizational History* 14, no. 4 (2019): 442–468.

Klein, Naomi. *The Shock Doctrine: The Rise of Disaster Capitalism*, 1st ed. New York: Metropolitan Books, 2007.

Komornicka, Aleksandra. *Poland and European East-West Cooperation in the 1970s: The Opening Up*. London: Routledge, 2023.

"Stable Support, Scant Initiative: European Business Associations and Economic and Monetary Union, 1946–1992." *Business History* 67, no. 4 (2025): 1021–1042.

Krotz, Ulrich, Kiran Klaus Patel, and Federico Romero, eds. *Europe's Cold War Relations: The EC Towards a Global Role*. London: Bloomsbury, 2020.

Krugman, Paul. *Geography and Trade*. 1st ed. Leuven: The MIT Press, 1992.

Paul Krugman, "Competitiveness: A Dangerous Obsession," *Foreign Affairs* 73, no. 2 (1994): 28–44.

Kurey, Gregory S. "GATT and the VRA: Japanese Automobile Imports and Trade Protectionism." *Dickinson Journal of International Law (Penn State International Law Review)* 5, no. 1 (1986): 51–80.

Kurtzman, Joel. "The Passionate Leader: An Interview with Jean Rene Fourtou." Strategy+Business. www.strategy-business.com/article/17726

Kurylko, Diana T. "No Fear: Europe's Makers Put Away Protectionism as Japanese Import Quotas Run Out." *Automotive News*, July 1, 1999.

Lafay, Gérard, Colette Herzog, Loukas Stemitsiostis, Deniz Unal, *Commerce international: La fin des avantages acquis*. Paris: Economica, 1989.

Laurens, Sylvain. *Lobbyists and Bureaucrats in Brussels: Capitalism's Brokers*. London: Routledge, 2018.

Laurent, Pierre-Henri. "The European Technology Community, the Meeting of the Elites, and the Completion of the Internal Market." *Il Politico* 52, no. 2 (1987): 309–316.

Laux, James M. *European Automobile Industry*. 1st ed. New York: Twayne Pub, 1992.

Law, Christopher M. *Restructuring the Global Automobile Industry*. Milton Park: Taylor & Francis, 2017.

Lee, W. R. "Economic Development and the State in Nineteenth-Century Germany." *The Economic History Review* 41, no. 3 (1988): 346–367.

Lehtimäki, Jonne, and David Sondermann. "Baldwin versus Cecchini Revisited: The Growth Impact of the European Single Market." Empirical Economics 63, no. 2 (August 1, 2022): 603–635.

Lenoir, Noëlle. "The Societas Europaea (SE) in Europe: A Promising Start and an Option with Good Prospects." *Utrecht Law Review* 4, no. 1 (2008).

Lerner, Paul. *The Consuming Temple: Jews, Department Stores, and the Consumer Revolution in Germany, 1880–1940*. Ithaca: Cornell University Press, 2015.

Levitsky, Steven, and Daniel Ziblatt. *How Democracies Die*. New York: Crown, 2018.

Levitsky, Steven, and Lucan A. Way. "The Myth of Democratic Recession." *Journal of Democracy* 26, no. 1 (2015): 45–58.

Link, Stefan, and Noam Maggor. "The United States as a Developing Nation: Revisiting the Peculiarities of American History." *Past & Present* 246, no. 1 (2020): 269–306.

Lipgens, Walter. *A History of European Integration: 1945–1947*. Oxford: Clarendon Press, 1982.

Lubinski, Christina. *Navigating Nationalism in Global Enterprise: A Century of Indo-German Business Relations*. Cambridge: Cambridge University Press, 2022.

Ludlow, N. Piers. "The Discomforts of Life on the Edge: Britain and Europe, 1963–1975." *International Affairs* 88, no. 6 (November 1, 2012): 1331–1340.

Lung, Yannick, ed. *Coping with Variety: Flexible Productive Systems for Product Variety in the Auto Industry*. Hampshire: Aldershot, 1999.

Lung, Yannick, Jorge Carrillo, and Rob van Tulder. *Cars, Carriers of Regionalism?* London: Palgrave Macmillan, 2004.

MacKinlay, Alan, Helen Mercer, and Neil Rollings. "Reluctant Europeans? The Federation of British Industries and European Integration, 1945–63." *Business History* 42, no. 4 (2000): 91–116.

Maier, Charles S. *The Project-State and Its Rivals: A New History of the Twentieth and Twenty-First Centuries*. Cambridge, MA: Harvard University Press, 2023.

Mallett, Robert L. "Why Standards Matter." *Issues in Science and Technology* 15, no. 22 (1998): 63–66.

Marina Schaufelbuehl, Janick. *Crusading for Globalization: US Multinationals and Their Opponents since 1945*. Philadelphia: University of Pennsylvania Press, 2025.

Mattson, Lars-Gunnar, and Bengt Stymne. *Corporate and Industry Strategies for Europe: Adaptations to the European Single Market in a Global Industrial Environment*. New York: Elsevier Science Publishers, 1991.

Mayes, David G., ed. *The European Challenge: Industry's Response to the 1992 Programme*. Hertfordshire: Harvester Wheatsheaf, 1991.

Mazey, Sonia, and J. J. Richardson eds. *Lobbying in the European Community*. Nuffield European Studies. Oxford; New York: Oxford University Press, 1993.

Mazower, Mark. *Governing the World: The History of an Idea, 1815 to the Present*. New York: Penguin Books, 2012.

Mazzucato, Mariana. *The Entrepreneurial State: Debunking Public vs. Private Sector Myths*. London: Demos, 2011.

Mission Economy: A Moonshot Guide to Changing Capitalism. New York: Harper Business, 2021.

Menz, Georg. *Varieties of Capitalism and Europeanization: National Response Strategies to the Single European Market*. Oxford; New York: Oxford University Press, 2008.

Merck, Ashton. "The Fox Guarding the Henhouse: Coregulation and Consumer Protection in Food Safety, 1946–2002." PhD dissertation, Duke University, 2020.

Michel, Hélène. "Businesseurope au-delà du 'lobbying': Le travail d'intégration européenne d'une organisation patronale." *Critique internationale* 59, no. 2 (2013): 133–155.

Milner, Helen. "Resisting the Protectionist Temptation: Industry and the Making of Trade Policy in France and the United States during the 1970s." *International Organization* 41, no. 4 (1987): 639–665.

Milor, Alice. "Non-documents for Big Decisions: The Commission and the EEC-Japan Automotive Agreement (1991)," *JCMS: Journal of Common Market Studies* 62, no. 6 (2024): 1654–1671.

Milor, Alice. "Whose Business Is Road Safety?: From a Fragmented to an Integrated Approach in France and Europe (1972–1998)," *Transfers* 9, no. 3 (2019): 41–60.

Milward, Alan, George Brennan, and Federico Romero. *The European Rescue of the Nation State*. Los Angeles: University of California Press, 1992.

Milward, Alan S. *The European Rescue of the Nation-State*. 2nd ed. London; New York: Routledge, 2000.

Moguen-Toursel, Marine. "Emergence and Transfer of Vehicle Safety Standards: Why We Still Do Not Have Global Standards." *Entreprises et histoire* 51, no. 2 (2008): 88–102.

Monnet, Jean. *Mémoires*. Paris: Artheme Fayard, 1976.

Moravcsik, Andrew. *The Choice for Europe: Social Purpose and State Power from Messina to Maastricht*. Cornell Studies in Political Economy. Ithaca: Cornell University Press, 1998.

"Negotiating the Single European Act: National Interests and Conventional Statecraft in the European Community." *International Organization* 45, no. 1 (1991): 19–56.

Morival, Yohann. "Reassessing the Historical Dynamics of European Business Associations: The Genesis of UNICE, Late 1940s to 1970s." *Business History* (published online October 26, 2022): 1–18.

Morrison, Allen J., David A. Ricks, and Kendall Roth. "Globalization versus Regionalization: Which Way for the Multinational?" *Organizational Dynamics* 19, no. 3 (1991): 17–29.

Mourlon-Druol, Emmanuel. *A Europe Made of Money: The Emergence of the European Monetary System*. Ithaca: Cornell University Press, 2012.

Mowery, David, and J. Khazam. "The Commercialization of RISC: Strategies for the Creation of Dominant Designs." *Research Policy* 23, no. 1 (1994): 89–102.

Mudde, Cas. "Populism in Europe: An Illiberal Democratic Response to Undemocratic Liberalism (The Government and Opposition/Leonard Schapiro Lecture 2019)." *Government and Opposition* 56, no. 4 (2021): 577–597.

"The Populist Zeitgeist." *Government and Opposition* 39, no. 4 (January 2004): 541–563.

Murphy, Craig. *International Organization and Industrial Change: Global Governance since 1850*. New York: Oxford University Press, 1994.

Nelson, Richard R. "Why Do Firms Differ, and How Does It Matter?" *Strategic Management Journal* 12, no. 2 (1991): 61–74.

Nilsson, Tony. "The Early IKEA Expansion, by Way of the German Speaking Markets." *Zeitschrift für das Archivwesen der Wirtschaft* 52, no. 4 (2019).

O'Neil, Shannon. *The Globalization Myth: Why Regions Matter*. New York: Council on Foreign Relations, 2022.

Ogle, Vanessa. "Archipelago Capitalism: Tax Havens, Offshore Money, and the State, 1950s–1970s." *The American Historical Review* 122, no. 5 (2017): 1431–1458.

"Governing Global Tax Dodgers: The 'Group of Four' and Taxation of Multinational Corporations." *Business History Review* 97, no. 3 (2023): 547–574.

Oh, Chang Hoon, and Jing Li. "Commentary: Alan Rugman and the Theory of the Regional Multinationals." *Journal of World Business* 50, no. 4 (2015): 631–633.

Oreskes, Naomi, and Erik M. Conway, *The Big Myth: How American Business Taught Us to Loathe Government and Love the Free Market*. London: Bloomsbury, 2023.

Osegowitsch, Thomas, and André Sammartino. "Reassessing (Home-) Regionalisation." *Journal of International Business Studies* 39, no. 2 (2008): 184–196.

Parsons, Craig. "The Extraordinary, Taken-for-Granted Achievement of Europe's Single Market." In Erik Jones ed. *European Studies: Past, Present, Future*. Newcastle upon Tyne: Agenda Publishing, 2020.

Patel, Kiran Klaus. *Project Europe: A History*. Cambridge: Cambridge University Press, 2020.

Provincialising European Union: Co-Operation and Integration in Europe in a Historical Perspective." *Contemporary European History* 22, no. 4 (2013): 649–673.

"Widening and Deepening? Recent Advances in European Integration History." *Neue Politische Literatur* 64, no. 2 (2019): 327–357.

Pelkmans, Jacques. *Market Integration in the European Community*. The Hague: Martinus Nijhoff Publishers, 1984.

"Mutual Recognition in Goods and Services: An Economic Perspective." *European Network of Economic Policy Research Institutes*, Working Paper no. 16, March 2003.

"The New Approach to Technical Harmonization and Standardization." *Journal of Common Market Studies* 25, no. 3 (1987): 249–269.

"The Significance of EC-1992." *The Annals of the American Academy of Political and Social Science* 531, no. 1 (January 1994): 94–111.

Pelkmans, Jacques, and A. Vollebergh. "Fifteen Years of Traditional Harmonisation: Accomplishments and Deficiencies." In Jacques Pelkmans and M. Vanheukelen, eds. *Coming to Grips with the Internal Market*, Working Document 85/05. Maastricht: European Institute of Public Administration, 1986.

Phelps, N. A. *Multinationals and European Integration: Trade, Investment, and Regional Development*. Regional Policy and Development 14. London; Bristol: J. Kingsley Publishers; Regional Studies Association, 1997.

Pitteloud, Sabine. *Les multinationales suisses dans l'arène politique, 1942–1993*. Geneva: Droz, 2022.

"Let's Coordinate! The Reinforcement of a 'Liberal Bastion' within European Industrial Federations, 1978–1987." *Business History* 65, no. 2 (2021): 345–365.

"Unwanted Attention: Swiss Multinationals and the Creation of International Corporate Guidelines in the 1970s." *Business and Politics* 22, no. 4 (December 2020): 587–611. https://doi.org/10.1017/bap.2020.10

et al. "Capitalism and Global Governance in Business History: A Roundtable Discussion." HBS Working Paper No. 22-081 (2022): 1–57.

Pitteloud, Sabine, and Pierre-Yves Donzé. "Swiss Multinationals versus the French Welfare State? The Social Security Deficit, European Integration, and the Battle for 'Fair' Drug Prices (1970–1990)." *Contemporary European History*, January 24, 2024, 1–20.

Ramirez Pérez, Sigfrido M. "Embedding the Market during Times of Crisis: The European Automobile Cartel during a Decade of Crisis (1973–1985)." *Business History* 62, no. 5 (2020): 815–836.

"La politique de la concurrence de la Communauté Économique Européenne et l'industrie: L'exemple des accords sur la distribution automobile (1972–1985)." *Histoire, économie & société* 27, no. 1 (2008): 63–77.

"Public Policies, European Integration and Multinational Corporations in the Automobile Sector." PhD dissertation, European University Institute, 2007.

Raytcheva, Stela, and Gilles Rouet, eds. *Les Entreprises et l'intégration européenne.* Paris: Harmattan, 2016.

Reckendrees, Alfred, Boris Gehlen, and Christian Marx, "International Business, Multinational Enterprises and Nationality of the Company: A Constructive Review of Literature." *Business History* 64, no. 9 (2022): 1567–1599.

Reich, Robert B. "Does Corporate Nationality Matter?" *Issues in Science and Technology* 7, no. 2 (1990): 40–44.

"Multinational Corporations and the Myth of National Origin." *Harvard International Review* 13, no. 4 (1991): 15–17.

Revzin, Philip. "Europe's Retailers Are Consolidating in Preparation for Post-1992 Market." *Wall Street Journal*, June 28, 1991, sec. International.

Rieger, Bernhard. *The People's Car: A Global History of the Volkswagen Beetle.* Cambridge, MA: Harvard University Press, 2013.

Rodrik, Dani. "How Far Will International Economic Integration Go?" *Journal of Economic Perspectives* 14, no. 1 (February 1, 2000): 177–186.

Roland, Stephen. *Vehicle of Influence: Building a European Car Market.* Ann Arbor: University of Michigan Press, 2000.

Rollings, Neil. *British Business in the Formative Years of European Integration 1945–1973.* Cambridge: Cambridge University Press, 2007.

"The Development of Transnational Business Associations during the Twentieth Century." *Business History* 65, no. 2 (February 17, 2023): 235–259.

"'The Vast and Unsolved Enigma of Power': Business History and Business Power." *Enterprise and Society* 22, no. 4 (2021): 893–920.

Rollings, Neil, and Laurent Warlouzet. "Business History and European Integration: How EEC Competition Policy Affected Companies' Strategies." *Business History* 62, no. 5 (July 2020): 717–742.

Rollings, Neil, and Matthias Kipping. "Private Transnational Governance in the Heyday of the Nation-State: The Council of European Industrial Federations (CEIF)." *The Economic History Review* 61, no. 2 (2008): 409–431.

Romano, Angela. "The EC and the Socialist World: The Ascent of a Key Player in Cold War Europe." In Ulrich Krotz, Kiran Klaus Patel and Federico Romero, eds., *Europe's Cold War Relations: The EC Towards a Global Role.* London: Bloomsbury, 2020, 51–71.

Romano, Angela, and Federico Romero, eds. *European Socialist Regimes' Fateful Engagement with the West: National Strategies in the Long 1970s.* 1st ed. Abingdon, Oxon; New York: Routledge, 2021.

Romano, Angela, and Federico Romero. *European Socialist Regimes' Fateful Engagement with the West: National Strategies in the Long 1970s.* London: Routledge, 2020.

Rosa, Benjamin, Philippe Gugler, and Alain Verbeke. "Regional and Global Strategies of MNEs: Revisiting Rugman & Verbeke (2004)." *Journal of International Business Studies* 51, no. 7 (September 1, 2020): 1045–1053.

Ross, Kristin. *Fast Cars, Clean Bodies: Decolonization and the Reordering of French Culture.* Cambridge, MA: MIT Press, 1996.

Rugman, Alan M. *The End of Globalization*. London: Random House Business Books, 2000.

The Regional Multinationals: MNEs and "Global" Strategic Management. Cambridge; New York: Cambridge University Press, 2005.

The Theory of Multinational Enterprises: The Selected Scientific Papers of Alan M. Rugman. Cheltenham: Edward Elgar, 1996.

Rugman, Alan M., and Alain Verbeke. "A Perspective on Regional and Global Strategies of Multinational Enterprises." *Journal of International Business Studies* 35, no. 1 (2004): 3–18.

Rugman, Alan M., and Richard Hodgetts. "The End of Global Strategy." *European Management Journal* 19, no. 4 (2001): 333–343.

Rugman, Alan M., and Simon Collinson. "Multinational Enterprises in the New Europe: Are They Really Global?" *Organizational Dynamics, Management Challenges in the New Europe* 34, no. 3 (2005): 258–272.

Ryner, Magnus, and Alan Cafruny. *The European Union and Global Capitalism: Origins, Development, Crisis*. London: Red Globe Press, 2016.

Sachwald, Fédérique. "De la libéralisation au néo-protectionnisme. Le cas de l'industrie automobile," *Politique Étrangère* 54, no. 4 (Winter 1989): 707–721.

Sadler, David. "Beyond '1992': The Evolution of European Community Policies towards the Automobile Industry." *Environment and Planning C: Government and Policy* 10, no. 2 (June 1992): 229–248.

"The Geographies of Just-in-Time: Japanese Investment and the Automotive Components Industry in Western Europe." *Economic Geography* 70, no. 1 (January 1994): 41–59.

Sally, Razeen. "The Basel Chemical Multinationals: Corporate Action within Structures of Corporatism in Switzerland." *West European Politics* 16, no. 4 (October 1993): 561–580.

Sandholtz, Wayne. *High-Tech Europe: The Politics of International Cooperation*. Berkeley: University of California Press, 1992. https://publishing.cdlib.org/ucpressebooks/view?docId=ft609nb394;brand=ucpress.

Sandholtz, Wayne and John Zysman. "1992: Recasting the European Bargain." *World Politics* 42, no. 1 (1989): 95–128.

Sargent, Daniel J. "Pax Americana: Sketches for an Undiplomatic History." *Diplomatic History* 42, no. 3 (June 1, 2018): 357–376.

Schaufelbuehl, Janick Marina. "'The Advantage of Being inside the Wall When It Is Built:' US Multinationals' Direct Investments in the Common Market, the Balance of Payments Deficit and Bretton Woods (1958–74)." *Journal of European Integration* 43, no. 6 (2021): 667–682.

"Becoming the Advocate for US-Based Multinationals: The United States Council of the International Chamber of Commerce, 1945–1974." *Business History* 65, no. 2 (2023): 284–301.

Schenck, Catherine, and Emmanuel Mourlon-Druol. "Banking Regulation and Supervision." In Youssef Cassis, Richard Grossman, and Catherine R. Schenck, eds., *The Oxford Handbook of Banking and Financial History*. Oxford: Oxford University Press, 2016: 395–419.

Schimmelfenig, Frank. "European Integration (Theory) in Times of Crisis: A Comparison of the Euro and Schengen Crises." *Journal of European Public Policy* 25, no. 7 (2018): 969–989.

Schmidt, Vivien. "European Political Economy: Labour Out, State Back In, Firm to the Fore." *West European Politics* 31, no. 1–2 (2008): 302–320.

Schröter, Harm G. *Americanization of the European Economy: A Compact Survey of American Economic Influence in Europe since the 1880s*. Dordrecht; Norwell: Springer, 2005.

The European Enterprise: Historical Investigation into a Future Species. New York: Springer Science & Business Media, 2007.

"The German Question, the Unification of Europe, and the European Market Strategies of Germany's Chemical and Electrical Industries, 1900–1992." *Business History Review* 67, no. 3 (1993): 369–405.

Servan-Schreiber, Jean-Jacques. *Le Défi américain*. Paris: Denoël, 1967.

Seth, Catriona, and Rotraud von Kulessa. *The Idea of Europe: Enlightenment Perspectives*. Cambridge: Open Book Publishers, 2017.

Sharp, Margaret, and Claire Shearman. *European Technological Cooperation*. London: Chatham House Papers, 1987.

Shimokawa, Koichi. "Reorganization of the Global Automobile Industry and Structural Change of the Automobile Component Industry" Massachusetts Institute of Technology, International Motor Vehicle Program, June 20, 2002. https://dspace.mit.edu/bitstream/handle/1721.1/1417/Shimokawa.pdf?sequenc

Sloniger, Jerry. *The VW Story*. Cambridge: Patrick Stephens, 1980.

Slobodian, Quinn, and Dieter Plehwe. "Neoliberals against Europe." In William Callison and Zachary Manfredi, eds., *Mutant Neoliberalism: Market Rule and Political Ruptures*. New York: Fordham University Press, 2019, 89–111.

Slobodian, Quinn. *Crack-Up Capitalism: Market Radicals and the Dream of a World Without Democracy*. New York: Metropolitan Books, 2023.

"Demos Veto and Demos Exit: The Neoliberals Who Embraced Referenda and Secession." *Journal of Australian Political Economy* 86 (2020): 19–36.

Globalists: The End of Empire and the Birth of Neoliberalism. Cambridge, MA: Harvard University Press, 2018.

Sluga, Glenda. *Internationalism in the Age of Nationalism*. Philadelphia: University of Pennsylvania Press, 2013.

Smits, René. "The European Community's Second Banking Directive." In Robert C. Effros, ed., *Current Legal Issues Facing Central Banks, Vol. IV*. Washington, DC: International Monetary Fund, 1997: Chapter 6, pp. 83–104.

Stiglitz, Joseph E. *Globalization and Its Discontents*. 2nd ed. New York: W. W. Norton and Company, 2003.

Stone, Jon. "Nigel Farage delivers first post-Brexit speech to the European Parliament in full." *The Independent*, June 30, 2016.

Strange, Susan. "Big Business and the State." In Lorraine Eden and Evan H. Potter, eds. *Multinationals in the Global Political Economy*. London: Palgrave Macmillan, 1993, 101–107.

Casino Capitalism. Oxford; New York: B. Blackwell, 1986.

Mad Money: When Markets Outgrow Governments. Ann Arbor: The University of Michigan Press, 1998.

The Retreat of the State: The Diffusion of Power in the World Economy. Cambridge Studies in International Relations 49. Cambridge; New York: Cambridge University Press, 1996.

States and Markets. Reprint ed. London; New York: Bloomsbury Academic, 2015.

"States, Firms and Diplomacy." *International Affairs (Royal Institute of International Affairs 1944–)* 68, no. 1 (1992): 1–15.

Streeck, Wolfgang, and Philippe C. Schmitter. "From National Corporatism to Transnational Pluralism: Organized Interests in the Single European Market." *Politics & Society* 19, no. 2 (1991): 133–64.

Streeck, Wolfgang. *How Will Capitalism End? Essays on a Failing System*. New York: Verso, 2016. Ebook version: 4.

"Successful Adjustment to Turbulent Markets: The Automobile Industry." In Katzenstein, Peter J., ed., *Industry and Politics in West Germany: Toward the Third Republic*. Ithaca: Cornell University Press, 2018: Chapter 5, pp. 113–156.

et al., eds. *Governing Interests: Business Associations Facing Internationalism*. London: Routledge, 2006.

Sturgeon, Timothy, Johannes Van Biesebroeck, and Gary Gereffi. "Value Chains, Networks and Clusters: Reframing the Global Automotive Industry." *Journal of Economic Geography* 8, no. 3 (2008): 297–321.

Suzuki, Hitoshi. "The New Politics of Trade: EU-Japan." *Journal of European Integration* 39, no. 7 (2017): 875–889.

Sylla, Richard. "United States Banks and Europe: Strategy and Attitudes." In Stefano Battilossi and Youssef Cassis, eds., *European Banks and the American Challenge: Competition and Cooperation in International Banking under Bretton Woods*. Oxford: Oxford University Press, 2002: 53–73.

te Broommelstroet, Marco, and Tobias Nowak. "How a Court, a Commissioner and a Lobby Group Brought European Transport Policy to Life in 1985." *GeoJournal* 72 (2008): 33–44.

Therborn, Göran, et al. "The 1970s and 1980s as a Turning Point in European History?" *Journal of Modern European History / Zeitschrift Für Moderne Europäische Geschichte / Revue d'histoire Européenne Contemporaine* 9, no. 1 (2011): 8–26.

Thompson, Grahame. "The Evolution of the Managed Economy." *Economy and Society* 21, no. 2 (1992): 129–151.

Thompson, James. "The Unassuming Empire-Builder." *The Independent*, February 26, 2011.

Thornton, Christy. *Revolution in Development: Mexico and the Governance of the Global Economy*. Los Angeles: University of California Press, 2021.

Tolliday, Steven, and Jonathan Zeitlin, eds. *The Automobile Industry and Its Workers: Between Fordism and Flexibility*. New York: St. Martin's Press, 1987.

Tracey, Peter. *My Life, My Business, and My Boats*. Self-published memoir, June 2020.

Trumbull, Gunnar. *Strength in Numbers: The Political Power of Weak Interests*. Cambridge, MA: Harvard University Press, 2012.

Vahlne, Jan-Erik, and Inge Ivarsson. "The Globalization of Swedish MNEs: Empirical Evidence and Theoretical Explanations." *Journal of International Business Studies* 45, no. 3 (2014): 227–247.

van Apeldoorn, Bastiaan. *Transnational Capitalism and the Struggle over European Integration*. Routledge, 2002.

"Transnational Class Agency and European Governance: The Case of the European Round Table of Industrialists." *New Political Economy* 5, no. 2 (2000): 157–181.

van de Grift, Liesbeth, and Koen van Zon. "The European Parliament and the Origins of Consumer Policy." European Parliament Think Tank, March 2024.

van Zon, Koen. "Battleground Brussels: The EU and the Regulation of Multinationals." PhD dissertation, Utrecht University, 2021.

Vauchez, Antoine. *Brokering Europe: Euro-Lawyers and the Making of a Transnational Polity*. Cambridge: Cambridge University Press, 2015.

Vaupel, James W., and Joan P. Curhan. *The Making of Multinational Enterprises: A Sourcebook of Tables Based on a Study of 187 Major U.S. Manufacturing Corporations*. Boston: Division of Research, Harvard Business School, 1969.

The World's Multinational Enterprises: A Sourcebook of Tables Based on a Study of the Largest U.S. and Non-U.S. Manufacturing Corporations. Boston: Division of Research, Harvard Business School, 1973.

Veblen, Thorstein. *The Theory of Business Enterprise*. New York: Charles Scribner's Sons, 1904.

Verbeke, Alain and Liena Kano. "The New Internalization Theory and Multinational Enterprises from Emerging Economies: A Business History Perspective." *Business History Review* 89, no. 3 (2015): 415–445.

Vernon, Raymond. *Sovereignty at Bay: The Multinational Spread of US Enterprises*. New York: Basic Books, 1971.

von Coudenhove-Kalergi, Richard. *Europa Erwacht!* Paris; Vienna; Zürich: Paneuropa-Verlag, 1934.

Vonyó, Tamás. *The Economic Consequences of the War: West Germany's Growth Miracle after 1945*. Cambridge: Cambridge University Press, 2018.

Wagnleitner, Reinhold. *Coca-Colonisation und Kalter Krieg. Die Kulturmission der USA in Österreich nach dem Zweiten Weltkrieg*. Wien: Verl. für Gesellschaftskritik, 1991.

Wallerstein, Immanuel M. *World-Systems Analysis: An Introduction*. Durham, NC: Duke University Press, 2004.

Warlouzet, Laurent, and Tobias Witschke. "The Difficult Path to an Economic Rule of Law: European Competition Policy, 1950–91." *Contemporary European History* 21, no. 3 (2012): 437–455.

Warlouzet, Laurent. "The Centralization of EU Competition Policy: Historical Institutionalist Dynamics from Cartel Monitoring to Merger Control (1956–91)." *JCMS: Journal of Common Market Studies* 54, no. 3 (2016): 725–741.

"Competition versus Planning: A Battle that Shaped European Integration (1945–2022)." In Mathieu Segers and Steven Van Hecke, eds., *The Cambridge History of the European Union, Volume 2, European Integration Inside-Out*. Cambridge: Cambridge University Press, 2023: Chapter 8, pp. 234–260.

Completing the Single Market: The European Parliament and Economic Integration, 1979–1989. Luxembourg: Publications Office of the European Union, 2020.

"The EEC/EU as an Evolving Compromise between French Dirigism and German Ordoliberalism (1957–1995)." *JCMS: Journal of Common Market Studies* 57, no. 1 (2019): 77–93.

Europe contre Europe: Entre liberté, solidarité et puissance. Paris: CNRS Editions, 2022.

"European Integration History: Beyond the Crisis." *Politique europeenne* 44, no. 2 (2014): 98–122.

"A Flanking European Welfare State: The European Community's Social Dimension, from Brandt to Delors (1969–1993)." *Contemporary European History* 33, no. 1 (2024): 23–36.

Governing Europe in a Globalizing World: Neoliberalism and Its Alternatives Following the 1973 Oil Crisis. 1st ed. Routledge Studies on Government and the European Union. New York: Routledge, 2017.

"La politique de la concurrence européenne depuis 1950: Surveiller les entreprises et les États." *CVCE*, University of Luxembourg (2012): 1–11.

"The Role of the European Parliament in the Single Market Programme: The Cost of Non-Europe and the Car Emission Directive." *Journal of European Integration History* 27, no. 1 (2021): 21–36.

"A Social Europe with a Greener Perspective: The Evolution of the Delors Commission around 1989." Studi Storici. *Rivista Trimestrale Dell'Istituto Gramsci* 62, no. 1 (2021): 189–209.

Liberty, Solidarity, and Community: Capitalism and European Integration, 1945 to the Present. Cambridge: Cambridge University Press, 2026.

Waterhouse, Benjamin C. *Lobbying America: The Politics of Business from Nixon to NAFTA*. Princeton: Princeton University Press, 2013.

Welch, Catherine, and Eriikka Paavilainen-Mäntymäki. "Putting Process (Back) In: Research on the Internationalization Process of the Firm." *International Journal of Management Reviews* 16, no. 1 (2014): 2–23.

Welch, Catherine, "Theorising from Case Studies: Towards a Pluralist Future for International Business Research." *Journal of International Business Studies* 42, no. 5 (2011): 740–762.

"Theory and Context: How the Case Study Can Set a New Agenda for IB Research." *Journal of International Business Studies* 53, no. 1 (2022): 4–26.

Westney, D. Eleanor. "The Regional Multinationals: MNEs and 'Global' Strategic Management." *Journal of International Business Studies* 37, no. 3 (2006): 445–449.

Wilkins, Mira, and Frank Ernest Hill. *American Business Abroad: Ford on Six Continents*. New York: Cambridge University Press, 2011.

Wilkins, Mira. "The Free-Standing Company, 1870–1914: An Important Type of British Foreign Direct Investment." *The Economic History Review* 41, no. 2 (1988): 259–282.

"The History of Multinationals: A 2015 View." *Business History Review* 89, no. 3 (2015): 405–414.

"Multinational Enterprises and the Varieties of Capitalism." *Business History Review* 84, no. 4 (2010): 638–645.

"The Neglected Intangible Asset: The Influence of the Trade Mark on the Rise of the Modern Corporation." *Business History* 34 (1992): 66–95.

Wilkins, Mira, and Harm Schroter, eds. *The Free-Standing Company in the World Economy, 1830-1996*. Oxford: Oxford University Press, 1999.

Winkler, Adam. *We the Corporations: How American Businesses Won Their Civil Rights*. New York: Liveright, 2018.

Wolf, Martin. *The Crisis of Democratic Capitalism*. 1st ed. London: Allen Lane, 2023.

Wrigley, Neil. "Pan-European Alliances Lead the Way for the Retail Sector." *International Journal of Retail & Distribution Management* 21, no. 2 (1993).

Yates, JoAnne, and Craig Murphy. *Engineering Rules: Global Standard Setting since 1880*. Baltimore: Johns Hopkins University Press, 2019.

Yates, JoAnne, and Craig N. Murphy. "Introduction: Standards and the Global Economy." *Business History Review* 96, no. 1 (2022): 3–15.

Zaccaria, Benedetto. "Personalism and European Integration: Jacques Delors and the Legacy of the 1930s." *Contemporary European History* (2023): 1–20.

Zuboff, Shoshana. *The Age of Surveillance Capitalism: The Fight for the Future at the New Frontier of Power*. 1st ed. London: Faber and Faber, 2019.

Zucman, Gabriel. *The Hidden Wealth of Nations: The Scourge of Tax Havens*. Trans. Teresa Lavender Fagan and with a foreword by Thomas Piketty. Chicago: University of Chicago Press, 2016.

Index

Printed in the United Kingdom by TJ Clays Ltd.